European Merger Control

European Merger Control

Do We Need an Efficiency Defence?

Edited by

Fabienne Ilzkovitz

Head of Unit, Directorate–General for Economic and Financial Affairs, European Commission and Associate Professor of Economics, University of Brussels and ICHEC, Belgium

Roderick Meiklejohn

Head of Section (Competition Policy), Economic Evaluation Service, Directorate–General for Economic and Financial Affairs, European Commission, Belgium

PUBLISHED ON BEHALF OF THE COMMISSION OF EUROPEAN COMMUNITIES

Edward Elgar

Cheltenham, UK • Northampton, MA, USA

Published by
Edward Elgar Publishing Limited
Glensanda House
Montpellier Parade
Cheltenham
Glos GL50 1UA
UK

Edward Elgar Publishing, Inc.
136 West Street
Suite 202
Northampton
Massachusetts 01060
USA

A catalogue record for this book is available from the British Library

Library of Congress Cataloguing-in-Publication Data
European merger control : do we need an efficiency defence / edited by Fabienne Ilzkovitz, Roderick Meiklejohn.
p. cm.
'Published on behalf of the Commission of European Communities.'
Includes index.
1. Consolidation and merger of corporations–Law and legislation–European Union countries. I. Ilzkovitz, F. II. Meiklejohn, Roderick. III. Commission of the European Communities.

KJE6467.E93 2006
346.24′06626–dc22 2005049827

The views expressed are purely those of the authors and may not, and in any circumstances, be regarded as stating an official position of the European Communities.

ISBN-13: 978 1 84542 491 6
ISBN-10: 1 84542 491 3
EU ISBN: 92-894-3486-4 Cat. number: KC-43-02-341-EN-C

Publications Office
Publications.eu.int

Printed and bound in Great Britain by MPG Books Ltd, Bodmin, Cornwall

Contents

Contributors

Fabienne Ilzkovitz, Directorate-General for Economic and Financial Affairs, European Commission, University of Brussels and ICHEC.

Roderick Meiklejohn, Directorate-General for Economic and Financial Affairs, European Commission.

Jrissy Motis, IDEI, Université des Sciences Sociales de Toulouse.

Damien Neven, Graduate Institute of International Studies, University of Geneva and CEPR.

Lars-Hendrik Röller, Directorate-General for Competition, European Commission, Humboldt University and Wissenschaftszentrum Berlin.

Paul Seabright, IDEI, Université des Sciences Sociales de Toulouse and CEPR.

Johan Stennek, Research Institute for Industrial Economics, Stockholm and CEPR.

Frank Verboven, Katholieke Universiteit Leuven and CEPR.

Acknowledgements

We are grateful to Klaus Regling, Director-General of Economic and Financial Affairs and Jan Host Schmidt, Director, for their support and for giving us the opportunity of communicating the results of this research programme to the policy and research communities. Daniel Vandewalle and Ramiro Gomez Villalba provided invaluable assistance with data processing and statistical analysis. Our thanks are also due to Sarah Vitiello and Kathia Dulieu for providing secretarial assistance. Last but not least, we would like to express our gratitude to numerous colleagues in the European Commission who made helpful comments on the studies published in this book. Nevertheless, the opinions expressed here are those of the authors and do not necessarily reflect the policy line of the Commission.

Foreword

Vigorous competition in the European internal market is the best guarantee of the efficiency of the economy in serving consumers' needs, innovation and the competitiveness of European firms in world markets. A large number of empirical studies confirm that companies that are exposed to effective competition in their home markets not only serve their domestic consumers better but also compete more successfully in foreign markets than firms that face little or no competition at home. An effective competition policy is therefore just as important today, in a context of rapid globalisation, as it ever was.

During my period of office as the member of the European Commission responsible for competition policy, I launched a programme of reforms designed to equip EU competition policy with the tools needed to face the challenges of enlargement and globalisation, while making greater use of the insights derived from theoretical and empirical economics. Prominent amongst these reforms was a thorough revision of the merger regulation, covering all aspects of merger control. One of the major changes introduced in the new regulation was the inclusion of a clear statement that substantiated and likely efficiences should be taken into account if they counteract the effects on competition, in particular the potential harm to consumers, that the merger might otherwise cause. Soon after the adoption of the new regulation in January 2004, the Commission issued guidelines, explaining how it would apply the regulation to horizontal mergers, that is, mergers between companies active in the same market. A section of those guidelines is devoted to the evaluation of the merging parties' efficiency claims, addressing questions concerning the sort of evidence needed to substantiate such claims, the assessment of the likelihood that the efficiency gains will be achieved and the extent to which the gains will be passed on to consumers.

It cannot be said that mergers generally lead to significant improvements in efficiency. Nevertheless, in important exceptional cases a merger may be a necessary step towards making substantial cost savings or significantly enhancing the parties' ability to innovate. Where benefits from such efficiency gains are passed on to the consumer, they should be taken into account in the merger appraisal, since consumer welfare is the ultimate object of EU competition policy.

Taken together, the new regulation and the Commission guidelines lay down two principles that are worthy of particular note in this context. The first is that efficiency gains can not be considered sufficient to counteract anti-competitive effects in cases where a merger eliminates effective competition. The second is that the benefit of the efficiency gains must be passed on to consumers, at least to the extent necessary to avert the danger that they will suffer harm as a result of the merger. Consequently, the Commission's willingness to consider efficiency arguments does not constitute a relaxation of competition policy nor is it an open door for the creation of would-be 'European champions' no longer subject to effective competition on home markets. Without sufficient competitive pressure, there can be no assurance either that the merged company will make the efforts needed to improve efficiency or that it will pass on any benefits from efficiency gains to its customers. Furthermore, as I have argued above, a firm enjoying unchallenged dominance at home is unlikely to be a dynamic player in world markets.

The introduction of the provisions for an efficiency defence in European merger control followed extensive debate and study, in which the considerations that I have outlined above figured prominently. The present volume brings together some significant contributions to the debate from an economic point of view. They examine in depth the theoretical and empirical foundations for the consideration of efficiencies in merger control while also proposing ways of resolving some important practical questions raised by the efficiency defence, such as the burden of proof, the nature and quality of the evidence required and methods for estimating the extent to which efficiency gains will be passed on to consumers.

Mario Monti

Introduction

For 15 years, the EU's merger control system, unlike most others in the world, offered only minimal possibilities for taking efficiency gains into account as a mitigating factor that might offset the anti-competitive effects of a merger. This changed in January 2004, when the EU Council of Ministers adopted a new merger regulation that for the first time explicitly recognizes the possibility of an efficiency defence. Shortly afterwards, the European Commission published its first guidelines for the assessment of horizontal mergers, explaining how it intends to apply the new regulation. In Part VII of the guidelines, the Commission outlines how efficiencies will be incorporated into merger appraisals.

What are the pros and cons of the efficiency defence? How do other merger control systems deal with efficiencies? What impact will the change in policy have on merging companies and the economy as a whole? How can the investigation process be organized to accommodate the analysis of efficiency gains? What are the main theoretical and practical problems which arise when anti-competitive effects have to be weighed against efficiency gains and how can they be resolved? This book aims to answer these questions or at least to indicate fruitful lines of further enquiry.

Although the old merger regulation included 'the development of technical and economic progress' among the criteria to be considered in the appraisal of mergers, it also stipulated that such progress could be taken into account only if it was to the consumer's advantage and if it did not form an obstacle to competition. The latter condition was generally viewed as allowing very little scope for efficiency arguments. Indeed, the Commission was sometimes criticized for regarding efficiencies as an aggravating factor, rather than an extenuating one. Many economists and business representatives argued in favour of revising the regulation to include an explicit provision which would allow the Commission to take account of the beneficial effects of efficiencies either on total welfare (the preference of many economists) or on consumer welfare. The proponents of the efficiency defence could point to the fact that almost all other merger control systems make such a provision or a more general provision for a 'public interest' defence. Some opponents, such as the German competition authority, argued that dominant firms have no incentive to pass efficiency benefits on to consumers. Others feared that the introduction of an efficiency defence would open the door for 'industrial policy' considerations to the detriment of consumers. Another objection was that, since the Commission would have access to very little independent information relevant to the assessment of efficiency gains, it would be easy for merging companies to pull the wool over the Commission's eyes.

The new regulation and the Commission's guidelines attempt to meet the main objections of the opponents of the efficiency defence. As a safeguard against the infiltration of industrial policy considerations, the regulation makes it clear that the relevant efficiencies are those which are passed on to consumers. The claim that dominant firms have no incentive to pass on cost savings is, of course, an exaggeration. However, the guidelines stress that the incentive for the merged entity to pass on efficiency gains to consumers is related to the competitive pressure from the remaining firms on the market and potential entry. In particular, the Commission states that it is highly unlikely that a merger leading to a monopoly or near-monopoly could be cleared on efficiency grounds. To address the problem of asymmetric information, the guidelines lay down the principle that efficiency claims must be verifiable and list the types of supporting evidence which are most likely to be considered credible.

In principle, the new regulation and the Commission's guidelines represent an important shift in European merger control policy as far as efficiencies are concerned. However, the practical impact of the changes will depend on the extent to which merging companies, when faced with the threat of a prohibition decision, are willing to make efficiency claims and able to substantiate them.

This volume brings together work on the subject of merger efficiencies undertaken by staff of the European Commission and three studies carried out on behalf of the Commission by academic consultants. All three of those studies have contributed to the policy-making process leading up to the adoption of the new regulation and the guidelines. Two of these studies (Chapters 3 and 4) were completed before the Commission made its proposal for a new regulation and the third was submitted before the Commission adopted its horizontal merger guidelines.

Chapter 1 is a general survey of statistical data on M&A and merger control activity since 1991. It provides the overall context for the specific discussion of efficiencies in the following chapters. The chapter starts by outlining the recent history of merger activity in the former fifteen-member EU (EU15) and in the New Member States. There are marked differences between countries in the intensity of M&A activity (the level of activity relative to the size of the economy). These disparities are not easy to explain as they result from a combination of numerous factors, such as the structure of share ownership, legal systems and stock exchange rules. As far as cross-border M&A are concerned, the main determinant of the level of activity between any pair of countries is the size of the countries, although proximity and historical or cultural ties are also important factors. When comparing EU15 and the New Member States, we observe marked differences between the two groups of countries, both in the temporal evolution and in the sectoral structure of M&A. With the exceptions of Malta and Cyprus, the New Member States have only recently made the transition to market economies and the development of M&A activity in these countries has been determined to a large extent by the progress of privatization. Cross-border M&A have played a very important role in the transition to capitalism in the Central and Eastern European countries, by providing not only much-needed capital but also managerial and technical expertise.

Chapter 1 also examines the available statistical information on mergers which have been subject to merger control procedures at EU level, in the Member States and in the USA. It looks at the numbers of mergers examined by the competition authorities, the sectors concerned and the outcome of the procedures. The percentage of M&A transactions covered by the EU merger regulation, although rising, is very small by comparison with the percentage of mergers scrutinized by the competition authorities of the largest Member States and the USA. Of the mergers notified under the regulation, a relatively small proportion (about 6 per cent) is subject to in-depth investigation and less than 1 per cent have been forbidden. Consequently, it does not seem that the merger regulation imposes an excessive burden on companies. However, the impact of the regulation varies between sectors. Sectors characterized by large companies and extensive cross-border trading or ownership links are the prime targets of the regulation. These are sectors such as chemicals, electrical equipment, telecommunications and financial services.

The last section of Chapter 1 examines the data on the merger wave of the 1990s in EU15 and the USA. The aim of this comparison is to see whether the wave behaviour of merger activity yields any general lessons about the motivation of mergers, in particular the role played by prospective efficiency gains. We find a striking contrast between the EU and the USA in the ways in which the merger wave developed. In the USA, the wave started and finished earlier and rose much higher. Moreover, almost every sector in the USA was strongly affected by the wave, whereas in EU15 most of the growth occurred in telecommunications and business services while manufacturing was largely unaffected and distribution and financial services responded relatively weakly. Gugler et al. (2002) have argued persuasively that merger waves are not caused by a generalized need for restructuring but rather by the interaction of stock market conditions and the private interests of company managers. However, as far as EU15 is concerned, the very large sectoral disparities in the growth rates of M&A activity do seem to suggest that sectoral shocks, such as privatization and liberalization of the network industries, may have been an important determinant of European M&A activity. To the extent that mergers enabled firms to adjust to such shocks, there is some reason to believe that the merger wave may have yielded efficiency gains in Europe.

In Chapter 2, Ilzkovitz and Meiklejohn give an overview of the economic and political arguments in favour of an efficiency defence. If the aim of competition policy is to maximize either total welfare or consumer welfare, a merger appraisal that is restricted to the anti-competitive effects, taking no account of productive efficiency gains, is clearly incomplete. The review of the empirical literature by Röller et al. (Chapter 3) shows that, although the average efficiency gain from mergers may be zero or even negative, the variance is very wide: some mergers yield very substantial efficiencies. Important welfare gains may therefore be forgone if the merger control system disregards effects on productive efficiency. From the political point of view, Chapter 2 examines the pressure to include efficiencies or international competitiveness in European merger control criteria. In some major cases there has been intensive lobbying, stressing industrial policy aspects of the cases. The authors argue that, without an explicit legal provision, clearly delimiting the scope of the efficiency defence, there is a danger that the Commission could be led into making unclear compromises between the objectives of competition policy and those of industrial policy.

The authors then survey the treatment of efficiencies by national competition authorities in the USA, Canada and the EU Member States, noting that most jurisdictions accept efficiency defences, some have vague 'public interest' provisions and a few take account of international competitiveness. The next section of the chapter discusses the choice of the welfare standard. This is a fundamental question that must be decided if provision is made for an efficiency defence. If the total welfare standard is applied, all efficiency gains can be taken into account, even if they only accrue to the merged entity and are not in any way passed on to customers. The consumer surplus standard, on the other hand, requires that the efficiency gains must be passed on to consumers at least to the extent that the consumer is no worse off after the merger than before. An intermediate position adopted in Canada takes account of both consumer and producer surplus but gives a greater weight to the former. On balance, the authors conclude that, for both legal and economic reasons, the case for the consumer surplus standard is strongest.

The last section of Chapter 2 examines the practical problems of implementing the efficiency defence. The first problem is the sheer amount of information needed to evaluate efficiency gains. As this requires a substantial effort on the part of the merging companies and the Commission, it is not practicable to make a thorough efficiency analysis of every notified merger. Following Röller et al. (Chapter 3), the authors therefore propose that, as far as possible, detailed consideration of efficiency claims should be limited to an intermediate class of cases, excluding both those which do not pose any important competition problems and those which, in the absence of efficiencies, would cause such serious harm to competition that no plausible efficiency gains are likely to compensate. When an efficiency defence is taken into consideration, an initial qualitative analysis has to be undertaken in all cases to establish whether the companies' claims are credible and whether the efficiencies could be achieved by means less harmful to competition than the proposed merger. If the merger passes the qualitative tests, a quantitative cost-benefit analysis should be carried out whenever possible. However, some types of efficiencies, in particular improvements in product quality and the creation of innovative products, do not lend themselves to quantitative analysis and the Commission may have to content itself with a rigorous qualitative appraisal. The authors conclude by noting that a number of methodological problems still need to be resolved.

Chapter 3 is an edited version of the report on a study carried out before the review of the merger regulation on behalf of the Commission by Röller, Stennek and Verboven. The aims of the study were to examine the evidence concerning the extent of efficiency gains resulting from mergers and to consider ways in which efficiency gains might be taken into account in EU merger control. The chapter first discusses the theoretical aspects: the types of efficiency gains which can be achieved through mergers, the welfare losses which can result from increases in market power and the problem of balancing the two effects. The next part examines the empirical evidence about the efficiency effects of mergers and comes to the conclusion that, while the average gain is probably close to zero, the dispersion about the mean is very wide. Consequently, failure to take account of efficiency effects may in some cases lead to prohibition of mergers which would lead to substantial welfare gains.

On the basis of their analysis and their knowledge of the practice in various merger control systems, Röller et al. propose a checklist of important factors which should be considered when taking efficiencies into account. In the last part of the chapter, the authors present a 'framework for merger analysis'. They suggest minimizing information costs by adopting a 'sequential approach', which would first assign each merger to one of three classes according to the gravity of its anti-competitive effects. It would be unnecessary to give detailed consideration to efficiency gains in cases where the anti-competitive effects are minor. Where there is very serious harm to competition, on the other hand, an efficiency defence would be most unlikely to succeed. Consequently, a thorough analysis of efficiencies should only be undertaken in those cases where the foreseeable harm is significant but not overwhelming. The authors then describe ways in which, given an estimate or presumption concerning a merger's effect on prices in the absence of efficiencies, one can estimate the minimum efficiency gain that would be necessary to counteract this effect. After this, they make a series of recommendations concerning the evaluation of the efficiency gains actually brought about by a merger and the chapter concludes by summing up the arguments for and against the efficiency defence.

The treatment of efficiencies in the new merger regulation and horizontal merger guidelines reflects many of the ideas to be found in Chapters 2 and 3 and, in particular, the following:

- Greater weight should be given to variable cost savings than to reductions in fixed costs, since the former have a direct effect on firms' pricing decisions.
- Merger appraisals must take account not only of cost savings but also of improvements in product quality.
- Cost savings that result from anti-competitive reductions in output should not be taken into consideration.
- The analysis should focus on efficiency gains achieved in the market where the competition problems arise.
- The burden of proof of efficiencies should lie entirely on the notifying parties.
- Greater evidential weight should be accorded to pre-merger estimates of efficiencies than to studies carried out after the beginning of the investigation procedure.

Chapter 4, by Stennek and Verboven, examines in more detail the questions of scale economies and pass-on. A general theme throughout the chapter is that efficiency gains, and their pass-on to consumers, may vary widely from merger to merger but in some cases the benefits to consumers may be substantial. For this reason it seems appropriate to allow the merging parties to present an efficiency defence. The authors provide a detailed examination of two main parts of an efficiency analysis: establishing the presence of efficiencies and estimating the extent to which any gains will be passed on to consumers. In the first part the focus is on economies of scale. The authors show that theoretical analysis can define the conditions which determine whether mergers will yield cost savings but they caution that more research is needed to make these conditions fully operational for competition policy purposes. In reviewing the empirical literature, they find evidence of wide variations in scale economies between industries. In addition, concentration in many industries has reached levels much higher than can be explained by scale economies. Consequently, in merger analysis it is very important to bear in mind that the merging firms may already have exhausted the available economies of scale. The authors suggest a two-step approach to the verification of scale economies. In the first step, the competition authority can use existing econometric evidence to check whether the order of magnitude of the cost saving justifies further investigation of the parties' efficiency claims. If a detailed study is warranted, the authority could commission engineering studies, which are better suited to the analysis of individual cases than econometric studies. The second part of the chapter considers the pass-on of efficiencies to consumers in the form of lower prices. Both the theoretical determinants and the empirical evidence are examined. The authors stress that empirical estimates of the pass-through of industry-wide cost savings are not useful in merger analysis, which has to focus on firm-specific cost savings. Whereas industry-wide cost savings are often fully passed on to customers, the pass-through of firm-specific savings varies widely but is almost always incomplete. The authors conclude that pass-through, like the cost savings themselves, has to be evaluated case by case. Finally, the authors develop a practical method for assessing pass-through and demonstrate its feasibility with a real-life example.

The last chapter is an edited version of the report on a study on synergies and dynamic efficiencies in mergers, carried out for the Commission in 2003 by Motis, Neven and Seabright. This study is a first attempt to come to grips with the difficult question of synergies and dynamic efficiencies, a subject that has hitherto received little attention from economists, since it is much less amenable to formal modelling than static efficiencies. The authors develop an analytical framework for identifying the sources of synergies, as distinct from static or 'technical' efficiencies, in mergers. They argue that true synergies occur in a merger when the parties find ways of combining their assets that enable them to achieve output/cost configurations that would not otherwise be possible. They contend that such recombinations of assets presuppose that at least one of the parties has substantial intangible assets to offer. The authors survey the relevant literature and summarize the empirical work they have undertaken to try to measure the importance of intangible assets in determining the size, variance and distribution of shareholder gains from mergers. The following hypotheses are tested:

- On average, mergers that combine important intangible assets yield higher gains than others.

- However, mergers which aim at synergies through new combinations of tangible and substantial intangible assets are more likely to fail than mergers that aim at merely technical efficiencies or the enhancement of market power.
- The gains from combining important intangible assets are more likely to be merger-specific, that is, associated with particular combinations of firms, than other types of gains from mergers. Auction theory suggests, therefore, that the acquiring firm should obtain a higher share of the gains when substantial intangible assets are involved.

Using an event study methodology, the authors are unable to confirm the first hypothesis but do find some limited support for the other two.

Against the background of their analytical framework and their empirical results, Motis et al. make some valuable recommendations concerning the approach that should be followed by competition authorities when considering an efficiency defence. They acknowledge that synergies are much more difficult to evaluate than technical efficiencies, because they are more complex and surrounded by greater uncertainties. Nevertheless, they argue that competition authorities would be wrong to refuse to consider synergies, since in some cases they offer potential efficiency gains that far exceed what can be achieved through technical efficiencies. Furthermore, synergies are much more likely to be merger-specific than other types of efficiencies. However, they advise that the uncertainties are such that an efficiency defence based on synergies should never be accepted if the anti-competitive effects of the merger are clearly very large. The presence of potential synergies and their nature can best be grasped by asking why the firms have chosen a merger rather than some other arrangement and considering the types of asset that each party brings to the merger. Since true synergies, as opposed to market power effects, cannot be achieved through a mere passive combination of those assets, an efficiency defence is only credible if the firms can show that they have precise plans for their integration. In conclusion, the authors suggest that the analysis of all mergers, regardless of the types of asset involved or the nature of the claimed efficiencies, should start by probing the business rationale. Management should be asked to explain clearly the sources of the shareholder gains that they project, so that the competition authority can form a judgement about the proportion of these gains that are of a kind that can be achieved without significant costs to consumers.

The contributions in this book cover a broad range of issues relevant to the introduction of an explicit efficiency defence in European merger control. They examine the background data on M&A activity and merger control, the political pressures, the theoretical underpinnings and the empirical findings. Last but not least, they contain a number of valuable practical suggestions for implementing the analysis of efficiencies in merger control. However, further work is still necessary to be able to better identify the conditions under which dynamic efficiencies are more likely to materialize and find some useful criteria in that respect.

Although the studies contained in this volume were carried out on behalf of the European Commission and some of the contributors are employed by the Commission, the views expressed are the authors' own and do not necessarily reflect the Commission's policy line.

REFERENCE

Gugler, K., D. Mueller and B. Burcin Yurtoglu (2002), 'The determinants of merger waves', working paper, University of Vienna.

1. M&A activity and merger control since 1991

Roderick Meiklejohn

The purpose of this chapter is to provide some background for the discussion which follows about the efficiency effects of mergers. We outline the recent history of merger activity in the former fifteen-member EU (EU15) and in the New Member States.[1] The New Member States are discussed separately, since most of them have only recently made the transition to market economies and their pattern of M&A activity is therefore quite idiosyncratic. Since this book is concerned in particular with the regulatory treatment of mergers, section 3 brings together some information on the number of mergers subject to merger control procedures in various jurisdictions, especially the EU, the sectors concerned and the outcome of the procedures. In the last section we compare the statistical data on the merger wave of the 1990s in the EU and the USA. The aim of this comparison is to see whether the wave behaviour of merger activity yields any general lessons about the motivation of mergers, in particular the role played by prospective efficiency gains.

1. M&A ACTIVITY IN THE EU15[2]

Overview of the Period 1991–2004

The merger wave of the 1980s reached its peak in the EU in 1991. In the following six years, the number of M&A fluctuated quite widely but remained below the 1991 level, although the total value of transactions began to increase steeply in 1995 (see Table 1.1). In the main, the early rise in transaction values was the result of very large deals in the network industries and the financial services sector. As far as the number of transactions is concerned, there were only three years of rapid growth, from 1998 to 2000. In the year 2000 the number of transactions recorded was 58 per cent greater than in 1991. In value terms, the merger wave peaked in 1999, when the total value in real terms was more than nine times that of 1991. By 2001

Table 1.1 M&A involving EU15 firms 1991–2004

	Number of M&A	Index 1991 = 100	Total value in billion euros (nominal)	Index of total value in real terms* 1991 = 100
1991	10 653	100	164.19	100
1992	10 084	95	166.48	97
1993	8 794	83	180.46	102
1994	9 070	85	187.05	103
1995	10 421	98	261.09	140
1996	9 437	89	316.50	166
1997	9 779	92	487.35	251
1998	11 228	105	853.28	432
1999	14 294	134	1860.63	929
2000	16 788	158	1623.39	799
2001	12 866	121	834.72	401
2002	9 529	89	564.78	265
2003	9 515	89	451.49	207
2004	9 811	92	627.36	282

Note: * Deflated by EU15 GDP deflator

Source: SDC

the boom was clearly over. The value of transactions fell by nearly 50 per cent in that year and there were further steep declines in the next two years. The number of M&A decreased by 23 per cent in 2001 and by 26 per cent in the following year, stabilizing in 2003. In 2004 there was some recovery in both the number and the value of transactions.

The Distribution of M&A Activity

The distribution of total M&A activity in the period 1991–2004 between the EU15 Member States is shown in Table 1.2. The UK accounts for by far the highest proportion (nearly one-third), followed at some distance by Germany and France and then by the Netherlands and Italy. The table compares the shares of M&A activity with the shares of GDP, showing that there is only a loose correlation between the size of a national economy and the number of M&A. Other factors that may play a role in determining the amount of M&A activity in a given country include the legal system, stock exchange rules, the structure of share ownership and taxation. However, it

Table 1.2 Distribution of M&A activity and GDP, 1991–2004*

Member State	Share of M&A (%)	Share of European Union GDP (%)
Belgium	2.8	3.2
Denmark	2.6	2.1
Germany	16.5	27.7
Greece	1.1	1.4
Spain	5.5	7.1
France	13.1	18.1
Ireland	1.7	1.0
Italy	6.2	12.4
Luxembourg	0.5	0.2
Netherlands	6.3	4.9
Austria	2.1	2.8
Portugal	1.3	1.3
Finland	3.9	1.6
Sweden	5.3	2.9
UK	31.2	13.3
EU15	100	100

Note: *Number of mergers involving EU15 firms, either as bidder or as target

Sources: SDC and AMECO

is difficult to identify the really important determinants (see European Commission 2000).

Domestic and Cross-border Operations

Most M&A are domestic operations, that is, all parties to the transaction are based in the same country. As Table 1.3 shows, domestic operations represented on average over the whole period 56 per cent of the total M&A involving EU15 firms and the fluctuations have been quite small. Community operations, that is, mergers between firms based in different Member States, account for 13 per cent, again with only small fluctuations from year to year. However, a different picture emerges when we look at mergers between EU15 firms and non-EU15 firms (international operations). Here there is a trend for the share of M&A targeting EU firms to decline (from 26 per cent in 1991 to 17 per cent in 2004) while the share of transactions in which EU firms are bidders rises (from 7 per cent to

Table 1.3 Breakdown of total M&A into domestic, Community and international operations (% of total number of M&A involving EU15 firms)

	Domestic	Community*	International** – EU target	International** – EU bidder	Total
1991	54.4	11.9	26.3	7.3	100
1992	58.0	11.6	23.9	6.5	100
1993	57.4	11.7	22.3	8.5	100
1994	58.6	13.0	18.5	9.9	100
1995	58.6	12.8	17.0	11.6	100
1996	56.0	12.5	18.9	12.7	100
1997	56.0	13.9	17.8	12.3	100
1998	53.7	14.0	17.4	14.9	100
1999	55.8	14.2	13.4	16.6	100
2000	54.8	15.2	13.2	16.9	100
2001	55.0	14.7	14.7	15.6	100
2002	58.4	13.8	14.4	13.4	100
2003	58.6	12.8	15.6	13.0	100
2004	57.5	12.7	16.7	13.2	100
Average	56.4	13.4	17.5	12.7	100

Notes:
* Mergers between firms based in different Member States
** Mergers between EU15 and non-EU15 firms

Source: SDC

13 per cent). In the peak year of 2000, the share of the latter type reached nearly 17 per cent. In absolute terms, the number of international M&A targeting EU15 companies fell by 20 per cent between 1991 and 2000, while the number of acquisitions made by EU15 firms outside the Community increased by 260 per cent.

It is possible that, in the early 1990s, the number of international M&A targeting firms in EU15 was inflated by a fear of the creation of a 'fortress Europe', causing foreign companies to make acquisitions in the Community in order to maintain their presence in European markets should the barriers to trade be raised. The successful completion of the Uruguay Round, together with continued liberalization measures taken by the Community, put an end to this fear and may consequently also have been a major cause of the declining interest of non-EU15 firms in acquiring companies in EU15.

Geographical Distribution of Cross-border Operations

As Table 1.4 shows, EU15 companies made slightly more acquisitions in other EU15 Member States than outside the area during the period 1991–2004. Overall, German firms are most frequently targeted in intra-EU cross-border operations. Given the size of the German economy and its central location, this observation is unsurprising. However, when we examine the data for individual countries, it becomes apparent that the size of the host country's economy is not the only determinant of the distribution of intra-EU merger activity. Proximity, historical and cultural links and the possession of a common language also seem to play important roles. Such factors clearly underlie, for example, the preference of Danish firms for Sweden and of Spanish firms for Portugal. An examination of international operations confirms this impression. Although the USA

Table 1.4 Cross-border M&A, 1991–2004 – number of acquisitions made by EU15 firms

Bidder country	Total cross-border M&A by country of bidder	Community operations		International operations*	
		Total number	Most targeted country (number)	Total number	Most targeted country (number)
Belgium	1 694	1 134	France (398)	560	USA (151)
Denmark	1 345	778	Sweden (212)	567	Norway (155)
Germany	6 191	3 125	France (608)	3 066	USA (742)
Greece	346	114	UK (32)	232	Romania (33)
Spain	1 446	570	Portugal (172)	876	Argentina (133)
France	5 118	2 760	Germany (626)	2 358	USA (600)
Ireland	1 114	697	UK (494)	417	USA (224)
Italy	1 775	1 031	France (284)	744	USA (155)
Luxembourg	503	344	France (77)	159	USA (26)
Netherlands	3 921	2 321	Germany (596)	1 600	USA (419)
Austria	1 194	574	Germany (331)	620	Hungary (110)
Portugal	329	182	Spain (132)	147	Brazil (72)
Finland	1 343	717	Sweden (279)	626	USA (126)
Sweden	2 752	1 577	Finland (403)	1 175	Norway (311)
UK	10 660	4 437	France (977)	6 223	USA (2557)
EU15 total	39 731	20 361	Germany (3559)	19 370	USA (5506)

Note: *Acquisitions of non-EU15 companies

Source: SDC

accounts for 28 per cent of all the acquisitions made outside the EU15, Danish and Swedish firms prefer Norway and Spanish firms favour Argentina, while Portuguese companies are attracted to Brazil and Austrian companies to Hungary.

Table 1.5, which gives a breakdown of cross-border operations by target country, shows a somewhat different picture.[3] Acquisitions of EU firms by non-EU firms outnumber intra-EU cross-border operations by a substantial margin. The USA appears as the principal bidder country for every EU target country. Indeed, the EU15 accounts for 43 per cent of all cross-border acquisitions made by US companies. In intra-EU operations, UK companies are the most frequent bidders, reflecting their generally greater propensity to engage in mergers and acquisitions.

Table 1.5 Cross-border M&A, 1991–2004 – number of acquisitions of EU15 firms

Target country	Total cross-border M&A by target country	Community operations		International operations*	
		Total number	Most frequent bidder country (number)	Total number	Most frequent bidder country (number)
Belgium	1 605	1 057	Netherlands (316)	548	USA (246)
Denmark	1 241	719	Sweden (274)	522	USA (171)
Germany	7 940	3 554	UK (936)	4 386	USA (1701)
Greece	449	152	France (33)	297	USA (43)
Spain	2 792	1 729	UK (400)	1 063	USA (390)
France	5 852	3 159	UK (977)	2 693	USA (1212)
Ireland	987	491	UK (377)	496	USA (222)
Italy	3 268	1 682	France (424)	1 586	USA (607)
Luxembourg	295	211	Germany (46)	84	USA (31)
Netherlands	2 818	1 597	UK (501)	1 221	USA (547)
Austria	1 183	715	Germany (453)	468	USA (93)
Portugal	804	477	Spain (172)	327	USA (58)
Finland	1 300	816	Sweden (403)	484	USA (155)
Sweden	2 403	1 262	UK (293)	1 141	USA (406)
UK	14 027	2 740	Germany (544)	11 287	USA (3574)
EU15 total	46 964	20 361	UK (4437)	26 603**	USA (9456)

Notes:
* Acquisitions made by non-EU15 companies
** N.B. For 41% of these operations, the database does not record the home country of the bidder

Source: SDC

Sectoral Distribution of EU Merger Activity

In this section we consider only the main sector of activity of the target company, on the assumption that this is likely to be the sector where the merger produces its main economic effects. The sectoral classification in the SDC data base is an old version of the US Standard Industrial Classification (SIC).[4]

During the period 1991–2004, the majority of operations involving EU companies took place in the service sectors,[5] which also showed much faster and more sustained growth in the boom period from 1997 to 2000 (see Figure 1.1).

More disaggregated data are given in Table 1.6, which shows that, at the one-digit level of classification, manufacturing accounted for by far the largest proportion (37 per cent) of all M&A involving EU companies in the period 1991–2004. At the two-digit level, however, the largest single sector, with 12 per cent, is business services. Information technology services account for nearly two-thirds of the mergers in that sector.

The share of service industries,[6] in particular IT services, increased rapidly during the 1990s, as Figure 1.2 shows, rising from 14 per cent in 1991 to 32 per cent in 2000 but falling away somewhat thereafter. The transport, utilities and communication sector increased its share from 8 per cent in 1991 to 12 per cent in 2004, mainly because of increased M&A activity by telecommunications firms. The share of manufacturing, on the other hand, fell steeply from 45 per cent to around 30 per cent. The shares of the other main sectors, including finance, insurance and real estate, remained quite stable.

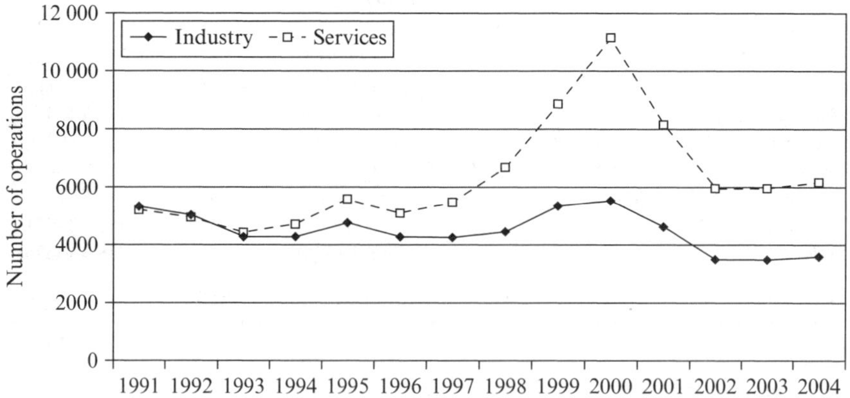

Source: SDC.

Figure 1.1 Sectoral composition of M&A involving EU15 firms

Table 1.6 Sectoral breakdown of M&A involving EU15 firms, 1991–2004 (number of deals)

Sector of target firm	SIC code	Percentage of M&A involving EU firms
Agriculture, forestry, fisheries	**0**	**0.7**
Mineral industries	10–14	2.0
Construction industries	15–17	2.5
Manufacturing	2 and 3	36.7
Of which:		
Food and kindred products	20	4.7
Industrial machinery and equipment	35	4.3
Chemicals	28	4.2
Total industry	**1 to 3**	**41.2**
Transportation, communication, utilities	4	10.4
Of which:		
Communications	48	3.2
Electric, gas and sanitary services	49	2.6
Wholesale trade	50–51	6.4
Retail trade	52–59	5.3
Finance, insurance, real estate	6	14.3
Of which:		
Banks and other credit institutions	60–61	3.5
Real estate	65	3.2
Holding and other investment offices	67	3.4
Service industries	7 and 8	21.4
Of which:		
Business services	73	11.9
Engineering and management services	87	3.9
Public administration	9	0.2
Total services	**4 to 9**	**58.1**

Source: SDC

2. M&A ACTIVITY IN THE NEW MEMBER STATES

Overview

At the beginning of the period under review, most of the New Member States (NMS), with exceptions of Cyprus and Malta, had just started their transition to capitalism. The level of M&A activity was therefore very low (see Table 1.7). Activity began to increase significantly in 1993 as more and

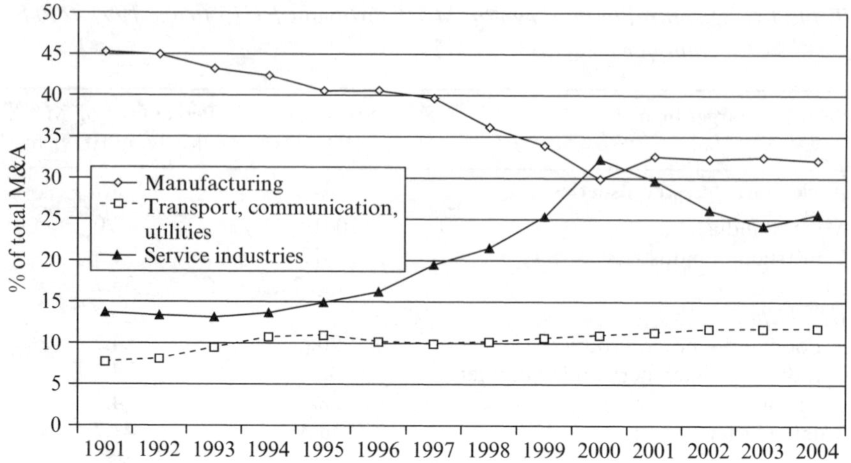

Source: SDC.

Figure 1.2 Sectoral distribution of M&A involving EU15 firms

Table 1.7 M&A activity in the New Member States, 1991–2004

	Number of M&A		Total value	
	Number	Index 1991 = 100	Million euros (nominal)	Index 1991 = 100
1991	186	100	1413	100
1992	204	110	1342	95
1993	435	234	3731	264
1994	463	249	1463	104
1995	960	516	6790	481
1996	843	453	4066	288
1997	595	320	6506	461
1998	591	318	6307	446
1999	1338	719	18442	1305
2000	1559	838	19745	1398
2001	1191	640	21955	1554
2002	813	437	17616	1247
2003	789	424	8352	591
2004	576	310	10512	744

Source: SDC

more firms were privatised. However, the growth has been extremely erratic, with very large increases in 1993, 1995 and 1999 but substantial declines (in terms of numbers of operations) in 1996 and 1997. These erratic movements do not seem to reflect macroeconomic developments. From 1994 to 2000, the GDP growth rate of the NMS was consistently above 3 per cent, with particularly high growth rates in the three years 1995–97. However, the sharp fall in the numbers of M&A after 2000 was associated with slower GDP growth (around 2.4 per cent per year). The wide fluctuations in M&A activity probably reflect the sporadic pattern of privatization in the Central and Eastern European countries.

By 2000, M&A activity had become much more intense in the NMS than in EU15. Over the period 2000–04, the ratio between the number of M&A and GDP (in billion euros) averaged 1.3 in EU15, where Finland had the highest value (3.8). For the NMS, the average ratio was 2.4, Malta having the lowest ratio (0.8) and Estonia the highest (9.8). To a large extent, this high level of activity is probably explained by the fact that most of these economies are still in transition and in need of substantial restructuring, as well as offering important new opportunities to foreign investors.

The distribution of M&A activity between the NMS (see Table 1.8) shows anomalies similar to those observed in EU15. The Baltic countries, especially Estonia, have much larger shares of the total M&A activity than the size of their economies would lead one to expect. The level of activity was also relatively high in the Czech Republic and Hungary, perhaps

Table 1.8 Distribution of M&A activity in New Member States, 2000–04

	Share of total number of M&A (%)	Share of GDP (%)
Cyprus	4.8	2.6
Czech Republic	18.9	17.3
Estonia	6.6	1.7
Hungary	17.6	15.3
Latvia	4.6	2.2
Lithuania	6.1	3.5
Malta	0.4	1.0
Poland	29.2	44.9
Slovak Republic	6.0	6.1
Slovenia	5.8	5.4
NMS Total	100	100

Source: SDC

Table 1.9 Shares of domestic and cross-border operations in total number of M&A in the New Member States

	Domestic (%)	Cross-border, as target (%)	Cross-border, as bidder (%)
1991	9.1	87.6	3.2
1992	9.8	86.8	3.4
1993	17.7	81.0	1.4
1994	37.1	59.7	3.2
1995	41.4	56.2	2.5
1996	45.2	50.4	4.4
1997	43.6	48.9	7.5
1998	37.8	57.1	5.2
1999	42.4	51.7	5.8
2000	40.7	52.9	6.4
2001	46.6	45.7	7.7
2002	41.5	47.9	10.6
2003	42.0	48.9	9.1
2004	31.8	52.5	15.7
Average 1991–2004	39.4	54.0	6.6

Source: SDC

mainly because of their attractive position in the middle of Europe. On the other hand, the level of activity in Poland is remarkably low. In Poland, the privatization of larger enterprises has been slow. At the end of 2002, the state still had a controlling stake in 2100 enterprises. This, together with a general perception that the Polish economy is over-regulated, may help to explain the low level of M&A activity.

As Table 1.9 shows, acquisitions by foreign companies accounted for the vast majority of M&A in the New Member States in the first half of the 1990s and still represent more than half of the total. However, the shares of the other types of operations have increased rapidly since 1994. It is understandable that domestic firms were initially not inclined to bid to acquire other companies, since newly privatized firms needed time to consolidate their position and managements needed to acquire the skills required to operate in a capitalist economy.

Geographical Distribution of Cross-border Operations

Tables 1.10 and 1.11 show even more clearly than in the case of EU15 the importance of proximity and historical links in determining the direction

Table 1.10 Cross-border M&A, number of acquisitions of firms in the New Member States, 1991–2004

Target country	Total	EU15 bidder		Non-EU15 bidder	
		Number	Most frequent bidder country (number)	Number	Most frequent bidder country (number)
Cyprus	71	40	Greece (30)	31	USA (11)
Czech Republic	1120	628	Germany (176)	492	USA (134)
Estonia	496	216	Finland (102)	280	Norway (24)
Hungary	1281	630	Germany (173)	651	USA (128)
Latvia	263	117	Finland (37)	146	Estonia (25)
Lithuania	325	146	Finland (35)	179	Estonia (25)
Malta	21	13	Netherlands/ UK (both 3)	8	Hong Kong (2)
Poland	1802	961	Germany (250)	841	USA (201)
Slovakia	308	158	Austria (39)	150	USA (22)
Slovenia	146	67	Austria (21)	79	USA (8)
All NMS*	5833	2976	Germany (686)	2857	USA (550)

Note: * For 25% of the overall total the database does not record the home country of the bidding firm

Source: SDC

of M&A flows. Although incomplete, the data show that well over a half of all acquisitions of firms in the NMS were made by companies based in EU15. The tables reflect the strong links between Cyprus and Greece, between the Nordic and Baltic countries, as well as between Germany and Austria and the Central European countries. Amongst the non-EU bidder countries, the USA naturally predominates.

Table 1.11 shows a marked preference for other transitional economies on the part of NMS-based firms making cross-border acquisitions. EU15 Member States were the targets of only 20 per cent of these M&A and the USA accounted for a mere 2 per cent. Russia is the most frequently targeted country, being favoured by Cypriot companies, which account for nearly one-fifth of the total number of cross-border acquisitions by NMS firms. The prominent position of Cyprus as a bidder country is accounted for by its relatively high per capita GDP and its unbroken history of integration in the world capitalist economy.

Table 1.11 Number of cross-border acquisitions made by NMS firms, 1991–2004

Bidder country	Total	EU15 target		Non-EU15 target	
		Number	Most frequent target country (number)	Number	Most frequent target country (number)
Cyprus	127	33	Greece (19)	94	Russia (24)
Czech Republic	90	18	Germany (8)	72	Slovakia (23)
Estonia	70	9	Finland (7)	61	Lithuania/Latvia (both 25)
Hungary	120	21	Austria (10)	99	Romania (15)
Latvia	35	4	DK/Germany/S/UK	31	Estonia (14)
Lithuania	32	9	Sweden (3)	23	Latvia (8)
Malta	14	4	Italy (3)	10	Russia (3)
Poland	93	23	Germany (6)	70	Lithuania (12)
Slovakia	54	6	Germany (2)	48	Czech Republic (26)
Slovenia	74	11	Italy (4)	63	Croatia (19)
All NMS*	709	138	Germany (23)	571	Russia (56)

Source: SDC

Sectoral Distribution

On the whole, the rates of growth of M&A in industry and services do not show such marked differences in the NMS as in EU15 (see Figure 1.3). Whereas service sector mergers in EU15 already exceeded industrial mergers by 1993, merger activity in the service sector got off to a slow start in the NMS and did not overtake industrial M&A until 1998. The slow initial growth of activity in the service sectors can be attributed to the priority accorded to industrial enterprises in the government privatization programmes. M&A in both branches of the economy showed strong growth in 1999 and 2000 and declined at similar rates in the following two years.

The more disaggregated data given in Table 1.12 shows that, at the one-digit level of the SIC classification, manufacturing accounted for 43 per cent of all operations involving NMS firms, a significantly higher proportion than in EU15 (37 per cent). Within manufacturing, food and drink was the most heavily represented sector with nearly 11 per cent, much more

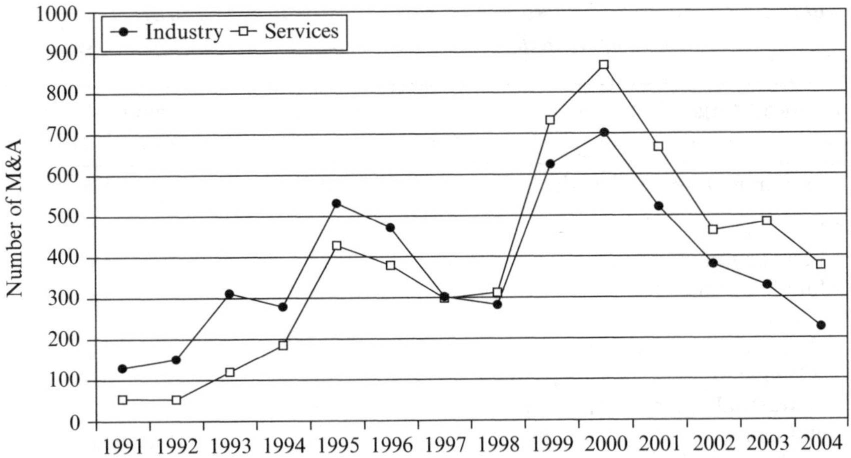

Source: SDC

Figure 1.3 Sectoral composition of M&A involving firms in the New Member States

than in EU15. As in EU15, the chemicals and industrial machinery sectors also figure prominently.

In the service sectors, the high share of banking (8 per cent) is noteworthy. This reflects the key role played by the banking sector in the transition to a market economy. On the other hand, the share of service industries is only half that observed in EU15, perhaps indicating that these sectors are somewhat underdeveloped in the NMS. Although the share of service industries[7] increased quite rapidly from 1998 onwards to average around 15 per cent in 2001–04, this percentage is still only about half of the corresponding figure for EU15. In both groups of countries, most of the growth in activity in service industries took place in the information technology sectors.

M&A and the Transition to Capitalism

In the New Member States, with the exceptions of Cyprus and Malta, the growth of M&A was a natural concomitant of the transition to capitalism. The structure of the economy had to be radically reorganized and the first step was privatization. In some countries, such as Hungary, where the preferred method of privatization was by direct trade sale, this led to an immediate development of significant M&A activity, particularly acquisitions by non-Hungarian companies. In other countries, such as Czechoslovakia before the split, the predominant method of privatization was the

Table 1.12 Sectoral breakdown of M&A involving NMS firms, 1991–2004 (number of deals)

Sector of target firm	SIC code	Percentage of M&A involving NMS firms
Agriculture, forestry, fisheries	**0**	**1.3**
Mineral industries	10–14	2.7
Construction industries	15–17	3.0
Manufacturing	2 and 3	42.8
Of which:		
Food and kindred products	20	10.8
Chemicals	28	5.0
Industrial machinery and equipment	35	2.8
Total industry	**1–3**	**48.5**
Transportation, communication, utilities	4	13.8
Of which:		
Communications	48	4.8
Electric, gas and sanitary services	49	4.8
Wholesale trade	50 and 51	4.5
Retail trade	52–59	3.8
Finance, insurance, real estate	6	16.5
Of which:		
Banks and other credit institutions	60–61	7.8
Insurance	63 and 64	3.1
Holding and other investment offices	67	3.1
Service industries	7 and 8	11.3
Of which:		
Business services	73	5.9
Engineering and management services	87	1.8
Public administration	9	0.2
Total services	**4–9**	**50.2**

Source: SDC

distribution of vouchers to the populace. This resulted in a wide dispersion of ownership, even though 60 per cent of voucher holders chose to assign their vouchers to investment funds rather than acquiring shares in specific firms. This dispersion of ownership delayed the development of M&A activity. In all these countries, however, the need for foreign capital and management expertise, together with the attractions of the local economies, led sooner or later to substantial levels of cross-border M&A. By the mid-1990s there was also significant domestic M&A activity. As noted above, Poland has been notably slower to privatize its enterprises and M&A activity there is consequently less developed than in most other NMS. Given that the Central and Eastern European Countries needed thoroughgoing restructuring, as well as foreign capital and expertise, it seems probable that M&A activity in these countries has, in general, helped to improve economic efficiency.

3. MERGER CONTROL IN THE EU

Overview

During the period 1991–2004, the European Commission dealt with 2636 merger notifications (see Table 1.13). Because the merger regulation defines mergers with a 'Community dimension' in a very restrictive way, this number represents less than 2 per cent of M&A involving EU firms over the same period and probably an even smaller proportion of the total number of M&A affecting markets in the EU[8]. In contrast, 35 747 transactions were

Table 1.13 Notified M&A in the EU and the USA, 1991–2004

	EU		USA	
	Number of notifications	Notifications as % of total M&A involving EU firms	Number of pre-merger filings	Notifications as % of total M&A involving US firms
1991	63	0.6	1 529	20.6
1992	60	0.6	1 589	20.7
1993	58	0.7	1 846	21.1
1994	95	1.0	2 305	21.9
1995	110	1.1	2 816	22.6
1996	131	1.4	3 087	21.7
1997	172	1.8	3 702	24.4
1998	235	2.1	4 728	27.1
1999	292	2.0	4 642	30.2
2000	345	2.1	4 926	33.1
2001	335	2.6	2 376	23.1
2002	279	3.0	1 187	13.1
2003	212	2.2	1 014	10.8
2004	249	2.5	n.a.	n.a.
Total	2636	1.7	35 747 (1991–2003)	23.4

Sources: European Commission, FTC, SDC

reported to the federal competition authorities in the USA between 1991 and 2003, representing 23 per cent of all M&A involving US companies.

The enlargement of the EU will result in an increase in the total number of cases notifiable under the merger regulation but is not likely to affect the proportion. Although enlargement will mean that there are more companies which exceed the threshold of €250 million for turnover within the Community, this effect will probably be counterbalanced by the smaller size of enterprises in the NMS.

Only about 5 per cent of cases notified to the European Commission raised serious competition issues that could not be resolved in the first phase of the procedure and therefore had to be subjected to in-depth investigation in a second phase (see Table 1.14). The US federal authorities challenge a much smaller proportion of mergers filed with them: less than 2 per cent in the period 1996–2003. However, because a much larger proportion of deals is subject to federal control, the percentage of the total number of M&A challenged is much greater in the USA than in the EU (about 0.4 per cent compared to 0.1 per cent).

Table 1.14 Phase II cases in the EU and challenges in the USA

	EU		USA	
	Number of Phase II cases initiated	Phase II cases as percentage of notifications	Number of challenges	Challenges as percentage of pre-merger filings
1991	6	9.5	n.a.	n.a.
1992	4	6.7	n.a.	n.a.
1993	4	6.9	n.a.	n.a.
1994	6	6.3	n.a.	n.a.
1995	7	6.4	n.a.	n.a.
1996	6	4.6	57	1.8
1997	11	6.4	59	1.6
1998	12	5.1	84	1.8
1999	20	6.8	77	1.7
2000	19	5.5	80	1.6
2001	22	6.6	50	2.1
2002	7	2.5	34	2.9
2003	9	4.2	36	3.6
2004	8	3.2	n.a.	n.a.
Total	141	5.3	n.a.	n.a.

Sources: European Commission, FTC

In the EU, many mergers that fall outside the Commission's jurisdiction are subject to control by the national authorities. Table 1.15 contains some data on mergers examined by the competition authorities in the three largest Member States, showing that national merger control laws cover a much larger proportion of deals in Germany than in France, while only 9 per cent of M&A are examined in the U.K. In the USA, merger control powers are exercised at the federal level not only by the Federal Trade Commission (FTC) and the Department of Justice (DoJ) but also by some sector-specific regulatory authorities such as the Federal Communications Commission. The Attorneys-General of the states also have powers in this field. Since, unlike the merger regulation, the federal statutes make no provision for a 'one-stop shop', the same merger may be subject to investigation by several authorities in the USA.[9]

Table 1.16 shows that less than 1 per cent of mergers dealt with by the European Commission under the merger regulation have been forbidden, while 88 per cent were approved unconditionally in the first phase of the procedure. In nearly 5 per cent of cases, the parties offered remedies early in the procedure to resolve competition problems and the Commission was able to accept these remedies already in the first phase. Of the 117 Phase II decisions, over 20 per cent were unconditional authorizations and more than 60 per cent were clearance decisions with remedies.

Table 1.15 *Mergers examined by EU national authorities, 1996–2003 (number and percentage of total M&A involving firms of the country concerned)*

	Germany		France		UK	
	Number	%	Number	%	Number	%
1996	1 286	59	472	33	531	15
1997	1 569	79	478	34	396	10
1998	1 691	98	505	34	425	9
1999	1 179	42	369	20	415	9
2000	1 429	45	342	14	315	6
2001	1 138	53	327	18	356	8
2002	1 317	80	125	10	355	11
2003	1 132	72	237	21	329*	8
Total	10 741	62	2855	22	3122	9

Note: *Includes first quarter 2004

Source: National competition authorities' annual reports and reports to OECD

Table 1.16 Final decisions under the merger regulation, 1991–2004

Type of decision	1991–95	1996	1997	1998	1999	2000	2001	2002	2003	2004	**Total**	%
Outside scope of regulation	32	6	4	6	1	1	1	1	0	0	52	2.0
Full referral to member state	1	3	1	1	3	2	1	4	8	2	26	1.0
Phase I clearance without remedies	307	109	118	207	236	293	299	240	203	220	2232	87.7
Phase I clearance with remedies	12	0	2	12	19	28	13	10	11	12	119	4.7
Phase II clearance without remedies	7	1	1	3	0	3	5	2	2	2	26	1.0
Phase II clearance with remedies	13	3	7	4	8	12	10	5	6	4	72	2.8
Prohibition	4	3	1	2	1	2	5	0	0	1	19	0.7
Total	376	125	134	235	268	341	334	262	230	241	2546	100

Source: European Commission

Our brief review of the statistics relating to Community merger control does not suggest that the merger regulation places a very heavy burden on business, nor that the Commission is exceptionally severe in its application of the regulation. Indeed, in an analysis of 164 cases dealt with under the merger regulation, Duso et al. (2003) find only four cases where they consider that the Commission erred in forbidding pro-competitive mergers (Type I errors) but 34 instances of mergers cleared unconditionally by the Commission that they judge to be anti-competitive (Type II errors). However, these authors use an event-study methodology which assumes that competitors' share prices will react positively if a merger is anti-competitive but negatively if it is pro-competitive. The reasoning behind this is that the increase in market power arising from an anti-competitive merger makes it profitable for the merged entity to raise its prices and reduce its output. This benefits competitors by enabling them to raise their prices while profiting from the diversion of some demand from the merged entity. By contrast, a pro-competitive merger damages rivals' profitability by creating a more aggressive competitor. This assumption is open to question, since a competitor's share price may fall on the announcement of a merger simply because that competitor was previously regarded as a potential candidate for takeover by the acquiring firm. The pre-announcement share price might therefore have been inflated by the expectation of a bid. In such circumstances, the share price would naturally fall when the market learns the true identity of the chosen target, regardless of the merger's effect on competition (see Stennek and Fridolfsson 2000). The details of the methodology applied by Duso et al. can also be criticized on the ground that it does not take account of the stock market's expectations concerning the treatment of the case by competition authorities other than the European Commission. The extent to which the competitors' share prices will react to the announcement of a merger depends on whether the market expects the merger to be cleared by all the relevant competition authorities. Very large mergers such as those that fall under the merger regulation often fall within the jurisdiction of authorities outside the EU. In addition, as the authors acknowledge, the number of Type I errors may be overestimated because a fall in the competitors' share prices may indicate either that the merger is pro-competitive or that it has anti-competitive foreclosure effects, which are not incorporated in their model.

Sectoral Distribution of Cases

Table 1.17 provides a breakdown of the sectoral distribution of cases dealt with under the merger regulation between 1991 and 2004. On comparing these figures with the data on the number of M&A involving EU firms, the

Table 1.17 Sectoral distribution of cases under the merger regulation, 1991–2004

	Percentage of total cases		M&A targeting firms in the sector as % of total M&A involving EU firms	
Agriculture, forestry, fisheries		**0.4**		**0.7**
Industry		**50.0**		**41.2**
Of which:				
Chemicals	8.8		4.2	
Electrical and optical equipment	8.0		5.3	
Mechanical engineering	4.8		4.3	
Food and kindred products	4.7		4.6	
Motor vehicles and parts	4.2		1.2	
Other industry	19.6		21.6	
Services		**49.6**		**58.1**
Of which:				
Post and telecommunications	7.9		3.2	
Banking	5.8		3.5	
Retail distribution	5.6		5.3	
Business services (inc. engineering and management)	5.2		15.8	
Insurance and pension funding	4.6		2.5	
Electricity and gas	4.5		1.8	
Wholesale distribution	3.8		6.4	
Other services	12.4		19.6	
Total		**100**		**100**

Sources: European Commission and SDC

first thing we notice is that industry is 'over-represented' in the cases notified to the Commission. This is because a larger proportion of industrial firms than of service-sector firms exceed the merger regulation thresholds. Not only are industrial firms more likely to have turnovers above the minimum levels specified in the regulation but they are also more likely to have sales in more than one Member State. Many parts of the services sector are composed largely of small or medium-sized firms operating at a local or, at most, national level.

Industrial sectors dominated by very large firms, such as chemicals, electrical and optical equipment and motor vehicles are particularly heavily represented amongst the notified cases. In the services sector, post and telecommunications mergers account for 8 per cent of notifications but only 2 per cent of the total number of mergers. Telecommunications companies are typically extremely large enterprises. Since 1990, technological changes, privatization and liberalization in the telecommunications sector have encouraged firms to expand but the opportunities for expansion by mergers or acquisitions within a single country are very limited. Consequently, cross-border mergers of large firms constitute a large proportion of the total M&A activity in this sector. On the other hand, mergers in the wholesale distribution sector and, especially, business services are 'under-represented' amongst the notified cases because firms in these sectors are generally much smaller and less likely to want to expand beyond their national borders.

4. THE MERGER WAVE OF THE 1990s: A COMPARISON WITH THE USA

This section considers only the period 1991–2002, in order to focus attention on the last merger wave. In those twelve years, EU companies were involved in nearly 133 000 mergers (see Figure 1.4). In the first half of the 1990s the pattern of M&A activity was rather erratic but a strong upsurge occurred in the period 1997–2000. In the year 2000 the number of mergers involving EU firms was 57 per cent higher than in 1991. In the following two years there was an equally dramatic decline as the number of transactions fell by 44 per cent to 9356 in 2002.

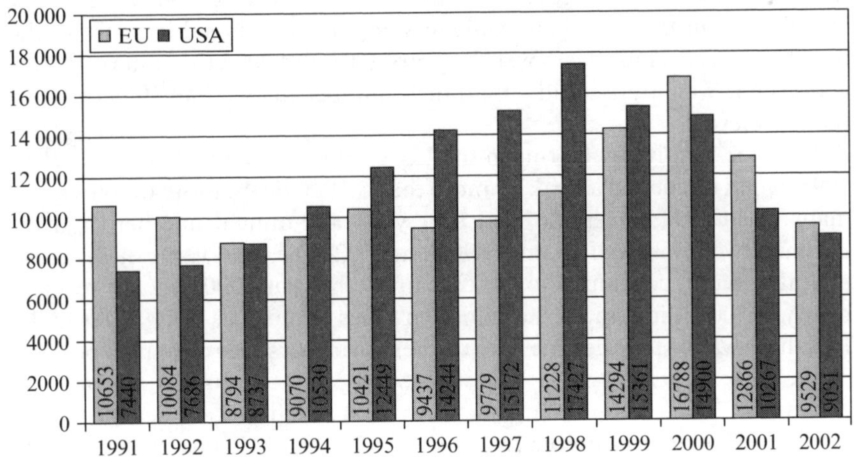

Source: SDC.

Figure 1.4 Number of M&A involving firms in the EU15 and the USA

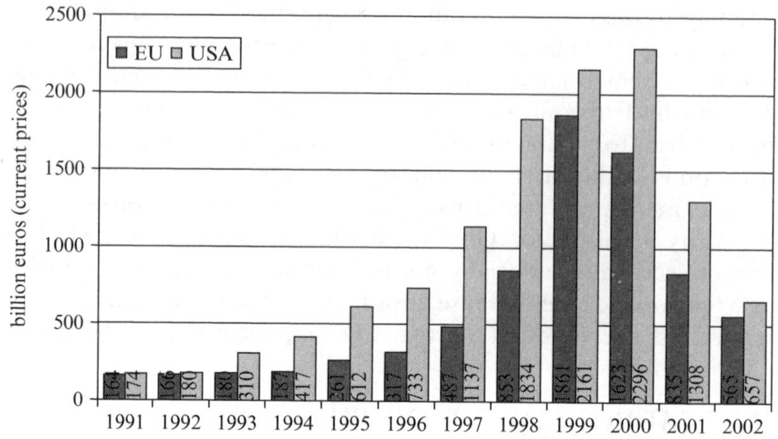

Source: SDC.

Figure 1.5 Value of M&A involving EU15 and US firms

The aggregate value of M&A transactions involving EU firms rose continuously between 1991 and 1999, the fastest growth occurring in the last three of those years (see Figure 1.5). The aggregate value in 1999 was more than eleven times greater than in 1991 but it should be noted that 1999 was the year of the record-breaking Vodafone/Mannesmann deal, which alone accounted for 11 per cent of the extreme value of €1860 billion reached in that year. It is therefore not surprising that the following year saw a 13 per cent decline in the aggregate value in spite of a continued increase in the number of deals. However, over the years 2001 and 2002 the value of transactions fell even more rapidly than their number to less than 30 per cent of the 1999 level.

The M&A activity of firms in the USA grew continuously from 1991 to 1998, when it reached a peak of more than 17 000 deals, more than twice as many as in 1991. Over the next four years the annual number of deals declined by almost half to under 9000 in 2002. The total value of deals, on the other hand, continued to increase up to the year 2000, when it reached nearly €2300 billion, more than thirteen times as much as in 1991. As in the EU, there was a steep decline over the next two years to less than 30 per cent of the peak value.

Years of weak economic growth are associated with a decline in the number of mergers, as in the EU in 1992–93, 1996 and 2001–02 and, in the latter two years, also in the USA (see Figure 1.6). However, transaction values may continue to rise strongly even if there is a sharp fall in the economic growth rate (see Figure 1.7). This was the case in the USA in 1995, when the total value of deals rose by nearly 50 per cent, while the GDP growth rate fell from 4.1 per cent to 2.7 per cent. Similarly, the value of deals involving EU firms grew by 20 per cent in 1996, in spite of a 9.5 per cent fall in the number of mergers and GDP growth of only 1.8 per cent.

Both the numbers and the values of M&A are positively correlated to movements in share prices[10] (see Figures 1.8 and 1.9). However, it is noteworthy that the number of M&A involving US firms peaked in 1998, one year before the peak in share prices and M&A values. In the EU, on the other hand, while share prices and the number of mergers both peaked in 2000, the aggregate annual value of mergers reached its maximum level in 1999.

There are basically three plausible explanations for the positive correlation between share prices and M&A activity. These explanations are not mutually exclusive. The first is that the share price index may be influenced by the level of merger activity, rather than the other way around. Indeed, as a general rule, the share prices of potential targets of takeover bids rise substantially, while those of bidders fall slightly on average. Although bidders are typically larger than targets, there is usually a net gain in the short run to the shareholders of both firms taken together. Moreover, when it is known that a firm is seeking to make an acquisition, there may be more than one potential target, all of which may benefit from an increase in their share prices during the run-up period. Consequently, it is quite probable that rises in the level of M&A activity could be a partial explanation of increases in the stock market index.

The second explanation is that a high share price index reflects a general mood of optimism that also infects managers who are assessing the risks and returns of a possible merger. The effect of market optimism can manifest itself in two main ways. Managers are aware that, in the short term, there is a reduced risk that the market will mark down the shares of an acquiring company heavily. Managers are also more confident of their ability to make a success of a merger in the longer term.

The third possibility is that stock market booms increase the differential between the best-performing firms and the rest in terms of Tobin's q (the ratio between the stock market valuation of a firm and its tradable assets) or the price/earnings ratio. The high-valued firms seize the opportunity of the wider differential to issue new shares in order to acquire companies whose shares are performing less well. Indeed, the proportion of acquisitions financed by exchange of shares increased significantly during the last merger wave. Shleifer and Vishny (2001) point out that the use of overvalued shares to make acquisitions can be in the interest of the bidding firm's shareholders, since the growth of the firm's asset base can limit the fall in the value of shares in the long run when stock market confidence declines. It is important to note, however, that the fact that acquiring firms usually

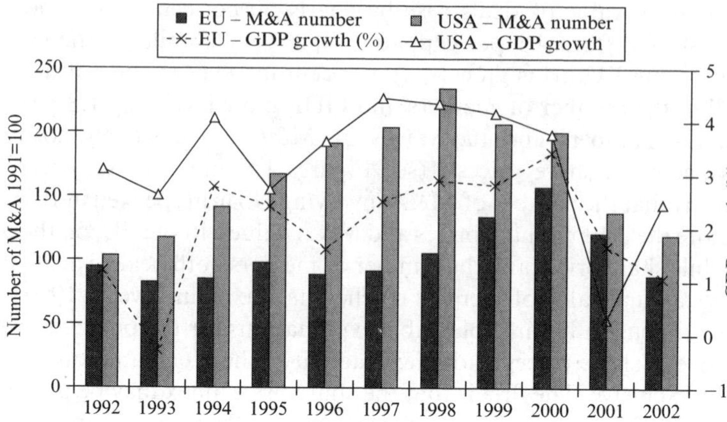

Sources: SDC and Eurostat.

Figure 1.6 Number of M&A and GDP growth

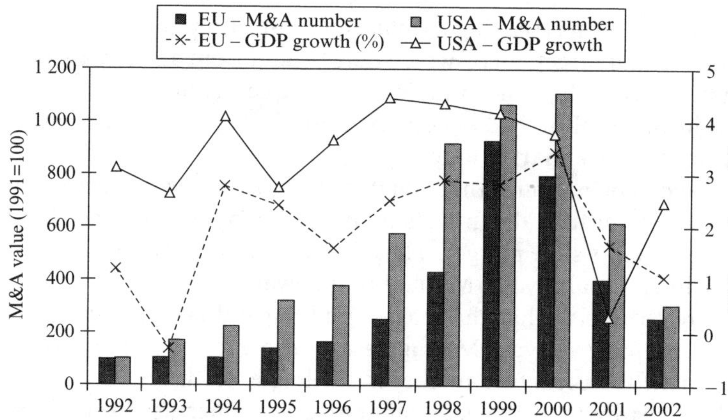

Sources: SDC and Eurostat.

Figure 1.7 M&A value (deflated by GDP deflator) and GDP growth

have a higher q than their targets does not imply that mergers will lead to efficiency gains. This would only be the case if the stock market valuations reflected the true capacities of each company's management and technology and if the supposed managerial or technological advantages of the acquiring firm can be successfully transferred to the firm that is taken over.

Gugler et al. (2002) point out that merger waves cannot be explained by sudden drives for efficiency, since the pressure to increase efficiency is

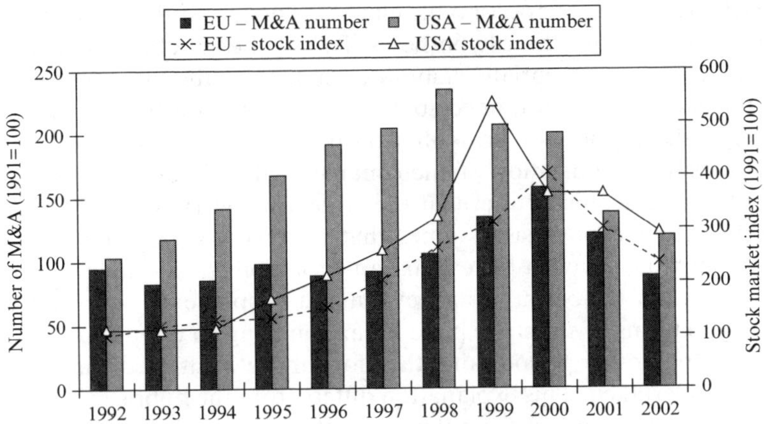

Sources: Own calculations on the basis of data from SDC and FIBV/WFE.
The stock indices are averages of the year-end stock market indices of:

- the main stock exchanges in each Member State for the EU
- Amex, NYSE and NASDAQ for the USA

re-based on 1991 and weighted by the market capitalization on each exchange.

Figure 1.8 Number of M&A and stock market index

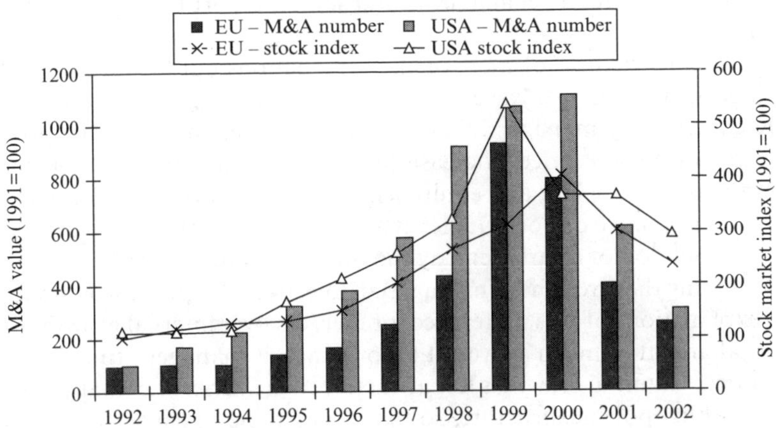

Sources: SDC and FIBV/WFE.

Figure 1.9 M&A value at constant prices (GDP deflator) and stock market index

greatest when the macroeconomic climate is poor and the stock market is depressed. They test three hypotheses. Two of these, hubris and managerial discretion, are essentially elaborate versions of the two aspects of the optimism explanation outlined above. According to the hubris hypothesis, the high share prices of firms that outperform the market are taken by managers as an indication of their managerial abilities and this induces them to make acquisitions even if the targets are overpriced. The managerial discretion hypothesis assumes that managers regard the growth of their companies, even at the expense of profitability, as a major objective. In a stock market boom, in a prevailing atmosphere of optimism,[11] the penalty in terms of the share price for announcing an unprofitable merger is less than in other periods and, therefore, more wealth-reducing mergers will be undertaken. This explanation differs from the hubris hypothesis in that managers are aware from the outset that the deal is unprofitable. The third hypothesis of Gugler et al. is overvaluation. The overvaluation hypothesis is a version of the explanation we have suggested above, based on widening differentials in Tobin's *q* and price/earnings ratios. The assumption that the differentials reflect overvaluation rests on the observation that, while acquiring firms' share prices tend to outperform the stock market before the merger, they tend to underperform afterwards.[12]

Using data on a large sample of US mergers and acquisitions between 1981 and 1999, Gugler et al. (2001) find some support for all three of their hypotheses.

The main weakness of most of the explanations put forward to explain the link between merger waves and stock market booms is that they do not fully explain why managers choose mergers rather than internal growth. Indeed, since share prices increase far more during stock market booms than the prices of plant and equipment, internal growth would seem to be the more attractive option. Gugler et al. make this point in discussing other theories but do not clearly remedy the problem in their own formulations.

Assuming that growth is a managerial objective in itself, we would suggest two explanations of this preference for mergers over internal growth. First, internal growth is much slower. It follows that, if managers' time-horizons are short,[13] internal growth is less attractive to them. Second, many markets have an oligopolistic structure, so that an increase in capacity is likely to depress prices and profits if demand is stagnant or growing only slowly. This problem is exacerbated for the expanding company if competitors are in a position to take retaliatory action.

Why should we assume that growth is a managerial objective in itself, which may be pursued even at the expense of profitability? One reason is that the structure of pecuniary incentives for executives is often not optimal: rewards may be more closely linked to the size of the firm than to its profitability.[14] Another reason is that managers seek not only pecuniary rewards but also status, that is, to improve their standing in the eyes of their peers, their subordinates and the media and also, perhaps, to increase their political influence. It seems plausible that managing a large company confers a higher status than managing a more profitable but significantly smaller company.

From this sociological point of view, we can tentatively advance an alternative explanation of merger waves. Since status is relative and since the main point of reference for a company manager is other company managers, the growth of one company can inspire managers of other firms with an urge to emulate in order to maintain their status. In times when business confidence is low, emulation may not be possible, because managers would be more risk-averse or because the penalty in terms of a negative stock market reaction would be too great. In periods of stock market booms, on the other hand, these constraints are less binding and merger waves could develop as a process of competition for status between company managers.

However, we should not ignore the possibility that that there is a two-way causal relationship between M&A activity and stock market conditions. If this is so, we may need additional explanatory factors to account for the rise and fall of merger waves. In the case of the EU in the 1990s, the main additional factors seem to be sectoral shocks, notably those arising from liberalization and privatization in network industries, the increasing integration of European markets for services and technological developments in the information technology sector. Important developments in all these fields coincided in the second half of the 1990s. A sectoral breakdown of M&A involving EU companies (see Table 1.18) shows that the network industries and the business services sector, especially computer-related services, accounted for most of the growth in the number of M&A between 1991 and the peak year 2000. The number of M&A increased in business services by 388 per cent and in the network industries by 126 per cent. In the extractive industries and in manufacturing, where the drive to create a single European market was largely completed by the beginning of the 1990s, the number of M&A was almost static. The marked asymmetry between the sectors seems to be strong evidence that sectoral shocks are important in explaining the European merger wave of the late 1990s. If this is the case, it is easier to believe that a substantial proportion of the mergers carried out during this period were aimed at maximizing shareholder value rather than the private benefits of managers. There is therefore a reasonable probability that a significant number of the mergers could have enhanced efficiency, although many may have been designed to strengthen market power and limit the impact of increased market integration. Nevertheless, these observations do not allow us to exclude the possibility

Table 1.18 Growth in M&A activity by sector between 1991 and peak year

Sector	Number of M&A involving EU15 firms			Number of M&A involving US firms		
	1991	Peak year (2000)	% change	1991	Peak year (1998)	%
Agriculture, forestry, fisheries (SIC 0)	118	96	−19	37	102	176
Mineral industries, construction (SIC 1)	555	541	−3	560	903	61
Manufacturing (SIC 2 and 3)	4770	4989	5	2685	4778	78
Transport, communication and utilities (SIC 4)	815	1841	126	672	1725	157
Distribution (SIC 5)	1382	1760	27	669	1811	171
Financial services, real estate (SIC 6)	1557	2147	38	1564	3361	115
Business services (SIC 73 and 87)	912	4450	388	733	3299	350
Other 'service industries' (SIC 7 and 8)	532	941	77	512	1428	179
Public administration (SIC 9)	12	23	92	8	20	150
Total*	10653	16788	58	7440	17427	134

Note: *The totals do not exactly equal the sum of the columns, because sectoral information on some mergers is missing from the database

Source: SDC

that hubris or the private interests of managers also played an important role in the European merger wave.

In the USA, on the other hand, the case for the sectoral shocks explanation is less strong. Over the period from 1991 to the US peak year of 1998, there was a 350 per cent increase in the number of mergers in the business services sector, where technological change may have played an important role. There were also large increases in the other 'service industries' (179 per cent), network industries (157 per cent) and financial services (115 per cent), which may be partly attributable to regulatory changes, although the regulatory environment in the network industries changed much less radically in the USA over this period than in the EU. However, one of the most striking features of M&A activity in the USA in this period is that it increased substantially in almost every sector. The number of M&A grew by 78 per cent in manufacturing and by 171 per cent in the distribution sector. At the two-digit level, the only sectors where there was a decline were metal mining (−34 per cent), air transport (−7 per cent) and fishing (a reduction from 4 operations to 1). However, these sectors never accounted for a significant proportion of M&A activity. By contrast, M&A activity in the EU fell in 29 of the 84 two-digit sectors between 1991 and 2000. It is therefore unlikely that sectoral shocks could explain as much of the merger wave in the USA as in the EU. Consequently, it is all the more probable that a substantial proportion of the mergers that occurred during this period in the USA were motivated by hubris or managers' private interests rather than shareholder value or efficiency.

5. CONCLUSIONS

This chapter has looked at M&A activity in the EU between 1991 and 2004, which covers the period of the last merger wave. We observe marked differences between countries in the intensity of M&A activity (the level of activity relative to the size of the economy). These differences are not easy to explain but probably result from a combination of numerous factors, such as the structure of share ownership, legal systems and stock exchange rules. As far as cross-border mergers are concerned, the level of activity between any pair of countries is strongly influenced by the size of the countries but proximity and historical or cultural ties are also extremely important factors.

We have found marked differences, both in the temporal evolution of M&A and in the sectoral structure, between the fifteen 'old' Member States of the EU and the ten New Member States. To a large extent, these differences can probably be attributed to the progress of privatization in the New Member States. In more general terms, the analysis of M&A in the Central and Eastern European countries has to take account of the process of transition to capitalism. M&A have played a very important – perhaps decisive – role in this process.

Section 3 of this chapter takes a look at merger control, both at the EU level and at the national level within the EU and in the USA. The percentage of mergers affected by the EU merger regulation, although rising, is very small by comparison with the percentage of mergers scrutinised by the competition authorities of the largest Member States and the USA. Of the mergers notified under the regulation, a relatively small proportion (about 6 per cent) is subject to in-depth investigation and less than 1 per cent have been forbidden. Consequently, it cannot reasonably be argued that the merger regulation imposes an excessive burden on companies. However, the impact of the regulation varies between sectors. Sectors characterized by large companies and extensive cross-border trading or ownership links are the prime targets of the regulation. These are sectors such as chemicals, electrical equipment, telecommunications and financial services.

The last section of this chapter compares the merger activity in the fifteen-member EU to that in the USA over the period 1991–2002. We find a striking contrast in the ways in which the merger wave of the 1990s developed. In the USA, the wave started and finished earlier and rose much higher. Moreover, almost every sector in the USA was strongly affected by the wave, whereas in EU15 manufacturing was largely unaffected, while distribution and financial services responded relatively weakly. We argue, following Gugler et al. (2002) that there are good reasons to believe that merger waves are not caused by a generalized need for restructuring but rather by the interaction of stock market conditions and the private interests of company managers. However, the disparities between sectors in EU15 do seem to suggest that sectoral shocks may have been an important determinant of European M&A activity. To the extent that this is true and that the mergers really enabled firms to take advantage of changed market conditions, M&A undertaken during the merger wave are more likely to have yielded efficiency gains in Europe than in the USA.

ACKNOWLEDGEMENT

The author thanks Gaëlle Garnier and Miriam Manchin for their helpful comments and Daniel Vandewalle for assistance with the statistical data.

NOTES

1. The New Member States, which joined the EU on 1 May 2004, are Cyprus, the Czech Republic, Estonia, Hungary, Latvia, Lithuania, Malta, Poland, the Slovak Republic and Slovenia.
2. Unless otherwise stated, the source of all M&A data used in this chapter is the SDC database of Thomson Financial Securities. See the appendix to this chapter for more information on the data.
3. It should be noted that the data concerning acquisitions of EU firms by non-EU firms are incomplete. For 41 per cent of these operations, the database does not record the bidder's home country.

4. The numbering and the grouping of sectors differ from the EU's NACE classification, the UN's ISIC system and the new North American Industry Classification System.
5. Here we follow the US practice of including the supply of electricity, gas and water amongst the service sectors.
6. The classification 'service industries' includes notably hotels, business services, amusement and recreational services, engineering and management services, accountancy and legal services.
7. See note 6.
8. The percentage has risen gradually, mainly because the turnover thresholds used to define 'Community dimension' have not been adjusted for inflation.
9. However, a protocol has been agreed between the federal authorities and the states' Attorneys-General to co-ordinate parallel investigations.
10. It is important, however, to bear in mind that a large proportion of deals are carried out by firms that are not listed on the stock exchange. In the year 2000 there were 7834 domestic firms listed on EU stock exchanges. In the same year there were nearly 17 000 M&A operations involving EU firms.
11. Or 'irrational exuberance' in the famous words of Alan Greenspan, Chairman of the US Federal Reserve Board.
12. Shleifer and Vishny (2001) allege also that 'bidders in stock acquisitions are likely to exhibit signs of overvaluation, such as earnings manipulation and insider dealing'.
13. This may often be the case, since many senior executives of major companies are employed on fixed-term contracts.
14. This question is discussed with specific reference to mergers in Girma et al. (2002). Using a sample of UK mergers, the authors find that the impact of a merger on the pay of the acquiring company's CEO is positive but small if the stock market reacts negatively to the merger. They also survey some other studies of US and UK mergers which yield mixed results, although none indicates that CEOs suffer an absolute fall in remuneration after carrying out unprofitable mergers. A study of 405 US firms that acquired other firms between 1993 and 2000 concludes that CEOs have clear pecuniary incentives to make acquisitions (Harford and Kai Li (2004)).

REFERENCES

Duso, T., D. Neven and L.-H. Röller (2003), 'The political economy of European merger control: evidence using stock market data', discussion paper FS IV 02–34, Wissenschaftszentrum Berlin.

European Commission, DG for Economic and Financial Affairs (2000), European Economy, Supplement A, no. 5/6.

Girma, S., S. Thompson and P. Wright (2002), 'Merger activity and executive pay', Centre for Economic Policy Research discussion paper no 3255, March, London.

Gugler, K., D. Mueller and B. Burcin Yurtoglu (2002), 'The determinants of merger waves', University of Vienna working paper.

Harford, J. and Kai Li (2004), 'Decoupling CEO wealth and firm performance: the case of acquiring CEOs', paper presented to the 2004 meeting of the Financial Research Association, Las Vegas.

Shleifer, A. and R.W. Vishny (2001), 'Stock market driven acquisitions', National Bureau for Economic Research working paper 8439, Cambridge, MA.

Stennek, J. and S.-O. Fridolfsson (2000), 'Why event studies do not detect anti-competitive mergers', Research Institute of Industrial Economics working paper, Stockholm.

APPENDIX DATA AND CONVENTIONS

A variety of information sources are available to monitor mergers and acquisitions activity. The press plays a key role, together with other sources such as company reports and announcements in official journals. Database providers have established networks of experts in several countries and devote considerable effort to collecting and cross-referencing information.

Although data providers endeavour to collect and present information which is as full as possible, the very nature of the information makes the coverage somewhat arbitrary. Whereas major operations affecting publicly listed companies are often officially published and widely reported in the press, the numerous purchases of smaller or unlisted companies are more difficult to detect. In addition, subjective assessments are often inevitable, for example, as regards the date and sectoral classification of an operation.

The data used in this chapter are based on the SDC database of Thomson Financial Securities. This base is very comprehensive, covering acquisitions of shareholdings of 5 per cent or more and with a value over US$1 million or an unknown value.

The figures include both deals that have been completed and those that are listed in the database as pending. Most pending deals are eventually completed but it is sometimes difficult to obtain confirmation of completion. Although the inclusion of pending deals results in some overestimation, their exclusion would probably lead to a much greater underestimation of the true figures.

Companies, and not only large conglomerates, are often too diversified to be classified in a single sector. The sectoral data in this chapter take account only of the main sector of activity of the target company. In general, as the target is smaller than the bidder, its main activity is usually better defined, and that activity is probably the one which interests the bidder. It is therefore assumed that this is the sector in which the effects of an M&A will be the greatest. The sectoral classification used by SDC is an old version of the U.S. Standard Industrial Classification (SIC). The numbering and, in some respects, the grouping of sectors differ from both the Community's NACE classification and the UN's ISIC system.

The database does not contain value data for a significant number of deals. However, since the value of large operations can usually be ascertained, the missing values relate mostly to small deals. The value data are therefore underestimated, though not by a large amount.

2. European merger control: do we need an efficiency defence?

Fabienne Ilzkovitz and Roderick Meiklejohn

Since the end of 1990, the European Commission has had specific powers to control mergers with a Community dimension under the merger regulation.[1] This system of merger control at the Community level was created because globalization and the dismantling of non-tariff barriers in the Single Market resulted in major corporate reorganizations in the Community, particularly in the form of cross-border mergers. Such restructuring is welcome if it enables firms to exploit the new opportunities created by a wider market and enhances their efficiency. However, mergers can also be a means to increase market power. The control of mergers at the Community level must therefore ensure that those mergers which do not enhance efficiency and which may distort competition in the Community are forbidden. However, the 1989 merger regulation was traditionally interpreted as requiring mergers to be judged on the basis of their anti-competitive effects alone and does not allow efficiency gains to be used to justify mergers which would otherwise be unacceptable.

In January 2004 the Council of Ministers adopted a new merger regulation.[2] Amongst other things, the new regulation changes the criteria (the substantive test) for deciding whether a merger should be permitted or forbidden and provides a somewhat firmer legal basis for the consideration of efficiency gains than existed in the old regulation. These aspects of the new regulation are described in Section 2.1 of this chapter.

Shortly after the adoption of the new regulation, the Commission published its first guidelines on the appraisal of horizontal mergers (European Commission 2004). These guidelines are, to a large extent, based on past practice. However, they include a section devoted to the analysis of efficiency gains, which confirms the Commission's new willingness to take efficiencies into account (see Section 2.1).

In the light of these recent developments, the purpose of this chapter is to discuss two questions. Should a merger control system take into account efficiency gains from mergers and how should a system be designed to balance the efficiency gains against the anti-competitive effects? These questions were already identified as important in the late 1980s (see Jacquemin et al. 1989) when the European merger control system was designed but, due to their complexity, they did not receive a clear answer. In the current context of rapid economic and technological change, it is important that the regulatory system should not impose unnecessary restrictions on the ability of companies to adapt and innovate. Sometimes, a merger between large firms may be a necessary precondition for such adaptation and innovation. Often, for example when the merging firms have small market shares or when the overlap between their activities is not significant, such mergers pose no competition problems. In a few cases, however, there may be a conflict between competition and efficiency. Such cases may be rare but their economic implications could be very important. The discussion must address the problems associated with dynamic efficiencies, such as synergies in R&D, as opposed to static efficiencies, which are easier to quantify but may be less important.

To help answer the questions posed above, we start by explaining the economic and political reasons that might justify the introduction of an 'efficiency defence' in a merger control policy. Next, we review the current legislation and practice in the European Union and its Member States, the USA and Canada. A comparison between the EU and the USA shows that, while the philosophy of these two jurisdictions has differed up to now in this regard, in practice, these differences seem to have little impact. In Canada and some EU Member States, on the other hand, defences based on efficiency, 'public interest' or international competitiveness have played a more important role. In Section 3 of this chapter, we discuss the fundamental question of the welfare standard: should the European Commission be solely concerned with efficiency gains that are passed on to consumers or should the gains to producers also be taken into account? Thereafter, we discuss the major problems of implementation raised by the efficiency defence, outline three possible approaches for its implementation and present some thoughts on how to implement our preferred approach.

From the start, it is important to emphasize that it is not possible to give a definitive answer to the questions posed above. First, the research on this issue is still incomplete. Second, the choices to be made cannot be based on objective criteria alone but also involve political considerations and value judgements.

1. REASONS FOR AN EFFICIENCY DEFENCE

1.1 Economic Reasons

BOX 2.1 THE ANALYTICAL FRAMEWORK

The analytical framework of this chapter is the standard one used by Williamson (1968). Figure 2.1 depicts the welfare effects of a merger, starting from a long-run equilibrium in a homogeneous good market where the competitive price P_1 is equal to average cost. The same general principles apply where there is already market power, so that P_1 is already above the competitive level. The merger creates (or increases) market power, so that the price rises to P_2. This results in a transfer from consumers to producers, represented by the rectangle B and a deadweight loss (triangle C).

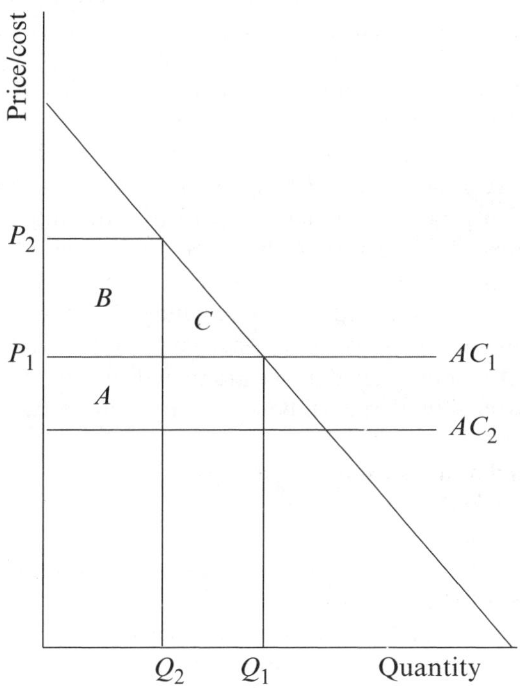

Figure 2.1 Welfare effects of a merger

However, if the merger lowers average cost from AC_1 to AC_2, there is also an increase in productive efficiency, represented by the rectangle A. To take account of cases where the efficiency gains are translated into product improvements, rather than lower costs, the prices and costs can be regarded as quality-adjusted.

This is a highly simplified schema, which assumes that the merging firms have the same costs before the merger and that the merger creates a monopoly, so that the effects on other suppliers do not have to be taken into account. Nevertheless, it is sufficient to illustrate the main points of the debate.

Williamson argued that a merger should be allowed provided that the productive efficiency gain (A), which is a real resource saving, exceeded the deadweight loss (C). Others have argued that more account must be taken of the interests of consumers and that the size of the transfer from consumers to producers (B) must also be taken into account. Supporters of the consumer surplus or price standard contend that efficiency gains should only be taken into account if they are so large as to obviate any increase in price, so that the transfer B and the deadweight loss C disappear.

Drawing on the analytical framework described in Box 2.1, an efficiency defence should make it possible to assess the net effects of mergers on welfare and the distribution of the gains and losses. There is a two-way interaction between productive efficiency and the conditions of competition. Increases in productive efficiency lead to more intense competition while competitive pressures push firms to find ways to improve their efficiency. For ease of presentation, however, the next section briefly summarizes the possible costs and efficiency gains of mergers under separate headings. The main results from empirical work and the lessons to be drawn for the design of an efficiency defence are then discussed. Finally, the main difficulties associated with a cost–benefit analysis are presented.

1.1.1 Costs and benefits from mergers

Anti-competitive effects

Mergers can reduce competition either as a result of a unilateral increase in market power of the new entity or by increasing the risk of collusion. On one hand, the combination of the merging firms' operations may create or increase substantial market power and on the other hand, the reduction in the number of firms in the market facilitates collusion because detection of cheating is easier and there are fewer co-ordination problems.

The main effect of a reduction in competition is an increase in price. This price increase implies a transfer of resources from consumers to producers (see Box 2.1). This distributional effect is accompanied by an allocative inefficiency (also called the deadweight loss) as production is reduced below its optimal level. The risk of price increases following mergers may be limited if the market share of the new entity is low, if entry into the market is easy and if strong buyers can exercise countervailing bargaining power.

The reduction in competition resulting from the merger may also diminish the disciplining power of the product market on productive efficiency. When product market competition is weaker, management and employees exert less effort. This leads to a sub-optimal allocation of human and financial resources and to higher production costs.[3] Similarly, reduced competition may also reduce firms' incentives to innovate because R&D decisions are taken strategically, in response to actions of competitors. In particular, if R&D are very risky, a dominant firm would rather enjoy the current monopoly rent than invest in it. In general, the relationship between innovation and the degree of competition in the market appears to take the shape of an inverted 'U'. Where many firms are competing on almost equal terms, the rents derived from innovation are soon competed away and so there is little incentive to invest in R&D. One may describe this situation as one of high static efficiency and low dynamic efficiency. The incentive increases with the degree of market power up to a certain, possibly quite modest, level, so that static efficiency declines while dynamic efficiency improves. Beyond this level of market power, both static and dynamic efficiency start to decline.[4]

Efficiency gains

Mergers can yield efficiency gains in several ways: by allowing a better exploitation of economies of scale, economies of scope and learning economies; by enhancing technological progress; by increasing the bargaining power of the merging firms; and by improving the efficiency of management.

A merger may give rise to economies of scale by eliminating a duplication of fixed costs. Rationalization, i.e. reallocating production between plants, may also yield economies of scale. These are short-term economies of scale, with physical capital held fixed.

Long-run economies of scale may also be realized through a merger if the merging firms' investments in physical capital are combined and integrated. Long-run economies of scale may arise in production (for example, energy requirements per unit of output for a large machine may be lower than those of a small machine), in research and development (for example, as the production of the firm increases, it becomes worthwhile to invest more in sophisticated technologies) and in marketing activities (a single brand name may be created to reduce advertising expenditures).

Economies of scope and learning effects may also result from mergers. Economies of scope arise when the cost of producing two products together is lower than the sum of the costs of producing them separately because they require a common input. Learning effects are the reduction in unit cost due to accumulated experience, as measured by cumulative past output.

A merger may also enhance technological progress by promoting the diffusion of know-how or by increasing the incentives for R&D activities among the merging firms. The diffusion of know-how across the participants may occur either by allowing the firm with less know-how to learn and adopt all skills from the partner with superior know-how, or by enabling the firms to pool complementary technological capabilities. The incentives to invest in R&D may increase because a merger could help to internalize the benefits from R&D among the participating firms and to secure sufficient rents to make it profitable to invest in innovation. For this reason, Bennett et al. (2001, p. 65) argue that:

> If mergers lead to market power in the short run, but are necessary in order to invest successfully in new technology, the current law can block the merger, leading to high static but low dynamic efficiency. Clearly, there is no market-driven way out of this state. European Competition Law should be modernised, in particular for a sector where technology and scale is [sic] important. Efficiency criteria and dynamic considerations should play an important part in merger decisions.

Some purchasing economies may occur after a merger. This happens when tariffs discriminate between large and small users, or when the merged firm increases its bargaining power and obtains quantity discounts. A merger may also lead to a lower cost of capital, especially for a small firm that joins a large corporation.

In Chapter 5, Motis, Neven and Seabright argue that the main purpose of mergers is to combine the non-tradable assets of the merging firms, such as reputation, awareness, relationships with customers and the corporate culture, since otherwise the firms could simply exchange tradable assets. They therefore suggest that the re-combination of non-tradable, intangible assets with other assets, both tangible and intangible, must be a major source of any efficiency gains. However, they note that this is also the major risk factor in any merger. Mergers inevitably disturb established customer relationships and relationships with the workforce. In addition, forging a common corporate culture out of two disparate ones, communicating it to managers and workforce and persuading them to accept it can be costly and time-consuming.

The threat of takeover may be an incentive for management to run the business in the best interest of the shareholders. A well-functioning market for corporate control could then reduce managerial inefficiencies. However, as takeovers are very costly, the credibility of this threat is low except in cases of severe mismanagement.

1.1.2 What about empirical evidence?

The available empirical evidence on the efficiency effects of mergers is poor, biased towards US mergers in manufacturing during the 1960s and 1970s and leads to somewhat contradictory results, due to methodological problems. The conclusions from empirical literature therefore need to be considered with caution.[5]

Empirical work mainly analyses the effects of mergers on the performance of the merging firms, as measured by accounting profits or share prices. If company performance is found to improve, this could be evidence that the merger created either market power or efficiency gains or a combination of both. Therefore, in order to discriminate between the two explanations, it is also necessary to have evidence on consumer prices, market shares and competing firms' share prices. If consumer prices and competing firms' share prices rise while the market share of the merged firm drops,[6] this suggests that increased market power is more important than efficiency gains.

The empirical evidence indicates that horizontal mergers increase market power. After a merger, prices tend to rise and the market share of the merging firms tends to fall. Empirical analysis also shows that mergers have very modest average effects on the profitability of the merging firms and that a large proportion of mergers reduce profitability.[7] An increase in profitability following a merger is not necessarily an indication of efficiency gains, since market power also plays a role. However, since mergers tend to increase the degree of concentration and thus to raise prices, a reduction in profitability can be taken as an indicator of a loss of productive efficiency. We can therefore assume that the number of efficiency-reducing mergers is even greater than the number of mergers which lead to lower profitability. This suggests that merger control should not be based on a general presumption that mergers create efficiency gains. In particular cases, however, mergers do enhance efficiency and there may be substantial variance in these gains. To conclude, therefore, empirical evidence tends to show that it is important to control mergers for their anti-competitive effects but the presence and magnitude of the efficiency effects also need to be examined on a case-by-case basis.

1.1.3 A cost–benefit analysis?

Given that there is a trade-off between the efficiency gains from mergers and the increase in market power, it is necessary to define a methodology for comparing the benefits and costs of mergers and assessing their net overall effects. This implies that one should not only be able to measure the expected efficiency gains from a merger but also calculate the anti-competitive effects.

This poses two challenges. First, it is necessary to define the policy goals of merger control. If the objective is the protection of consumer interests, the central focus of merger analysis is on the price effects of mergers.[8] On the other hand, if the objective is to enhance total surplus (generally defined as the sum of producer and consumer surplus), then the overall effects of the merger must be analysed. Furthermore, as we argue in section 4.2.4, simple formulae for efficiencies can be misleading if they do not take account of quality and a price increase cannot necessarily be equated with a reduction in consumer surplus.

The second challenge is that the consideration of efficiency defences accentuates the need to model competitive conditions in the relevant market more explicitly and precisely than has hitherto been thought necessary in European merger control. Even in the easier case of a price standard, one has to assess the expected price increase arising from increased (unilateral or collusive) market power. This presupposes a model of the current and expected intensity of competition. But there are many different modes of competition and, accordingly, many different models to be used. The old structure–conduct–performance paradigm has been replaced by the new industrial organization theory which allows a more sophisticated analysis of the interdependence between the players in a market and which has stressed the dynamic framework within which the competitive process should be placed. As mentioned by Jacquemin (1997), the new industrial organization theory has improved the criteria and tools that can be used to measure the effects of mergers but the new dimensions to be taken into account are very complex and the results obtained are very sensitive to the assumptions made. This implies that it is not possible to present a simple model of cost–benefit analysis applicable to all mergers. Furthermore, the information the antitrust authorities possess is generally insufficient to permit a rigorous cost–benefit analysis. A new process has thus to be implemented in order to allow the collection of the data necessary for this analysis. In spite of these difficulties, the introduction of an efficiency defence could have the beneficial side-effect of increasing the overall rigour of the analyses undertaken in European merger control.

1.2 Political Reasons

As we have seen, current economic analysis shows the difficulty of introducing an efficiency defence in a merger control system. However, other arguments can be advanced in favour of an efficiency defence. Basically, two kinds of argument can be distinguished. The first line of argument stresses the importance of the international competitiveness of enterprises, especially given the globalization of markets. The second is based on considerations of transparency.

Some critics of the old merger regulation argued that a merger control policy which takes no account of efficiency gains may be harmful to European competitiveness, in particular in high-tech industries.

Indeed, some of the Commission's communications on industrial policy could be interpreted as advocating mergers as a means of improving competitiveness. For example, in the communication on the aerospace industry (European Commission 1997, p. 13), we read that '[t]here are few, if any, other industries where size is as important as it is in aerospace. . . . The nature of the aerospace market is such that in many, though not all, sectors it will only be possible for one entity to remain viable in Europe . . .' Commenting on this communication, a committee of the European Parliament expressed its belief that 'European competition law, and in particular the merger regulation, must now be interpreted in the context of international competitiveness within increasingly globalised markets' (European Parliament 1998b).

Similarly, in a communication on globalization (European Commission 1999), the Commission points out that the EU is underperforming in high-technology industries, such as the information technology industry. It goes on to express the opinion that alliances, mergers and acquisitions are necessary to gain access to additional know-how, to share risks and to extend distribution networks and that, in this respect, European companies are less dynamic than US ones. It also mentions an alleged relaxation in US merger control, leading to the approval of many important consolidations in the US defence industry. The communication makes no explicit reference to an efficiency defence but rather a general plea in favour of a modernization of competition policy to keep up with globalization. However, an earlier parliamentary report on the competitiveness of European industry specifically advocates that 'competition policy must encourage the regrouping of European companies in so far as that influences their competitiveness on world markets'.[9]

The debates in the European Parliament on the Commission's Competition Policy report for 1999 exemplify the strong political pressure to take efficiencies and competitiveness into account. Point 15 of the

Parliament's resolution on this report[10] calls for 'efficiency and other pro-competitive elements' to be taken into account in competition cases. Point 18 is particularly interesting. In this, Parliament:

> stresses that large companies based in small Member States must not be categorically excluded from merging in order to be competitive throughout Europe and globally; notes that it is, in particular large firms in small Member States that may see their competitiveness decline relative to that of firms in the rest of the world as a result of the internal market not being completed in full; calls, therefore, on the Commission to remove the remaining barriers aimed at preventing or delaying the removal of borders in the market, so that the whole of the EU can be regarded as one market as far as mergers are concerned.

This part of the resolution was inspired by the controversy aroused in the Nordic countries by the prohibition of the Volvo/Scania merger on the grounds that it would create dominant positions in several national markets. This point is carefully worded as a plea for more vigorous action to break down trade barriers, while ignoring the fact that many of these barriers are created by the companies in question. However, some of the speeches made during the debate imply that the Commission should manipulate the market delineation, and hence the analysis of the anti-competitive effects, in order to clear mergers which are considered desirable from the point of view of global competitiveness. It is reported that the Swedish government strongly advocated such an approach when the Volvo/Scania case was under investigation.

This debate was revived at the end of 2004, when Commissioner Günther Verheugen was quoted as giving the following answer to the question 'What else can the Commission do to promote champions?'

> It is a question of basic priorities. Do we want European firms to achieve global market positions? Or do we want to follow bureaucratic rules literally? In the past the EU competition authority often defined markets too narrowly and thereby prevented promising mergers. The case of Scania and Volvo is an example. (*Handelsblatt*, 1 November 2004, p. 1)

Given the Commission's responsibilities in the field of industrial policy and the external political pressures, it could be argued that merger control decisions will almost inevitably be influenced by efficiency (or 'competitiveness') considerations, even if only subconsciously.[11] If this is true, the danger is then that, without an explicit analysis of efficiency effects, unclear compromises between competition policy and industrial policy will be made. It would follow from this that the introduction of an efficiency defence in the merger regulation and the horizontal merger guidelines will improve the clarity and transparency of the decision-making procedure and rigour of the analysis, without extending the range of considerations that are, in reality, already taken into account.

From an economic point of view, the political arguments based on 'competitiveness' are not convincing. On one hand, by expanding the relevant geographic market, globalization makes it less likely that a merger will be found to have significant anti-competitive effects. Consequently, globalization in itself does not increase the need for an efficiency defence. On the other hand, the notion of 'competitiveness' can be used to disguise the promotion of national (or European) champions at the expense not only of trading partners' businesses but also of domestic customers.[12] Furthermore, both theory and experience have shown that reducing competition in the home market rarely improves competitiveness in foreign markets. In spite of this, as we shall see in our survey of national rules in section 2 of this chapter, a number of jurisdictions explicitly consider international competitiveness in their assessment of mergers. To the extent that decision makers are influenced by such considerations, the introduction of an efficiency defence in EU law could have a salutary effect if it obliges them to justify their decisions on the basis of a well-defined concept of efficiency.

2. A COMPARISON OF LEGISLATION AND CURRENT PRACTICE IN THE EU, THE USA AND CANADA

An important part of the analysis of a proposed merger made by the antitrust authorities involves its effect on market power, which is often linked to its effect on concentration. Under US law, the decision to investigate and challenge a merger is mainly based on the initial level of concentration and the predicted change in concentration due to the merger. This reflects a view that anti-competitive effects increase with concentration, which is measured by the Herfindahl–Hirschman index (HHI). However, concentration is a necessary but not sufficient condition for a merger challenge.

The Canadian Competition Bureau challenges mergers which seem likely to result in a substantial (5 per cent) price increase or which would result in a concentration of buying power likely to depress prices substantially below the prevailing level. The main indicators used to screen mergers are the market share of the merged entity and the combined market shares of the four largest firms (C4 ratio). Normally, the Bureau will not challenge a merger if the merged entity's market share is less than 35 per cent, unless the C4 ratio is 65 per cent or more.

Under the old European merger regulation, mergers were prohibited if they created or strengthened a dominant position. An important factor for the assessment of dominance is the existence of very large market shares but the European Court of Justice has made it clear that dominance may derive from a combination of several factors, which are not necessarily decisive when taken separately. The approach used in the application of the old merger regulation is less clear-cut than the HHI approach of the USA. The new merger regulation replaces the dominance test with a wider one. Article 2.3 stipulates that '[a] concentration which would significantly impede effective competition, in the common market or in a substantial part of it, in particular as a result of the creation or strengthening of a dominant position, shall be declared incompatible with the common market'. Thus, the primary test is now whether the merger would significantly impair competition and it is no longer essential to show that a dominant position would be created or strengthened. However, the Commission's guidelines on horizontal mergers make it clear that the Commission's interpretation of 'significant impediment' is still to a large extent inspired by the past practice relating to dominance.[13] However, the guidelines explain that the new test makes it possible to take account of 'non-coordinated effects' in oligopolistic markets. Non-coordinated effects are increases in market power that result simply from the removal of an important competitive constraint. For example, if one of the merging firms had raised its price before the merger, it would have lost some sales to the other party in the merger. After the merger, this particular constraint disappears and a price increase may become profitable. In these circumstances, some demand is likely to be diverted to the other firms in the market, which may then also find it profitable to raise their prices. Thus a merger can do substantial harm to competition even if the merged entity is not the largest supplier in the market and even if the firms in the market do not coordinate their behaviour. This type of effect, often called a 'unilateral effect', can happen in particular in markets where products are strongly differentiated and when the merging firms are each other's closest competitors, while other firms' products are less close substitutes. In such circumstances, it is often possible for the merged company to raise its prices by a substantial amount without the danger of losing so many sales to rivals that the price rise will be unprofitable.[14]

All three approaches refine their preliminary analysis of the possible anti-competitive effects by taking into account other factors such as entry barriers, potential competition and the structure of supply and demand. The European Commission's approach to the analysis of the anti-competitive effects does not differ strongly from those of the North American authorities.

2.1 The Treatment of Efficiency Gains in the EU Merger Regulation

Amongst the factors which the Commission is required to take into account in examining mergers, Article 2.1(b) of the EU merger regulation includes 'the development of technical and economic progress provided that it is to consumers' advantage and does not form an obstacle to competition'. This provision is found in both the old and the new regulations.

The wording of this sub-paragraph of the merger regulation is quite different from that of Article 81(3) of the EC Treaty, concerning agreements between enterprises. The latter allows the Commission to authorize agreements if, *inter alia*, they contribute to 'improving the production or distribution of goods or to promoting technical or economic progress, while allowing consumers a fair share of the resulting benefit' and provided that they do not give the companies concerned 'the possibility of eliminating competition in respect of a substantial part of the products in question'. It is noteworthy that efficiencies are not a defence under Article 81 but a *requirement*. In this respect, Article 81 is far stricter than anything so far envisaged in the field of merger control.

The other differences are also significant. First, the merger regulation includes technical and economic progress but eschews the more general reference to improvements in production and distribution. It could be inferred, therefore, that 'technical and economic progress' is to be interpreted narrowly as referring only to efficiency gains brought about through innovation.

According to the traditional interpretation of the old regulation, the stipulation, as a separate condition, that the technical and economic progress resulting from the merger should not form an obstacle to competition makes it almost impossible to accept an efficiency defence for a dominant enterprise, since any improvement in the merged entity's efficiency is likely to enhance its market power. Consequently, commentators sometimes spoke of an 'efficiency offence' under the merger regulation and, indeed, in some cases the Commission has argued along these lines.

The Commission's traditional interpretation of Article 2.1(b) was clearly expressed in its decision on the Danish Crown/Vestjyske Slagterier case[15]. In this case, the main reason given by the Commission for rejecting the parties' efficiency arguments was as follows:

> As far as those efficiencies are concerned, it should be noted that under Article 2(1)(b) of the Merger Regulation the Commission may take account of the development of technical and economic progress only to the extent that it is to consumers' advantage and does not form an obstacle to competition. *The creation of a dominant position in the relevant markets identified above,*

> *therefore, means that the efficiencies argument put forward by the parties cannot be taken into account in the assessment of the present merger* (p. 28; emphasis added).

In other words, the Commission considered that it was inherently improbable that efficiency gains made by a dominant firm would be passed on to the consumer and would not weaken competition.

In a note to the OECD in 1996, the Commission stated quite plainly that, 'there is no real legal possibility of justifying an efficiency defence under the Merger Regulation' (European Commission 1996, p. 53).

Nevertheless, it has always been acknowledged that the provisions of Article 2.1(b) would not prevent the Commission from taking efficiency gains into account when assessing whether or not a merger would create or strengthen a position of joint dominance. In this respect, efficiencies could be relevant in cases where the post-merger structure of the market seems to be conducive to collusion between the major players, so that the merger would normally be expected to create or strengthen joint dominance. In such circumstances, it is possible that the efficiency gains resulting from a merger would give the merged company such a substantial advantage over other firms in the market that it would not, in fact, have an incentive to collude.

The new regulation, on the other hand, offers a wider scope for the consideration of efficiencies. Recital 29 of that regulation states that, when assessing a merger's impact on competition, 'substantiated and likely efficiencies' should be taken into account, since 'it is possible that the efficiencies brought about by the concentration counteract the effects on competition, in particular the potential harm to consumers, that it might otherwise have'.

The interpretation of this text may be controversial. Since Article 2.1(b) remains unchanged, it could be argued that the traditional approach, which precludes the consideration of efficiencies if the parties have a dominant position, is still valid. On the other hand, the recital can be read as equating 'effects on competition' with 'potential harm to consumers'. The section on efficiencies in the Commission's horizontal merger guidelines is based on this interpretation. According to this interpretation, the charge that a merger will significantly impede competition can be rebutted if sufficient efficiencies are passed on to consumers. In other words, even if the post-merger competitive constraints would be extremely weak, a merger could be allowed, provided that, as a result of efficiency gains, the merged company would have no presently foreseeable incentive to raise prices, reduce the quality of its product or otherwise harm consumers.

However, the Commission's horizontal merger guidelines narrow the possibilities for a successful efficiency defence by noting that 'the incentive on the part of the merged entity to pass efficiency gains on to consumers is often related to the existence of competitive pressure from the remaining firms and from potential entry.' Consequently, the greater the increase in market power resulting from a merger, the greater the burden of proof on the notifying parties to show that the efficiencies are substantial, likely to be realized and likely to be passed on to consumers to a sufficient extent.

The guidelines also stipulate that efficiencies will be taken into account only on the following conditions:

- They are of direct benefit to consumers, either because they lead to lower prices or because they lead to new or improved products or services;
- They are merger-specific, i.e. they cannot realistically be achieved by less anti-competitive means;
- They are verifiable and, as far as possible, quantified.

In accordance with economic theory, reductions in variable or marginal costs are considered to be more likely to be passed on to consumers than reductions in fixed costs. Since the merger regulation is based on the consumer surplus standard, the former are therefore given more weight in the analysis than the latter.

2.2 EU Member States

In France, merger cases are analysed in two stages: the *bilan concurrentiel* (competition balance-sheet) and the *bilan économique* (economic balance-sheet). In the first stage, the Competition Council considers whether the merger harms competition, in particular by creating or strengthening a dominant position. If it finds that the merger harms competition, it draws up the *bilan économique*, which amounts to an assessment of the effects of the merger on the French economy as a whole. If the *bilan économique* is positive, the Council recommends to the Minister that the merger should be cleared. In effect, therefore, French law accepts an efficiency defence based on the total welfare standard. It is noteworthy, however, that the Council is specifically required to take account of the international competitiveness of the firms in question.

In Germany, the competition authority (Bundeskartellamt or BKA) applies the test of creation or strengthening of a dominant position with no allowance for an efficiency defence. However, companies can appeal against a prohibition decision to the Minister of Economic Affairs, who can authorize a merger on the grounds of advantages for the whole economy or 'public interest'. As in France, there is a specific requirement to take account of the international competitiveness of the merging firms. The Minister rarely overrides decisions of the BKA but he did so in one highly controversial case, that of E.ON/Ruhrgas (2002), partly on the basis of international competitiveness considerations, as well as the alleged contribution that the merger would make to safeguarding Germany's natural gas supplies. According to the Minister's decision, the merger would improve Ruhrgas' position as a buyer in international gas markets and allow it to make the investments needed to penetrate downstream foreign markets as a supplier (Bundesminister für Wirtschaft und Technologie 2002).

In the United Kingdom, under the Enterprise Act 2002, mergers are generally prohibited if they lead to a substantial lessening of competition. One exception is made for cases where 'customer benefits . . . outweigh the substantial lessening of competition concerned and any adverse effects of the substantial lessening of competition concerned.' In its 'Substantive assessment guidance' (OFT 2003), the Office of Fair Trading (OFT) states that efficiency gains can be taken into account at two points in the assessment of a merger. First, if merger-generated efficiencies increase the intensity of rivalry in the market, they may lead the OFT to conclude that there is no significant lessening of competition. The OFT cites the example of a merger between two of the smaller firms in the market, generating efficiencies which enable them to exert greater competitive pressure on the larger firms. Second, efficiencies may be taken into account where they do not avert a significant lessening of competition but will nonetheless be passed on to customers. The consultation paper warns that the OFT expects that successful efficiency defences in such cases will be rare. In particular, it notes that one precondition for sufficient pass-on is that sufficient competition or buyer power remains after the merger. However, the customer benefits do not necessarily have to arise in the market where the substantial lessening of competition occurs.

The Irish Competition Act 2002 also applies the 'significant lessening of competition' test to mergers. In a consultative document published in August 2002 (Competition Authority 2002), the Irish Competition Authority does not make a sharp distinction between the two types of efficiency consideration identified by the OFT. For the Irish authority, a significant lessening of competition can be equated with an increase in price or a reduction in output. However, the consultative document claims that pass-on is generally higher, the more intense the rivalry in the market. It also notes that any reduction in rivalry as a result of the merger may damage the incentives to achieve efficiency gains. Consequently, merging firms will be required to demonstrate that these incentives will be sufficiently strong after the merger. Firms making use of the efficiency defence will also be required to show that the efficiencies will be directly achieved by the merger, cannot be achieved by less anti-competitive means and will be realized with sufficient likelihood within a reasonable timeframe.

Amongst the other EU countries, efficiency defences are explicitly provided for in the legislation of Spain, Greece and Portugal. Spain applies the total welfare standard, while Greece and Portugal apply the consumer welfare criterion. Interestingly, the conditions for accepting an efficiency defence in Portugal are the same as the conditions for granting exemptions to agreements between companies, modelled on Article 81(3) of the EC Treaty (see Section 2.1). In Finland, the competition authority is willing to consider efficiency defences, applying the consumer welfare standard, even though the relevant law does not explicitly mention such a possibility. In Belgium, the relevant law makes provision for the consideration of 'technical and economic progress' but it is not clear how this is intended to be applied. Greek competition law contains a provision similar to Article 2.1 of the present EU merger regulation, requiring the Competition Committee to take into account 'technical and economic progress provided it is to the consumer's advantage and does not form an obstacle to competition'.

In Spain, Italy, Austria and Portugal, the competition authorities or courts are required to take account of the international competitiveness of the merging firms. Finally, in Belgium, Greece and the Netherlands, the government can overrule a prohibition decision of the competition authority on 'public interest' grounds. In the case of Belgium, as in Germany, international competitiveness is explicitly mentioned as one of these grounds. The law in Denmark and Sweden makes no explicit provision for an efficiency defence.

Summing up this survey, we find that competition authorities or courts can consider efficiency defences in at least six national jurisdictions[16] and possibly also in Belgium and Greece. In four of the six Member States, the consumer welfare standard is applied but Spain and France use the total welfare standard. A rather worrying finding is that the law in five Member States[17] requires the competition bodies to take account of the international competitiveness of the merging firms. Finally, we note that the government can override prohibition decisions of the competition bodies in four Member States[18] in the 'public interest'. The notion of 'public interest' may be intended primarily to cover efficiency considerations but it may also, either explicitly or implicitly, include considerations of international competitiveness.

2.3 Merger Control in the USA

Under the Clayton Act, a merger may be forbidden if it would substantially lessen competition in the future. This test, which implies a much stricter control than the EU merger regulation, is interpreted by the courts to mean essentially that mergers should be forbidden if they make it easier for firms to force prices above, or further above, the competitive level. In US merger control, therefore, it is clear that efficiency arguments have to concentrate on the effects of the merger on consumer surplus.

Concerning efficiencies, the horizontal merger guidelines of the Federal Trade Commission (FTC) and Department of Justice (as revised in 1997) find that 'the primary benefits of mergers to the economy is their potential to generate . . . efficiencies. Efficiencies generated through merger can enhance the merged firm's ability and incentive to compete, which may result in lower prices, improved quality, enhanced service, or new products . . . and efficiencies may result in benefits even when price is not immediately and directly affected.' According to these guidelines, efficiency gains can be taken into account in assessing mergers under the following conditions:

- The gains must be 'merger-specific', i.e. it must be unlikely that they could be achieved by another means having a less anti-competitive effect.
- The merging firms must substantiate their efficiency claims so that the likelihood and magnitude of each gain can be verified by reasonable means.
- The gains must not arise from anti-competitive reductions in output or service.
- The gains must be sufficient to reverse the merger's potential to harm consumers in the relevant market. Normally this means preventing price increases, but the authorities may also consider other benefits, such as new and improved products.

The guidelines remark that efficiencies can enhance the merged firm's ability and incentive to compete, for example, when two weak competitors combine to form one effective competitor. In a co-ordinated interaction context, marginal cost reductions may make co-ordination less likely or effective by creating a 'maverick' firm or enhancing the incentive of an existing maverick to lower its prices. In a unilateral effects context, efficiency gains may reduce the merged firm's incentive to raise its prices.

Some types of efficiencies are more likely to be taken into account than others. In particular, marginal cost reductions resulting from shifting production amongst facilities formerly owned separately are considered to be more likely to be verifiable, merger-specific and substantial, and less likely to result from anti-competitive reductions in output. On the other hand, gains resulting from merging R&D activities are deemed to be difficult to verify and more likely to result from anti-competitive output restrictions.

In practice, however, it appears that the US authorities rarely acknowledge having taken efficiencies into consideration when deciding whether or not to challenge a merger (see Camesasca 1999). On the other hand, the Federal courts, after having initially considered that efficiencies were not relevant to the application of the Clayton Act, have given serious consideration to efficiency arguments during the 1990s. Federal court rulings on the subject have accepted the principle of the efficiency defence,[19] confirmed the consumer surplus standard[20] and stressed that efficiencies may only be taken into account if they are merger-specific.[21]

2.4 Merger Control in Canada

Sub-section 96(1) of the Canadian Competition Act provides that the Competition Tribunal may not forbid a merger or order the dissolution of a merger 'if it finds that the merger . . . has brought about or is likely to bring about gains in efficiency that will be greater than, and will offset, the effects of any prevention or lessening of competition that will result or is likely to result from the merger . . . and that the gains in efficiency would not likely be attained if the order were made.' Sub-section 96(2) specifies that, when applying this provision, the Tribunal must consider whether the efficiency gains will lead to a significant increase in the real value of exports or a significant substitution of domestic products for imported products.

Initially, the Competition Bureau appears to have interpreted these provisions as implying the application of the total welfare standard, i.e. that the merger should be allowed if it increases the sum of consumer and producer surplus.[22] However, in the Hillsdown case of 1992, the Competition Tribunal (the court of first instance in merger cases) seemed to favour a consumer surplus standard.[23] The only other case in which the Competition Tribunal considered an efficiency defence was that of Superior Propane. In this case, the Competition Bureau seems to have deviated from its own guidelines by proposing that the loss to consumers should be weighed against the efficiency gains according to the 'balancing weights' approach developed by Professor Peter Townley (1999).

This approach involves calculating the weight w that would just balance producer gains and consumer losses. In terms of Figure 2.1, w is such that $A + B = w(B + C)$. The merger is allowed if w seems 'reasonable' in the light of the objectives of the Competition Act and the unquantified factors.

Although the Competition Tribunal (2000) initially rejected this approach and applied the total welfare standard, the Federal Appeals Court ruled that the 'balancing weights' approach seemed to be an appropriate test, although the presiding judge remarked that 'for all I know, the same standard may not be equally apposite for all mergers' (see Competition Bureau 2001). In the aftermath of the Propane case, the Competition Bureau published new merger enforcement guidelines in 2004. These new guidelines take a very cautious approach to the trade-off between efficiency gains and anti-competitive effects. The Bureau seems undecided as to whether and how redistributive effects (i.e. transfers from buyers to sellers resulting from higher prices) should be taken into account. It recognizes that 'there is currently no statutory basis for assuming an equal weighting of redistributive effects, deadweight losses and efficiency gains' but gives no criteria for choosing alternative weighting schemes. Indeed, merging parties are encouraged to propose their own weightings.

Other aspects of the efficiency defence have not been controversial. The Competition Bureau's insistence that efficiencies must be merger-specific has not been contested. The interpretation of Sub-section 96(2), quoted above, which requires that increases in exports and import-substitution effects should be taken into account, has so far not been an issue in any case. According to the Bureau's interpretation, this sub-section does not expand the class of efficiency gains that may be considered in the trade-off analysis nor does it require any special weighting of the efficiency gains in question (Competition Bureau 1991). Nevertheless, since it is unusual for a law to contain provisions which are not intended to have any practical effect, there is a danger that this sub-section may give rise to disputes in the future.

At the time of writing, the Canadian Senate was examining a bill (Bill C-249) radically limiting the scope of the efficiency defence under the Competition Act. The proposed amendments would allow the consideration of the efficiency gains only if most of the gains are likely to be passed on to consumers within a reasonable time. The bill also stipulates that the pass-on must be in the form of lower prices. Furthermore, the efficiency defence would not be available if the merger is likely to create or strengthen a dominant position.

3. THE FUNDAMENTAL PROBLEM: CHOICE OF A WELFARE STANDARD

Under the European merger regulation, as under US law, merger control takes account only of consumer welfare. Benefits to the merging companies are disregarded, as are any spillover effects on other firms, except insofar as these may affect the intensity of competition in the market. It has been argued, most notably by Williamson (1968), that the goal of competition policy should be to maximize total welfare. A variant of the latter approach, considered by Farrell and Shapiro (1990), is to assess mergers on the basis of their effects on consumers and competitors jointly, on the assumption that the merger will be privately profitable to the merging firms. If mergers yield a net positive external effect, they should be allowed, even if the effect on consumers alone is negative. As Farrell and Shapiro admit, this approach would mean clearing output-reducing mergers, if they lead to the closure of plants with relatively high marginal costs. Furthermore, the Farrell–Shapiro approach does not take account of the strong evidence that a large proportion of mergers are not privately profitable (cf. Section 1.1.2) and their analysis does not allow for product differentiation or for any increased probability of explicit collusion.

The choice between the consumer welfare and total welfare standards is primarily a political one. The consumer welfare criterion would be favoured by those who consider that competition authorities should avoid trading off the welfare of one group against that of another. The consumer welfare standard avoids such a trade-off by accepting the efficiency defence only where the nature and size of the efficiency gains are such that, even with reduced competition in the market, the consumer will be no worse off than before the merger. However, a trade-off could occur if the merger affects more than one market, the anti-competitive effects and the efficiencies being distributed differently between the markets. In theory, this might raise the question whether benefits to one set of consumers should be weighed against harm to another set of consumers. In most cases, however, it would probably be possible to find a remedy for the adversely affected market without substantially reducing the efficiencies in the other market.

Furthermore, the consumer surplus standard conforms to the underlying philosophy of existing EU competition law as reflected notably in Article 81 of the EC Treaty. It would be anomalous to accept a diminution of consumer surplus in merger cases while maintaining the provision that agreements and concerted practices falling under Article 81(1) may only be accepted if consumers have a 'fair share of the resulting benefit'.

In support of the wider criterion, it can be argued that, in practice, since Pareto improvements are difficult to achieve, public bodies frequently make trade-offs between different groups. However, it is also true that, in doing so, they often give different weights to the welfare of different groups. Hence, the Williamson approach, which follows traditional welfare economics in giving equal weight to all groups, is not necessarily politically realistic.

The strongest argument in favour of the total welfare standard is that consumers and producers do not constitute distinct groups but overlap to a large extent. Consumers can also be shareholders, even if only indirectly through pension funds and the like, or employees who may stand to gain from a merger. Furthermore, even if the exercise of market power leads to an undesirable distribution of income, this problem could, in principle, be rectified by the tax system.[24] However, as we explain below, this argument has somewhat less force when the competition authority has to appraise mergers between foreign companies.

The Canadian 'balancing weights' approach gives the merger control authorities much more discretion than the simple consumer surplus and total surplus standards. It requires them to address the question of the appropriate weights to be given to consumers and producers and to different objectives of competition policy. It can be criticized for allowing the competition authorities to decide questions which should have been resolved by the legislature and for creating legal uncertainty. It will also certainly be criticized by those who believe that, in the last analysis, efficiency is the only legitimate goal of competition policy.

The choice of the total welfare standard or the 'balancing weights' approach would pose problems in defining the geographical scope of the assessment of the welfare effects of a merger. The merger regulation requires the Commission to forbid a merger only if it would 'significantly impede effective competition in the common market or in a substantial part of it', while the EEA Agreement requires the Commission to consider also the impact on other signatories. Consequently, Community law does not permit a prohibition if a merger does not seriously affect competition within the EEA but would create or strengthen a dominant position in foreign markets. Thus the present consumer welfare standard applies only to consumers within the EEA. This geographical restriction simplifies the task of merger control.

If the regulation were to be amended to take account also of producer surplus, it would be essential to decide whether this geographical limitation should be maintained. Clearly, it would be irrational to weigh the effects on European consumers against worldwide producer surplus gains but the idea of adopting a standard which takes account of worldwide costs and benefits to producers and consumers is unlikely to appeal to European politicians. At the very least, they would insist that such a change should not be made unless all of Europe's major trading partners agreed to follow suit. On the other hand, in cases involving multinational enterprises it would often be somewhat artificial to try to allocate the efficiency gains between different geographic markets or between parts of a global market. A way out of this dilemma might be to take account only of gains made by

European companies but this would almost certainly give rise to complaints of discrimination from trading partners,[25] since the principle of 'national treatment' of foreign companies has hitherto been generally accepted by most countries with well developed competition policies. Difficult problems of definition could also arise. For example, should local subsidiaries of American multinational enterprises be considered as EEA enterprises? Should a distinction be made between the benefits to shareholders resident within the EEA and other shareholders?

Some economists have put forward arguments tending to show that, in practice, the consumer welfare standard (CWS) may yield better results in terms of total surplus than the total welfare standard (TWS) itself. Besanko and Spulber (1993) suggest that the CWS is needed simply because the merging parties have an incentive to make exaggerated efficiency claims and competition authorities lack sufficient information with which to assess the credibility of these claims. The stricter standard is therefore justified as a means of redressing the imbalance. Neven and Röller (2001) also argue that competition authorities may be systematically biased in favour of large mergers by lobbying activity. When the costs of lobbying are taken into account, the CWS may lead to a generally better outcome in terms of total welfare when the regulatory environment is favourable to lobbying.

Fridolfsson (2002) and Lyons (2002) take a different approach. They both start from the assumption that an alternative merger is usually possible in the event of prohibition of the acquirer's preferred merger. Lyons looks at the implications of the two welfare standards for sequences of mergers leading to various equilibrium market structures in a differentiated products setting. In Lyons' model, all mergers yield some efficiency gains but only in the form of fixed cost savings. Because they do not directly affect prices, these savings are not taken into account by the CWS. In addition, mergers between firms with neighbouring products are assumed to lead to greater savings, as well as greater increases in market power, than mergers of firms whose products are less close substitutes. The assumption that higher efficiency gains go together with greater anti-competitive effects might be expected to lead to a less favourable outcome in terms of total welfare when the CWS is applied. Nonetheless, given the possibility of alternative mergers, which also yield some – albeit smaller – efficiencies, Lyons finds that the range of scenarios over which TWS is superior to CWS in enhancing total welfare is in fact rather limited. His conclusion is that the consumer welfare standard has strong advantages in large, complex economies, where there are socially preferable but privately less profitable alternative merger opportunities. Fridolfsson comes to a similar conclusion using a simple duopoly model where the two firms transfer assets between each other. In essence, these findings can be explained by the following mechanism. By applying the CWS, the competition authority blocks the firms' preferred – anti-competitive – mergers even if they increase total welfare. As a result, firms undertake alternative mergers, which increase total welfare more, even if the efficiency gains are smaller, because they have no significant anti-competitive effects. Thus, even if the overall objective is to maximize the total surplus, it may be optimal to apply the CWS standard to the examination of individual cases.

4. IMPLEMENTATION OF AN EFFICIENCY DEFENCE

4.1 Possible Approaches

Three different approaches can be used to incorporate efficiency considerations in merger analysis (see Camesasca (1999) and Röller et al. (see Chapter 3, this volume): the general presumptions approach, the case-by-case approach and the sequential approach. In this section, the pros and cons of these three approaches are presented and we conclude in favour of the sequential approach.

4.1.1 The general presumptions approach

The general presumptions approach makes use of indicators (such as market shares or a concentration index) and implicitly considers that below a certain threshold for these indicators, efficiency gains are always sufficient to outweigh the anti-competitive effects of the mergers. For example, if the indicator is the merging firms' joint market share, a market share of 25 per cent might be considered as the upper limit for acceptance of mergers under the assumption that up to this limit of market shares mergers are efficiency-enhancing or at least neutral. Thus this approach is based on the implicit recognition of efficiencies and assumes that the indicators used contain some (albeit imperfect) information about the likely net effects of mergers. Not all mergers are prohibited. Only those that significantly reduce competition may be challenged. For mergers that reduce competition only marginally, efficiency gains are presumed to be more important than anti-competitive effects. On the other hand, if a merger leads to a substantial increase in market power, the anti-competitive effect is assumed to outweigh any efficiency gain. This approach eliminates the high information costs involved in assessing the efficiency effects on a case-by-case basis. But it assumes that there is a set of indicators that measure adequately the net effects of mergers.

If the threshold for the indicators is fixed at a low level, for example, if all mergers leading to a combined market share of 10 per cent and more are challenged, this reflects the merger control authority's belief that low values of the indicators predict net effects with a reasonable degree of confidence and that efficiencies have a low average. This corresponds to a stricter merger control policy. If the threshold is fixed at a high level (e.g. a market share of 50 per cent and more), this implies that the merger control authority believes that efficiency effects have a high average and that they normally dominate up to a high level of market power.

The general presumptions approach corresponds to the old EU model with no explicit efficiency defence and a relatively high threshold for the indicators. Thus the old EU model was based on the wrong assumption that mergers usually generate large efficiency gains. Above the threshold, however, it made no allowance for exceptional cases where the efficiency gains might be large enough to compensate even for large increases in market power.

4.1.2 The case-by-case approach

The second approach directly incorporates an explicit efficiency defence for each individual merger. Such a case-by-case approach explicitly recognizes the possible presence of efficiencies in every single case and balances these efficiencies against anti-competitive effects. This approach eliminates the need to use proxies for the net effects of mergers as these effects are assessed individually but it entails very high information costs and raises many methodological and practical problems if a thorough cost–benefit analysis is to be undertaken. Since a large proportion of mergers present no significant competition problems or do not involve large efficiencies, such an approach is unnecessarily costly and time-consuming.

4.1.3 The sequential approach

The sequential approach is an intermediate approach that combines aspects of both previous approaches and aims to limit the number of cases for which an explicit efficiency defence is considered and thus minimize the information costs involved. The idea is to attempt to identify those cases for which it is relevant to carry out an in-depth efficiency investigation. This approach starts by assessing the competition effects of mergers on the basis of more or less sophisticated criteria. For mergers that only reduce competition insignificantly, efficiency gains are presumed to be more important than anti-competitive effects and these mergers will be automatically accepted. Similarly, one uses general presumptions to define a threshold above which anti-competitive effects are presumed to dominate. Thus, both a low and a high threshold are defined and a more detailed investigation, including an explicit efficiency defence, is made only in intermediate cases.[26]

Of course, even if the threshold above which anti-competitive effects are likely to dominate is exceeded, one cannot exclude the possibility that the parties involved in a merger would invoke efficiency arguments. In such a case, however, the competition authority would start from the presumption that the efficiencies created by the merger would not be sufficient to counterbalance its market power effects and the burden of proving that this is not the case would be particularly heavy for the parties. This presumption of the competition authorities could also be justified by the fact that the incentives for companies to be more efficient would be lower if the degree of competition on the market is significantly reduced.

The sequential approach would be compatible with the new European merger regulation and the Commission's guidelines for the appraisal of horizontal mergers. The guidelines structure the analysis of mergers around five components:

- The likelihood of anti-competitive effects in the absence of countervailing factors;
- Countervailing buyer power;
- The contestability of the market (potential entry);
- Efficiencies;
- The failing firm defence.

The guidelines comment that efficiencies and the failing firm defence will be examined only if the notifying parties demonstrate that they are relevant and, furthermore, that it may be unnecessary to analyse all the elements in the same detail. This would leave room to exclude efficiencies from detailed analysis both when the merger raises no serious competition problems and where the claimed efficiencies are small in comparison with the anti-competitive effects. In addition, the section of the guidelines devoted to efficiencies states that 'It is highly unlikely that a market position approaching that of a monopoly, or leading to a similar level of market power, can be declared compatible with the common market' on efficiency grounds. Although this does not amount to a categorical exclusion of an efficiency defence when some upper bound of tolerance is reached, it is likely to deter firms from putting forward such a defence in such circumstances. Initially, however, firms may try to test exactly what level of market power constitutes 'a market position approaching that of a monopoly'.

4.2 Implementation of the Sequential Approach

Economic theory can provide analytical techniques for assessing the net beneficial effects arising from mergers but these techniques require a lot of data and are still being tested by economists. Therefore, while quantitative evidence should be used whenever it is sufficiently sound, the assessment of efficiencies would, in the large majority of cases, be based on a mix of qualitative and quantitative evidence. In practice, one could thus consider three stages for the sequential approach: the screening tests, the qualitative analysis of efficiencies and the quantitative cost–benefit analysis. Where the qualitative evidence is particularly convincing, an efficiency defence could already be implemented without a complex quantitative cost–benefit analysis, which still poses some unresolved problems (see below, Section 4.2.3).

Within this framework, we suggest the following basic principles for the analysis of efficiencies:

- The analysis should be based on a consumer welfare standard, which ensures that the positive welfare effects a merger may entail are transmitted to the consumers.
- The types of efficiencies considered should include static and dynamic efficiencies. This means that efficiencies that do not necessarily lead to price reduction, such as R&D synergies, should be taken into account. However, it should also be made clear that international competitiveness is a policy objective distinct from static and dynamic efficiency considerations even if the latter can contribute to the former.
- The analysis should not be arbitrarily limited to a short time horizon, since this would lead to excessive emphasis on static effects at the expense of dynamic efficiencies. However, the longer the time span considered, the more uncertain are the effects.
- The efficiencies need to be merger-specific, i.e. they would not materialize without the merger.
- The merging parties have to claim and be in a position to demonstrate that, as a result of their merger, sufficient efficiencies will be created to outweigh the anti-competitive effects. For the sake of transparency, the competition authorities should precisely define the information they need and the approach they will follow to assess such a claim.

4.2.1 The screening tests

The screening tests should aim at minimizing the errors of selection while economizing on information costs. At this stage, there is no explicit analysis of efficiencies and the appraisal concentrates on the anti-competitive effects that may be expected in the absence of efficiencies. However, it is usually considered useful to ask the notifying parties at an early stage to give some explanation of the benefits they expect from the merger. Although this explanation need not initially be subject to rigorous scrutiny, any failure to present an at least superficially plausible argument on efficiency grounds may be taken as an indication that the merger's effects on competition should be examined with care. It would probably be useful to include in the notification form an explicit requirement to explain, in a page or two, the efficiency gains expected from the merger. Relevant questions would include: What are the expected gains of the merger? Why are these gains merger-specific? At what time horizon could they materialize? How would they be passed to consumers (price reduction or non-price effects)?

There is no reason to carry out an in-depth efficiency analysis if there are no serious doubts about the anti-competitive effects of a merger. Similarly, such an analysis should not be made for mergers which reduce competition significantly. In that case, efficiency can be assumed to be insufficient to outweigh the anti-competitive effects of the merger. In addition, in markets with low competition, even if the potential efficiencies are relatively high, the incentives to achieve these efficiencies are weak. To identify mergers with large anti-competitive effects, criteria such as market share or concentration index can be used. However, market shares and concentration measures alone cannot be considered as providing a reliable guide to potential market power. Other market characteristics should be taken into account in order to reduce the risk of rejecting mergers having net beneficial effects for consumers. For example, in markets where technological development is rapid, the market share of companies offering new products can be high just because there are not yet other competitors on the market. These markets may, however, be highly contestable and the potential for dynamic efficiencies can also be high, provided that the merger does not deter future entry. Therefore, one should avoid rejecting a merger in these markets just on the basis of market shares without considering the potential efficiency gains. This was already acknowledged in the Cyanamid/Shell case where a finding of dominance was avoided as 'an analysis focusing on market share alone is not particularly probative in a dynamic and R&D-intensive industry'.[27]

It is thus essential to supplement the market share and concentration indicators by other criteria indicating a risk of market power. Amongst the former, one can find indicators such as entry barriers, existence of sunk costs, inelasticity of demand and the degree of differentiation of products. The latter could include large economies of scale and learning effects, important intangible assets and rapid technological development.[28]

Finally, the information provided by the parties at the screening stage should already enable the Commission to indicate whether an efficiency defence is likely to succeed. Where the parties have failed to provide any plausible reasons to expect significant efficiency gains, they can be discouraged from pursuing this line of defence in the rest of the procedure.

4.2.2 The qualitative analysis of efficiencies

If the competition authority suspects that the merger could cause significant harm to competition, it would be open to the notifying parties to invoke an efficiency defence. Only then would the efficiency gains be analysed in depth. The burden of proof of efficiencies must clearly lie with the parties, since only they possess the necessary information. It would be for the parties to show that their efficiency claims are realistic, that the efficiencies can be achieved within an appropriate time frame and that they can be sufficient to counterbalance the anti-competitive effects of the merger. Because of the complexity of the issues involved, there is probably a need for competition authorities to provide guidance to firms about the information they will be expected to provide if they invoke an efficiency defence. This information would include an explanation of the nature of the expected efficiency gains (economies of scale and scope, rationalization of research and development, improvement in management, etc.); their possible effects on costs, prices, the quality of products and innovation, as well as the time horizon for these positive effects to be realized. Companies should also show that the efficiencies cannot be obtained without the merger, for example, by internal growth or by licensing of technology. In Chapter 5 of this volume, Motis, Neven and Seabright suggest that efficiency claims are not really credible unless the notifying parties can support their claims by showing evidence that they have planned the necessary reorganizations of their management structure, production facilities, marketing and R&D departments and designed appropriate incentive structures for their staff.

4.2.3 The quantitative cost–benefit analysis

At this final stage, a more complex analysis would be carried out to quantify the net beneficial effects of the merger by comparing the anti-competitive effects due to a change in market power of the parties with the efficiencies expected from the merger. Röller, Stennek and Verboven (Chapter 3, this volume) consider that conceptually, this cost–benefit analysis should include the two following components: the calculation of the minimum efficiencies required to outweigh the anti-competitive effects and the measurement and verification of expected efficiencies.

To define the minimum required efficiencies, it is necessary to start from the effect of a merger on price. This effect can be divided into three separate components. First, there is the price increase stemming from an increase in market power, holding the merging firms' cost constant. Second, there is a possible price reduction stemming from the cost savings due to the merger. Third, there is the degree of pass-on of cost savings into consumer price. The percentage price increase divided by the pass-on elasticity represents the minimum cost savings necessary to outweigh the anti-competitive effects of the merger.[29] For example, if 50 per cent of the cost savings are passed on to consumers, then a merger decreases price if the realized cost savings are larger than twice the absolute price rise that would result from increased market power in the absence of efficiencies. In fact, these three components can all be affected by the degree of market power of the merging firms. First, an increase in market power will tend to lead to a higher mark-up and, hence, to an increased price in the absence of efficiencies. Second, a weakening of competition may reduce the incentive to realize efficiencies. One can expect that companies have a greater incentive to be efficient when competition on the market is more intense. However, this is not necessarily true for some dynamic efficiencies such as those resulting from innovation. Increasing competition encourages innovation but at some point, when competition becomes more intense, innovation is less worthwhile because there is less rent to be taken. Finally, an increase in market power will affect the absolute pass-on, i.e. the proportion of any cost saving that is passed on to customers.[30]

In Section 1.1.3, we pointed out that the measurement of the competition effects of a merger presents major difficulties, not least that of selecting the appropriate models to describe the modes of competition before and after the merger. Under the existing EU merger regulation, a qualitative assessment of the likely change in the conditions of competition is sufficient. The introduction of an efficiency defence, which would require quantification not only of the efficiency gains but also of the competition effects, would therefore represent a major change in the whole process of the EU merger analysis. However, even without an efficiency defence, a shift towards more explicit modelling of competitive conditions would probably improve the quality of decision-making.

Röller, Stennek and Verboven (Chapter 3, this volume) suggest that a way around this problem would be to assume a worst-case scenario. This scenario might consist of an increase in price, in the absence of efficiency gains, of 5–10 per cent.[31] Such a baseline would require very substantial efficiency gains, particularly if the merger is to be assessed on the basis of its impact on consumer welfare rather than total welfare. Using the consumer welfare standard, the projected percentage reduction in marginal cost[32] has to be multiplied by the pass-on elasticity, given the post-merger market structure and price-elasticity of demand. In an imperfectly competitive market, the pass-on elasticity is always less than 1. If the pass-on elasticity is 0.5, marginal cost has to be reduced by 10–20 per cent to satisfy the test proposed by Röller, Stennek and Verboven.

However, a good estimate of the post-merger pass-on elasticity can only be arrived at with the help of a model describing competition in the market, since the extent of the pass-on depends on several factors, including the presence of capacity constraints, the price elasticity of demand, the degree of market power, and the market share of the merging firms. Consequently, the Röller-Stennek-Verboven approach simplifies the analysis only if an average (or minimum) pass-on elasticity is assumed. The introduction of this additional assumption adds a further element of arbitrariness to the test. Furthermore, the pass-on elasticity must be consistent with the assumed or estimated price increase in the absence of efficiencies. Consequently, it seems that any application of the efficiency defence based on the consumer welfare standard requires a simulation analysis using a technique such as that developed by Crooke, Froeb, Tschantz and Werden (see Werden and Froeb 1995), allowing simultaneous estimation of the price increase in the absence of efficiencies and the degree of pass-on. A thorough simulation analysis requires detailed data permitting the estimation of all the relevant elasticities, as was done by the US Department of Justice in the Interstate Bakeries Corporation/Continental Baking Company case (see Shapiro 1995) and the FTC in the Staples/Office Depot case (see Baker 1997). However, as Shapiro (1995) remarks, 'the data are rarely available to do this type of full-blown simulation analysis with assurance'. In most cases, therefore, it will still be necessary to rely on some rather rough and ready quantitative procedures.

This kind of quantitative cost–benefit analysis needs to be tested before being implemented. However, it seems difficult to test it *ex post*, that is, for completed mergers, because the necessary information has not been collected. Therefore, it seems more promising to try to test the methodology *ex ante* by applying it to new cases. A major difficulty is to identify appropriate cases at an early stage so that sufficient time is available to collect the necessary data. As the cost–benefit methodology developed so far relates to efficiency gains that have an impact on prices, that is, reductions in marginal cost, the cases used to test the methodology must satisfy three preconditions. First, the merging parties must be willing to cooperate, since the merger regulation does not oblige them to furnish information on efficiencies. Second, they have to claim and be in a position to demonstrate that, as a result of their merger, price reductions will follow. Third, there must be adequate raw data from independent sources to assess the credibility of such claims.

4.2.4 Measurement of actual efficiencies

Any provision for an efficiency defence must define what types of efficiencies can be considered. The selection of the types of efficiency gains that should be taken into account depends partly on the choice of the welfare standard, partly on the time horizon adopted for the analysis and partly on the relative difficulty of verifying the parties' claims.

Efficiencies come not only from cost savings. They can also be generated by improved quality or improved services. Those efficiencies that do not lead to cost reductions are more difficult to quantify but they can play an important role. In practice, the measurement of effects on consumer surplus is often restricted to price effects, because these are easier to predict and quantify. However, this exclusive attention to price effects has been criticized by Jacquemin (1997), who points out that new research in industrial organization has shown that such simple formulas for efficiency are misleading. Consumer welfare does not depend only on prices but also includes aspects such as variety, the quality of the product and the speed and security of supply. Therefore, mergers leading to technological change and improvement in the quality of product can improve consumer welfare even with price increases. Unfortunately, these aspects are difficult to measure and cannot be taken into account with the usual quantitative methods, which require that the effect of a merger should be translated into price terms.

The problem is that, although the traditional approach can be applied to cost-saving process innovations, it is less relevant for mergers in high-tech industries characterized by rapid product innovation, where efficiency gains are more likely. Moreover, in industries characterized by short-lived high technology and rapidly expanding demand, all other things being equal, the danger of monopoly is limited. Jacquemin also points out that, even in the application of the total welfare criterion, as exemplified by Williamson, the consumer surplus gains tend to be evaluated purely by reference to price. In principle, quality can be incorporated into the framework of the traditional analysis by means of hedonic pricing, for example. However, the methodologies used to make such price adjustments are of little use for forecasting future developments. There is therefore a danger that an over-reliance on quantitative methods may lead competition authorities to place too much emphasis on short-term price effects.

Nevertheless, claims that a merger will accelerate innovation have to be examined with care. A merger will yield the greatest economies of scale in R&D when the merging firms are conducting overlapping research programmes, because the opportunities to share knowledge and to eliminate duplication are greatest in this case. One might therefore expect such a merger to yield faster innovation at a lower resource cost. However, where the merging firms are major 'poles of innovation' in relation to a particular product, the merger could significantly reduce the competitive pressure to innovate. Furthermore, even if the total resources devoted to R&D increase, the fusion of two research departments under a single management may reduce the likelihood of successful innovation by reducing the number of research trajectories being followed. Finally, it is intuitively probable that the merger will reduce spillovers to other firms in the industry. Where the other firms are much smaller and dependent on such spillovers for the development of new generations of products, there is a risk that one or more of them could be forced out of the market, thus weakening competition in the market for the final product.

It is also important to distinguish between true social efficiencies and redistributive gains. Only the first category should be included in an efficiency defence, if we follow a traditional welfare economics approach. For example, tax gains or wage concessions should not be counted as social efficiencies.

Another issue concerns the distinction between efficiencies at the level of the merging firm and efficiencies at the level of the market or even in other markets. For example, a merger may affect the R&D incentives for competitors. In practice, firm-level efficiencies are easier to verify but, in theory, there is no reason to consider only these efficiencies.

A central question is also whether efficiencies can be achieved through other means than the proposed merger, for example, internal growth, a joint venture, another merger or another contractual agreement. In many cases, it may be difficult for competition authorities to judge what alternatives are feasible and to assess whether an alternative should be preferred. As a first step towards answering these questions, the merging firms must be required to disclose as much information as possible about these alternatives whenever efficiency arguments are used. However, it is clear that the information and analyses they submit are likely to be heavily biased.

4.2.5 Burden of proof and verification of actual efficiencies

As one of the key problems with an efficiency defence is information, the firms should have the burden of proving that a merger (already found to be anti-competitive) produces sufficient efficiency gains not to be blocked. A good reason for this is that the firms have the best information. Nevertheless, this raises three types of problems: what standard of proof to require, how to check the validity of the firm's assertions, whether and how to check *ex post* if the alleged efficiency gains have been actually realized and whether they have been passed on to consumers.

Brodley (1996), for example, argues that the *ex ante* analysis of mergers is subject to so much uncertainty that the competition authority should carry out 'an after-the-fact audit to determine whether efficiencies have in fact been achieved'. If the efficiencies have not been achieved, the authority should obtain appropriate remedies to restore competitive conditions. At first sight, this suggestion seems attractive but it poses difficult problems. First, it is by no means easy to estimate the efficiency gains resulting from a merger when the whole economic environment is changing constantly.

Brodley's proposal therefore offers wide scope for legal and economic dispute. Second, in the European context, the implementation of this proposal would imply a major innovation in Community law, which at present does not even give the Commission power to break up a company which persistently abuses a dominant position. Last but not least, it may prove very difficult and socially costly to unscramble the assets of a company several years after a merger.

5. CONCLUSION

A new European merger regulation came into force on 1 May 2004, replacing the 1989 regulation. Many of the changes made in the new regulation relate to questions such as the division of responsibility between the Commission and the Member States and procedural matters. However, the modifications also address two major economic issues: the substantive test for prohibiting a merger and the efficiency defence. As explained in Section 2.1, although the EU clearly wishes to open the door to the efficiency defence, the precise scope for such a defence is not yet clear.

Economic theory shows that mergers can reduce competition by creating or increasing unilateral or collusive market power but that they can also create efficiencies. An efficiency defence should make it possible to compare these costs and benefits from mergers and to reject those mergers for which the anti-competitive effects are stronger than the efficiency gains. This kind of analysis is particularly relevant for the development of the European Single Market, where mergers can be a means to take advantage of wider markets. Similarly, some mergers can lead to synergies in R&D, facilitating the development of innovation, which is very important in the current context of rapid technological change.

If economic theory can be used to justify the relevance of an efficiency defence in a merger control system, empirical evidence suggests that mergers have very modest average effects on the profitability of the merging firms and that a large proportion of mergers reduce profitability. In addition, in many cases, the gains in profitability result from increases in market power rather than efficiencies. Nevertheless, in some cases, mergers may yield substantial efficiency gains. This indicates that one should not make the general presumption that mergers create efficiency gains but rather analyse efficiency effects on a case-by-case basis.

However, the cost–benefit analysis of mergers raises many methodological and implementation problems. First, it is necessary to make the choice of welfare standard. Even if the ultimate goal of competition policy is to maximize total welfare, without concern for distributional effects, it is not certain that a total welfare standard applied to the evaluation of individual mergers would necessarily yield the optimal result. For this reason and for a number of political and legal reasons, the EU applies the consumer welfare standard. However, even in the case of the consumer standard, simple formulas for efficiencies can be misleading, as a price increase cannot necessarily be equated with a reduction in consumer welfare, particularly in markets where technological change is rapid. The traditional approach, with its emphasis on modelling price effects, may lead to an overemphasis on short-run static effects at the expense of longer-term considerations of dynamic efficiency.

A second difficulty with the cost–benefit analysis is that one has to balance the efficiency gains against the anti-competitive effects and thus one needs to have a clear idea of the current and expected intensity of competition in the relevant market. The best solution is to use simulation analysis. This presents many difficulties, not least that of selecting the appropriate model to describe the modes of competition before and after the merger. In addition, there is so far no comprehensive model which assesses, within a consistent framework, the price variation resulting from the increase in market power and the degree to which the cost savings will be passed on to consumers. Finally, even assuming that one has the appropriate model, it cannot be taken for granted that the antitrust authorities will possess the necessary information for a comprehensive cost–benefit analysis. Other implementation problems to be solved are how to check the validity of firms' assertions, what types of efficiencies to consider and how to check that these efficiencies are merger-specific.

Given these problems, one might ask whether it is worthwhile to have an efficiency defence in the merger regulation. However, it seems reasonable to suppose that, within the Commission, efficiency considerations already influence the thinking of at least some of the participants in the decision-making process. Some Commission communications on industrial policy suggest that, within the Commission services, there is support for the view that a merger control policy which takes no account of efficiency gains may be harmful to European competitiveness. The Commission is also subject to strong external pressure, for example from the European Parliament, to take account of 'competitiveness'. In the absence of an explicit efficiency defence, there is therefore a risk that unclear compromises between competition policy and industrial policy may be made. Furthermore, efficiency gains are taken into account by the competition authorities in the USA, Canada and a number of other countries when assessing mergers, even if efficiency considerations seem to play a relatively minor role in practice in North America.

Therefore, a strong argument in favour of an explicit efficiency defence in the merger regulation is that it will improve the clarity and transparency of the decision-making procedure. The provisions made in the new merger regulation avoid the uncertainties that have surrounded the efficiency defence in Canada, by clearly specifying that the consumer surplus standard is to be applied. In addition, the regulation eschews any reference to considerations of international competitiveness, such as those contained in the Canadian Competition Act, thus avoiding the danger of abuse in order to promote European champions.

The efficiency defence may also yield two side-benefits. First, the need to make a trade-off between anti-competitive effects and efficiency gains may increase the pressure on the merger control authority to apply rigorous methods of analysis. Second, as Motis, Neven and Seabright argue in Chapter 5, shareholders often seem to exercise a rather weak control over managers even in important matters such as mergers. The knowledge that the rationale of a merger will be scrutinized by a competition authority may, therefore, induce managers to think more carefully before embarking on a course of action which entails substantial risks.

Since the magnitude of the information costs required for an efficiency defence is high, it should be carried out in a very limited number of cases. Furthermore, while quantitative evidence should be used whenever it is sufficiently sound, the qualitative assessment will play a predominant role in the large majority of cases. Consequently, if an efficiency defence were to be incorporated in the merger regulation, we would favour using a sequential approach distinguishing three stages: the screening tests, a qualitative analysis of efficiencies and a quantitative cost–benefit analysis. We would suggest starting implementation of the two first stages and testing the feasibility of implementing the last one.

In the first stage there is no explicit analysis of efficiencies. Criteria indicating a risk of market power are used to identify the mergers for which the consideration of efficiencies could tilt the balance of the decision. Essentially, the screening tests are the same as the existing Phase I procedure of the merger regulation, with the difference that the Commission might indicate to the notifying parties that an efficiency defence would be unlikely to succeed if the market power effects of the merger are perceived to be very large or if the claimed efficiencies are small or implausible. If the merger passes the screening tests and if the parties claim that it will create efficiencies, a comprehensive qualitative analysis of efficiencies is made. It will be for the parties to show that the efficiencies are likely to be achieved and that they are sufficient to counterbalance the anti-competitive effects of the merger.

At the final stage of this process, a more complex analysis might be carried out to quantify the net effects of the merger taking account of both the anti-competitive effects due to the increase in market power and the efficiencies expected from the merger. As a number of methodological problems still need to be resolved, we recommend testing the cost–benefit methodology by means of case studies.

NOTES

1. Council Regulation (EEC) No 4064/89. This regulation was amended by Council Regulation (EC) 1310/97.
2. Council Regulation (EC) No 139/2004.
3. According to Röller et al. (see Chapter 3, this volume), there is a small literature that has analysed the different linkages between product market competition and firm efficiency but none of these studies explicitly examines the effect of mergers on X-efficiency. Therefore these authors conclude: 'In our view, the issue of whether and how mergers, through their effects on competition in the product market, affect the X-efficiency of firms is still an open question'.
4. See Bennett et al. (2001). A decline in dynamic efficiency (innovation) may not necessarily be identified with a decline in R&D effort, since companies may engage in a race to obtain blocking patents.
5. See Tichy (2001) for a comprehensive overview and Gugler et al. (2001) for an analysis of a large panel of data on mergers throughout the world between 1981 and 1998.
6. After a merger driven by market power, the merged entity will increase its price and reduce its output and in general, its market share will decrease. Competitors will increase their output, but not sufficiently to compensate fully for the merged firm's reduction in output. Competitors therefore benefit not only from the price increase but also from an increase in their market shares. The resulting improvement in the competitors' profitability is likely to be reflected in their share prices.
7. However, mergers tend to increase the combined stock value of firms (at least in the short term). It is difficult to reconcile the evidence that a large proportion of mergers reduce profitability and that share prices rise. A possible explanation is the preemptive merger motive: a merger between A and B takes place to avoid a merger between B and C (which would reduce A's profit even more). If the pre-merger share prices reflect the risk that the merging firms may become outsiders, the announcement of a merger removing this risk will lead to a rise in the share prices.
8. Ideally, one should also take account of effects on quality, innovation, variety, and so on.
9. European Parliament (1998a, p. 22). See also European Parliament (1998c, p. 29), which urges that the Community and Member States should encourage consolidation of defence-related industries by means of cross-border mergers in order to create 'a strong, integrated and competitive European defence technological and industrial base'.
10. Minutes of 24 October 2000 (A5-0290/2000).
11. See, for example, Neven et al. (1993), Jacquemin (1997) and Camesasca (1999 and 2000).
12. See Eleanor Fox's remarks about American proponents of the efficiency defence (Fox (1995)).
13. Recital 26 of the new merger regulation states that 'A significant impediment to effective competition generally results from the creation or strengthening of a dominant position.'
14. For a more detailed explanation of this type of non-coordinated or unilateral effect see Bishop and Walker (2002) and NERA (1999).
15. Commission Decision no. 2000/42/EC of 9 March 1999, OJ no. L20 of 25/01/2000.
16. France, Spain, Ireland, Portugal, Finland and the UK.
17. Spain, France, Italy, Austria and Portugal.
18. Belgium, Germany, Greece and the Netherlands.
19. FTC vs. University Health Inc (1991) and FTC vs. Butterworth Health Corp and Blodgett Memorial Medical Center (1996).

20. U.S. vs. United Tote Inc (1991).
21. U.S. vs. Rockford Memorial Corp (1989).
22. In the terms of Figure 2.1, this means A > C.
23. Competition Tribunal (1992). We interpret this judgment as favouring the consumer surplus standard. McFetridge (1998), on the other hand, considers that there is a specific 'Hillsdown standard', which allows losses of consumer surplus provided that they are less than the efficiency gains.
24. One might also argue that, for example, there is no justification on equity grounds for favouring the buyers of expensive luxury goods rather than the shareholders of the companies that make them.
25. The Canadian Competition Tribunal raised, but did not answer, this question in the Hillsdown judgment (Competition Tribunal (1992)).
26. Two variants of this sequential approach can be considered. In the first one, mergers are always accepted if the structural indicator does not exceed a certain threshold and an explicit efficiency defence is always allowed if the structural indicator exceeds the threshold. In the second one, mergers are always rejected if the structural indicator exceeds the threshold and an explicit efficiency defence is allowed below that threshold.
27. Cyanamid/Shell (Case IV/M354), 1 October 1993, *Official Journal* 9 October 1993.
28. Farrell and Shapiro (2001) dispute whether the scale economies are important for the analysis of merger efficiencies. In their view, efficiency gains arising from scale economies are unlikely to be merger-specific.
29. Assume that the merger tends to increase price by dP/P per cent as a result of the increase of market power. Then, for the net effects of this merger to be beneficial to consumers, it is necessary that $(dC/C)\beta > dP/P$, where dC/C is the percentage cost reduction due to the efficiencies created by the merger and $\beta = (dP/dC)(C/P)$ is the pass-on elasticity. The pass-on elasticity indicates by what percentage the price would be reduced if cost were reduced by 1 per cent. It is a function of the absolute pass-on and the mark-up.
30. According to Stennek and Verboven (see Chapter 4, this volume), there is an inverted U-shaped relationship between the absolute pass-on and the degree of market power as measured by market shares: the pass-on in an industry is typically the largest for firms with intermediate market share, i.e. not the very small firms and the dominant firms.
31. The worst-case scenario is based on the assumption that all the firms in the market will increase their price by 5–10 per cent. This increase in price has been chosen on the basis of the principles for market definition set out in the Commission Notice on the definition of the relevant market (published in the *Official Journal* 372 on 9 December 1997). According to this Notice, the relevant anti-trust market consists of the minimum number of products for which a hypothetical joint price increase in the range of 5–10 per cent above the competitive level would be profitable (assuming no change in efficiencies). This justification is not really convincing and therefore, the worst-case scenario price increase is rather an arbitrary choice.
32. More precisely, incremental costs. The longer the time horizon, the more costs will be incremental, rather than fixed.

REFERENCES

Baker, J.B. (1997), 'Econometric analysis in FTC v. Staples', Federal Trade Commission, 18 July, accessed at www.ftc.gov/speeches/other/stspch.htm.

Bennett, M., P. de Bijl and M. Canoy (2001), 'Future policy in telecommunications: an analytical framework', Centraal Planbureau document no. 005, The Hague.

Besanko, D. and D. Spulber (1993), 'Contested mergers and equilibrium antitrust policy', *Journal of Law, Economics and Organization*, **9**(1), 1–29.

Bishop, S. and M. Walker (2002), *The Economics of EC Competition Law: Concepts, Application and Measurement*, 2nd edn, London: Sweet & Maxwell.

Brodley, J. F. (1996), 'Proof of efficiencies in mergers and joint ventures: testing ex ante claims against ex post evidence', statement of Joseph H. Brodley, Federal Trade Commission hearings on global and innovation-based competition, 7 November 1995 (revised January 1996).

Bundesminister für Wirtschaft und Technologie (2002), Ministererlaubnis vom 18. September 2002, Gesch.-Z.: IB1 – 22 08 40/129 [German Federal Minister of Economics and Technology, ministerial authorisation of the E.ON/Ruhrgas merger].

Camesasca, P.D. (1999), 'The explicit efficiency defence in merger control: does it make the difference', *European Competition Law Review*, **20**(1) (January), 14–18.

Camesasca, P.D. (2000), *European Merger Control: Getting the Efficiencies Right*, Antwerp, Groningen and Oxford: Intersentia-Hart.

Competition Authority (2002), 'Guidelines for merger analysis: a consultative document', Irish Competition Authority, August, Dublin.

Competition Bureau (1991), *Merger Enforcement Guidelines*, Ottawa: Government of Canada.

Competition Bureau (2001), The Commissioner of Competition v Superior Propane Inc. and ICG Propane Inc., CT-98/2, memorandum of the Commissioner of Competition on the redetermination proceedings, 25 June 2001 (Canada).

Competition Bureau (2004), *Merger Enforcement Guidelines*, Ottawa: Government of Canada.

Competition Tribunal (1992), Director of Investigation and Research v Hillsdown Holdings (Canada) Ltd et al., CT 91/1, Reasons and Order, 9 March 1992 (Canada).

Competition Tribunal (2000), The Commissioner of Competition v Superior Propane Inc. and ICG Propane Inc., CT 1998/002, Reasons and Order, 30 August 2000 (Canada).

Competition Tribunal (2002), The Commissioner of Competition v Superior Propane Inc. and ICG Propane Inc., CT 1998/002, Reasons and Order following Reasons for Judgment of the Federal Court of Appeal dated 4 April 2001 (Canada).

Council Regulation (EEC) no. 4064/89 of 21 December 1989 on the control of concentrations between undertakings, *Official Journal* no. L395, 30 December 1989, page 1.

Council Regulation (EC) no. 1310/97 of 30 June 1997 amending Regulation (EEC) No 4064/89 on the control of concentrations between undertakings, *Official Journal* no. L40 , 13 February 1998, page 17.

Council Regulation (EC) no. 139/2004 of 20 January 2004 on the control of concentrations between undertakings, *Official Journal* no. L24, 29 January 2004, page 1.

European Commission (1996), 'European Commission: Contribution to Efficiency Claims in Mergers and Other Horizontal Agreements', O.E.C.D./GD(96)65.

European Commission (1997), 'The European aerospace industry: meeting the global challenge', communication from the Commission, COM (1997)466 of 24 September 1997.

European Commission (1999), 'The competitiveness of European enterprises in the face of globalization – how it can be encouraged', communication from the Commission, COM(98)718 of 20 January 1999.

European Commission (2004), 'Guidelines on the assessment of horizontal mergers under the Council regulation on the control of concentrations between undertakings', *Official Journal* no. C31, 5 February 2004, page 5.
European Parliament (1998a), report of the Committee on Economic and Monetary Affairs and Industrial Policy on the competitiveness of European industry, PE 223.973/fin. of 21 April 1998.
European Parliament (1998b), report of the Committee on Economic and Monetary Affairs and Industrial Policy, PE 223.989/fin. of 13 October 1998.
European Parliament (1998c), report of the Committee on Foreign Affairs, Security and Defence Policy on a communication from the Commission 'Implementing European Union strategy on defence-related industries', PE 227.720/fin. of 8 December 1998.
Farrell, J. and C. Shapiro (1990), 'Horizontal mergers: an equilibrium analysis', American *Economic Review*, **80**(1), 107–26.
Farrell, J. and C. Shapiro (2001), 'Scale economies and synergies in horizontal merger analysis', *Antitrust Law Journal*, **68**, 685–710.
Fox, E.M. (1995), 'Antitrust and competitiveness: efficiencies, failing firms and the world arena', statement of Eleanor M. Fox, Federal Trade Commission hearings on global and innovation-based competition, 13 December (revised 29 December).
Fridolfsson, S.-O. (2002), 'A consumers' surplus defence in merger control', paper presented to the 29th Annual Conference of the European Association for Research in Industrial Economics, Madrid.
Froeb, L., S. Tschanz and G. Werden (2001), 'Pass-through rates and the price effects of mergers', Owen Graduate School of Management working paper, Vanderbilt University, 12 July.
Gugler, K., D.C. Mueller, B. Burcin Yurtoglu and C. Zulehner (2001), 'The effects of mergers: an international comparison', discussion paper FS IV 01–21, WZB, Berlin.
Jacquemin, A. (1997), 'Theories of industrial organization and competition policy: what are the links?' in *Economic Science: An Art or an Asset*?, Cheltenham, UK and Lyme, USA: Edward Elgar.
Jacquemin, A., P. Buigues and F. Ilzkovitz (1989), *Horizontal Mergers and Competition Policy in the European Community, European Economy no 40*, March, Brussels: European Commission.
Lyons, B. (2002), 'Could politicians be more right than economists? A theory of merger standards', Centre for Competition and Regulation working paper CCR 02–1, University of East Anglia, Norwich.
McFetridge, D.G. (1998), 'Merger enforcement under the Competition Act after 10 years', *Review of Industrial Organization*, **13**, 25–56.
National Economic Research Associates (NERA) (1999), 'Merger appraisal in oligopolistic markets', OFT research paper 19, Office of Fair Trading, London.
Neven, D. and L.-H. Röller (2001), 'Consumer surplus vs. welfare standard in a political economy model of merger control', WZB discussion paper FS IV 00–15.
Neven, D., R. Nuttal and P. Seabright (1993), *Merger in Daylight. The Economics and Politics of European Merger Control*, London: Centre for Economic Policy Research.
Office of Fair Trading (OFT) (2003), 'Mergers – substantive assessment guidance', OFT516, Office of Fair Trading, May, London.
Shapiro, C. (1995), 'Mergers with differentiated products', US Department of Justice, 9 November, accessed at www.antitrust.org/law/shapSpeech.html.

Tichy, G. (2001), 'What do we know about success and failure of mergers', *Journal of Industry, Competition and Trade*, **1**(4), 347–94.
Townley, P. (1999), The Commissioner of Competition v. Superior Propane Inc. et al., affidavit of Peter G.C. Townley, Competition Tribunal, file no. CT 98/2, 16 August 1999.
US District Court for the District of Columbia (1997), FTC v Staples, Inc. and Office Depot, Inc., Civ. No 97–701(TFH).
Werden, G. and L. Froeb (1995), 'Simulation as an alternative to structural merger policy in differentiated products industries', US Department of Justice Economic Analysis Group discussion paper EAG 95–2, September, Washington, DC.
Williamson, O. (1968), 'Economies as an antitrust defense: the welfare trade-offs', *American Economic Review*, **58**, 18–36.

3. Efficiency gains from mergers

Lars-Hendrik Röller, Johan Stennek and Frank Verboven

The purpose of this chapter is to contribute to the analysis of two questions: Should a merger control system take into account efficiency gains from horizontal mergers, and balance these gains against the anti-competitive effects of mergers? If so, how should a system be designed to account for efficiency gains?

There are several reasons why efficiency gains from horizontal mergers are an important issue today. Business conditions are changing rapidly, for example as a result of the internal market, increased global competition, and the deregulation of many industries. The consequent need to adapt the industry structure has generated a wave of mergers in Europe as well as in the rest of the world. The current wave is of historical proportions.

All mergers with a so-called Community dimension must be notified to the Commission and are subsequently reviewed under the merger regulation.[1] According to Articles 2(3) of the regulation, a concentration which 'creates or strengthens a dominant position as a result of which effective competition would be significantly impeded' shall be prohibited. Otherwise it shall be allowed. According to Article 2(1)(b), the Commission shall, in making this appraisal, amongst other things take into account 'the development of technical and economic progress provided that it is to consumers' advantage and does not form an obstacle to competition'. The latter clause has triggered a debate whether the merger regulation allows for a so-called efficiency defence. Can important cost savings (or other efficiencies) save an otherwise anti-competitive merger? The Commission has, in policy statements, argued that, 'there is no real legal possibility of justifying an efficiency defence under the merger regulation' (European Commission 1996). Many economists, starting with Williamson (1968), have argued that competition authorities should take efficiency gains into account.

Another reason why it is important to discuss an efficiency defence under the merger regulation is the introduction of the concept of joint dominance. According to the Merger Regulation, a merger can only be blocked if it creates or strengthens a dominant position. A firm is dominant if it has a large degree of market power – a monopoly-like situation. In such cases one talks more precisely of single-firm dominance. The Commission has widened the concept of dominance to include also joint, or oligopolistic, dominance. The relevance of joint dominance in merger cases was confirmed by the Court in the Kali+Salz decision. This suggests that merger policy has become stricter. Economic theory suggests that cost savings (and other efficiencies) are more likely to dominate the anti-competitive effects of a merger, the lower the concentration is. Hence, the introduction of the concept of joint dominance makes it more natural to consider efficiencies today.

Recent developments in economics may make an efficiency defence more tractable. For example new computer-based simulation techniques can be used as a way to estimate the likely anti-competitive effects of a merger and, at the same time, balance these effects against possible efficiency gains. Such techniques are starting to be used in the USA and in Canada.

One may note that the treatment of efficiencies in merger control also has been debated in the USA. That discussion gave rise to a revision of the merger guidelines to clarify how the US Department of Justice and the Federal Trade Commission treat efficiencies. Before this, several revisions of the merger guidelines have occurred that show a gradually more positive attitude towards efficiencies. One can also notice a similar development in the Federal Courts' treatment of efficiencies. In the 1960s the Supreme Court seemed to reject an efficiency defence. In the 1990s lower courts started to analyse efficiencies in a way similar to the merger guidelines.

To help answer the two questions whether EU merger control should allow an efficiency defence, and if so, how it should be designed, we start with an extensive review of the relevant economic research, including both theoretical and empirical work. Next, we draw up a 'checklist' of relevant dimensions that need to be considered when assessing the possible role of efficiencies. Finally, we compare alternative approaches to include efficiencies in a merger control system, emphasizing the central role of informational limitations.

We should emphasize that although the insights provided by economic research are vital inputs for answering the questions, the final choice necessarily involves value judgements. For this reason, this report cannot come to a definite answer to the above two questions. We should also emphasize, already here in the beginning, that various issues addressed in this report are still the subjects of intense academic research. Many of the facts require more detailed analysis.

1. THEORETICAL ANALYSIS

This section provides a discussion of the theory that is necessary to obtain a coherent understanding of mergers and the role played by efficiencies. We start from a typology of possible efficiencies that may arise from mergers. The effects from mergers on consumer or total surplus may depend on the type of efficiency. We distinguish between five categories, based on the concept of the production function:

1. Rationalisation of production, which refers to cost savings from reallocating production across firms, without increasing the joint technological capabilities;
2. Economies of scale, i.e. savings in average costs associated with an increase in total output;
3. Technological progress, which may stem from the diffusion of know-how or increased incentives for R&D;
4. Purchasing economies or savings in factor prices such as intermediate goods or the cost of capital;
5. Reduction of slack (managerial and X-efficiency).

Next, we review the anti-competitive effects that may arise from mergers, either due to an increased unilateral market power, or due to an increased likelihood of successful collusion.

Finally, in this section we discuss both the price effects and total surplus effects arising from mergers, taking into account the role played by efficiencies. We argue that internal efficiencies often need to imply sufficiently large savings in marginal costs for price to decrease. Not all types of efficiencies guarantee that this will be the case. The required amount of efficiencies for price to decrease depends on various variables, such as the merging firms' market share and the price elasticity of demand. For total welfare to increase, all types of internal efficiencies may in principle be considered, although the required amount may depend on which type of efficiency is realized due to the merger. It is important to stress that the precise amount of efficiencies required for price to decrease or total welfare to increase is dependent on the specific assumptions one makes about how firms behave in the market, both before and after the merger. This does not make it possible to present a simple and unique formula, applicable to all mergers.

1.1 Typologies of Efficiency Gains

Efficiencies from mergers may come about in a variety of ways. In order to obtain a clear and systematic understanding of the consumer and welfare effects of mergers, discussed in section 1.3, it is important to make a typology of the various kinds of efficiencies that may be created. Naturally there are many different ways in which one may categorize efficiency gains from mergers. Different typologies are useful for the different discussions in this chapter.

The first typology is based on the concept of the production function. It is extensively used in the literature on productivity measurement.

- Rationalization
- Economies of scale
- Technological progress
- Purchasing economies
- Slack.

This typology is useful for the identification of different efficiencies. This typology is described in detail in sub-sections 1.1.1 to 1.1.5 below.

A second distinction that is often made in the context of merger analysis is:

- Real cost savings
- Redistributive (or pecuniary) cost savings.

This distinction is important since typically only real cost savings are considered in an efficiency defence. Redistributive gains are cost savings that the firms may achieve for example in the form of lower taxes. However purchasing economies may also be redistributive (see below). Real cost savings are those savings that correspond to some savings of productive resources in the economy. Rationalization, economies of scale, technological progress, and slack reduction are all real cost savings. Also some purchasing economies are real cost savings.

A third distinction that is often made in the context of merger analysis is:

- Fixed costs
- Variable costs.

This distinction is important since savings in variable costs, but not savings in fixed costs, may almost immediately benefit not only the merging firms, but also the consumers (see below). Savings in fixed costs normally come in the form of economies of scale, technological progress and purchasing economies. Savings in variable costs may come in all five forms.

A fourth distinction that is useful in the context of mergers is:

- Firm-level efficiencies
- Industry-level efficiencies.

An example of efficiencies at the level of the industry would be cost savings due to a reallocation of production from the merging firms to their competitors – a common effect of mergers (see below). This distinction is important since it is mainly in the first category that the merging firms have an informational advantage over competition authorities. All the five categories above can occur at both the level of the firm, and at the level of the industry.

Finally, one may distinguish between:

- Efficiencies in the relevant market
- Efficiencies in other markets.

According to some, only the first category can be taken into account in an efficiency defence. At a minimum, including also the second type introduces some additional complications.

1.1.1 Rationalization

Rationalization of production refers to the cost savings that may be realized from shifting output from one plant to another, without changing the firms' joint production possibilities. As the term indicates, rationalization of production refers to an optimal allocation of the production levels across the different plants of a firm.

Before the merger, the firms may differ in their marginal cost of production. This may be the case for at least three reasons. First, one of the firms may have a higher amount of physical capital. Second, one firm may have some inherent competitive advantage, for example due to a patent or other superior knowledge. Finally, when marginal cost is increasing in output due to capacity constraints, firms may differ in their marginal costs because they are producing at different output levels.

After the merger, the new company becomes a multi-plant firm, and cost savings can be realized by shifting production from the plants with a high marginal cost to the plants with a lower marginal cost. A firm fully rationalizes its production if the marginal costs at all its plants are equalized: in this case it no longer pays to further reallocate production across plants. For example, when cost differences arise from differing capacity constraints, output rationalization implies that the firm, which is most capacity-constrained, reduces its production in favour of the firm with more excess capacity.

The most drastic case of rationalization occurs when one firm operates at such a low marginal cost (for all relevant levels of total production) that it is optimal to reallocate all production to that firm. The merger then effectively involves the shutdown of the other, less efficient firm. In this case, the merger also leads to an elimination of the fixed set-up costs that are required to keep a plant operational.[2] Such fixed cost savings are discussed in the next sub-section on economies of scale.

1.1.2 Economies of scale (and scope)

A firm is said to have economies of scale when its average cost falls as output increases. Economies of scope generalize the concept of economies of scale to the case of the multiproduct firm (see 1.1.2.3). Economies of scale and scope are frequently used as an argument to defend a proposed merger. To assess the validity of the argument in each case, it is important to understand the sources of economies of scale, and assess whether they cannot be realized otherwise.

Economies of scale, realized through a merger, may be the result of coordination of the (formerly separate) firms' investments in physical capital – called long-run economies of scale. Other realizations of economies of scale may, however, come already in the short run (when physical capital is held fixed). Chapter 4 contains a more detailed discussion of economies of scale in mergers.

1.1.2.1 Short-run economies of scale

There are two types of short-run economies of scale that potentially can be realized through a merger, namely the elimination of duplication of indivisible tasks, and a form of rationalization.

First, indivisibility occurs when it is technically impossible to scale down an input below a certain minimum size, even when the level of output is very small. No matter how small the size of a firm, some minimum expenditure on essential tasks is required to keep the firm operational. These include certain administrative and support routines, such as the purchasing of materials, the billing of customers, personnel service, etc. These tasks involve fixed costs, i.e. costs that do not increase as total output increases. Before the merger, all firms wastefully duplicate the fixed costs. After the merger, they may be spread over the larger combined output of the merging firms. The merger then realizes scale economies by avoiding a duplication of fixed costs. Note that a spreading of these fixed costs may be feasible both when the firms produce identical and when they produce different products.

Second, short-run economies of scale may be realized by a reallocation of production between plants (rationalisation). We categorize such cost savings as economies of scale rather than as rationalization, if the reason for the reallocation is that short-run marginal costs are decreasing with higher output.[3]

1.1.2.2 Long-run economies of scale

Long-run economies of scale occur when a doubling of *all* inputs (including physical capital) leads to more than a doubling of total output. Product-level (or specific) returns to scale are related to the total production of a single product variety. Plant-level returns to scale are related to the total production of all product varieties within a plant. Firm-level returns to scale are related to economies realized by managing many plants within the same firm.

Long-run economies of scale may arise for several reasons. First, when the output of a firm is small, it is usually preferable to invest little, and operate at an inferior technology with a higher marginal cost. As the production of the firm increases, it becomes worthwhile to invest more in automated technologies that yield lower marginal costs. Long-run economies of scale may also arise because of the benefits from specialization. Each worker can concentrate his or her efforts on certain specific tasks that can be implemented more efficiently. Similarly, the energy requirements for a large machine may be proportionally lower than those of a small machine. Due to certain physical laws, material requirements may also be decreasing in size.[4]

To realize long-run economies of scale through a merger, it is essential that the assets of the partners are combined and integrated. Such a restructuring may not be desirable, in the short run: the plants are already built and it is costly to unbuild them, reallocate capital and achieve the economies of scale. Therefore, in the short run, adjustment costs may impede a full integration of the firms' activities. In contrast, in the long run, it may be less costly to integrate the future investment decisions within the newly created firm. Future investments occur for two reasons. First, the firms' current capital depreciates and old plants need renovation. This includes both physical capital and intangible assets such as brand name. Second, new investment opportunities may arise if the size of the market increases.

Economies of scale (Scherer et al. 1975; Panzar 1989) also apply to a context where the merging firms produce differentiated products. After a merger between firms selling similar product lines, it may be desirable to concentrate the production of certain products within the same plant, rather than to have each former firm continue to produce the whole product line within the same plant. Such a specialization of production allows the plants to reduce down-time due to shifting production (run-length economies).

Long-run economies of scale may arise in both production and in research and development. They may also arise in marketing activities. A single brand name may be created to economize on advertising expenditures. The sales forces or the distribution network may be combined (see, for example, Kitching 1967).

The exploitation of economies of scale through a merger between firms that are producing differentiated products may involve a reduction in product diversity. This potential loss to consumers should also be taken into account when measuring the net benefits from economies of scale.

1.1.2.3 Economies of scope

Economies of scope arise when it is advantageous to produce goods that are related in one way or another within the same plant. Economies of scope may for example arise when multi-product production requires a common 'public' input. For example, the production of wool and mutton requires the common input, sheep; the production of beef and hides requires the common input, cattle. When economies of scope are present, it may not be desirable to have plants specialize in the production of single products even if there are product-specific economies of scale.

1.1.3 Technological progress

In the analysis of technological progress a distinction is often made between process and product innovations. A process innovation reduces the cost of producing an existing product; a product innovation increases the value (quality) of an existing product.[5] Both types of innovation are essentially equivalent in that they imply an improvement in the firms' joint production possibilities frontier. In the discussion below, we often refer to technological progress as process innovations with corresponding cost savings. However, it should be clear that similar conclusions can be drawn for product innovations and corresponding quality improvements.

1.1.3.1 Diffusion of know-how

Firms may have different technological or administrative capabilities due to different patents, different experiences, a different management or organization, etc. A merger between firms with different characteristics may then lead to a diffusion of know-how across the participants. This can bring the firms closer to their joint production possibilities frontier, without shifting the frontier itself.[6]

First, it may be the case that one of the merging firms has superior know-how in all dimensions. The merger then allows its partner(s) to learn and potentially adopt all the skills of the firms with superior know-how. For example, the better management may teach the bad management.

Alternatively, the better management may replace the old management and make all decisions by itself. In these examples, the diffusion of know-how goes in one single direction, and the superior firm does not learn.

Second, there may be two-way diffusion of know-how. In this case, both firms can benefit from the merger and improve their technological or administrative capabilities. A two-way diffusion of know-how is possible when firms have complementary skills or own some other complementary assets. For example, the merging firms may own complementary patents, which taken together further improve the production process on the quality of the product. A merger in this instance effectively implements a cross-licensing agreement. Similarly, the management of each firm may have built up different experience or expertise. As another example, consider a relatively young R&D-intensive firm that has developed a superior product but lacks the marketing know-how or a distribution network. A merger with one of the existing competitors, with an established brand name and a solid distribution network, may then ensure a fast diffusion of the new (or improved) product.

Two-way diffusion of know-how may also occur when firms have different capabilities in the production of intermediate outputs. For example, consider two car manufacturers which both produce (or purchase from suppliers) several intermediate outputs such as brakes or gears. One of the firms may be more efficient in producing brakes (or can buy them cheaper from a supplier), whereas the other firm may be more efficient in producing (or purchasing) gears. Specialization then leads to a reduction in costs, below either of the firms' costs before the merger.[7]

As a final example of two-way diffusion of know-how, consider an industry in which there is learning by doing. Learning by doing means that the firms' average costs are declining in their cumulative (past) output (as a measure of experience). It is sometimes referred to as 'dynamic economies of scale'. A merger may facilitate learning by causing spill-overs, allowing firms to learn better from each other's experience.

1.1.3.2 Incentives for research and development

An important activity of many firms involved in mergers is research and development (R&D), in either cost-reducing production processes or in product improvement or in the development of new products. As discussed above, the integration of investment and R&D activities after the merger may sometimes create significant economies of scale. In addition, a merger may alter the incentives for R&D expenditures. R&D decisions are frequently taken strategically, that is, dependent on the actions of competing firms. It is often argued that the presence of too much competition destroys the incentives to spend money on R&D. The most popular argument is that the outcome of R&D is highly non-proprietary, due to imitation or information spill-overs of the R&D results (d'Aspremont and Jacquemin 1989). If this is indeed important, a merger could help to internalize the benefits from R&D among the participating firms, thereby creating an increased incentive for R&D.

Even in the absence of R&D spill-overs, the intensity of competition influences incentives for R&D. The industrial economics literature has addressed the question whether a large dominating firm still has sufficient incentives to spend money on R&D, compared to its smaller rivals. The answer depends on the expected payoffs from R&D (assuming no spill-overs). Consider first the case in which the outcome of R&D involves little risk, so that R&D looks much like traditional investment. In this case, a dominating firm would have greater incentives to invest in R&D, so as to retain its competitive advantage and associated monopoly rents. In contrast, if R&D is very risky, then the dominating firm cannot guarantee success even for disproportionately large amounts spent on R&D. As a result, the large firm would rather 'rest on its laurels', enjoy the current monopoly rents and accept the risk of being leapfrogged.[8]

1.1.4 Purchasing economies

Cost savings may also be involved in the merger because of the presence of imperfectly competitive factor markets. Small firms often need to purchase their inputs such as materials and energy at prices above marginal costs. When the firms merge, their bargaining power may increase and more pressure can be put on upstream input suppliers to cut their prices and obtain quantity discounts. In the automobile industry, for example, manufacturers sometimes form alliances to purchase their components in larger amounts to increase their discounts. Similarly, significant advertising discounts may be obtained when large contracts can be made. To assess the social effects from increased bargaining power towards suppliers, it is important to know the degree of power at the supplier side. If there is little power on the supplier side, the increased bargaining power of the merging firm may be socially harmful. If, however, the increased bargaining power becomes a form of countervailing power to an already strong supply side, then the private benefits from the merging firm may coincide with the social benefits. Unfortunately, economic theory has not yet analysed these issues in detail.[9]

Note that mergers may also create discounts when there is no increase in bargaining power (that is, when the upstream supplier would retain all the bargaining power to set prices). This happens when suppliers offer two-part tariffs, consisting of a fixed fee, and a price per unit (or some other non-linear pricing schemes). Such tariffs are used to price-discriminate between low and high users. When firms merge, they become high users, and thereby can spread the fixed fee and obtain a lower average price for their supplies.

A merger may also lead to a lower cost of capital since capital markets do not function perfectly. For a variety of reasons, such as asymmetric information about risk and expected return, firms cannot always borrow at a competitive interest rate. Small and expanding firms, in particular, often face stringent liquidity constraints, while large corporations usually have better access to the outside capital markets, and big firms in declining industries may even generate 'excess' liquidity. A small firm that joins a large corporation, or is being bought by a firm with limited possibilities for internal expansion obtains new possibilities in raising capital.

1.1.5 Slack

Large public corporations are characterized by a separation of ownership and control. This creates problems of asymmetric information between the shareholders of the firm and the management to whom control is delegated. A failure by the management to maximize the profits of the firm leads to internal inefficiency, sometimes called X-inefficiency.[10] Why may the goals of management diverge from profit maximization, despite the fact that they are often given profit maximizing incentives through profit sharing, stock option plans, and so on? Other interests of management may be the personal ambitions to obtain power, become the leader of a big or growing company; or not to change a chosen strategy and thereby admitting old mistakes; or to avoid having to fire excess personnel. These goals conflict with the shareholders' goals. The shareholders can exercise some control over the management through the board of directors. However, the management is usually much better informed about its projects, and the board may have only a limited possibility to challenge the management's decisions. To collect all the necessary information is not necessarily profitable. After all, the whole idea of delegating power to the management is to avoid these information costs.

The firm's internal efficiency is partly determined by the management (administrative) techniques, such as incentives systems, used to mitigate the problems caused by the separation of ownership and control. We view such techniques as defining the firm's production possibility frontier, and hence improvements in such techniques as technological progress. A merger may lead to improvements in such techniques (for example if one firm can learn them from the other). Such gains, we classify as technological progress, and not slack reduction.

However, the firm's internal efficiency is also determined by other factors, and these other factors may be affected as a result of a merger. One commonly mentioned example is that mergers are an important part of the disciplining power of the capital market (discussed in sub-section 1.1.5.1). Another example, pointing in the opposite direction, is that a horizontal merger reduces competition in the product market and hence the disciplining power of the product market on firm efficiency (discussed in sub-section 1.1.5.2). A third example is that a merger may increase the possibilities for the merged entity to use relative performance evaluations between the formerly separately owned plants.[11] If that should happen, slack would be reduced as a result of the merger.

1.1.5.1 The market for corporate control

Slack makes a firm undervalued and lowers the firm's stock price. This may induce another company to buy the firm, reorganize and bring the firm back to profit maximizing behaviour. Actually, Manne (1965) and Marris (1964) argue that the mere threat of a takeover can be sufficient to discipline the current management, despite the presence of asymmetric information between shareholders and management.

The threat of corporate takeovers may then serve as a disciplining device to the management. Yet management is usually not punished after a takeover; often they even obtain large compensation ('golden parachutes'). The punishment mainly lies in the loss of the enjoyed managerial rents, including prestige or on-the-job consumption, such as private jets and excessive representation expenses. See Scharfstein (1988) for a detailed analysis. Provided there is a sufficiently high punishment threat to management involved, a well-functioning market for corporate control could then ensure that managerial inefficiencies could not be long lived.

The disciplinary power of takeovers is, however, limited for several reasons. First, there is a free-rider problem involved in disciplining the management, as pointed out by Grossman and Hart (1980b). A raider needs to collect costly information to identify managerial inefficiencies. The raider can then make a profit only if the tender price of the shares (at which he buys) is lower than the post-raid price. However, each single current shareholder may not be willing to sell at a tender price, in anticipation of a higher stock price after the raid.[12] One solution to this free-rider problem is dilution, which allows a majority shareholder (the raider) to sell part of the firm to another company he owns at terms that are disadvantageous to minority shareholders. Shleifer and Vishny (1986) point out that a raid may be successful if it is done by a large existing shareholder, who then at least enjoys an increase in the value of its own shares (the other shareholders would then benefit more, of course).

A second limit to takeovers arises because of possible actions by the existing management in response to takeover bids. For example, poison pills are sometimes used as a defence. These are preferred stock rights that may be used in the event of a tender. Scherer (1980, cited in Holmström and Tirole 1989) also questioned the strength of the disciplining power of takeovers. Takeovers are very costly so that they may be used only in cases of severe mismanagement.

The theory of the disciplining role of takeover threats is also problematic in that it is difficult to test empirically. Studies of actual takeovers cannot provide sufficient information, since the theory is about the disciplining threat, which is difficult to measure as long as it is not realized.

As discussed by Manne (1965), the theory of the disciplining role of takeover threats is potentially important for the design of merger control. Unfortunately, to our knowledge there has been little or no research on this topic. Nevertheless, a few general remarks can be made. By making takeovers more difficult, competition policy may reduce the disciplining role of the takeover threat. Presumably, the firm's closest competitors form the most effective takeover threat, since they are likely to possess the best information about mismanagement. Without the allowance of an efficiency defence, such disciplinary mergers may not be carried out. As a compromise, one may argue that a takeover should be temporarily allowed, to replace current management; after the re-organization the target should be sold again as soon as possible. The problem with such as compromise is however that a raider would be strengthening the position of its own competitors, so that the raid would not be carried out in the first place. Hence, if a disciplinary threat of mergers mainly comes from competing firms, there may be a real trade-off between efficiency gains and anti-competitive effects.

1.1.5.2 Product market competition and the internal efficiency of firms

When product market competition is soft, management and employees exert low effort and production costs are high. Moreover, the low efforts and the high costs are too low and too high respectively, from a social welfare point of view. These ideas are widespread among economists as well as policy-makers. Actually, these ideas motivate policies to promote competition such as deregulation and trade liberalization. For example, the European Commission (1988, p. 134) argued that 'the new competitive pressures brought about by the completion of the internal market can be expected to . . . produce appreciable gains in internal efficiency . . . [which will] constitute much of what can be called the dynamic effects of the internal market.' According to Scherer and Ross (1990) the empirical evidence is fragmentary but points in the same general direction: X-efficiency is more apt to be low when competitive pressures are strong than when firms enjoy insulated market positions. Moreover, these X-inefficiencies are at least as large as the welfare losses from resource misallocation.

There is a small literature that has analysed the different linkages between product market competition and firm efficiency. Some studies focus on financial linkages between competition and firm efficiency. Grossman and Hart (1982) argue that if there exists a bankruptcy risk, and a receiver who is able to recover all funds that are not invested, leaving the manager with no perquisites in case of bankruptcy, the manager invests more to reduce the risk of bankruptcy. Any changes in product market competition that affect the risk of bankruptcy also affect managerial incentives. Schmidt (1997) makes this intuition more precise. In his model, increased competition has two effects on managerial incentives: it increases the probability of liquidation, which increases managerial effort, but it also reduces the firm's profits, which may make it less attractive to induce high effort. Stennek (forthcoming) argues that limited liability may serve as a disciplining device on the internal efficiency of a firm, and the tougher the product market competition, the higher the disciplining power.[13] However, even if policies that promote competition enhance X-efficiency, the social gain may be outweighed by a less efficient allocation of risk. Other studies focus on informational linkages between competition and firm efficiency. Holmström (1982) and Nalebuff and Stiglitz (1983) argue that cost shocks normally should be positively correlated between competitors. Then, by using relative performance evaluations, the moral hazard problem is mitigated within each firm. However, even if more firms increases the amount of available information and hence increase the overall efficiency of the firms, the effect on effort is ambiguous.[14] Hermalin (1992) focuses on wealth linkages between competition and firm efficiency. He argues that managers often have substantial bargaining power in negotiations over their employment contracts. Since increased competition decreases the 'pie' over which the principal and agent bargain, increased competition also reduces the manager's wealth. If 'shirking' is a normal good, then competition reduces shirking. Finally, some papers focus on output and strategic linkages between competition and firm efficiency. Martin (1993) and Horn et al. (1994, 1995) argued that a reduction in marginal cost saves more money for larger firms. Since the size of firms decreases with competition, managers exert more effort into cost-reduction under soft competition – an output effect. Horn et al. (1994) also demonstrate a strategic effect when the compensation scheme is public information.[15]

Perhaps surprisingly, the emerging picture from these studies is that the effect of competition on internal efficiency may be both positive and negative. Moreover, even in the cases where the effect is positive, the welfare consequences may be negative. The picture is rather complex. Unfortunately, none of the studies explicitly examines the effect of mergers on X-efficiency. The reason for the change in competition in these studies is instead lowered entry barriers or trade liberalization. Hence, it is not clear to what extent the studied linkages between competition and X-efficiency are also relevant in merger analysis. In our view, the issue of whether and how mergers, through their effects on competition in the product market, affect the X-efficiency of firms is still an open question.

1.2 Anti-competitive Effects from Mergers

The prime reason why competition policy authorities are concerned with horizontal mergers is that they reduce competition, which may have many unwanted repercussions in the affected markets. The most well-known effect of a reduction of competition is that prices may increase. This effect will be discussed in detail below. Another effect is that a reduction of competition may lead to X-inefficiency (or slack) in the firms (see sub-section 1.1.5 above). Reduced competition may also reduce firms' incentives to provide product diversity and to innovate (see sub-section 1.1.3.2 above). Finally we should mention an aspect which is often mentioned but not yet studied in any detail. Firms' managers have only limited cognition (or bounded rationality). As an unavoidable consequence, many of their decisions are based on their beliefs and prejudices, and not on facts and reasoning. As a result of these individual imperfections, competition in the marketplace has an important role to fill as a selection device. If competition is intense, only those firms survive and expand that are run by managers who (by coincidence) happen to be equipped with the most accurate beliefs and prejudices. These are the firms that produce the product varieties that consumers want at a low cost. In contrast, if competition is soft, high-cost firms that produce inferior product varieties may also survive.

As already argued, the most well-known effect of a reduction of competition is that prices may increase. There are two possible reasons to be concerned with price increases. First, there is the obvious fact that a price increase implies a transfer of wealth from consumers to producers. This is a distributional consideration. Second, an increase in the price of a product above its marginal cost creates (or strengthens) an allocative inefficiency, also called the dead-weight loss. Indeed, whenever the price of a product exceeds its marginal cost, it would be socially desirable to increase production. The social value of increasing production by one unit equals the current price minus the marginal cost (the difference between what consumers are willing to pay for an additional unit, and what this additional unit costs to producers).

Competition authorities in most countries have been primarily concerned with the distributional effects of price increases. Economists, in contrast, tend to argue that one should focus on total welfare, and therefore focus on the allocative inefficiency (or dead-weight loss) caused by the merger. Whatever the policy concern behind price increases, a proper assessment of the competitive effects from mergers requires a good understanding of the nature of competitive interaction in the industry.

Generally speaking, oligopoly theory confirms the common intuition that prices increase as the number of firms is reduced. Abstracting from cost reductions, the fear of price increases following mergers may thus be justified. Two reasons for price increases may be distinguished. First, a merger between two or more firms may increase the firms' unilateral market power. Before the merger, the firms compete and do not take into account the effect of their quantity or price decisions on the profits of their competitors. After the merger, the firms maximize their joint profits, and thereby take into account the detrimental effect of quantity increases or price cuts on the market share of each others' products.

Second, a merger may shift the nature of conduct from competitive to collusive behaviour, or facilitate collusion at a higher price level. As the number of firms decreases, it may become easier to sustain implicit cartel agreements, for example because it becomes easier to monitor cheating. When a shift in conduct takes place, the merger increases the joint market power of the firms in the industry.

The risk of price increases following mergers may be limited for several reasons. The presence of actual competitors producing similar products is an obvious first constraint. Second, the possibility of new-firm entry in the long run may effectively constrain the firms' willingness to raise prices. Third, particularly in intermediate goods markets, strong buyers may exercise countervailing bargaining power that may limit the merging firms' potential to raise prices. Finally, it may be the case that one of the merging firms is failing,[16] perhaps due to a drop in demand for its product. In the absence of a merger such a firm would eventually have to leave the market, so that market power would increase irrespective of whether the merger took place.

In the following discussion, we will assume that entry is difficult, and that none of the firms is failing. Efficiency considerations are usually only made when these assumptions hold true. We will also assume that buyers take prices as given, and hence do not exercise countervailing power. This assumption is an unfortunate consequence of the fact that economic theory is lagging behind. The theory of oligopoly that is used to assess the competitive effects of mergers has generally assumed that one side of the market (typically the consumer side) is price taking, and that only the other side of the market exercises market power.

1.3 Welfare Effects of Mergers and the Role of Efficiencies

The previous section sketched out some general considerations on the competitive effects of mergers. This section goes into more detail, and in particular examines the role of efficiencies. In order to assess the overall effects of mergers it is necessary to first make explicit the policy goals of merger regulation. In the policy debate several objectives are frequently mentioned.

- *Consumer surplus* A first objective upon which merger analysis may be based is the protection of consumer interests. If this is the case, the central focus of merger analysis is on the competitive, or price effects, of mergers.
- *Total surplus* Another objective may be to further both consumer and producer interests. Total surplus may operationally be defined as the sum of consumer and producer surplus. More generally, one may give different weights to consumer and producer surplus.
- *Other objectives* These include the promotion of European integration, employment, regional balance, viability of small firms, and competitiveness of national firms on international markets. The concern with the preservation of employment has often been a political concern in proposed mergers. In principle, employment considerations should be taken into account in a full cost–benefit analysis of mergers. In practice, a merger policy designed to preserve an old production structure is presumably not the best way to deal with the employment objective in the long run. See for example Crampton (1994) for more on the employment objective.

In the analysis below we focus on the first two policy goals. This makes it natural to split our analysis into two distinct parts. The first part analyses the price effects of mergers. Of particular interest is the role played by efficiencies. Is the relationship between efficiency gains and consumer interests necessarily a trade-off? Or are there circumstances in which efficiency gains also benefit consumers? To answer these questions, the typology of efficiency gains provided above will prove to be very useful. Depending on the specific type of efficiency, a merger may sometimes lower prices, to the benefit of consumers. To assess the price effects of a merger, it is therefore crucial to identify the specific types of efficiencies that are involved, and, less obviously, to quantify the magnitude of these efficiencies.

The second part analyses the total welfare effects of mergers. To focus ideas, we assume in this part that the efficiency gains are insufficient to ensure price reductions (pro-competitive effects). We then follow a trade-off approach in which the possible efficiency gains need to be weighted against anti-competitive effects from the merger. Once again, the typology of efficiency gains proves useful to assess the trade-offs involved.

1.3.1 Price effects of horizontal mergers

This section considers the price effects of horizontal mergers in the presence (or absence) of cost savings. In practice, horizontal mergers may also generate product (quality) improvements. In this case, consumers may benefit from a merger even without price decreases, provided that quality increases sufficiently. The discussion in this section may thus be rephrased in terms of 'quality-adjusted' price effects of horizontal mergers (e.g. Rosen 1974). The spirit of the various results will therefore also apply to mergers with product (quality) improvements.

Since horizontal mergers reduce the number of competing firms in the industry, the common view is that mergers tend to increase price. However, to obtain a thorough understanding of the price effects of mergers, it is necessary to examine this common view under various modes of competition and alternative types of efficiency.

First, consider a simple industry in which all firms have identical and constant unit costs. Consider a merger with no efficiency gains. In this case, most theories of oligopoly imply that the price will increase.[17] The only exceptions are if firms have a 'perfect' cartel before the merger, if one firm is failing, or if the merger triggers immediate entry. In these cases, the price would be unaffected by the merger. What, then, is the role played by internal efficiencies? To what extent can they ensure that price decreases will take place after merger?

1.3.1.1 Non-collusion theories

Farrell and Shapiro (1990) consider a Cournot model, in which firms compete by setting quantities. To simplify, they assume that all firms produce the same homogeneous good. In this set-up they analyse the nature and the magnitude of internal efficiencies that are required for a merger to reduce price and increase output to the benefit of consumers. From their analysis it is possible to draw the following conclusions:

- For price to decrease after a merger, the merged firm must realize a *substantially* lower marginal cost than did either of its constituent firms before the merger. Farrell and Shapiro (1990) provide a more precise formula for the required reduction in marginal costs.
- If the internal efficiencies only consist of output rationalization or fixed cost savings, then there will be a price increase after the merger.[18] Rationalization, but not fixed cost savings, may, when combined with other cost savings, lead to lower prices.

Given the negative result on rationalisation and fixed cost savings, one may wonder which type of efficiencies may be responsible for price reductions. The typology of efficiency gains described in section 1.1 provides an answer. The following types of efficiencies may ensure price reductions after mergers, at least provided that they are 'sufficiently large':

1. Long-run economies of scale, and product-specific economies of scale;
2. Technological progress, either achieved by a transfer of know-how, or by increased incentives for R&D;
3. Purchasing economies.

All these efficiencies have in common that they may lead to a (long-term) reduction in the marginal costs below those of the formerly separate firms. The question is of course how large the reduction in marginal costs is required to be. Interestingly, Farrell and Shapiro show that the required reductions in marginal cost depend on relatively easy to observe variables, that is the firms' pre-merger market shares and the elasticity of demand. We return to this question in more detail in section 4, where we discuss a framework for merger analysis, including operational criteria for determining the likelihood that mergers will not increase prices.

The analysis of Farrell and Shapiro, as with most static theories of oligopolies, stresses the importance of marginal costs rather than fixed costs in reducing prices. In a dynamic setting, when new entry may occur, it may be possible that fixed cost savings also have an impact on prices. At this point, there has however been little theoretical work on this issue.

These authors establish general results for the Cournot model.[19] Some industries are however better described by the Bertrand model, in which firms compete by setting prices rather than quantities. Does the main result of Farrell and Shapiro generalize to this alternative setting? In particular, can a price reduction after a merger only be achieved through a significant reduction in the marginal cost below the pre-merger level of either participating firm? General results cannot be easily obtained since the degree of price competition depends on the nature of product differentiation.[20] Nevertheless, the results of Werden and Froeb (1994) teach us some interesting results for an industry with symmetric product differentiation. They assume that a unit price increase by one firm increases the market share of all competitors by the same percentage amount.[21] Werden and Froeb demonstrate the following result:

- If there are no internal efficiencies generated by the merger, except for fixed cost savings or output rationalization, then the prices of all products in the industry will increase after the merger; the magnitudes of the price increases are dependent on the market share of the different products.[22]

Since products are differentiated, each product may have a different price. Therefore, the effects of a merger on prices are more involved. Werden and Froeb find the following results on the magnitudes of price changes for the various products. First, the prices of the merging firms' products (weighted by their sales) increase by more than any of the competing firms' prices. In particular, the price of the small firm's product involved in the merger increases. Second, competing firms with a large market share (for example due to a relatively low marginal cost) will increase price by more than competing firms with a small market share. Moreover, a similar picture seems to emerge as in the general Cournot model considered by Farrell and Shapiro: significant savings in marginal costs, below the lowest marginal cost of either partner involved in the merger, are required for prices to drop after the merger.

Stennek (2001) modifies the assumptions of the Cournot model in a different way, namely by introducing incomplete information between firms about each other's marginal costs. He shows that, under these conditions, the market is inefficient (in particular, more inefficient than under symmetric information) in short-term allocation of production between firms. As a result, a merger may increase efficiency due to the pooling of information. Such information synergies may be large enough for prices to fall and consumers to benefit from the merger (see also Gal-Or (1988)).

1.3.1.2 Collusion theories

Firms may, under certain circumstances, sustain a cartel-like agreement without the opportunity to write legally binding contracts.[23] A precondition is that the firms are able to detect and punish any firm undercutting the agreed-upon price, without the help of the legal system. Firm-organized punishment may, for example, take the form of a price war that is limited in time. Economic models of collusion (notably the super-game literature) attempt to delineate the exact conditions under which such cartel-like agreements can be sustained by the firms. These models may also allow us to assess whether mergers affect the degree of joint market power in the industry.

A first approach to analysing the role of mergers for collusion assumes that there is initially no collusion, and asks whether and under what circumstances collusion is likely to be facilitated as a result of the merger. Recent theories of collusive behaviour predict that there exists a positive relationship between market concentration and the likelihood of collusion. Formal and informal contributions by Stigler (1964), Friedman (1971), Davidson and Deneckere (1984), among others, indicate that more concentrated market structures facilitate collusion for a variety of reasons. Increased concentration implies reduced profits from cheating by 'stealing' competitors' market shares; increased possibilities to detect cheating; and less co-ordination problems. Compte et al. (2002) emphasize the role of capacity constraints for the sustainability of collusion. A firm's capacity constraint determines how attractive it is for the firm to undercut the collusive price. The capacity constraint also determines how easy it is to flood the market to punish other firms that deviate. Compte et al. show how merger-induced asymmetries in capacity may affect the sustainability of collusion.

Economic models of collusion have far less predictive power than the non-collusive Bertrand and Cournot models, as discussed for example also by Hay and Werden (1993). The lack of predictive power is almost inevitable, since the mere fact that one collusive outcome is sustainable implies that a variety of other collusive outcomes are sustainable as well. The problem thus is to predict on which specific collusive arrangement, if any, firms would co-ordinate. If one is willing to make some more specific assumptions on which collusive arrangement firms will co-ordinate, one can obtain stronger predictions about the effects of mergers in collusion models. Following this approach, it has been demonstrated that – perhaps surprisingly – the cost savings requirements for mergers to reduce price are smaller if firms collude rather than compete. The intuition behind this result is that firms do not compete anyway before the merger and already succeed in (partial) collusion before the merger. Furthermore, the existing collusion before the merger may create particular inefficiencies that are eliminated after the merger.

To explain the nature of these existing inefficiencies, consider first the analyses of Schmalensee (1987) and Harrington (1991). They study fully collusive regimes based on models of (successful) bargaining.[24] To illustrate, assume there are two firms, one with a low (constant) marginal cost, and another with a high (constant) marginal cost. In a fully collusive agreement firms will bargain to allocate production such that the price lies in between two hypothetical monopoly prices: the price that the low-cost firm would choose if it were a monopoly, and the – higher – price that the high-cost firm would choose if it were a monopoly.[25] Now consider a merger between the two firms in such a fully collusive industry. A merger would simply rationalize production by transferring all production from the high-cost to the low-cost plant. As a consequence, the price drops to the lower monopoly price. Therefore, under full collusion a merger leading to monopoly reduces price even without any efficiencies other than output rationalization.

One may argue that this reasoning assumes that firms can enforce a perfect cartel before the merger. Yet Verboven (1995) shows that this result generalizes to industries in which – more plausibly – only partial collusion can be sustained before the merger, that is, a price above the Cournot level but below the optimal cartel allocation. In his model, the collusive outcome is determined by the sustainability constraints ensuring that no firm would defect, independent of the exact bargaining process. Verboven also shows that the condition for prices to decrease is that the market share of the merging firms is sufficiently small. Furthermore, as the degree of sustainable collusion increases, the market share tolerated for the merging firms also increases.

1.3.1.3 Conclusion

The above discussion shows that there are many different modes of (price) competition, and accordingly, many different models of (price) competition. Actually, any description of competition, including ours, is bound to be stylised. Just to mention one example, the mode of competition is much affected by the exact information that the firms have about themselves, about their competitors, and about their market. The effect of mergers on prices has been studied for some such cases, but not for all of them. Another, but related, problem is that some aspects of competition have hardly begun to be analysed in economic theory. (That is, there are still too few models of competition!) One example is that almost all economic models of competition are based on the assumption that the firms' managers are fully rational, while they in reality only are boundedly so.

This multiplicity of modes and models of competition creates a problem for policy design. Should policy be based on only one of the models? If so, which one? Or, are there ways in which policy can be made more flexible? The ideal choice, of course, would be if competition authorities, in each individual merger case, apply that model which conforms best to the actual mode of competition. In our policy discussion in section 4, we will describe some methods that can be used that are based on explicit models of competition. We also describe simulation analysis, a flexible technique that may be tailored to fit the situation at hand even better. However, these methods presume that the competition authority is fairly well informed about the mode of competition in the market that they investigate. If that is not the case, we suggest that the authority may use an approach that is based on a worst-case scenario. Hereby, the authority may combine flexibility with limited information. We also suggest that if the firms, that presumably are more informed about the details of the competitive situation, are not satisfied with such an analysis, and can provide a more well-tailored (and verifiable) analysis, then the agency may use that instead.

1.3.2 Total surplus

Most economists take the view that competition policy should not be designed solely to protect the interests of consumers. A common policy goal formulated by economists is the maximization of 'total surplus', the sum of consumer surplus and producer surplus. Under this policy goal, transfers from consumers to producers due to price increases are not considered as a problem. However, increased prices yield an allocative inefficiency, i.e. a dead-weight loss due to sub-optimal production and consumption.

1.3.2.1 Williamsonian merger analysis

Perhaps the most influential contribution which advocated the total welfare approach in merger analysis is by Williamson (1968). Williamson proposed to compare the dead-weight losses due to price increases after a merger with the internal efficiencies that are generated. Williamson concluded that cost savings need not be very high to compensate for dead-weight losses induced by price increases. We now illustrate Williamson's analysis in Figure 3.1. We will show that the 'trade-off' framework is useful, though the conclusion that only small cost savings are required is not general, since this depends on how intense one assumes competition is before and after the merger. This conclusion is similar in spirit to the one obtained when discussing the price effects of mergers. The degree of competition, both before and after merger, is essential in examining the price effects of mergers.

Consider a homogeneous goods industry where unit costs are constant and equal to AC_1 before the merger, and drop to AC_2 after the merger, as illustrated in Figure 3.1. Consider three alternative scenarios on how behaviour changes due to the merger:

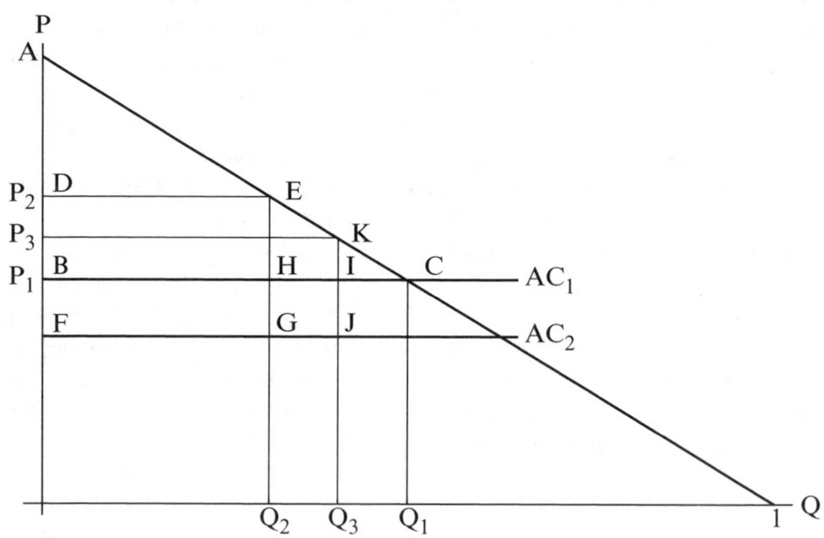

Figure 3.1 Williamsonian merger analysis

Scenario 1 From perfect competition to monopoly

This is the simplest case to analyse. Total welfare before the merger coincides with total consumer surplus at the competitive price P_1, indicated by the triangle ACB. At the competitive price, there is no producer surplus. After the merger, unit costs drop and the monopoly price P_2 is charged. Total welfare is now the sum of consumer surplus, AED, and producer surplus, DEGF. As a result, the *change* in welfare due to merger is the difference between the rectangle, BHGF, and the triangle, ECH. Intuitively, the cost savings evaluated at post-merger production (BHGF) need to be traded off against the net losses from reduced consumption (ECH). The specific example on Figure 3.1, which considers a unit cost reduction by 25 per cent, shows that the internal cost savings outweigh the losses from reduced consumption. But note that if we had considered a unit cost reduction by only 12.5 per cent, the reverse would have been true.

Scenario 2 From perfect competition to 'partial monopoly'

This is the original scenario, considered by Williamson's article of 1968. There, Williamson assumed that a merger in an initially competitive industry 'extends market power', but not to the monopoly extreme. Consider for example a price rise to P_3 instead of P_2. The result is a higher output after the merger, implying higher internal cost savings than in the first scenario, amounting to BIJF. These need to balance against the losses from reduced consumption, which are now only the triangle KCI. The unit cost reduction by 25 per cent generates internal cost savings which by far exceed the losses from reduced consumption on Figure 3.1. In fact, under the assumed price increase of this example, total welfare would increase for any reduction in unit cost by more than 2 per cent. This confirms the claim made by Williamson.

The difference between scenario 1 and scenario 2 shows that it is important to know the extent of the price increase after the merger. Scenario 1 had been considered by DePrano and Nugent (1969) in a critical review of Williamson's analysis. Williamson (1969) replied that the drastic price rise to the monopoly level considered by DePrano and Nugent is unrealistic, since a merged firm needs to take into account the risk of entry of new firms into the market when raising its prices. Entry can almost never be blockaded, argues Williamson, and therefore one may expect that a merged firm will follow a 'limit pricing strategy', taking into account potential competitors as well as actual competitors.

The debate between Williamson and DePrano and Nugent illustrates the importance of predicting the extent of the price increase after a merger. In other words, it is necessary to properly assess the nature of post-merger competitive interaction. The third scenario stresses that one should also properly assess pre-merger conduct.

Scenario 3 From 'partial monopoly' to monopoly

To illustrate the importance of considering *pre-merger* market power in the same Figure 3.1, consider a merger in which the initial price is P_3, which exceeds marginal cost AC_1. After the merger the marginal cost is AC_2, and the monopoly price P_2 is charged.

In this scenario, total welfare changes from the area AKIB before the merger to the area AEGF afterwards. Therefore, the trade-off is between internal cost savings of BHGF and losses from reduced output of LKIH. In the example in Figure 3.1, which assumed a 25 per cent reduction in unit costs, the internal cost savings would be sufficient. In fact, in the example, any reduction in unit costs by 9 per cent would suffice for welfare to increase.

A general insight into the trade-off between internal cost efficiencies and the losses due to output reduction can be achieved by considering a merger in industry which is initially non-competitive, and which causes a 'small' reduction in total industry output, accompanied by a 'small' internal cost efficiency. Generally speaking, the gain due to internal cost savings is proportional to the industry output, and the loss due to reduced output is proportional to the price-cost margin.[26] To assess the welfare trade-off, one therefore needs to have a good estimate of both pre-merger output and of pre-merger price-cost markups. Pre-merger output times the expected cost reduction would be approximately equal to the expected welfare gains. Pre-merger markups times the expected output reduction would be approximately equal to the expected welfare losses. Of course, the main empirical difficulty in comparing the expected gains to the expected losses is in the assessment of the expected cost reduction and the expected output reduction.

Which types of cost savings are valid to apply the framework of Williamson? Note that Williamson's formula does not depend on the actual type of efficiency that is realized; it is sufficient that the efficiency implies a reduction in average costs. Therefore, all types of efficiency, in principle, qualify for a Williamsonian type of defence, provided, of course, that they involve sufficiently large average cost reductions. Nevertheless, a case may be made that efficiencies that involve a marginal cost reduction are superior to those that do not. This is because in this case, it may generally be expected that the price increase will be lower than when there is no reduction in marginal cost.

1.3.2.2 Externality analysis

Williamsonian analysis evaluates the efficiency gains from unit cost savings over the total industry output. This approach is justified under the assumption that all firms in the industry participate in the merger. Of course, in practice, most mergers only take place among some of the firms in the industry. In this case, one should evaluate the internal cost savings at the – smaller – output of the merging firms. Another difficulty with Williamsonian analysis is that one needs to be able to measure the actual cost reduction that will be generated by the merger. It is, of course, in the interest of the merging firm to claim as high efficiencies as possible.

Farrell and Shapiro (1990) propose a methodology for evaluating mergers among some of the firms in the industry without a need for relying on internal efficiency claims. In a general Cournot setting, they propose to evaluate the externality that is created by the merger. The externality of a merger consists of the sum of the effect on consumers and on the rival firms which did not participate in the merger. Farrell and Shapiro argue that if the externality is positive, then the merger must also increase total welfare since the proposed merger may also be expected to be profitable (otherwise it would not be proposed in the first place).

Farrell and Shapiro derive conditions under which price-increasing (i.e. output-reducing) mergers will generate a positive externality. In particular, they find that the market share of the merging firms should be sufficiently small. The intuition for their result is clear. When two (or more) firms merge in order to reduce output, there is an expansion of output by the competitors. The expansion by the competitors is less than the contraction of the merging firms. The result is an overall fall in output, accompanied by a reallocation of output from the merging firms to their competitors. Such a reallocation of output would be desirable if the merging firms are relatively inefficient (that is, operate at a higher marginal cost) as compared to their competitors. A relative inefficiency of the merging firms would indeed exist if they have a relatively small market share. In sum, a small market share by the merging firms indicates their relative inefficiency, making a merger which reallocates output to the competitors desirable.[27] The opposite is of course also true: when two large firms merge to reduce output, there will be a reallocation to relatively inefficient competitors so that the merger will create a negative externality. In this case, total welfare will only be positive if large internal efficiencies can be proven by the merger.

The main contributions of the approach of Farrell and Shapiro are twofold: (1) they point out a potentially important effect that has traditionally been ignored in assessing merger: a reallocation of output to competitors; (2) they demonstrate that due to this effect, mergers may be beneficial even when there are no internal efficiencies (or when internal efficiencies cannot be proven). Their analysis applies to Cournot competition.[28]

In fact, the general message of their results also applies to other forms of oligopolistic interdependence. In particular, in the models of Bertrand competition with differentiated products of both Deneckere and Davidson (1985a), and Werden and Froeb (1994), a price increase by the merging firms triggers price increases by the competitors. These positive responses are, however, typically less than the original price increase initiated by the merging firms. As a result, the market share of the merging firms decreases and a reallocation of production from the merging firms to the competitors takes place. In a similar way to the Cournot model, such a reallocation of output would be desirable if the merging firms are relatively inefficient, as would be the case when they have relatively small market shares.

The relatively simple specific conditions on the market shares that are provided in Farrell and Shapiro's Cournot analysis do not generalize to Bertrand models with product differentiation. This is natural, since the product differentiation is market-specific, and no simple general description can be provided. In section 5, where we discuss the framework, we nevertheless attempt to provide some operational sufficient criteria that will hold for all oligopoly models.

1.3.2.3 Other studies

There has also been some literature that tries to draw inferences on the welfare from the mere fact that merger is proposed and thus is profitable.

Levin uses a model with homogeneous goods and quantity-setting firms to show that output-reducing mergers are never profitable if market share is less than 50 per cent (assuming no internal efficiencies other than output rationalization). Furthermore, any proposed (thus profitable) merger with a market share less than 50 per cent increases welfare, whether it increases or decreases output.

Werden and Froeb (1998, p. 541) consider the entry-inducing effects of mergers. Entry reduces the possibilities of raising prices and thus profitability. Hence, if we observe a (profitable) merger, it seems more likely that it will reduce prices (and thereby deter entry). The entry possibility thus allows us to infer price-reducing efficiencies. As stated by Werden and Froeb:

> If firms are rational and informed, they merge only if they expect significant efficiency gains generated from merger, or they perceive substantial entry obstacles such as sunk costs. Consequently, the entry issue can be collapsed into efficiency considerations, and in the absence of strong evidence that an otherwise anti-competitive merger generates significant efficiency gains, there is a sound basis for presuming that entry obstacles will prevent entry in response.

(Thus the best way for courts to treat entry in many mergers may be not to consider it at all.)

2. EMPIRICAL EVIDENCE

This part of the chapter reviews the empirical evidence on mergers. Most of this literature has not attempted to directly identify efficiency gains from mergers. The available empirical evidence may nevertheless help us to shed some indirect light on the existence and the magnitude of efficiency gains. Many studies have considered the effect of mergers on company performance, as measured by the accounting profits or the share prices of the firms. If company performance is found to increase, there is evidence that the merger created either market power or efficiency gains, or a combination of both. Unfortunately, such evidence is not sufficient to discriminate between the two explanations. Additional information needs to be gathered to obtain more conclusive results. For example, evidence on consumer prices and market shares are also potentially useful in disentangling the market power and efficiency effects. There are also some papers that study the effect of mergers on the competing firms' share prices. If these also rise, this suggests that market power is more important than efficiency gains, since increased market power tends to benefit the competitors, whereas reduced production costs tend to harm competitors.

The evidence on share prices, profitability and consumer prices may not only tell us something on the relative importance of market power and efficiency motives for mergers. It may also indicate how the gains or losses from mergers are distributed between different groups in the economy. Since competition policy in the EU and other jurisdictions is partly motivated by distributional concerns, such knowledge is crucial for the proper design of merger control.

Section 2.1 considers the evidence on company performance, measured by accounting profits and stock prices. Section 2.2 discusses the literature that has attempted to disentangle the two motives, market power and cost reductions. Finally, in section 2.3 we provide evidence from a limited number of studies that have attempted to *directly* quantify the importance of efficiency gains.

The main impression is that the available evidence is very limited in many respects. First, there are surprisingly few studies of the effect of mergers on productivity, price and market shares. Second, the evidence on company performance is contradictory, and troubled by methodological problems. Third, most studies concern mergers in manufacturing during the 1960s and 1970s, with a clear bias towards mergers in the USA. This evidence is not sufficient to draw any conclusions about the likely effects of mergers in different sectors.

Bearing in mind the above reservations, our main conclusions are the following. First, the empirical literature does provide some support for the fear that horizontal mergers increase market power. Second, there seems to be no support for a general presumption that mergers create efficiency gains. Third, in particular cases, however, mergers do create efficiencies. Moreover, empirical evidence indicates that cost savings are passed on to consumers in the form of a downward push on price. It appears that there may be substantial variance in the efficiency gains from mergers. (Unfortunately, however, there does not exist any formal statistical testing that clearly indicates that the variance is high.) In sum, the empirical evidence suggests that controlling mergers is important, and that the presence and magnitude of efficiency gains may need to be examined on a case-by-case basis.

To complement this picture we believe that a follow-up study would be valuable. Such a study should, in our view, focus on empirical estimates of returns to scale. It could also be used at least as indirect evidence for the efficiency gains from mergers. It would also be desirable to deepen the survey into pass-on. In both cases, it should be possible to obtain results for specific industries.

2.1 Overall Company Performance

2.1.1 Effects of mergers on profits

The industrial economics approach studies merger performance by measuring the (accounting) profits of the merging parties before and after the integration. From a theoretical point of view, a merger may increase or decrease profitability. On the one hand, oligopoly theory predicts that horizontal mergers increase market power, that is, the firms' ability to set a price above marginal cost. On the other hand, mergers tend to lower the merging parties' market shares, since the rival firms may have an incentive to expand their production as a result of the merger. The net effect of an increased mark-up but decreased sales is ambiguous. In addition, the effects of mergers on the internal efficiency of the firms are also ambiguous. A merger may lead to rationalization or scale efficiencies, but it also reduces competition in the product market, and may hence increase or create slacks in the organization. Hence, the effect of a merger on the merging firms' profits is an empirical issue.[29]

In sub-sections 2.1.1.1 and 2.1.1.2 we review individual studies in detail. We treat the European and the non-European (mainly US) experiences separately to see if there are any systematic differences.

2.1.1.1 The European experience

A large-scale project consisting of studies from several European countries is reported in Mueller (1980a). The study by Mueller (1980b), discussed below, on US mergers, is also part of this international comparison. An important advantage of this project is that all the studies use the same methodology. The data cover firms undertaking mergers during the period 1962–72, for the five years preceding the merger and the five years afterwards. All studies use several different tests for the effect of mergers on profitability. Two measures of profitability are adopted, namely the rate of profit on equity, and the rate of profit on total assets. Two alternative methods are used to control for external shocks. First, the merging firms' profits are compared with a control group consisting of a pair of firms that are similar to the merged ones. Second, they are compared to the industry average.

Kumps and Wtterwulghe (1980) studied 21 mergers in the manufacturing and retail sectors in Belgium during the period 1962 to 1974. They show that the merging firms performed better than a control group of non-merged companies. Their profit rates declined by less between the five-year pre-merger period and the five-year post-merger period, than those of the control group firms. Cable et al. (1980) studied around 50 mergers in Germany during the period 1964 to 1974. They find that the merging firms did better than the control firms, although not in a statistically significant way. Jenny and Weber (1980) studied 20–40 (depending on the test) horizontal mergers in France during the period 1962–72. They showed that the merging firms experienced decreasing profitability between the four-year pre-merger and four-year post-merger period. This reduction was larger than the reduction of the control firms, although the difference is not statistically significant. Peer (1980) studied around 30 mergers in the manufacturing and retail sectors in the Netherlands during the period 1963 to 1973. He found that the merging firms did worse than the control firms did, although not in a statistically significant way. Rydén and Edberg (1980) studied 25 large mergers in Sweden during the period 1962 to 1976. They showed that the merging firms experienced a reduction in the profitability between the five-year pre-merger period and the five-year post-merger period. At the same time a control group of non-merged firms increased their profitability. Cosh et al. (1980) studied 211 mergers in the UK during 1967 to 1969. They showed that the merging firms experienced an increase in profitability between the five-year pre-merger period and the five-year post-merger period. At the same time a control group of non-merged firms decreased their profitability. Meeks (1977) studied takeovers by large UK listed firms during the period 1964 to 1972. The typical target is small in comparison with a control group, but has average profitability. The typical buyer is large in comparison with a control group, and has a higher profitability. During the seven years following the takeover, the profitability of the integrated firm is typically reduced.

To summarize, the evidence on the European mergers during the 1960s is mixed. Profitability improved on average, in comparison with control firms, in two countries (Belgium and Germany) and it deteriorated in three countries (France, Netherlands and Sweden). The evidence on the profitability of UK mergers is mixed. One study found that profitability had increased, another that profitability decreased, and it is not clear what causes the different results. Often the changes in profitability are small and insignificant.

2.1.1.2 The US and Japanese experience

As a part of the international comparison, discussed above, Mueller (1980b) studied around 250 mergers in the USA during the period 1962 to 1972. He compared profitability five years before and three years after the merger. The merged firms experienced a loss in comparison to the non-merged firms.

Perhaps the most famous study – or actually, collection of studies – is by Ravenscraft and Scherer (1987). They considered a large sample of US mergers over a long time period. In one study, Ravenscraft and Scherer estimated the pre-merger profitability of 634 targets (Chapter 3). All targets were manufacturing companies and they were acquired in 1968, 1971 or 1974. Their sample included small and privately-held companies, not listed on major stock exchanges. Profitability was measured by the ratio of annual operating income to total end-of-period assets. The average profitability of the targets was 20 per cent. The average profitability of all manufacturing corporations was at the same time 11 per cent. Hence, the targets were substantially more profitable. The difference is also statistically significant. Ravenscraft and Scherer also separately studied the pre-merger profitability of 95 targets of 1962–76 tender offers. These targets were slightly less profitable than the industries to which they belonged.

In another study, Ravenscraft and Scherer examined post-merger performance, using so-called line of business data (1987, ch. 4). That is, the unit of observation is not the acquiring firm, but the branch of the firm that made the acquisition. Branches are defined according to three- or four-digit level of the US Standard Industrial Classification. Hereby, the sample consists of 4409 lines of business observations. For each line of business, they have data on profitability for the years 1974–77, and on the merger history – as measured by ratio of the value of the acquired assets to total assets – between 1950 and 1977. (In total more than 7000 acquisitions were undertaken, and the median acquisition was made eight or nine years before the date for measuring profitability.) In an ordinary least squares regression model, they show that merger intensity has a negative effect on profitability.

Ravenscraft and Scherer also studied sell-off of acquired units (1987, ch. 6). They estimated that between 19 and 47 per cent of the acquired units were subsequently sold off. They also showed that these units experienced a fall in profitability preceding sell-off, and that their profitability was below the profitability of non-divested lines in the same industry. Combining these observations with the observation from their Chapter 3 that the acquired units were twice as profitable as the industry average, Ravenscraft and Scherer concluded that these units were in good health at the time of their acquisition, but became gravely ill thereafter.

Healy et al. (1992) studied the post-acquisition performance of the 50 largest US mergers between 1979 and mid-1984. They used pre-tax operating cash flow returns on assets, and they used industry performance as a benchmark. Data were collected for each of the five years before the merger and each of the five years after the merger (leaving out the year of merger). In the period before the merger, the merging firms earned a median annual return around 25 per cent. After the merger the return had declined to around 20 per cent. However, this decline was smaller than the decline experienced by other firms in the same industries. Hence, the industry-adjusted median annual return was around zero per cent before the merger. After the merger the industry-adjusted return has increased to around 3 per cent.

Ikeda and Doi (1983) studied the performance of 49 merging firms in the Japanese manufacturing industry 1964–75. Profit rate was measured by the average current profit before tax as a percentage of end-of-year equity and end-of-year total assets. Data was collected for the five years before and after the merger. One test concerned the merging firms' absolute performance, and another test concerned the merging firms' performance in comparison with the performance of rival firms in the industry to which the merging firms belonged. The absolute test shows that around 60 per cent of the merging firms increased profitability, while 40 per cent decreased profitability. In relative terms, 60 to 70 per cent of the merging firms experienced an increased profitability.

2.1.2 Effects of mergers on share prices

A second strand of literature has assessed the performance of mergers by studying the effects they have on the stock prices of the participating firms at the time of the merger announcement. The empirical methodology is called event study analysis. Basically, event study analysts estimate whether there is a significant difference in stock prices a few weeks before and after an 'event' such as a merger announcement. The change in stock prices is measured net of market-wide price movements.

An important potential advantage of event studies is that stock prices reflect the present value of expected future profits created by firms, under the assumption that the stock market is efficient. This approach differs fundamentally from the profitability studies based on accounting data. Accounting profits only refer to current profits, which may be subject to exceptional temporary gains or losses; in addition, the accounting profits depend on the precise methods that have been used to classify revenues and costs.

The evidence is summarized and discussed in sub-section 2.1.3. In the three sub-sections that precede it we review individual studies in more detail. As is conventional, we report results on returns to targets (2.1.2.1), bidders (2.1.2.2) and total returns (2.1.2.3) separately.

2.1.2.1 Returns to targets

The results concerning targets are relatively clear. The average target shareholder gain varies between 20 and 35 per cent. The target gains more in tender offers than in mergers. The gain is higher if there is more than one bidder. The gains have varied over time, due to changes in the legal and institutional environment.

Jensen and Ruback (1983) reviewed 13 early event studies. Six studies concerned mergers, and seven concerned tender offers. The period was 1956 to 1981. The abnormal percentage stock price changes associated with successful corporate takeovers was 30 per cent for tender offers, and 20 per cent for mergers. Jarrell et al. (1988) surveyed event studies that cover takeovers in the 1980s. (Many of their conclusions came from a study of 663 successful tender offers from 1962 to 1985.) The target premiums averaged 19 per cent in the 1960s, 35 per cent in the 1970s, and from 1980 to 1985 the average premium was 30 per cent. Bradley et al. (1988) used a sample of 236 successful tender offers occurring over the period 1963 to 1984. The mean target gain for the whole period was 32 per cent. They also showed that competition among bidding firms increased the returns to targets, and decreased the returns to acquirers. Schwert (1996) studied 1814 targets in successful and unsuccessful takeovers during 1975 to 1991. The average gain in tender offers was 36 per cent and in mergers 17 per cent. He also showed that the total return to the target consisted of two approximately equal parts, namely the mark-up (which is the increase in the stock price beginning the day the first bid is announced), and the run-up (which is the increase in the stock price in the period of 40 days before the first bid). The mark-ups are essentially unrelated to the size of the run-up. One interpretation of this result is that the run-up reflects information held by other potential bidders, rather than insider trading or information leakage. If this interpretation is correct, then previous event studies may have exaggerated the gains from mergers since they normally include the run-up as a part of the merger premium.

2.1.2.2 Returns to bidders

The event study evidence on bidder gains is mixed, but it suggests that bidders on average break even, or do slightly better. Naturally, however, there is some variance, meaning that some bidders gain while others lose.

In the study of Jensen's and Ruback (1983), the abnormal percentage stock price changes associated with successful corporate takeovers was 4 per cent for tender offers, and zero per cent for mergers. In Jarrell et al. (1988) bidders realized small, but statistically significant, gains of about 1 to 2 per cent. They also showed that these gains had declined, to become negative (statistically insignificant) in the 1980s. Bradley et al. (1988) confirm this pattern.

2.1.2.3 Total returns

The evidence indicates that shareholders of target firms realize large positive abnormal returns in takeovers. The evidence on the rewards to bidding firms is mixed, but suggested that they break even. Since targets gain, and bidders do not appear to lose, the evidence seems to suggest that takeovers create value to the participating firms. However, as pointed out by Jensen and Ruback (1983) the bidding firms tend to be larger than target firms. Hence, the sum of the returns to bidding and target firms does not measure the gains to the merging firms. The dollar value of small percentage losses for bidders could exceed the dollar value of large percentage gains to targets. Or, as Roll (1986) says, in some cases the observed increase in the target would correspond to such a trivial loss to the bidder that the loss is bound to be hidden in the bid/ask spread and in the noise of daily return volatility. Roll reviews the evidence up to 1985 and argues that it is inconclusive.

More recent studies provide more conclusive evidence. Bradley et al. (1988) explicitly constructed their sample so as to match pairs of targets and bidders in order to measure synergistic gains. During the whole period, the average combined gain is 7 per cent, and statistically significant. Stulz et al. (1990) studied 104 tender offers during the period 1968 to 1986 and found an average gain of about 11 per cent, which is statistically significant. Berkovitch and Narayanan (1993) found that 76 per cent of 330 successful tender offers from 1963 to 1988 achieved positive total gains. Houston and Ryngaert (1994) demonstrated that the overall gains from a sample of bank mergers announced during the period 1985 to 1991 were slightly positive, but statistically indistinguishable form zero. Banerjee and Eckard (1998) showed that the participants in the great US merger wave of 1897–1903 gained between 12 and 18 per cent. Based on the more recent evidence, we conclude that the total gains on average are positive.

However, the long-term effects may be different. Rau and Vermaelen (1998) showed that bidders in mergers under-perform (while bidders in tender offers out-perform) the market in the three years after the acquisition. The long-term under-performance of acquiring firms is not uniformly distributed across firms. It is predominantly caused by the poor post-acquisition performance of low book-to-market 'glamour' acquirers.[30] To explain their findings, Rau and Vermaelen proposed a performance extrapolation hypothesis. The management, as well as the market, the board of directors, and the large shareholders over-extrapolate the past performance of the bidders' management when they assess the benefits of an acquisition. That is, the market overestimates (underestimates) the ability of glamour bidders (value firms) to manage other companies' assets.

2.1.3 Summary and conclusions

Profit-flow studies

If a generalization is to be drawn from the profit-flow studies, it would have to be that mergers have but modest average effects on the profitability of the merging firms. A robust finding, however, reappearing in many studies is that the profitability of mergers is not guaranteed: a large proportion of mergers reduces profitability.

This result can be interpreted in several ways. The worst-case scenario is that in many mergers market power is increased, but that the mergers create internal inefficiencies in the firm that offset any profit increases. Another possibility is that there were no effects on production costs on average, and that losses are due to competitors expanding their production in response to mergers. This is a very surprising result. It is not difficult to understand that a merger can be socially undesirable. But why should firms engage in activities that are even bad for them? This is an issue to which we will return below.

It is important to keep in mind that there is variance around the mean profit effects. Some mergers are profitable, and some mergers are unprofitable. This result is consistent with the view that some, but not all, mergers do create efficiencies. This is important, since it suggests that policy should not count on general cost savings from mergers, but that policy somehow should allow for cost savings in specific cases – perhaps an efficiency defence.

The available evidence is limited in several respects. Most studies concern mergers in manufacturing during the 1960s and 1970s. The evidence is not sufficient to draw any conclusions about the likely effects of mergers in different industries.

The empirical methodology adopted in the above mentioned and other studies is not homogeneous. For example, some studies simply consider the profitability of the merging firms before and after the merger. Other studies are more sophisticated in that they compare the profitability of the merging firms with other firms in the same industry in order to control for other changes that may have affected profitability during the studied period. However, as Fridolfsson and Stennek (2000) point out, the use of competing firms to control for exogenous shocks creates its own problems. The reason is that a merger normally confers an externality on the outsiders. When two firms merge and reduce competition, the remaining competitors also gain. In fact, the outsiders may gain more than the merging firms (so-called strong positive externalities). The reason is that the outsiders gain from the increase in the price, without having to reduce their own production. Thus, what appears to be an unprofitable merger may simply be a profitable merger with a strong positive externality. The reverse is also true. What appears to be a profitable merger may be an unprofitable merger with strong negative externalities. These problems warn us that one should interpret the results of the studies with care.

Event studies

The event study evidence shows that the target firms' shareholders benefit (20–35 per cent), and the bidding firms' shareholders generally break even (in the short run). Moreover, the combined gains are mostly positive (up to 10 per cent gains). The increased total gains seems to suggest that merging firms either increase market power or experience efficiency gains, such as cost savings.

Unfortunately, almost all event studies discussed above use data from the USA. It is not clear to what extent these studies are also representative for Europe.

Furthermore, recent results invite some caution concerning the event study methodology. First, Rau and Vermaelen (1998) show that the bidders' long-term performance is often negative. This may be interpreted to say that the short-term price movements in the stock market are not very good at predicting merger performance. If this interpretation is correct, Rau and Vermaelen's results should be perceived as evidence against the efficient market hypothesis underlying the (short-term) event study methodology.[31] If the efficient market hypothesis is rejected, it is not clear how one should interpret the results in the earlier literature discussed above. Second, empirical evidence suggests that the measures of target gains may include other information than just the takeover (Schwert 1996). Third, Fridolfsson and Stennek (2000) argue that, theoretically, changes in share prices may reflect other information than the profitability of the merger (see below). There are also some general problems associated with event study methodology that do not only affect studies of mergers. For example, the practical measurement of the stock price effects of certain events is clouded by other factors influencing stock prices. Furthermore, it is not obvious exactly which event should be taken as the (merger) event.

From this evidence, our two main conclusions are:

1. Merger control should not be based on a general presumption that mergers create cost savings. The presence and magnitude of efficiency gains may need to be examined on a case-by-case basis.
2. The available evidence on profitability and share prices does not point at any easily observable conditions under which to expect efficiency gains.

We have already argued that both studies of profitability and studies of share prices are troubled by methodological problems. Furthermore, if one combines the evidence from studies of profitability and studies of share prices the emerging picture is mixed, and perhaps even confusing. The available evidence indicates that a large proportion of mergers reduce profitability, but that share prices rise. If the evidence from both types of studies is correct, we are left with two empirical puzzles (cf. Caves 1989; Scherer and Ross 1990): Why do unprofitable mergers occur? How can share prices increase when profitability falls? Most theoretical explanations for the occurrence of unprofitable mergers rely on the idea that owners of the firms lack the instruments to discipline their managers, and that the managers consistently overestimate their abilities (Roll 1986), or that the managers are motivated by a desire to build a corporate empire (Shleifer and Vishny 1988). Neither the hubris nor the empire building hypothesis explains why the share prices may increase at the same time as the profit flows decrease. In an attempt to answer both puzzles, Stennek (1999) proposes a hypothesis called the pre-emptive merger motive. Firm A may merge with firm B, even if the merger reduces their combined profit flow as compared with the status quo. This would happen if the relevant alternative is that firm B merges with firm C, and this alternative merger would reduce firm A's profit flow even more. Expressed differently, even if a merger reduces the profit flow compared to the initial situation, it may increase the profit flow compared to the relevant alternative – another merger. Furthermore, even though such a pre-emptive merger reduces the profit flow, the aggregate value of the firms – the discounted sum of all expected future profits – may actually increase. The reason is that the pre-merger value of the firms accounts for the risk that the firms may become outsiders. Under the hypothesis that the stock market is efficient – in the sense that share prices reflect firm values – these results demonstrate that the two strands of the literature may be consistent. In particular, the event studies can be interpreted to show that there exists an industry-wide anticipation of a merger, and that the relevant information content of the merger announcement is which firms are insiders and which are outsiders. To sum up, these theories give a rather pessimistic picture of mergers. They may be motivated by hubris, or empire building, or an attempt to pre-empt other mergers. According to these interpretations of the available evidence, both market power and cost savings may be secondary motives for mergers. Nevertheless, even if the motives are different, the mergers still affect both market power and costs.

2.2 Disentangling Market Power and Cost Reductions

2.2.1 Effects of mergers on product prices

2.2.1.1 Direct studies

There are surprisingly few studies of the effect of mergers on product prices. But the few studies that have been made unambiguously indicate that prices tend to rise as a result of a merger. These results are of course not inconsistent with mergers leading to more efficient operations. Yet, the impact of efficiency gains on price is more than offset by increased market power, at least in the cases studied in the economics literature. One may conclude that wealth gains to the stockholders of merging firms do not arise through value creation alone, and relaxation of antitrust policy may result in non-trivial wealth transfers from consumers.

A general methodological difficulty with a study of the price effects of mergers is that one should properly take into account other conditions that may have changed after the merger, for example changes in factor prices. This problem has been tackled by studying how the prices of the merged firms' products have changed in comparison to other prices.

Barton and Sherman (1984) estimate the price effects of two acquisitions that resulted in substantial increases in the market share of the acquiring firm. Both acquisitions were made by Xidex Corporation, the world's largest producer of duplicating microfilm. In 1976 Xidex acquired its major rival in so-called diazo microfilm, and thereby increased its US market share from 40 per cent to 55 per cent. In 1979 it acquired its main rival in vesicular microfilm, thereby increasing its US market share from 67 per cent to 93 per cent. The study uses data on actual transaction prices during the ten-year period 1973 to 1982. To control for the influence of general inflation, costs of inputs, and gains in productivity, they used price ratios of vesicular and diazo microfilm. This methodology biases the results against finding any effects from the mergers to the extent that the two products are good substitutes. The results indicate that the increase in the price of diazo film at the first merger was around 11 per cent, and that the increase in the price of vesicular microfilm at the second merger was around 23 per cent. Both estimates are significant at the 0.01 level. One may also note that the latter merger, which almost created a monopoly, increased the price more than the former merger.

Kim and Singal (1993) examine price changes associated with all airline mergers, and all routes affected by those mergers for which data are available, in the USA during 1985–88. This is a natural experiment since during that period the USA government did not contest any proposed merger in the airline industry. Another advantage of studying the airline industry is that each route can be considered a separate market. Moreover, each merger affects hundreds of routes. Thus, each of the 14 mergers generates a large number of observations. To identify price changes that can be attributed to mergers, they compared the fare change of a sample route with the average fare change in a control group. There are, on average, 196 unaffected routes for each merger to be included in the control group. The results show that over the period from merger talks through to merger completion, the merging firms increased airfares by an average of 9 per cent relative to a control group of routes unaffected by the merger. Rival firms responded by raising their prices by an average of 12 per cent.[32] The fare changes are also positively related to the distance of routes, suggesting that airlines exploit greater market power on longer routes for which substitution by other modes of transport is less likely. Kim and Singal also study the announcement and completion periods separately to identify the effects of market power and synergy. They show that during the announcement period – when changes are primarily due to the market power effect – prices are increased (plus 11 per cent), but that during the completion period – when changes are primarily due to efficiency – prices decrease (minus 9 per cent). These results concern mergers that do not include failing firms.[33] Another interesting result is that Kim and Singal show that there exists a significant positive relation between fare changes and changes in concentration. Finally, they reject the idea that the mergers generated gains in quality that offset the price increases. The number of customer complaints filed with a governing agency increased almost threefold during the studied period.

Borenstein (1990), and Werden et al. (1991) study the effect on airfares of two airline mergers that occurred in 1986: the TWA-Ozark and Northwest-Republic mergers. They find a significant increase in relative airfares on routes affected by the Northwest-Republic merger, but little or no evidence on fare increases associated with the TWA-Ozark merger.

Finally, we should mention a very different type of study. Cotterill (1990) studied the effect of six horizontal mergers, among supermarkets in the USA, on concentration, the price level and the consumer food bill. First, he observes pre- and post-merger market concentration, and computes how the mergers change market concentration, as measured by the Herfindahl index. Second, he uses a previously established empirical relationship between market concentration and the market price level, to predict the impact of the mergers on the price level. Finally, he computes the implied increase in the consumer food bill. Using this methodology, and depending on the size of the merger, Cotterill predicts price changes in the range from fractions of a per cent up to 3 per cent. This methodology is obviously very indirect, and it does not perhaps provide much evidence about the price effects of mergers. However, it is interesting since it could be used by competition authorities as a way to predict the likely effect of a merger on price. However, to do so one first needs to validate the methodology by comparing predictions with actual results.

2.2.1.2 Indirect studies

The number of empirical studies of the effects of mergers on prices is surprisingly small. For this reason it is worth considering also the indirect but complementary evidence obtained in studies that compare prices between geographically separated markets with different concentration levels. If high concentration is associated with high prices, this is indirect evidence that horizontal mergers increase price, that is the market power effect dominates the efficiency effect.

Schmalensee (1989) has previously surveyed this cross-section literature. According to him the main stylized fact that appears from these studies is that there exists a positive relation between concentration and the price level (his stylized fact 5.1). Bresnahan (1989) also argues that the cross-section studies confirm the existence of a relationship between price and concentration. In order to provide some feeling for these studies, we describe some of them here as well.

The US food retailing industry has been the subject of two studies. Lamm (1981) studies 18 major Standard Metropolitan Statistical Areas in the USA, covering the period from 1974 to 1977. He identifies a positive relationship between food prices and market concentration. Moreover, the results indicate that increases in the market shares of any of the three largest firms increase price, while an increase in the size of the fourth largest firm reduces market price. This evidence may indicate that three firms may collude, but that collusion becomes more difficult when there are four or more large firms. Lamm also finds that increased average store size reduces the market price. To be more exact, increasing average store size by 10 per cent reduces the price by around 5 per cent. This is consistent with the existence of scale efficiencies. Hence, to the extent that a merger realizes scale efficiencies it may actually reduce price. Using individual firm price levels, Cotterill (1986) studies 18 local food retail markets in Vermont, each market being served by between one and 17 supermarkets. He shows that different firms in the same market charge different prices that are based upon firm-specific characteristics, such as chain-dependence, capacity utilization, and store size. After controlling for these factors, market concentration has a significant impact on a firm's price level. Marvel (1978) studies the retail gasoline market in 22 US cities for the years 1964 to 1971, and finds a statistically significant relation between concentration, as measured by the Herfindhal index, and price. In particular, he finds that high concentration leads to relatively high prices in the 'low-price segment' of the markets. Geithman et al. (1981) review and extend some previous papers and search for so-called critical concentration ratios. They look at the markets for underwriting, gasoline retailing, and supermarkets. If a critical concentration ratio were found, below which concentration had no effect on price, it would be of great importance because of its implications for competition policy. It would seem to follow that a horizontal merger in a market where concentration was below the critical level and where the merger could not increase concentration above the critical level could not increase market power, or at least would lead to efficiencies that outweigh increased market power. They show that critical concentration ratios may exist in certain industries, for example, a four-firm concentration ratio about 50. In other industries, for example supermarkets, no critical level was found. They conclude that a single critical concentration ratio for all of manufacturing is likely to be incorrect.

More recently, two studies on European markets appeared. Verboven (1996) analyses international differences in automobile prices in five European countries: Belgium, France, Germany, Italy and the United Kingdom. He estimates price-cost margins and finds that they tend to be larger for firms with higher market shares. In particular, domestic firms with a large market share, such as the Fiat Group in Italy, have strong domestic market power. Belgium, which has the lowest concentration, shows the lowest price-cost margins for most automobile models. Asplund and Sandin (1996a) studied 543 driving schools in 250 local Swedish markets for 1995. Driving schools are generally small, family-owned businesses with a median of two cars and two employees. The mean market price per minute varies from 4.5 to 8.0 Swedish kronor. However, there is almost no variation within a market. The results show that if prices in nearby markets are low and the distances to them are short, prices tend to be lower. It is also shown that local markets with high concentration tend to have higher prices than local markets with low concentration.

Bresnahan and Reiss (1990, 1991) propose another methodology. The novelty is that it can be applied in cases when data on prices are not available. Again, the idea is to study different geographically separated markets. In particular, they focus on how the number of firms in each market relates to market size. To enter into a market a firm must be able to cover its fixed costs. A monopolist can charge a high margin, that is, it can set a high price in relation to its marginal cost. As a result, the monopolist may need a relatively small market to cover its fixed costs. For example, if the fixed cost is 100, and if the (constant) marginal cost is 1, and if a monopolist can charge a price of 2, it must sell at least 100 units to break even. If consumers buy at most one unit of the good, the market size must be at least 100 consumers. Consider two scenarios. Assume first that the data reveal that in order for a market to support two firms, the market size must be at least 400 consumers. Then we can infer that the duopoly price is 1.5. (That gives a margin of 0.5. This margin multiplied by 200 consumers (per firm) gives 100 which is exactly enough to cover fixed costs.) Assume next that the data reveal that in order for a market to support two firms, the market size must be at least 200 consumers. Then we can infer that the duopoly price is 1 (equal to the monopoly price). In short, by studying how the number of firms relates to market size, we may infer how market power relates to the number of firms. Using this methodology, Bresnahan and Reiss study several markets (medical, dentists, plumbers and tyre-sales) in the USA. They suggest that competition is significantly increased when the second or the third firm enters into the market. At lower concentration levels, however, the effect of the number of firms on the margins appears to be marginal. Asplund and Sandin (1996b) obtain similar results for Swedish driving schools. In the context of mergers, this may be taken to indicate that mergers in a market with three or two firms are detrimental to allocative efficiency. Such an interpretation requires of course that new entry is not immediate.

2.2.2 Effects of mergers on market shares

There have been a few studies that analysed the effects of mergers on the market share of the merged entity. If a merger is driven by market power, the merged firm will increase its price and lower its output. This initial change will increase the residual demand for the competitors. As a response to the demand increase, the competitors will normally increase both their prices and their output. The exact mix of these two elements depends on the nature of competition.[34] A robust prediction is that the market share of the merged firm will drop if the merger is driven by market power. In contrast, if the merger generates sufficient variable-cost synergies, the merging firms may increase their market share. Actually, mergers that tend to increase the price level should also tend to reduce the merging firms' market share, and mergers that tend to decrease the price level should also tend to increase the merging firms' market share.[35] Hence, studying the effect of merger on market shares, in principle, gives very similar information as a study of prices.[36]

Again, the number of studies is very small. Nevertheless, the available evidence, if anything, seems to suggest that the market shares of firms engaged in horizontal mergers decline. The evidence on the effects on market shares from non-horizontal mergers is mixed.

Goldberg (1973, cited in Mueller 1985) examined a sample of 44 companies acquired in the 1950s and 1960s and found no significant change in market shares or growth rates in the (median three and a half) years following the mergers. Mueller (1985) uses surveys for 1950 and 1972 of sales at the 5-digit level for the 1000 largest companies in the USA. He constructs a sample of 209 acquired firms and 123 acquiring firms together with a control group of firms that did not participate in mergers. Control groups are formed to match the merging firms' characteristics. The control-group to firms participating in conglomerate or vertical mergers retained 88.5 per cent of their 1950 market share in 1972. Firms participating in a non-horizontal merger on the other hand only retained 18 per cent of their market share. The corresponding figures for horizontal mergers are 55 per cent and 14 per cent respectively. Baldwin and Gorecki (1990, cited in Mueller 1997) find significant declines in market shares for plants acquired in horizontal mergers, but no significant changes for plants acquired in other sorts of mergers.

2.2.3 Effects of mergers on outsiders' share prices

The results on the merging firms' stock price performance do not disentangle the gains attributable to increased market power and the gains attributable to, for example, technological efficiencies. As a solution, Eckbo (1983) proposes to indirectly disentangle both types of effects on profitability by also considering the effect of stock prices on the competitors that are not involved in the merger. The idea is that mergers driven by market power motives are beneficial to competitors: any attempt to raise prices or restrict production by the merging firms also benefits the competitors. In contrast, some types of efficiencies should hurt the competitors, for example cost efficiencies that induce the merged firm to lower its prices, in which case the stock price of the competitors would drop.

Unfortunately, the available evidence on this point is not conclusive. Stillman (1983) finds no statistically significant effect on outsiders' share prices. Eckbo (1983) finds a small but statistically significant increase. However, the latter study is also inconclusive: in those cases where competition authorities announce an investigation of the merger, the outsiders' share prices are not affected in a significant way. Schumann (1993) confirms this pattern.

Banerjee and Eckard (1998) show that the competitors during the great merger wave of 1897–1903 suffered significant value losses, around 10 per cent. This result may be interpreted as evidence for the existence of price-reducing efficiencies. A potential criticism of this approach is that anti-competitive mergers without efficiencies may hurt the rival firms if they are of a predatory nature. Banerjee and Eckard (1998) argue that the competitors' losses during the great merger wave are not associated with predatory practices of the merged firm. The reason is that there is no statistically significant difference between the returns to outsiders when the merging parties have high market shares (and where predation is more likely to be effective) and when the merging parties have low market shares. These results are consistent with the idea that efficiency gains were involved in the great merger wave.

Singal (1996) develops this methodology even further by combining stock-price data with product market data. The study concerns 14 airline mergers in the USA during 1985–88. Singal relates changes in stock prices of merging and rival firms to the change in market concentration (measured by the Herfindhal index), and to the number of common airports of the merging firms. The latter is considered to be an indication of the presence of efficiency gains from a merger. The results show that common airports are positively related to gains for insiders and losses for outsiders – interpreted as evidence of efficiency gains. The results also show that a large increase in concentration is associated with gains for outsiders and no effect on insiders – interpreted as the classical free-rider problem, associated with mergers that increase market power.[37]

2.2.4 Summary and conclusions

There is considerable dispute concerning the welfare effects of mergers. Are mergers mainly motivated by market power or efficiency gains? The two strands of the empirical literature, industrial economics and financial economics, reach apparently contradictory results.

The industrial economics literature studies the effect of mergers on product prices and market shares. There are surprisingly few such studies,[38] but they unambiguously indicate that prices tend to rise, and that insiders' market shares tend to fall as a result of horizontal mergers. A reasonable interpretation of this evidence is that mergers create market power, and that any cost reductions are insufficient to dominate (from a consumer's perspective). However, the evidence is also consistent with the idea that mergers increase rather than reduce costs. These studies indicate that horizontal mergers reduce consumers' welfare, by transferring wealth to firms, and by creating dead-weight losses.

Financial economists use event study methodology to disentangle market power and cost saving effects in horizontal mergers. Eckbo (1983), Eckbo and Wier (1985), Banerjee and Eckard (1998) and others use event studies to evaluate the welfare effects of horizontal mergers, by examining how the outsiders' share prices move in response to the announcement of a horizontal merger, and a subsequent announcement of an antitrust complaint. If the outsiders' share prices increase (decrease) at the time of the first (second) announcement, then the merger is deemed anti-competitive. The reason is that an anti-competitive merger raises the product price, thereby increasing the outsiders' profits. Unfortunately, the available evidence on this point is not conclusive. All studies of modern mergers find no or only small effects on outsiders' share prices. This can be interpreted as either the absence of both market power and efficiency effects, or their offsetting presence.[39]

The event study approach has been criticized by McAfee and Williams (1988), and Fridolfsson and Stennek (2000). McAfee and Williams turn the event study procedure around and ask whether rival firms' stock prices move in the predicted directions when a horizontal merger with *ex post* known anti-competitive effects is announced and, subsequently, challenged. The empirical results show absolutely no evidence of the merger being anti-competitive. Indeed, the signs of the estimated coefficients are generally opposite to their predicted values, given that the merger was anti-competitive. This finding casts doubts on event studies being able to detect anti-competitive mergers, and the policy implications of such studies. McAfee and Williams argue that their result is probably due to the fact that the outsiders, in their sample, were large multi-product firms that derived only a small fraction of their revenues from the affected market. The theoretical model of Fridolfsson and Stennek provides an additional explanation why event studies fail to detect anti-competitive mergers. In fact, they show that the effect of an anti-competitive merger on the rivals' stock value may be the opposite to what is generally believed, exactly as is suggested by the empirical evidence of McAfee and Williams. If a merger increases the price and has a positive externality on the outsider, but becoming an insider is even more advantageous, then the outsiders' value is always reduced. Assuming that the stock market is efficient, anti-competitive mergers may reduce the outsiders' stock market value. Intuitively, the pre-merger value of the outside firm is high, since it reflects the possibility of becoming an insider. Once the merger has taken place, this possibility is excluded, and the outsider's share price is reduced. The new information in the merger announcement is which firms are insiders and which are outsiders.

As a consequence, of this critique, we believe that the direct studies of the effect of merger on prices are more reliable than the Stillman-Eckbo methodology.

A study by Singal (1996) combines stock price data with product market data (for example concentration). This study provides some evidence that 14 airline mergers in the USA during 1985–88 did create both market power and reduce cost.

2.3 Studies of Efficiency Gains and Pass-on

2.3.1 Effects of mergers on productivity

The most direct way of assessing the efficiency gains from mergers is by measuring productivity gains and economies of scale realized following a merger.[40] Some studies do this using statistical techniques, others confine attention to particular cases.

Berger and Humphrey (1992) study 57 US banking mega-mergers from 1981 to 1989. They estimate a neoclassical cost function which allows them to consider two types of efficiencies, namely scale economies, and X-efficiency (or slack).[41] Earlier studies have shown that there are not substantial cost efficiency gains to be make simply by increasing the size of already large banks. In fact, there may be slight diseconomies of scale. On the other hand, a growing literature on X-inefficiencies in banking, or variations in cost ascribed to differences in managerial ability, finds that these efficiencies account for cost variations of 20 per cent or more and that these differences are stable over time. Thus, if more efficient banks take over less efficient banks, a merger could create substantial efficiency gains. Berger and Humphrey produce three main results. First, the *ex ante* choice of merger partners often did satisfy the condition for being conducive to improving X-efficiency. In 55 to 72 per cent of the cases, the acquiring bank was more efficient than the acquired. Also, more than 70 per cent of the mergers partners has some geographical market overlap. Second, the mergers were not successful on average in improving cost efficiency. The average X-efficiency improvement was less than five percentage points and was not statistically significant. Moreover, because of diseconomies of scale, the consolidated firms actually performed slightly worse on average after the mergers, although this effect was also small and often not statistically significant. However, there do appear to be some very successful mergers as well as some very unsuccessful ones. Third, Berger and Humphrey go one step further and relate their *ex post* efficiency results to some *ex ante* conditions that are commonly believed to be indicators of expected efficiency effects (large difference in X-efficiency between the acquiring and the acquired banks, and a large degree of deposit market overlap). They find that *ex post* cost efficiency gains are not significantly positively associated with these *ex ante* conditions.

A couple of papers study how productivity varies according to the diversification of firms' activities.[42] Their results show that productivity declines as firms become more diversified. However, since these studies concern diversification mergers, they need not carry much information concerning the efficiency effects of horizontal mergers.

An example of a case study is provided by Scherer et al. (1975, cited in Scherer and Ross 1990). He studied the 1969 merger of three English anti-friction bearing manufacturers. The firms sold extensively overlapping lines of general-purpose bearings. Immediately following the merger, production assignments were revamped to eliminate duplication and lengthen runs. Within three years, output per employee had been improved by some 40 per cent, at least partly as a result of the increased specialization. Further improvements were expected after some time, as a result of increased mechanization. Similar, but less dramatic cases of cost savings are described in the same study.

Some economists argue that capital-raising (a form of purchasing economy) is much cheaper for large than small firms. As a consequence, when a small firm joins a large firm, the smaller firm is likely to benefit from the larger enterprise's lower cost of capital. Case studies by Ravenscraft and Scherer (1987) reveal that this may be one of the most compelling advantages of mergers.

Finally, Fisher and Lande (1983) review a set of case studies of mergers (many from the trade and general business press). They emphasize that it is dangerous to generalize from examples. Nevertheless, they argue that many individual mergers create substantial efficiencies, that many others are notable failures, and that the record of prediction is too poor to give any confidence that we can predict the level of cost saving on a case-by-case basis sufficiently accurately to make this prediction a major basis for public policy.

2.3.1.1 Indirect evidence

There exists an empirical literature that estimates returns to scale. This literature may be used to assess indirectly the possibility that mergers realize cost savings related to returns of scale. A second advantage with this literature is that it can be used to say something about individual industries. This evidence is reviewed in, for example, Scherer and Ross (1990).

We can use the study by Scherer et al. (1975) to illustrate the types of results that are obtained. The study is based on an interviewing programme covering twelve major industries in seven industrialized nations. The industries are brewing, cigarettes, cotton, paints, oil refining, leather shoes, glass bottles, Portland cement, integrated steel, anti-friction bearings, refrigerators and automobile batteries. They report estimates of the minimum efficient scale, the percentage of 1967 US demand covered by a minimum efficient scale plant, and the percentage increase in cost that would result from operating a plant at one-third of the minimum efficient scale. The estimates indicate that the minimum efficient scale constitutes between 0.2 per cent of US demand (leather shoes) and 14.1 per cent (refrigerators). The percentage cost increase of running at a smaller scale ranges from 1.5 per cent (leather shoes) to 26 per cent (Portland cement). In half the industries the cost-elevation is 5 per cent or less.

The relevance of such results in assessing the efficiency gains from mergers is not obvious. However, we believe that numbers like these may provide useful background information for antitrust authorities when evaluating the likely consequences of a merger. It may therefore be useful to complement our preliminary description with an in-depth investigation in to this literature, and to synthesize the results (i.e. collect more studies, in particular more updated studies, arrange them by industry, and compare them with relevant demand figures for Europe and parts of Europe) so that they may be used in merger analysis.

2.3.2 Effects of mergers on innovation

According to Schumpeter (1942), it is essential to distinguish between the organization of industries most conducive to solving the problem of excessive pricing and those organizational forms most conducive to rapid technological progress. In his view, a large firm operating in a concentrated market is the most powerful engine of progress and long-run expansion of output. There are several theoretical arguments to substantiate the Schumpeterian claim. Large firms may have larger and more stable internal funds to finance R&D projects. There may be scale economies in R&D. The returns from, for example, process innovation may be higher if the firm is producing large quantities. Finally, there may exist complementarities between R&D and other activities in the firm. However, there are also some counter-arguments, for example, the loss of control in large organizations.

Since horizontal mergers increase the size of the merging firms and also the concentration in the relevant market, horizontal mergers may potentially create important efficiencies in promoting technological progress. Unfortunately we are not aware of any empirical studies that focus directly on the effects of merger on technological progress. However, there exists a large empirical literature that tests Schumpeter's two hypotheses: (1) innovation increases with firm size and (2) innovation increases with market concentration. This literature may be used as indirect evidence. However, one should point out that there are many methodological problems in this work. For example, one fundamental problem is the absence of satisfactory measures of new knowledge and its contribution to technological progress. The main conclusion from this literature is that the effects of firm size and market concentration on innovation, if they exist at all, do not appear to be important (Cohen and Levin 1989).[43]

2.3.3 Pass-on

In order to understand the welfare effects of a merger, it is not sufficient to know whether the merger creates any efficiency gains. It is also important to know if, for example, cost savings are passed on to consumers in the form of a lower price. This is important in order to assess the effect of a merger on the distribution of wealth in society. Pass-on is also important since it affects the dead-weight loss of a merger.

From an empirical perspective, pass-on studies appear in various applications. In international economics, for example, there exists a detailed literature estimating the effects of exchange rate changes on prices, see for example, Goldberg and Verboven (1998) and, for an overview, Goldberg and Knetter (1997). These studies show that foreign firms generally do not fully pass-through exchange rate changes into local consumer prices. Also in international economics, there are studies that analyse the effects of import tariffs on prices. Feenstra (1989), for example, finds a symmetric degree of incomplete pass-through of import tariffs as of exchange rate fluctuations, consistent with theory. In public economics, there exists an empirical literature on tax incidence, that is, who bears the burden of value added taxes and excise taxes. Most of the traditional literature focuses on tax incidence under perfect competition. More recently, Verboven (1998) considered a model of imperfect competition for the car market, and found significant tax incidence stemming from imperfect competition. Finally, in agricultural economics there is a large literature on the incomplete transmission of raw goods prices into final consumer prices; see, for example, McCorriston et al. (1998). The results from this literature should however be interpreted with care in the present context, since raw goods typically constitute only part of marginal costs. For an attempt to take this into account empirically, see, for example, Bettendorf and Verboven (2000).

The general empirical finding from this literature is that pass-on is indeed incomplete. The examples cited above suggest that pass-on roughly varies between 30 per cent and 70 per cent.[44] Chapter 4 of this volume, sections 2 and 3 contains a more detailed treatment of the question of pass-on. Yet we stress that more study is necessary to obtain a complete picture.

2.3.4 Summary and conclusions

In our view, the empirical picture on the effect of merger on productivity and technological progress is too incomplete to allow any far-reaching conclusions. The general picture remains: there does not exist clear evidence that mergers, as a general rule, create efficiency gains. However, at least some mergers do create efficiencies. Moreover, empirical evidence indicates that (between 30 and 70 per cent of) costs savings are passed on to price.

To complement this picture we believe that it would be valuable to have a follow-up study. Such a study should, in our view, focus on empirical estimates of returns to scale. Such studies can be used at least as indirect evidence for the efficiency gains from mergers. It would also be desirable to deepen the survey into pass-on. In both cases, it should be possible to obtain results for specific industries.

2.4 Distribution

The discussion above has primarily focused on the issue of whether mergers create any efficiency gains. However, we are also interested in how the social surplus (or losses) created by the merger is divided between the firms' different interest groups. Typically one would expect that a merger would affect the wealth of all the interest groups, including suppliers, buyers, competitors, bondholders, employees and management. Actually, some of the studies reviewed above also have implications for the distribution of the social surplus created by the merger. In particular, two results are noteworthy.

First, studies of consumer prices (and the merging firms' market shares) indicate that horizontal mergers reduce consumers' welfare. Hence, if mergers create efficiency gains, consumers do not, at least as a general rule, receive a share of that surplus.[45]

Second, the event study evidence shows that the target firms' shareholders benefit, and that the bidding firms' shareholders generally break even.[46] The unequal distribution suggests that competition authorities may want to condition the approval of an international merger on whether the national firm is buying or being bought. In particular, the competition authorities may look more favourably on a merger in which the national firm is being bought.[47] Also in national mergers, the unequal distribution may have some consequences for distribution between wealth groups. The bidder is often the bigger and financially stronger party, and the target may be a smaller (perhaps family-owned) firm.

Apart from the impact on consumers and shareholders, it may be of special interest to analyse the effects of mergers on employees. In particular, for policy-makers, potential job losses are an important issue. Unfortunately, not much useful empirical or theoretical work has been done to analyse what impact horizontal mergers, and the efficiency gains from such mergers, have on wages and employment. Therefore we confine ourselves to sketching what these effects may be.

The effect of mergers on employees is a complex issue. A purely anti-competitive merger reduces output and thus employment. A merger that creates some efficiency gains does so either because the assets in the two firms (including employees) are complementary in some sense, or because some duplicated functions can be eliminated. In the first case the marginal products of the employees are increased. In the short run, that could lead to higher wages. But in the longer run, when the firm can hire more people, marginal productivity should be forced back to the level determined by the market wage rate. Thus the anti-competitive effect and the efficiency effect go in opposite directions. The total effect, one may expect, goes in the same direction as output. That is, if the merger reduces output and increases consumers' prices, then employment is likely to be reduced. (A complication is that since productivity has increased, by assumption, output change is an upward biased estimate of employment change.) Empirical results indicate that horizontal mergers, on average, reduce output. Hence, one may expect that horizontal mergers, on average, lead to reduced employment. In the second case, one would expect that the firms lay off some employees. In this case, the anti-competitive effect and the efficiency effect both point at reduced employment.[48]

We thus conclude that horizontal mergers, on average, may be expected to reduce employment in the merging firms. At the same time, one should note, competitors to the merging firms are likely to expand their output (if the merger increases consumers' prices). Hence, the first effect is likely to be mitigated by this response. However, the first effect may still be likely to dominate. Now, if employment is reduced, we need to know where these former employees go. If there is no unemployment (or only unemployment due to frictions), they will soon get a new job at a similar wage. However, if there is unemployment, the laid-off workers may be hurt in a very significant way by the merger.

The above discussion has presupposed that wages are set by the market, and that the firms only adjust employment as a result of the merger. However, if wages are truly negotiated, and if the employees have bargaining power in wage negotiations, the analysis becomes more complicated. In this case, one may expect that the surplus the firms gain from having market power in the final goods markets is, to some extent, transferred to the employees. A merger that increases market power thus has the potential to increase wages to those that remain employed in the firms. (Another way for employees to extract these rents is to negotiate fewer lay-offs.) On the other hand, the merger may increase the firms' market power in the labour market (buying power). Hence, the effect on wages is ambiguous. There is a larger surplus to bargain over, but the firms have increased their bargaining power. Much of the empirical evidence seems to support the employer bargaining strength hypothesis (Hekmat 1995; Gokhale et al. 1995; Becker 1995; Peoples et al. 1993). Some evidence points in the opposite direction (Kole and Lehn 1997).[49]

3. A 'CHECKLIST'

On the basis of a review of the efficiency defences in seven OECD merger control systems, we now synthesize the discussion to produce a 'checklist' covering the important dimensions that must be considered in order to design a control system that takes efficiencies into account. Our checklist consists of 19 points, arranged under five headings. We should emphasize that the main purpose of this part of the chapter is to identify the important dimensions, and to illustrate them with examples from the practice of competition authorities. The purpose is not to describe what every competition authority is doing in every dimension.

The discussion also includes some preliminary economic analysis. We often refer to what competition authorities 'should do' if they aim for a full cost–benefit analysis of the merger.

Our discussion is often phrased in terms of cost savings, however that should only be viewed as an example of efficiencies in general.

3.1 Objectives

Any merger control system is, at least implicitly, based on some welfare considerations. A merger affects the well-being of many individuals. In fact, any person that belongs to at least one of the firms' interest groups (consumers, shareholders, management, workers, suppliers, creditors and also competitors) is likely to be affected. The purpose of an explicit welfare standard is to indicate which of these effects are to be taken into account by competition authorities, and how one is to weigh the positive effects for some individuals against the negative effects for others. If a complete cost–benefit analysis is to be made, all effects must be considered, and added to a social net effect. Furthermore, if the policy-maker is concerned with the distribution of wealth in society, the effect on each individual should be given a weight corresponding to that individual's position in the wealth distribution.[50] In practice, however, competition authorities analyse the effects of a merger at the level of interest groups, and not at the level of individuals. Moreover, they do not include all interest groups in the analysis.

Point 1. Welfare Standard. All competition authorities analyse the effects of a merger on two interest groups, namely consumers and shareholders.[51] At least four different welfare standards have been used (or discussed) in different jurisdictions to weigh consumers' interests against shareholders' interests.

1. *Total surplus (or Williamson's) standard* According to this standard a merger should be allowed if it creates more wealth to producers than it destroys for consumers. Hence, distribution does not matter. It should be emphasized that, in addition, according to this standard a merger that raises the price may be approved.
2. *Consumers' surplus (or price) standard* According to this standard a proposed merger should be allowed if and only if consumers gain. The reason for adopting this standard is if one is concerned with distribution, and if consumers in general are poorer than the owners of the firms.
3. *Hillsdown standard* According to this standard, efficiencies must exceed the losses to consumers. It can be shown that this standard is stricter than the total surplus standard, but allows more than the price standard. Expressed differently, this means that there are distributional concerns, but not as strong as in the consumer's surplus standard.
4. *Killer standard* According to this standard, a merger should be allowed only if all efficiencies are passed on to consumers. This standard is built on very strong distributional concerns.

One may rank these standards according to the strength of distributional concerns: total surplus (distribution does not matter), Hillsdown, consumer's surplus, killer (distribution very important). The total surplus standard is articulated in the Canadian merger guidelines.[52] However, in Hillsdown this interpretation of the Canadian Competition Act has been questioned by the courts. According to McFetridge (1998), a reasonable interpretation of the court's decision is a 'new' standard – called Hillsdown above. The US merger guidelines apply the consumer's surplus standard. It appears that the courts in Sweden employ the total surplus standard, while the Swedish competition authority applies the consumer's surplus standard.

The choice of welfare standard affects how often an efficiency defence can be expected to be used. For example, in the USA (consumers' surplus standard) there are numerous cases where efficiencies have been an issue. However, the US choice of fairly strict concentration thresholds also matters. In the EU, where dominance is looked at, many of these mergers would not be contested in the first place. Those that would be contested would require large cost savings to meet a consumer's surplus standard (cf. McFetridge 1998, p. 52). The killer standard is only applicable when the market is perfectly competitive anyway. Hence, with the killer standard an efficiency defence would never be used.

Point 2. International Competitiveness. In international markets the welfare trade-offs are somewhat different from the welfare trade-offs made in national markets. There are two reasons for this. First, in a market where mainly national firms sell to mainly foreign consumers, an anti-competitive merger enhances national welfare, even if there are strong distributional concerns (within the country). Second, in a market where national firms compete with foreign firms, a merger of national firms that leads to substantial cost savings enhances the national firms' competitiveness. In some jurisdictions, the international competitiveness[53] of the domestic firms is considered a consideration in the merger control.

The Canadian Competition Act stipulates that, in the determination of whether a merger is likely to bring about gains in efficiency, account should be taken of whether such gains will result in: (1) a significant increase in the real value of exports or (2) a significant substitution of domestic products for imported products. In France, the efficiency defence explicitly states that, in addition to economic progress, a contribution to international competitiveness is considered a part of the efficiency defence. In the UK[54] and in Sweden international competitiveness is also a consideration in merger control. In the USA, on the other hand, international competitiveness is not taken into account.

Although related, international competitiveness is a distinct policy objective from productive efficiency (cost savings). For analytical clarity it may be convenient to treat them separately.

Point 3. Future Viability. Cost savings may also be necessary for the merging firms to survive in the long run. An example of such a situation is if there are important returns to scale, and if the merging firms are small in comparison to their competitors. Such considerations are made in Sweden. Taking the firms' future viability into account, as a part of an efficiency defence, is not necessary if the merger control includes a failing firm defence.[55]

Point 4. Inefficiencies. In some cases the competition authorities suspect that a merger will produce net inefficiencies rather than net efficiencies. Our review of the empirical and the theoretical literature has shown that such mergers do occur. The question is then, should competition authorities condemn a merger based *inter alia* on the argument that the merger creates inefficiencies. Expressed differently, should competition policy be used as a means to eliminate mergers that reduce firms' internal efficiency. Merger control in the UK includes such a possibility.[56]

3.2 Identification and Measurement of Efficiencies

Point 5. Types of efficiencies. An efficiency defence must state what types of efficiencies are included. If a complete cost–benefit analysis is to be made, any social efficiency that the merger generates should be included. Efficiencies may come in the form of cost savings, improved quality or improved services. Cost savings, in turn, may stem from rationalization or scale economies or technological progress, and so on.

In this section we discuss six forms of restrictions that competition authorities, nevertheless, may put on what types of efficiencies they consider.

(a) *Redistributive (or pecuniary) gains* It is important to distinguish between true social efficiencies and redistributive gains. This is, for example, done in a clear way in the Canadian merger guidelines.[57] Only the first category should be included in an efficiency defence. For example, cost savings should only be included if they represent a saving of resources. If firms save on costs because the merger increases their bargaining power and enables the merged entity to extract wage concessions, or discounts from suppliers (not corresponding to cost savings), that is only a wealth transfer and it should not be counted as a social efficiency. Another example would be tax gains.[58]

(b) *Quantity reductions* Another issue concerns cost savings that stem from an anti-competitive reduction in quantity. In a complete cost–benefit analysis, such cost savings should be considered. Of course, they should be balanced against the reduction of consumer's surplus, and if these are the only cost savings they will never suffice to make the merger socially desirable. But the point remains, they should be counted as a cost saving. However, there are two different ways to do this. One way is to include these cost savings in the 'stage-one' analysis that attempts to compute the dead-weight loss due to the merger. If that is done, these cost savings should not be counted once again in the efficiency defence. The other way is to exclude these cost savings from the first stage, and to include them instead in the efficiency defence.[59]

(c) *Fixed costs* If competition authorities use a consumer's surplus standard, only savings in variable costs are normally to be considered. This means that some types of efficiencies, e.g. duplication of administrative routines, usually do not need to be discussed, since they do not usually affect variable costs.

(d) *Other markets* Another subtle issue is cost savings (or other efficiencies) that are realized in other markets. On one hand, one may argue that it does not matter where the saving of resources occur.

In a complete cost–benefit analysis, these savings should be included. This view is taken in the Canadian merger guidelines.[60] However, there are at least two arguments against this view. First, if competition authorities need to study the effect of the merger on more markets (than the so-called relevant market), the analysis would be more complex and hence costly. Moreover, if cost savings in other markets are included one may argue that other issues related to these other markets should also be addressed by the competition authorities.[61] Second, including efficiencies in other markets makes it necessary to weigh the gains for consumers in those other markets against the losses for consumers in the market where competition is harmed. In the US case Lucy Lee/Doctors Regional Medical Center, the court held that pro-competitive effects in one market could not justify anti-competitive effects in a different market. In Germany and the UK, on the other hand, the competition authorities balance anti-competitive effects in one market against pro-competitive effects in other markets.

(e) *Industry level efficiencies* Another issue concerns the distinction between efficiencies at the level of the merging firms and efficiencies at the level of the market. An example of the efficiencies at the level of the merging firms could be cost savings as a result of specialization between the plants that are owned by the merged entity. An example of efficiencies at the level of the industry is that the merger between two firms may affect the R&D incentives for the competitors (see subsection 1.1.3). It appears that US and Canadian efficiency considerations only refer to firm-level efficiencies, while Swedish efficiency considerations, in principle but perhaps not in practice, include both types.[62] A possible reason why only firm-level efficiencies are considered is that they are easier to verify. Even if both types are considered, one may argue that market-level efficiencies should be treated separately, at least in assigning the burden of proof. The reason is that it is probably only concerning the firm-level efficiencies that the firms are (much) better informed than the competition authorities.

(f) *Problem of proof* In practice some efficiencies are more difficult to verify. Some competition authorities have chosen to state explicitly which types of efficiencies are less likely to be considered due to such problems (see below).

Point 6. Net effects. An efficiency defence may take into account retooling and other costs that must be incurred to achieve efficiency gains, and deduct them from the total value of the efficiencies – computing the net efficiency. That is done in the USA, Canada and Sweden. Note, however, that if these costs only affect fixed costs, they will not be passed on to consumers.

Hence, including these costs is not important if competition agencies use a consumer's surplus standard.

Point 7. Measurement. In some jurisdictions it is explicitly indicated what firms should prove, and what kind of documentation they should use.

In the US merger guidelines it is said that the merging firms must substantiate efficiency claims so that the agencies can verify (1) the likelihood and magnitude of each asserted efficiency; (2) how and when each would be achieved (and any costs of doing so); (3) how each would enhance the merged firm's ability and incentive to compete; and (4) why each would be merger-specific.

In the Canadian merger guidelines[63] it is said that objective verification of particular sources of efficiency gains may be provided by (1) plant and firm-level accounting statements; (2) internal studies; (3) strategic plans; (4) capital appropriation requests; (5) management consultant studies (where available); or (6) other available data.

Point 8. Merger specificity. In some jurisdictions, it is argued that an anti-competitive merger should only be approved because of the efficiencies that it creates, if those efficiencies would not be realized through less anti-competitive means.

It may be difficult for competition authorities to judge what alternatives should be considered. For this reason it is explicitly stated in the Canadian merger guidelines[64] that only if the other means is a common industry practice will it be considered. Examples of alternatives are: internal growth; a merger with an identified third party; a joint venture; a specialization agreement; or a licensing, lease or other contractual arrangement.

Note that the 'merger-specificity' requirement entails that an efficiency defence is invoked only if the anti-competitive concerns cannot be resolved through divestiture or other remedies.

Point 9. Discounting. In the Canadian merger guidelines[65] it is explicitly stated that to compare efficiencies and anti-competitive effects that occur at different points in time, one needs to remove the effects of anticipated future inflation, and apply a standard real discount rate.

3.3 Analysis of Competition

In this section we discuss how to analyse the linkage between efficiency gains and competition.

Point 10. Mode of competition. Already an analysis of the effect of a merger on competition (assuming that there are no cost savings) requires that competition authorities have information about the mode of competition in the market. The analysis of the effect of cost savings brought about by the merger also depends on the mode of competition.

There are several issues involved. The first issue concerns whether the firms on the market compete or whether they collude. In the US merger guidelines the first possibility is discussed under the heading 'unilateral effects' and the second under the heading 'co-ordinated effects'. Second, if firms compete, analysis of oligopolistic interaction can be performed either according to the Bertrand model or the Cournot model (see the Theory section 1.3). In the USA it appears that the agencies use the Cournot model for homogeneous goods markets, and the Bertrand model for differentiated products. Third, in some markets (typically markets for intermediate goods) the buyers (or sellers, if the merging firms are buyers) also have market power. In that case, the analysis needs to take countervailing power into account.

Point 11. Efficiencies as an offence (anti-competitive effects). Cost savings are *per se* desirable. However, cost savings can have negative side effects. In particular, if two firms merge and thereby lower their variable costs, they become a tougher competitor. Actually, if the cost reduction is big enough, the merger may imply that competitors are driven out of the market, or that new entry is blocked. In this sense, cost savings may be anti-competitive. In a complete cost–benefit analysis such anti-competitive effects should be included in the analysis of a merger, and there is no inconsistency if efficiencies are treated both as an offence and as a defence. Cost savings have been treated as an offence both in the USA (Brown Shoe) and in the EU (MSG Media Service).

The fact that cost savings may have anti-competitive effects may complicate the analysis. It means that the analysis of the merger's anti-competitive effects cannot be completely separated from an analysis of the merger's effect on costs. That is, a preliminary analysis of the effect of the merger on competition, based on the assumption that costs are not affected, may underestimate the true anti-competitive effects of the merger. If a merger is cleared at this stage, before cost savings have been estimated, there is a risk that mergers that should have been blocked are never detected as anti-competitive.

Point 12. Pass-on (pro-competitive effects). Competition authorities do not only need to assess the existence and magnitude of efficiencies. They also need to assess the extent to which the cost savings are passed on to consumers.[66]

In a non-collusive market (unilateral effects), four issues are important for assessing pass-on. First, it is necessary to distinguish between variable and fixed costs. Only reductions in variable costs are (directly) passed through to consumers. Second, it is necessary to estimate the degree of post-merger competition. The more competition there is *ex post*, the more the cost savings will be passed on to consumers. For example, if competition is very intense, a reduction of marginal cost by €1 would lead to a reduction of the price by €1. If the merger creates a monopoly (and if demand is very price-insensitive) the price may essentially be unaffected by the cost savings. Third, pass-on also depends on the exact 'shape' of the demand function. In particular, if the price elasticity of demand is higher at higher price levels, then the effect of a reduction in cost on price tends to be small (everything else equal). Fourth, the slope of the marginal cost function also affects pass-on.

In a collusive market, all four aspects mentioned above are still crucial. In order to estimate the degree of post-merger competition, it is also necessary to estimate the degree of post-merger collusion. The more collusion there is, the less a given reduction in cost will be passed on to consumers (much like the non-collusive case). It may be more difficult to assess the effect of efficiencies on the price level in a collusive market. The reason is that cost savings may reduce the likelihood that collusion is successful.[67] However, economic theory is not well developed to analyse these issues.

In one US case (Long Island Jewish Medical/North Shore Health) pass-on was considered likely since the merging parties were not-for-profit organizations.

3.4 Informational Aspects

In this section we discuss issues related to the fact that competition authorities have little (in particular, less than the firms) information concerning the efficiency gains from mergers.

Point 13. General-presumptions versus case-by-case methodology. Essentially all horizontal mergers increase market power and reduce allocative efficiency. If this was the only effect of horizontal mergers, a general prohibition against horizontal mergers would be the natural policy. However, mergers also lead to cost savings and other efficiencies. There are two main methods by which efficiencies are balanced against the reductions in allocative efficiency in merger control today:

> *The general-presumptions method* Not all horizontal mergers are prohibited. Typically, only those mergers that significantly reduce competition may be challenged. For mergers that only reduce competition insignificantly (according to some indicator such as the Herfindahl measure of concentration or the merging firms' market shares), cost savings are presumed to be more important than the anti-competitive effects. The global method is used by the Bundeskartellamt in Germany. According to some, including the EU Commission, the global method is used in the EU merger control.

The case-by-case method Efficiencies may be balanced against anti-competitive effects on a case-by-case basis (efficiency defence). Elements of the case-by-case method are used in the USA, Canada, France, the UK and Sweden.

The main argument in favour of the global method is that the case-by-case method requires a lot of information and hence may be costly, or even impossible, to implement. Against this argument one may say that the global method only produces a reasonable outcome if the indicators (such as the Herfindahl measure of concentration or the merging firms' market shares) that are used to indirectly assess anti-competitive effects are reliable and if the threshold is set in a reasonable way. This also requires information. The type of information needed is, however, different. It is not necessary to collect data about the proposed mergers. It is sufficient to use statistical information, for example from economic research. Unfortunately, as we have already argued, there is not much such information.

Typically, case-by-case considerations of efficiency gains are combined with some general presumptions about the effect of merger on efficiency. This intermediary form may be called the sequential method.

The sequential method For mergers that only reduce competition insignificantly, cost savings are presumed to be more important than the anti-competitive effects. Case-by-case considerations of efficiencies are initiated as a second step, in case the analysis of a first step suggests that the proposed merger causes non-negligible concern for anti-competitive effects.

Symmetrically, one may use general presumptions to define a level above which anti-competitive effects are presumed to dominate (and case-by-case analysis is not allowed). In a case where both a high and a low threshold are defined, case-by-case considerations are allowed only in intermediate (or perhaps marginal) cases. For example, according to the US merger guidelines, efficiencies almost never justify a merger to monopoly or near-monopoly. Similarly, according to Article 81(3) of the Treaty of Rome, an anti-competitive agreement cannot be exempted if the agreement gives the firms the possibility of eliminating competition in respect of a substantial part of the products in question.

The motive for the two-step procedure is that efficiencies are difficult to evaluate. The two-step procedure means that efficiencies need only be assessed in those cases where the anti-competitive effects are neither negligible nor very strong.

However, there is a potential risk with such a procedure. Since efficiencies may have anti-competitive effects, those effects may not be noted (see the discussion about efficiency offence above). Naturally, if the thresholds are strict, this problem is less important.

Point 14. Burden of Proof. The key problem with an efficiency defence is information. In many jurisdictions, it is the firms that have the burden of proving that a merger (already found to be anti-competitive) produces sufficient efficiencies not to be blocked. This is the case in the USA and Canada, and in the EU concerning exemptions for agreements that restrict competition. A likely reason for this is that it is the firms that have the best information.

In some jurisdictions it is explicitly indicated what firms should prove, and what kind of documentation they should use (see above). Nevertheless, even with such clarifications, lack of information remains as the key problem with an efficiency defence. For example, Kinne (1998) argues that it is the problem of proof that is the principal reason why courts in the USA have repeatedly rejected efficiency claims.

Point 15. Standard of Proof. Whenever decisions are to be based on evidence, one of the fundamental questions is what standard of proof to require. As it is difficult to predict efficiencies precisely before a merger is consummated, one should rather talk about a persuasion standard. But the question remains, for an efficiencies defence, should one require that the cost savings be possible, probable, or virtually certain? In the USA the standard has changed over time, from requiring 'clear and convincing evidence' to requiring that claims are 'credible' or 'clearly demonstrated' (see Kinne 1998).

Point 16. Full versus Partial Defence. In practice some efficiency gains are more difficult to verify. Some competition authorities have chosen to explicitly state which types of efficiencies are less likely to be considered due to such problems. That may help to clarify the standard of proof that is used, and it may save time for both firms and the competition agency (see also Fisher and Lande 1983).

According to the US merger guidelines: efficiencies resulting from rationalization and multi-plant economies of scale, that is shifting production among facilities formerly owned separately, which enable the merging firms to reduce the marginal cost of production, are more likely to be susceptible to verification. Efficiencies relating to research and development are potentially substantial but are generally less susceptible to verification.

The Canadian guidelines[68] use two broad classes of efficiency gains: production efficiencies and dynamic efficiencies. Production efficiencies are generally the focus of the evaluation, because they can be quantifiably measured, objectively ascertained, and supported by engineering, accounting or other data. Dynamic efficiencies include gains attained through the optimal introduction of new products, the development of more efficient productive processes, and the improvement of product quality and service. However, claims that a merger will lead to dynamic efficiencies are ordinarily extremely difficult to measure. Accordingly, the weight given to claims regarding such efficiencies will generally be qualitative in nature.

3.5 Other Procedural Aspects

Point 17. Prosecutorial discretion versus Litigation. Efficiencies may be considered either by the competition agencies, or by the courts, or by both (see Fisher and Lande 1983).

Point 18. Rebuttal versus Defence. There are at least two different ways that one may *frame* an efficiency justification for a merger, namely as rebuttal or as defence. The difference between the two frames originates from the fact that the term 'competition' can be used in two different meanings.

According to one definition, the degree of competition is measured by the price level (or perhaps consumers' satisfaction). Using this definition, horizontal mergers can be both pro-competitive (those that reduce price) and anti-competitive (those that increase price).

According to another definition, the term 'competition' refers to the degree of market power. Market power may be measured by the price to cost mark-up that firms charge. With this definition, all horizontal mergers reduce competition (that is, increase mark-ups) at least slightly,[69] and some of them significantly reduce competition.

Merger control forbids mergers that reduce competition (significantly). The exact meaning of this prohibition depends on which of the two meanings that one gives the term 'competition'. Consider a merger that increases mark-ups significantly, but reduces price (due to large counteracting cost savings). Since mark-ups are increased, such a merger would be blocked using the second interpretation of the term 'competition'. Since price is reduced, such a merger would be permitted using the first interpretation of the term 'competition'.

Furthermore, depending on the interpretation of the term 'competition', an efficiency justification of a merger must be framed differently. If competition refers to the price level, a merger should be blocked if, and only if, it raises the price (significantly). With this definition one may justify a horizontal merger by rebutting a claim that it reduces competition.

Rebuttal Because of the efficiencies, the merger does not lessen competition (it does not increase price), and should be allowed.

In contrast, if competition refers to the degree of market power (mark-up), almost all horizontal mergers reduce competition, and are consequently hit by the prohibition. With this definition, rebuttal is not available.[70] Instead, one may express the justification of a horizontal merger as an efficiency defence.

Defence The merger lessens competition (it increases mark-ups). However, due to the efficiencies, it is nevertheless desirable, and should be allowed.

As we see it, the difference between the two frames is only a difference in terminology.[71]

It seems that there has been a drift away from the defence-frame to the rebuttal-frame in the 1997 revision of the US 1992 merger guidelines (see FTC Staff Report 1997). It also seems that the rebuttal frame was used in the landmark case FTC v University Health (see above). It is not possible for us to say if there has been any related change in the substance (for example that pass-on to consumers is considered more important now, or that the timing of the analysis has changed[72]). One may speculate that such a change in terminology may make it easier to reconcile the Supreme Court case law (negative to efficiency justifications of mergers) with FTC-DOJ policy and the emerging lower court case law (more favourable to efficiencies).

Actually, the rebuttal frame may also provide a more convenient setting than the defence frame for efficiency justifications under the EU merger regulation (see section 4.4.2.1).[73]

Point 19. Merger guidelines/Notices. Several competition agencies, notably in Canada and the USA,[74] have chosen to publish the way they analyse mergers, including the way efficiencies are considered. In Europe, the Commission has published Notices concerning certain aspects of its analysis, for example market delineation. If the firms have the burden of proving the existence of efficiencies, such merger guidelines may help the firms, the competition agencies and the courts. Apart from reducing the firms' uncertainty, it may help them to focus on the relevant matters.

4. A FRAMEWORK FOR MERGER ANALYSIS

The previous sections of the chapter discussed theoretical aspects, empirical evidence and the practices of competition authorities concerning the treatment of efficiencies from mergers. This section aims to bring the threads together and propose a framework that may be used in incorporating efficiencies into merger analysis. Broadly speaking, three approaches may be distinguished. The case-by-case approach explicitly analyses the magnitude and effects of efficiencies in every merger case. The general presumption approach makes use of general structural indicators (such as market shares) with an implicit recognition on the existence of average efficiencies in mergers. The first approach has the potential problem of high information costs in measuring efficiencies and their effects. The second approach has the potential problem that there is a lot of aggregate uncertainty concerning efficiencies from mergers, in which case the structural indicators are not perfect predictors of the net benefits from mergers.

A third approach is the 'sequential' approach, which aims to combine the relative advantages of both extremes by minimizing on both information costs and errors that may arise from the unreliability of structural indicators. In a first step, structural indicators are used to arrive at an initial decision. In a second step, an 'efficiency defence'[75] with a more detailed investigation may be allowed.[76]

Section 4.1 of this chapter reviews in detail the various approaches to incorporate efficiencies. Based on our conclusions from the empirical literature that efficiencies may need to be assessed on a case-by-case basis, we construct an information-economizing framework for evaluating mergers. In a first stage, notified mergers are assessed using routine tools with modest information requirements. Mergers that do not pass the first stage test are subject to further investigation, including an efficiency defence. We note that the transition from a general presumptions approach (where explicit efficiency arguments are ruled out) to a sequential approach with explicit efficiency considerations for some mergers, does not imply a more lax policy towards mergers. Generally speaking, such a transition does require a revision of the currently used threshold criteria. Rather than a single 'dominance' threshold level, delineating acceptable from unacceptable mergers, two thresholds levels are now required: a first threshold to delineate automatically acceptable mergers from those subject to an efficiency defence; and a second threshold to delineate the mergers subject to an efficiency defence from those that are automatically unacceptable. The first threshold typically lies below the currently used 'dominance' threshold level, whereas the second threshold level would lie above the current level.

Sections 4.2 and 4.3 go into more detail in informational aspects that need to be addressed if one decides to incorporate an efficiency defence in merger evaluation. This analysis is partly based on our theoretical findings and partly based on the practice in OECD countries. We focus on the implementation of an efficiency defence assuming that the merger authority has a price standard, rather than a total welfare standard. We emphasize that there are two essential components to the analysis of efficiencies: the calculation of minimum required efficiencies or MREs (section 4.2), that is, efficiencies required to compensate for market power effects; and the measurement and verification of actual efficiencies (section 4.3). An efficiency investigation should explicitly balance these two components in as transparent a way as possible.

The calculation of MREs requires essentially an assessment of the likely expected market power (or anti-competitive) effects. The difficult task for the merger authorities is to obtain a good idea of the nature of competitive interaction before and after the merger. This is not an obvious task, given the various possible models of competition as shown in the theoretical part. To resolve this problem, we propose that the merger authorities focus on calculating the MREs in a worst-case scenario about anti-competitive effects. We provide a simple methodology to implement this idea, which essentially only requires information on the expected degree of pass-on of cost changes into consumer prices. Our worst-case scenario approach may yield efficiency standards that are too high for the merging firms. We therefore also provide formulae for MREs based on specific and simple models of competition, requiring information on market shares, concentration and price elasticities; in addition we outline the simulation approach for computing MREs in more complicated models of competition. Nevertheless, these alternative procedures require a considerably more complex investigation (including robustness analysis) than our proposed simple worst-case scenario approach. For this reason, it seems desirable to place the burden of proof on the merging firms when these more complex techniques are used.

The computed MREs may then be confronted with the actual expected efficiencies involved in the mergers. To measure actual efficiencies in a direct way, it is important to assess the various types of efficiencies, since not all types will have the same effects. Given the verifiability issues, it would be desirable to put the burden of proof regarding the types and the magnitude of expected efficiencies on the merging firms, who should follow procedures set out by the merger authority.

Section 4.4 synthesizes the discussion and provides informational arguments for and against the efficiency defence. Political arguments are also considered. Finally, section 4.4 provides some suggestions on what needs to be done to incorporate the possible presence of efficiencies. In order to improve merger policy regarding the account of efficiencies, various concrete actions seem worth considering. First, it would be important to think carefully about Article 2(1)(b) of the merger regulation. Either a reinterpretation of this article or a modification would be desirable to recognize the potential role of efficiencies, without outlining how efficiency considerations should be taken into account. A separate notice (similar to 'Guidelines') could then be published in which more detailed procedures are formulated on how efficiencies are to be treated in the evaluation of mergers. Finally, we argue that it would be desirable to systematically perform post-merger evaluation, which could, for example, include an analysis into actually realized efficiencies from mergers, and their pass-on to consumers.

4.1 The Treatment of Efficiencies

The purpose of this section is to provide possible alternative approaches to the treatment of efficiencies in merger analysis. The central problem for the merger authorities is to economize on information costs, without relying too heavily on indicators of expected net benefits in circumstances where these are unreliable.

4.1.1 Merger decision-making and types of errors

By its very nature, merger policy offers only a limited set of choices for influencing competition. The competition authority either accepts the merger, rejects it, or, as a compromise, accepts the merger conditional on certain requirements such as divestiture. The limited, discrete set of alternatives in merger policy is in stark contrast with regulation, where a larger and more flexible set of policy instruments is available to influence competition. The regulation of prices, for example, allows for an infinite number of alternatives.

Whatever the goals of merger policy are (to protect consumer interests, international competitiveness, or total surplus), the merger authority faces the tremendous task of computing the net effects of a merger, by comparing the effects on market power with the effects on various types of efficiencies. The empirical evidence in section 2 indicates that even for firms it may not be a straightforward task to compute their net private benefits from merger. For the merger authority the problem is even greater, since they have considerably less knowledge regarding the markets in which the firms operate.

Given the difficulties in computing the net effects of a merger, and given the limited set of alternatives available to the competition authority, one may distinguish between two types of error:

- Type I error: Reject a merger that has net beneficial effects.
- Type II error: Accept a merger that has net harmful effects.

The challenge is to design and apply a policy that minimizes the consequences of the two types of errors. This does not mean that it is necessary to minimize the number of errors *per se*. Rather, it means that a good policy should minimize Type I errors in those cases where significant net harmful effects are likely; and minimize Type II errors in those cases where significant net beneficial effects are likely. At the same time, it is necessary to economize on information costs.

4.1.2 Alternative approaches

4.1.2.1 The case-by-case approach

A first way to analyse the net effects of mergers, including both market power and efficiencies, is to simultaneously consider all factors for each individual merger that is proposed. Such a case-by-case approach explicitly recognizes the possible presence of efficiencies in every single case. One cannot speak, however, of an efficiency defence, since efficiencies are considered in the merger analysis in a fully integrated way. A case-by-case approach would, in principle, allow one to keep type 1 and type 2 errors at a minimum, at least to the extent that the investigation is successful without any unforeseen consequences.

In practice, however, a case-by-case approach entails tremendous information costs. Broadly speaking, there are two types of information gathering activities: information gathering regarding market power effects, and information gathering regarding efficiencies. First, it is necessary to quantify the market power effects associated with the merger. We will introduce the concept of minimum required efficiencies, that is, the quantity of efficiencies necessary to compensate for the market power (or anti-competitive) effects of the merger. In principle, this requires a good understanding of the nature and the degree of competitive interaction in the industry. However, we will propose a tractable and general procedure which requires that the merger authorities focus on a 'worst-case scenario', which does not require the anti-trust authority to make specific behavioural assumptions.

Second, it is necessary to identify and measure the actual efficiencies that will be realized. Both types of information-gathering activities may involve significant costs if there is a lot of uncertainty associated with future effects. Furthermore, the merging parties are likely to be in a better position to assess certain aspects of the merger effects than the merger authorities. Problems of information costs are discussed in detail in sub-sections 4.1.2 and 4.1.3.

4.1.2.2 The general presumptions approach

An alternative approach to evaluating mergers and incorporating efficiencies is by relying on general presumptions about their likely effects. An extreme example would be to forbid all horizontal mergers (net effects are presumed to be negative) or to allow all mergers (net effects are presumed to be positive). A better variant, however, is to make the approval contingent on some easily observable indicators that contain some (but imperfect) information about the likely net effects of the merger. In particular, based on past experience regarding the types, the magnitude and the effects of efficiencies associated with mergers, one may construct structural indicators, such as market shares or concentration indices, that measure the average net benefits from mergers. The general presumptions approach is therefore based on the implicit recognition of efficiencies.

The general presumptions approach obviously eliminates the high information costs involved in assessing mergers on a case-by-case basis. Instead, there is now a need for a set of structural indicators that measure the average net expected benefits from mergers. The quality of these structural indicators as a predictor of the net benefits from a specific merger depends on the degree of aggregate uncertainty regarding merger effects. A high aggregate uncertainty may arise for two main reasons: uncertainty related to average market power effects and uncertainty related to average efficiencies.

First, as documented in the theoretical section 1, each oligopolistic industry is characterized by its own behavioural peculiarities, such as price-setting versus quantity-setting behaviour, collusive or non-collusive behaviour, homogeneous goods or product differentiation, etc. Simple and general formulae of a merger's market power effects, in terms of observables such as market shares and concentration indices, can therefore not be expected to be a good approximation for every industry.[77]

Second, mergers generally differ in the actual efficiencies they realize. Mergers generally create different types of efficiencies with different effects on competition. Moreover, the size of efficiencies (and inefficiencies) may differ significantly across mergers.

4.1.2.3 The sequential approach

The information costs associated with the case-by-case approach and the aggregate uncertainty problems associated with the general presumptions approach raise the question whether there exists an intermediate approach that combines the advantages of both extremes. The sequential decision-making approach aims to combine aspects of both approaches. Broadly speaking, a sequential decision approach starts by assessing mergers based on general structural criteria. If the merger meets the criteria, then it is accepted. If not, a more detailed analysis is allowed into some, though not necessary all, aspects of the merger.

Most countries do, in fact, adopt some version of the sequential approach in evaluating mergers. For example, a first stage of the procedure consists of some routine tasks to check whether, for example, the total turnover of the merging firms does not exceed a critical level. Only if the firms do not meet these criteria is a further investigation instigated. The reason for this procedure is that information costs are too high to justify a detailed investigation of all (even 'minor') cases, yet aggregate uncertainty about the merger's effect is too high to limit the analysis to a routine test on all (in particular borderline) cases.

Once a merger fails the routine tests in the first stage, a more detailed investigation starts. Again the question arises whether the merger authorities should simultaneously consider all factors to assess the net benefits of the merger, or whether, in contrast, a more limited investigation based on general presumptions is preferable. In principle, the various dimensions that may be investigated either simultaneously or in sequential steps include: the definition of the relevant market and a market share test, an entry barriers test, a more detailed test on expected market power effects (e.g. a collusion test), a failing firm test.[78]

At one of these stages a detailed test on the presence of efficiencies may also occur. This then amounts to the recognition of an efficiency defence. The decision on whether or not to consider various dimensions simultaneously, sequentially, or not at all, will in general depend on the relative importance of the information costs and aggregate uncertainty associated with structural criteria. We now discuss in more detail the implications of applying a sequential approach for the treatment of efficiencies.

4.1.3 The efficiency defence

For simplicity, we limit our attention to two central dimensions in merger analysis: market power (or 'anti-competitive') effects and efficiencies. The sequential approach then amounts to a two-step approach. In the first step, simple structural indicators are computed which implicitly aim to incorporate both market power effects and efficiencies. During this step, there is no explicit analysis of efficiencies, but rather some general presumptions. If the structural indicators meet certain thresholds, then the merger is automatically accepted or rejected. In other cases an efficiency defence is allowed in a second step. In this step market power and efficiency effects are balanced in a detailed and explicit manner.[79]

Two central questions arise in the implementation of the efficiency defence:

1. How should the thresholds for the structural indicators be determined in the first step?
2. How should the detailed analysis of market power and efficiency effects be performed in the second step?

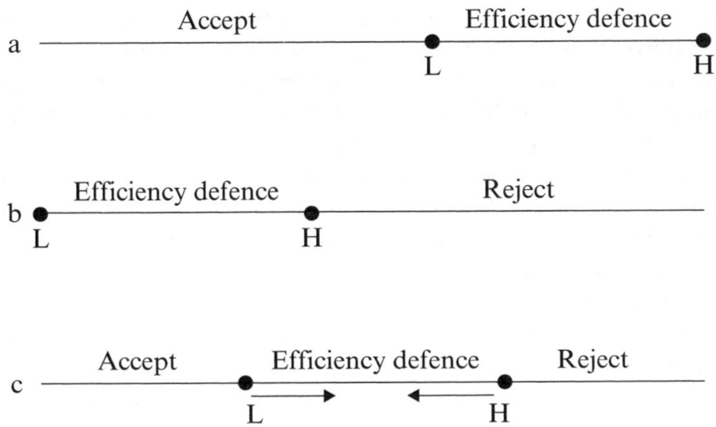

Figure 3.2 *Alternative efficiency defences*

We go into detail regarding the second question in sections 4.2 and 4.3. In the present sub-section we discuss the merger analysis in the first step, in particular the determination of the thresholds for the structural indicators. The determination of the thresholds is of course also of importance in the general presumptions approach. However, as we will show, the actual criteria for acceptance or rejection may differ because of the possibility of a defence in the second step.

To focus ideas, assume that the merger authorities use a specific structural indicator as a measure of the expected net benefits from a merger. For example, the European Commission generally uses market shares of the merging firms. In the United States, the use of concentration indices, in addition to the market share of the merging firms has been popular. In particular, the Herfindahl index of concentration (defined as the sum of all firms' squared market shares) has received a lot of attention.

Figure 3.2 considers three possible ways on how these structural criteria may be set in the first stage of the investigation. Each line describes the range that the structural indicator may take. For example, if the structural indicator is the merging firms' joint market share, the range is between zero and one. The points L and H depict the lower and upper threshold levels between which the merger authority decides to pursue a more detailed investigation into efficiencies in the second step.

Consider first Figure 3.2a. In this case, mergers are always accepted without a further investigation if the structural indicator (e.g. the merging firms' joint market share) does not exceed a certain threshold level L. An efficiency defence is always allowed if the structural indicator exceeds the threshold L. This is what is most commonly understood under an efficiency defence. It would mean for example that the merger authorities always pass a merger that does not lead to a dominant position; in case of a dominant position an efficiency defence is required. This type of efficiency defence reflects the merger authorities' belief that low structural indicators predict net benefits with a reasonable degree of confidence, whereas high structural indicators have little predictive power on net benefits. This may occur for example when the structural indicator is a very good measure of market power effects, and when the merger authorities believe that efficiencies have a high average and a high variance.

Figure 3.2b considers the other extreme case in which mergers are always rejected if the structural indicator exceeds a certain threshold level H. An efficiency defence is allowed for sufficiently low levels of the structural indicator. It would mean for example that a merger authority never allows a merger to bring about monopoly; other mergers are allowed an efficiency defence. This type of efficiency defence reflects the merger authorities' belief that a high structural indicator predicts net harmful effects with a reasonable degree of confidence, whereas a low structural indicator has little predictive power. This may occur for example when the structural indicator is again a very good measure of market power effects, but when the merger authorities believe that efficiencies have a very low (possibly negative) average combined with a high variance.

Figure 3.2c considers a two-sided efficiency defence. Mergers are always accepted if the structural indicator is below a threshold L, and always rejected if it is above a threshold H. Intermediate levels of the structural indicator require an efficiency defence before a decision is made. This would mean, for example, that all mergers among small firms are automatically accepted, whereas all mergers which bring about monopoly are always rejected, and a detailed investigation into efficiencies is required in intermediate, or marginal, cases. Note that if the thresholds L and H are moved closer to each other in Figure 3.2c (as indicated by the arrows), then the scope for an efficiency defence becomes more limited. In the extreme case when L and H would become equal to each other, there is no longer an efficiency defence, and instead a general presumption approach is applied. The two-sided efficiency defence may thus be viewed as the most immediate generalization of the general presumptions approach, where the strict single threshold for acceptance and rejection is broadened to a 'grey' zone in which an efficiency defence is allowed. A two-sided efficiency defence would thus reflect the merger authorities' belief that the structural indicators perform relatively well, except in borderline cases.

The above discussion shows that an efficiency defence in a second step may be implemented in various different ways. As discussed in the above paragraphs, the specific type of efficiency defence to be used, one-sided or two-sided, depends on the expected net benefits that are predicted by the observed structural indicator. A preliminary question is however whether it is worthwhile to adopt an efficiency defence in the first place. If information costs in carrying out an efficiency investigation are considered to be prohibitively high, then an efficiency defence should not be adopted and we are essentially in the extreme case of Figure 3.2c, in which L is equal to H (assuming both thresholds are not at the left or right extreme at which all mergers would either be accepted or rejected). Now consider a drop in the information costs that induces the merger authorities to introduce an efficiency defence. Such a drop in information costs may for example stem from improved measurement methods such as simulation analysis, to be discussed in the next section. When information costs drop sufficiently, the threshold levels L and H no longer coincide: L starts to shift to the left and H starts to shift to the right (i.e. the reverse movement of the arrows indicated on Figure 3.2c).

The introduction of an efficiency defence, if induced by a drop in information costs, thus calls for two threshold standards instead of one: (1) a threshold level L, which is lower than the previous single threshold so that fewer mergers should be automatically accepted; (2) a threshold level H, which is higher than the previous single threshold so that fewer mergers are automatically rejected once an efficiency defence is introduced. In this sense one could say that the introduction of an efficiency defence in the European Union (based on the consideration that information costs are no longer prohibitive) should also lead antitrust authorities to revise their current threshold approach based on the notion of dominance. On the one hand, the threshold level of dominance (H) above which mergers are automatically blocked without appeal to efficiency considerations should be increased. On the other hand, a 'new' threshold level referring to lack of any dominance (L) would need to be installed, below which mergers are accepted without efficiency considerations.

As we have seen in the discussion of the case-by-case approach, information costs in computing both market power and efficiency effects may in fact be high, and may thus make an efficiency defence impractical (so that L equals H). In sections 4.2 and 4.3 we turn to the issue of how a detailed investigation can be implemented, in particular the question how to compute the actual efficiencies and the efficiency standards that are required to compensate for the market power effects. This discussion should also serve to indicate the potential importance of information costs in introducing an efficiency defence.

4.2 Calculating Minimum Required Efficiencies

4.2.1 Introduction

If a merger has failed the test for acceptance or rejection in the first step, then a second step with an efficiency defence may be started. This step requires a more thorough, case-by-case investigation into the possible net beneficial effects arising from efficiencies. It should be emphasized that this step does not simply require an adequate measurement of the actual (expected) efficiencies from the merger, but also a good calculation of the market power (or anti-competitive) effects. Both aspects should be measured in comparable units so as to arrive at an overall assessment of the net benefits. Conceptually, one may thus distinguish between:

1. The measurement of actual efficiencies; and
2. The calculation of minimum required efficiencies (MREs) in order to compensate for market power effects.

In this sub-section we consider the calculation of MREs[80] in more detail. We focus on MREs for price to decrease, since we interpret the merger regulation to be founded on a consumer welfare standard. Nevertheless we also briefly consider MREs for a positive externality.

4.2.2 Minimum required efficiencies in a worst-case scenario

4.2.2.1 Expected price increase in a worst-case scenario

The expected percentage price increase following a merger may be broken down into two separate components. First, there is the expected price increase arising from increased (unilateral or collusive) market power, holding costs constant. Second, there is the reduction in marginal cost multiplied by the expected pass-on to consumers.[81]

The problem with computing the first component is that one needs to have an idea of the current and future expected intensity of competition. Are firms currently competing according to the Cournot model or according to the Bertrand model? Are they currently colluding or behaving in another, less well-defined way? How will firms behave after the merger? Is the merger likely to increase the likelihood of collusion, or are only unilateral market power effects to be expected?

To avoid these difficult questions, the merger authorities may opt for a 'worst-case scenario'. Such a worst-case scenario can actually be formulated quite naturally from the way the size of the relevant market is currently defined by the European Commission. A Commission Notice of 1997[82] sets out the basic principles for market definition. The relevant antitrust market consists of the minimum number of products for which a hypothetical joint price increase above current levels – in the range of 5–10 per cent – would be profitable (assuming no changes in efficiencies).[83] Thus if the two merging firms would not be able to profitably increase their prices by 5–10 per cent, then the relevant antitrust market would be larger than these two firms, and one can conclude that there is at least no merger leading to 'monopoly'. The competition agency has to continue to include additional competing products in the definition of the relevant market until a sufficient number of products is reached so as to make the hypothetical joint price increase profitable.

If the relevant antitrust market is defined according to this procedure, the worst-case scenario would be that all firms in the market would increase their price by 5–10 per cent (assuming no changes in efficiencies). This is because a larger price increase would by the definition of the relevant antitrust market, not be profitable to the firms. Generally speaking, it seems likely that firms would in fact not increase their prices by as much as 5–10 per cent. Even if a collusive (i.e. joint profit maximizing) price is set after the merger, this would generally result in a price increase of less than 5–10 per cent. Lower price increases may also be expected if the merger does not result in collusive price setting.

It might be argued that the worst-case scenario price increase of 5–10 per cent is an arbitrary number; if the competition agencies had chosen the number of, say, 20 per cent to define the relevant antitrust market, then the market definition would have included more firms but the worst-case scenario price increase would also have been higher. However, such a reasoning fails to take into account why the competition agency has chosen the 5–10 per cent number for market definition in the first place. We now go into some detail in how one may interpret this number.

One may view the figure of 5–10 per cent as the intolerance level for maximum price increases, to be used during the initial phase of the investigation. This intolerance level is set at this, based on some (implicit) general presumption that efficiencies are very likely going to be insufficient to compensate for the 5–10 per cent price rise that would take place without any change in efficiencies. The important question for the competition agency is what is the size of the merger, relative to the size of the relevant antitrust market. First, the proposed merger may involve all firms or more firms than those that are included in the definition of the relevant antitrust market, that is, a merger leading to monopoly or 'beyond'. Our interpretation is that the competition agency would (almost) certainly reject such a merger during the initial phase of the investigation because the intolerance level of 5–10 per cent price increases (without efficiencies) would have been exceeded.[84]

Second, the proposed merger may involve only part of the firms included in the definition of the relevant antitrust market, that is a merger to less than monopoly. The merger may then be accepted or rejected depending on the outcome of a test whether or not the merger creates or strengthens dominance in the relevant market. If the merger passes the dominance test, it would be approved without a more detailed investigation. One may thus interpret the dominance test as the tolerance level for price increases, below which there is a general presumption that the expected anti-competitive effects are small relative to the expected efficiencies.[85]

If the merger fails to pass the dominance test, then it is made subject to a more detailed investigation. In particular, we know that such a merger will, without cost savings, be likely to lead to a moderate or significant price increase of at most 5–10 per cent. Expressed differently, the worst-case scenario for these mergers is that they increase price by 5–10 per cent.

4.2.2.2 The importance of pass-on

By how much does marginal cost have to drop in order to compensate for the expected worst-case scenario price increase? As indicated above, this will depend on the degree of pass-on of costs into consumer prices. For example, suppose that pass-on is 50 per cent. In other words, suppose that if cost is decreased by, for example, 10 per cent, then price is reduced by only 5 per cent. A 50 per cent pass-on would imply that the minimum required reduction in marginal cost, i.e. the MRE, is in the range of 10–20 per cent, i.e. the 5–10 per cent range divided by 50 per cent. More generally, suppose that we know that pass-on of a marginal cost reduction into consumer prices is equal to the parameter β.[86] The required drop in marginal costs to compensate for the price increase in a worst-case scenario is then equal to the 5–10 per cent range divided by β. Thus the greater the pass-on parameter β, the greater will be the efficiency standard for price to increase.

Using the procedure of the worst-case scenario, the question of computing MREs boils down to estimating the degree of pass-on. This greatly simplifies matters since this is a question that has received a lot of attention in the economic literature. A detailed review on the size of the pass-on parameter β is beyond the scope of this study. Nevertheless, we want to emphasize that there exist several studies that have analysed pass-on from both a theoretical and an empirical perspective.

4.2.2.3 Assessing pass-on in practice

The empirical literature on pass-on is large, and is scattered over various fields in economics; see Chapter 4, Section 2 for a more detailed discussion. The general empirical finding from this literature is that pass-on is indeed incomplete. The examples cited above suggest that the pass-on parameter

β varies roughly between 30 per cent and 70 per cent. Yet we stress that a more detailed study is necessary to obtain a more complete picture. If the conclusions do turn out to be robust, then one could conclude that the efficiency standard for price to increase would vary between 7 and 17 per cent if a 5 per cent rule for defining the relevant market is used; it would vary between 14 and 33 per cent if a 10 per cent rule is used. One may note that these numbers are rather high. The reason is that they come from the worst-case scenario. Nevertheless, there are mergers that may meet such stringent requirements.

The more confidence one could gain regarding the estimate of the pass-on parameter across sectors, the easier it would be for the merger authority to revert to a general presumptions approach regarding the MREs (though not necessarily, of course, regarding actual efficiencies). For example, if it would be found from empirical studies that it is fairly safe to assume a pass-on parameter of 50 per cent, then the efficiency standard would simply amount to twice the hypothetical joint price increase that was used when defining the relevant market. If, in contrast, a detailed review of the literature revealed that the pass-on parameter varies substantially across sectors, then the merger authority might prefer to do a case-by-case analysis in the second step for determining the pass-on parameter. The following considerations may be taken into account under such a case-by-case investigation.

1. Previous empirical results on pass-on may be used if these are available for the sector in which the merger takes place.
2. The merging firms may be requested to provide the necessary information for estimating pass-on based on historical data. A descriptive empirical approach to estimating past pass-on behaviour would require fairly standard econometric procedures based on data that the firms should have readily available.
3. A qualitative analysis may be undertaken on the likelihood that pass-on in the sector of the merging firms will deviate from the mean pass-on parameter in the economy. Such a qualitative analysis may be based on several theoretical arguments.

Theory predicts the importance of the following three variables in determining the degree of pass-on of a marginal cost reduction into consumer prices: the slope of marginal costs, the intensity of competition and the curvature of the price elasticity of demand. First, assume there is perfect competition and marginal costs are constant. In this case marginal cost changes will be fully passed on into consumer prices ($\beta = 100$ per cent). Second, assume there is still perfect competition but that marginal costs are increasing (reflecting capacity constraints). In this case pass-on will be incomplete, provided at least that industry demand is not perfectly inelastic ($\beta < 100$ per cent). Intuitively, suppose that the competitive firms decide to lower their prices by the extent of the reduction in marginal costs. This price increase would raise industry demand (unless it is perfectly inelastic). In order to meet the increased demand the firms would need to produce more. When marginal costs are increasing due to capacity constraints, this requires firms to charge a higher price than the original decreased price, so that pass-on is incomplete.

Third, assume that there is imperfect competition. In this case firms may have incentives to absorb cost changes by adjusting their mark-ups. The degree of mark-up absorption depends on the curvature of the price elasticity of demand. To see this, note that percentage mark-ups over marginal costs are given by the inverse of the price elasticity of demand. If the price elasticity of demand is constant, then percentage mark-ups will also be constant. In this case there is no mark-up absorption of cost changes. If, in contrast, the price elasticity of demand is increasing in price, then firms find it optimal to reduce their mark-ups when costs increase, and increase their mark-ups when costs decrease. Consequently, pass-on is incomplete.[87]

These theoretical considerations teach us that pass-on is expected to be weak when the industry is characterized by increasing marginal costs (capacity constraints), when there is a significant degree of market power, and when there is mark-up absorption due to an increasing price elasticity of demand. The first two conditions are intuitive and possibly variables that are relatively easy to observe. The third condition seems more difficult. Nevertheless, even for this case there are some interesting theoretical results that suggest a link between the degree of mark-up absorption and the firms' market shares. For example, Feenstra et al. (1996) show that the degree of mark-up absorption depends on the market share of the firms according to a U-shaped pattern.

4.2.2.4 Caveats regarding the worst-case scenario approach

The above procedure proposes a computation for the MRE, that is, the required drop in marginal cost for price to decrease, by focusing on a worst-case scenario about the anti-competitive effects from the merger. The MRE in this worst-case scenario is equal to the maximal profitable joint price increase divided by the pass-on parameter β. The maximal profitable joint price increase is equal to 5–10 per cent, because that is how the relevant market has been delineated based on an (implicit) intolerance level of the competition agency, above which a merger would be almost certainly rejected. In this sub-section we are more explicit about possible objections against our worst-case scenario approach.

First, it should be noted that the 5–10 per cent method for market delineation used by the Commission presupposes that the competition agencies, explicitly or implicitly, make an assumption (or know) how the firms outside the (candidate) relevant market respond to a joint increase in price by the firms inside the (candidate) market. For example, the competition agency may presume that the outsiders keep their prices constant when the insiders increase their price by 5–10 per cent. Alternatively, the competition agency may presume that the outsiders respond collusively (i.e. also by 5–10 per cent). Finally, the competition agency may presume that outsiders respond according to Bertrand or Cournot or some other model of strategic behaviour. When we construct our worst-case scenario, we assume that the merger authority did use correct information in the market delineation step, also about possible responses by outsiders. This is also how theoretical work prescribes the definition of the relevant market; see Sleuwaegen (1994) for a discussion. If, however, this is not the case in practice, our methodology may need to be modified. This would occur, for example, if the competition agencies incorrectly assumed that all outsiders keep their prices constant, whereas in practice some would respond collusively to the 5–10 per cent price increase.

A second difficulty with the worst-case scenario approach is that the 5–10 per cent price increase is only a lower bound for the maximal jointly profitable price increase, and may thus not always be a good approximation of the worst-case scenario price increase. To see this, suppose that the 5–10 per cent procedure leads one to find that the market consists of N firms. Strictly speaking, one can only be certain that $N-1$ firms would not find it profitable to raise their price by 5–10 per cent. If potential joint market power rises extremely rapidly with the inclusion of the Nth firm, then it may be that firms would now suddenly find a joint price increase of drastically more than 5 per cent profitable.[88] One may refer to this problem as the integer problem from moving from $N-1$ to N firms.

In practice, this integer problem should not be exaggerated if one accepts that adding additional firms to the market definition increases joint market power in a more or less smooth manner. The main exception would be in the case where the definition of the relevant market is just equal to the number of merging firms, so that it concerns a merger to monopoly (in the sense of the relevant market definition). In this case, the two merging firms may indeed possibly find it profitable to increase their prices by significantly more than 5–10 per cent; the 5–10 per cent price increase is still a lower bound to the worst-case scenario, but the actual worst-case price increase may be even higher. The intolerance level of the competition agency is then likely to be exceeded and the merger would need to be rejected without an efficiency defence.

Finally, we note that the European Commission notice defines the relevant market by considering maximum profitable joint price increases; in other countries, the relevant market is defined by considering optimal joint price increases.[89] Both approaches may however be interpreted as a worst-case scenario, although one needs to make a somewhat different assumption on the firms' rationality. In the first approach, one assumes that the worst that can happen is that firms increase their price up to the point where this is no longer profitable compared to the pre-merger situation. In the second approach, one assumes that the worst that can happen is that the firms set their price in a jointly optimal way.

4.2.3 Minimum required efficiencies based on specific models of competition

4.2.3.1 Introduction

The procedure outlined in the previous sub-section requires a minimal amount of information in order to compute the MREs for price to decrease. Essentially, only the degree of pass-on needs to be estimated. A disadvantage of the approach is that it starts from a worst-case scenario. In reality, it is possible and perhaps even likely that firms would raise their price by less than the assumed 5–10 per cent amount (ignoring changes in efficiencies). This would especially be the case when the relevant market includes a high number of firms, since in this case post-merger collusion can presumably be ruled out, and a non-collusive model of oligopoly may be more likely to apply. Therefore, the procedure outlined in the previous sub-section may impose MREs that are too high and lead to a rejection of mergers with potential net benefits.

Nevertheless, the construction of MREs based on specific non-collusive models of competition is subject to some reservation. In the EU, a merger can only be blocked if it creates or strengthens a dominant position. Hence, only in case of dominance is there need for an efficiency defence. A firm is dominant if it has a large degree of market power. In such case one talks more precisely of single-firm dominance. The Commission has widened the concept of dominance to also include joint, or oligopolistic, dominance. The relevance of joint dominance in merger cases was confirmed by the Court in Kali + Salz. According to Morgan (1996) joint dominance has, using economic terminology, been interpreted as collusion. If this is correct, only mergers that create single-firm dominance, or that lead to collusion, risk being blocked in the EU. Hence, there may only be a need to construct an efficiency defence for collusive markets, and not for markets characterized by, for example, Cournot or Bertrand type of competition. If this is correct, then the worst-case scenario described above is appropriate.

It is nevertheless instructive to also consider the construction of MREs based on non-collusive models of competition. One reason for this is that the interpretation of joint dominance as only including collusion, and not non-collusive oligopolies, might be subject to revisions in the future. In fact, there is no obvious economic ground for this restriction. If a merger leads to increased prices and harms consumers, it is not important to the consumers if the price increase is due to a unilateral action by the merging firms, or if it is due to co-ordinated actions among all firms.

In what follows, we consider some specific models of competition to derive explicit formulae of the MREs for price to decrease. If these models of competition can be shown to apply with a reasonable degree of confidence to the industry in which the merger takes place, then these derived MREs may be more accurate. However, we would recommend placing the burden of proof for applying these formulae to the merging firms rather than to the merger authorities. First, the merging firms are likely to have better information about the nature of competition in their industry. Furthermore, the merging firms may be supposed to have carefully assessed anti-competitive effects of the mergers (see, for example, Song Shin (1998), for a formal argument along these lines).

We distinguish between two types of models: industries with homogeneous goods and Cournot competition, and industries with product differentiation and Bertrand competition.[90] We make some simplifying assumptions in order to derive explicit formulae. The derived formulae for the efficiency standards are easy to interpret; they are based on relatively easy to observe variables, and they can be easily and quickly implemented. The disadvantage is that the formulae for the efficiency standards may be quite sensitive to the assumptions regarding pre-merger and post-merger competition. In the next sub-section we describe the computationally more complex simulation approach. This approach shares much of the economic intuition of the simple models, and at the same time allows for significantly more flexibility and realism in modelling competition.

4.2.3.2 Homogeneous products and Cournot competition

Consider a merger between firm A and firm B. Farrell and Shapiro (1990) consider a homogeneous goods market with Cournot competition. Denote the (single) pre-merger price of the homogeneous good by P; the marginal cost of firm A and B by MC_A and MC_B, respectively; and the marginal cost of the merged entity (at the pre-merger production level) by MC^M. Farrell and Shapiro find that a merger reduces price if, and only if, the merged firm's mark-up (at the pre-merger production level) would be greater than the sum of the mark-ups of the constituent firms before the merger, that is, $P - MC^M > (P - MC_A) + (P - MC_B)$. Let us say that firm A has a marginal cost that is lower than (or equal to) firm *B*'s. The condition may then be rewritten in terms of the required cost reduction below the lowest cost firm:

$$MC_A - MC^M > P - MC_B.$$

In other words, the reduction in the marginal cost of the lowest cost firm, firm A, must exceed firm B's pre-merger mark-up. This condition is intuitive: the required marginal cost reduction is larger the larger is the firms' pre-merger market power. A problem with the formula is that it depends on variables that are not so easy to observe: marginal cost data cannot easily be retrieved from accounting cost data. Yet, using the equilibrium conditions for mark-ups of the Cournot model it is possible to rewrite the above condition as:

$$\frac{MC_A - MC^M}{MC_A} > \frac{s_B}{\varepsilon - s_A},$$

where s_A and s_B are the market shares of firm *A* and *B*, and ε is the price elasticity of market demand, that is, the effect of an increase in *P* by 1 per cent on market demand in per cent (in absolute terms). In other words, the required percentage reduction in marginal cost below the low-cost firm *A*'s marginal cost must exceed an easy-to-compute threshold $s_B/(\varepsilon - s_B)$. All one needs to know is the market share of each partner before the merger, and the market elasticity of demand. Intuitively, as the market share of either firm *A* or firm *B* increases, or as the price elasticity of market demand decreases, the required percentage cost reduction increases.[91]

One may distinguish between two extreme cases. On the one hand, if the market share of firm *B* becomes very small, then the required reduction in the marginal cost below the low-cost firm *A*'s pre-merger marginal cost can be very small. The acquisition of a small firm thus implies very low MREs. On the other hand, if the joint market share of the merging firms exceeds the price elasticity of market demand ($s_A + s_B > \varepsilon$), then the merger can never reduce price, even if the marginal cost dropped to zero after the merger.[92] In less extreme cases, the threshold efficiency level needs to be computed. For example, if firm *A* and *B* have a market share of 30 per cent and 10 per cent, and if the price elasticity of market demand equals one, then the required percentage reduction in *A*'s marginal cost is 33 per cent; if the merging firms' joint market share of 40 per cent is evenly distributed (that is, each firm has 20 per cent), then the required marginal cost reduction is 25 per cent.

From a practical perspective, it is necessary to compute the firms' market shares and the price elasticity of market demand. A prerequisite for both is a proper definition of what constitutes the relevant market. In the previous sub-section we discussed how the relevant market is defined according to the Commission's notice.[93] To compute the price elasticity of demand (once the market is defined), one may follow an econometric approach after gathering historical information on prices, total market demand and other variables such as income. In many cases, price elasticities of market demand may also be available from academic publications or from industry sources. If none of these possibilities is available, reasonable values for elasticities may be assumed and the robustness regarding alternative assumptions will need to be assessed.

4.2.3.3 Differentiated products and Bertrand competition

The above simple formula applies if firms produce homogeneous goods. When products are differentiated several modifications need to be made. There is no longer a single price for both products. As a consequence, there is no single notion for the price elasticity of market demand. More fundamentally, one needs to address the issue of how products are differentiated. At the one extreme, products may be differentiated symmetrically, with all products in the industry being equally close (or distant) substitutes for one another. At the other extreme, product differentiation may be asymmetric, with each product having only one or two direct competitors and competition being highly localized.

Generally speaking, with product differentiation the effects of mergers on prices may be phrased in terms of own- and cross-price elasticities of demand for the products. The own-price elasticity of demand for product A, ε_{AA}, is the effect on the demand for product A(in percentage terms) when its price is increased by 1 per cent. The cross-price elasticity of demand for product B with respect to the price of product A, ε_{AB}, is the effect on product B's demand (in percentage terms) when the price of product A is increased by 1 per cent. The diversion ratio δ_A is the ratio $\varepsilon_{AB}/\varepsilon_{AA}$, that is, the proportion of lost sales that is captured by product B, when product A's price is increased. Put differently, the diversion ratio is the proportion of consumers for which product B is the second-best alternative to product A. Similar concepts may be defined to measure the effect of changes in the price of product B (ε_{BB}, ε_{BA}, δ_B).

The diversion ratio δ_A is very important in merger analysis since it provides a measure of the intensity of pre-merger competition between A and B. Suppose that products A and B are merged into a single company. If the diversion ratio is very small, then A and B are not close competitors and the merger should have no significant impact on product A's market power. If the diversion ratio is high, and if, in addition, firm A and B do not face much competition from other products in the market, then a significant increase in market power may be expected. What cost efficiencies are required for the merger to reduce price despite a possible increase in market power? If one is willing to assume that the own- and cross-price elasticities do not vary as prices increase, then the following formula for the MRE may be derived:[94]

$$\frac{MC_A - MC_A^M}{MC_A} > \frac{1}{\varepsilon_{AA} - 1}\left[\frac{\delta_B(1+\delta_A)}{1-\delta_A\delta_B}\right].$$

In the special case in which products A and B are symmetric, this formula would simplify to:

$$\frac{MC_A - MC_A^M}{MC_A} > \frac{1}{\varepsilon_{AA} - 1}\left[\frac{\delta_A}{1-\delta_A}\right].$$

For example, suppose that the price elasticity of demand ε_{AA} is 3 (implying a pre-merger mark-up of 33 per cent); and that the diversion ratio δ_A is 0.2 (20 per cent of the sales lost go to product B when A increases its price). The efficiency standard is then a marginal cost reduction of 12.5 per cent. More generally speaking, the above formulae imply that the efficiency standard for the price of product A to decrease is greater, as the elasticity of product A's demand decreases and as the diversion ratio increases. This is intuitive since a low price elasticity reflects high pre-merger market power, and a high diversion ratio reflects intense competition between the merging products.

If one makes the further (strong) assumption that the ratio of two products' market shares is independent of the available products in the market, then one can compute the diversion ratio in terms of market shares. Under this independence assumption the diversion ratio δ_A would equal $s_B/(1 - s_A)$, that is, the probability that B is second-best for product A equals the market share of product B relative to the joint market share of all goods except A. Willig (1991) has made this observation to provide a foundation of traditional merger analysis based on market shares. Indeed, substituting out the diversion ratio δ_A in the above formula, one obtains:

$$\frac{MC_A - MC_A^M}{MC_A} > \frac{1}{\varepsilon_{AA} - 1}\left[\frac{s_A}{1-2s_A}\right].$$

This formula shows some resemblance to the efficiency standard formula for homogeneous goods (and Cournot competition). It emphasises once again that information on the price elasticity and market shares is critical in assessing the required efficiencies.

The above formulae assume that the elasticities of demand are constant. This may be a good approximation for evaluating small changes around the initial pre-merger equilibrium. However, when mergers occur, a non-trivial change in equilibrium takes place, so that the constant elasticity assumption is no longer innocuous. To the extent that the elasticity of demand for a product increases as the price of that product increases, post-merger market power would be overestimated under a constant elasticity assumption, and the required efficiencies for price to decrease may be less than implied by the above formulae. If the constant elasticity assumption is believed to be unrealistic, then a more general approach needs to be adopted, presumably requiring simulation analysis (see below).

4.2.3.4 Assessing elasticities of demand

An important practical problem with the above formulae is how to compute the own- and cross-price elasticities of demand, and the implied diversion ratio. We provided a simple procedure above to compute the diversion ratio in terms of market shares in a simplified model of product differentiation. Such a procedure may be useful as a first approximation, or when data are not easily available. Similarly, one may make use of survey data or 'common sense' to estimate the diversion ratio as the proportion of consumers for which product *B* would be the second choice to product *A*.

If detailed data on prices and market shares of all products in the market are available, then one may be able to estimate all own- and cross-price elasticities (and the implied diversion ratio) through an econometric model of product differentiation. Such models of product differentiation have been estimated econometrically for the automobile market by Bresnahan (1981), Berry et al. (1995) and Verboven (1996), among others; and for the ready-to-eat cereal industry by Nevo (1998). The limited number of studies is largely due to the high data requirements, but more studies may be expected as more data become available (for example due to the detailed scanner data from supermarkets).

Another approach that has been used to estimate elasticities is called 'residual demand analysis'. This approach[95] proposes focusing only on the own- and cross-elasticities faced by the merging firms, after substituting out the responses by the competitors. The other elasticities need not be known for the purposes of merger analysis, so that the information requirements are greatly reduced. The only data that are needed are historical data on the merging firms' market shares and prices (which may be requested during the investigation), as well as some market-level variables affecting the industry. Data on the competitors' prices and market shares are not needed. Intuitively, residual demand analysis makes it possible to determine whether or not the firms proposing to merge have been close competitors in the past and face little competition from others (in which case the merger would require high efficiencies). In fact, the obtained estimates for the own- and cross-price elasticities may be used to compute the diversion ratio and substituted into the simple formulae for minimum required efficiencies derived in sub-section 4.2.3.3. Such a procedure would require a careful analysis by economists.

4.2.4 Minimum required efficiencies using simulation analysis

4.2.4.1 Introduction

As shown above, for some special cases of oligopolistic behaviour it is relatively easy to compute the efficiency standards for prices to decrease. Several simplifications were necessary to derive these formulae, such as the assumption that goods are homogeneous, or, under differentiated products, the assumption of a constant elasticity of demand. Furthermore, we did not consider models in which there is both product differentiation and Cournot behaviour (capacity constraints). Finally, we did not consider explicit formulae for total welfare to increase. No simple formulae to compute efficiency standards for welfare to increase are available. For these reasons, these formulae should only be treated as indicators, not as definite tests in borderline cases. A thorough robustness analysis, by considering alternative (plausible) values of elasticities, market shares, and so on, would certainly help in obtaining greater confidence in the obtained threshold conditions.

At the same time, it may be worthwhile in certain cases to follow a more realistic, in-depth calculation of efficiency standards by applying simulation analysis. Simulation analysis allows one to specify the nature of competitive interaction in the industry without a need to make strong simplifying assumptions. The approach has become increasingly popular in evaluating mergers in the USA in response to increasing criticism of the use of simplified formulae that do not apply to the industry under investigation. More recently, simulation analysis has also been applied in Canadian investigations. As computer programs develop and become more user-friendly, there seems to be little reason for not considering simulations in merger analysis in various cases.

A simulation analysis for mergers can be broken down into three separate steps: (1) development of the model of competitive interaction, (2) model parameter calibration, and (3) simulation of post-merger equilibrium, including the computation of efficiency standards.[96]

4.2.4.2 Development of the model of competitive interaction

In this step, one investigates how the nature of competitive interaction can be best described. In section 2 various models where discussed. First, one needs to determine whether products are homogeneous or differentiated. If they are differentiated, it is necessary to find out the precise nature of differentiation, that is competition symmetric between all firms in the industry, or is competition localised between smaller subsets of products or firms. Second, it is necessary to specify the cost conditions of the firms. Can firms compete in prices without accounting for capacity constraints? Or do firms face binding capacity constraints and so resemble Cournot quantity-setting firms? Do firms set prices (or quantities) unilaterally, or in a co-ordinated manner? A great advantage of simulation analysis is that it allows one to consider, at least in principle, all these possibilities.

To facilitate the task in this step, the investigator may decide to apply one of the existing programs that has been used in other investigations. For example, Werden and Froeb (1994) have intensively used the logit and nested logit model of product differentiation. The first model allows for product differentiation, but assumes that all products compete symmetrically; the second model allows for localised competition between groups or subgroups of products.

4.2.4.3 Model parameter calibration

In this step, data on the products' current prices and markets shares are substituted into the model, as well as a measure for the price elasticity of market demand. The data requirements are thus limited and are no larger than needed when the simple threshold conditions discussed in the previous sub-section are used. After these data are substituted into the model, it is possible to calibrate the model and retrieve the firm-specific parameter values for marginal cost and demand.

To understand this, suppose there are ten products in the market. Assume that each product has a different marginal cost and possibly also a different valuation (quality), which are not directly observed by the investigator. Assume that other parameters, such as a measure for the price elasticity of market demand, have known values. The investigator observes each product's own price and its own market share, which are interpreted as the equilibrium outcome of consumer demand and firm pricing decisions. Calibrating the model now consists of inverting the system of ten demand and pricing equations to retrieve ten firm-specific valuations and marginal cost parameters. Intuitively, if two products have the same price but one has a higher market share, then calibration would reveal that the more popular model has a higher valuation. The unobserved marginal cost and demand parameters may thus be inferred from the observed equilibrium values for prices and demand, assuming any other parameters are known.

In fact, the own- and cross-price elasticities are thus retrieved from the current data on the firms' prices and market shares, usually augmented with some indication of the price elasticity of the overall market demand. There is thus in principle no need for detailed data to econometrically estimate all elasticities. A disadvantage may be that the retrieved elasticities are not as reliable as those obtained through an econometric procedure. This issue can be overcome through a detailed sensitivity analysis.

4.2.4.4 Simulation of post-merger equilibrium

The previous two steps fully quantify the model of competitive interaction through a mixture of specification assumptions and parameter calibrations based on the pre-merger equilibrium. The final step is to specify the changes to the model as implied by the merger and compute the new prices and market shares. One may then easily compute changes in prices, consumer surplus and total welfare following the merger.

The first change that needs to be made to the model is the assumption of price-setting. Where the merging firms previously set prices independently, they now may be expected to act in a co-ordinated way and take into account the effects on each other's profit. This change will tend to increase prices.

A second change may be the presence of efficiencies realized by the merger. The most direct way of simulation analysis would be to re-compute the equilibrium prices and market shares for alternative levels of efficiencies that may be involved in the merger. In particular, as the reduction in marginal cost realized by one or both of the firms increases, the expected price increase falls. There will be a critical level for marginal costs for which the merger just leaves the prices of the merging products unaffected. This critical level is a generalization of the efficiency standards for price to decrease derived in the discussion based on simple formulae. A simulation analysis also allows one to compute minimum required reductions in marginal or average costs for mergers to exhibit a positive externality or to increase total surplus. We are thus left with a very powerful and generally applicable instrument for analysing the likely effects of mergers and calculating the efficiency standards for price to decrease or total surplus to increase.[97]

4.2.4.5 A hypothetical example

To illustrate the simulation approach regarding merger analysis, Werden and Froeb (1994) simulate the effect of mergers of long-distance telecommunication carriers. They start from an oligopoly model with product differentiation and price-setting firms. They use the logit model as the specific model partly because the US 1992 merger guidelines use this as the reference model for differentiated products analysis, and partly because it has modest data requirements: prices, market shares, a measure of aggregate price elasticity of demand, and a cross-elasticity parameter. Furthermore, even though the logit model does not generate analytic solutions for equilibrium prices, consumer surplus and welfare, it has proved to be a tractable model for numerical analysis.

The model has various general predictions regarding mergers: (1) prices of all products increase as a result of the merger, but the magnitudes of the price increases are very different across products. The price of the small merging partner increases by more than the price of the larger partner. The weighted average of the merging partners' prices increases much more than the prices of the non-merging outsiders. The larger non-merging firms increase price more than the smaller firms. Mergers that increase price may at the same time increase welfare because of output reallocation effects. To understand the net outcome for consumer surplus and/or welfare, a simulation analysis can be very helpful.

Froeb and Werden consider hypothetical mergers among US long-distance carriers. For this industry good data on market shares and prices are available; commonly accepted measures on price elasticities are available. In a first scenario they assume that the merger has no effect on costs. Under this scenario, they find that all mergers involving AT&T have significant adverse welfare effects, and mergers not involving AT&T have only small effects. In a second scenario, they assume that the merging partners' marginal costs equal the minimum of the two merging firms' marginal costs before the merger. In this scenario all mergers of pairs of long-distance carriers increase social welfare, except a merger between AT&T and MCI. Table 3.1 below illustrates these computations.

A merger between AT&T and MCI has significant price effects both with and without the above mentioned possible cost savings. Also a merger between AT&T and Sprint has significant price effects. Regarding welfare effects, only a merger without cost savings between AT&T and MCI would cause significant adverse effects.

Note that these computations are only hypothetical and one should not generalize their findings to hypothetical mergers in other industries. Yet the calculations illustrate that simulation analysis does provide a potentially powerful tool for merger analysis. An extension of Froeb and Werden's analysis could have been to simulate the minimum required cost savings for consumer surplus or welfare to increase. These would than fit directly into our framework. In addition, it would be wise to perform a more detailed robustness analysis regarding merger effects. For example, one could redo their calculation based on the hypothesis that the industry becomes collusive after the merger.

4.2.4.6 Simulation analysis in practice

Simulation analysis has been applied several times in the USA. In US vs. Interstate Bakeries, the Justice Department blocked a merger between

Table 3.1 Price and welfare effects of hypothetical mergers in the US long-distance telecommunications carrier market

Change in:	No cost advantage from merger		Cost advantages from merger	
	consumer surplus	total welfare	consumer surplus	total welfare
AT&T – MCI	−5.63	−2.296	−5.06	−0.587
AT&T – Sprint	−3.40	−1.243	−2.91	0.130
AT&T – Minor	−1.45	−0.488	−1.21	0.162
MCI – Sprint	−0.98	−0.046	−0.56	0.306
MCI – Minor	−0.43	−0.011	−0.20	0.195
Sprint – Minor	−0.27	−0.000	−0.20	0.047
Minor – Minor	−0.12	+0.003	−0.13	0.003

Notes:
All numbers are in per cent of premerger revenues. Minor = representative other firm.

Source: Werden and Froeb (1994), Tables 3 and 5.

white pan bread companies in Chicago using this analysis. In the L'Oreal acquisition of Maybelline, the methodology was again used by the Justice Department to allow a merger between competing cosmetics firms, a merger that probably would have been blocked using the structural analysis of the guidelines. More recently, simulation analysis has also been applied in Canadian merger cases. The explanation for the recent trend towards simulation analysis is related to the recent theoretical advances in modelling the competitive effects of mergers, combined with improvements in computational methods.

4.2.5 Minimum required efficiencies for a positive externality

The efficiency standard for price to decrease may of course not always be met. Economists often argue that the relevant objective for the government is total social surplus, which is the sum of both consumer and producer surplus. For this reason one may allow the merging firms to appeal to the fact that the merger could create a positive externality to the consumers and the competing firms jointly. Farrell and Shapiro (1990) considered this possibility (assuming homogeneous goods). As explained in section 2, mergers that increase price may still create a positive externality since the outsider firms may expand their output after the merger. To the extent that these outsider firms are relatively more efficient than the insiders, the merger may exhibit a positive externality. A positive externality is a sufficient (though not a necessary) condition for total surplus to increase, assuming that the proposed merger is privately profitable.

Farrell and Shapiro derive the condition that the sum of the merging firms' market shares $s_A + s_B$ should not exceed a concentration index CI_O of the outsider firms' market shares for the merger to create a positive externality. More specifically, the critical index is:

$$CI_O = \sum_{i \in O} s_i^2 \left(\frac{1 - s_i \eta}{s_i + \mu_i(\varepsilon - s_i)} \right),$$

where η is the elasticity of the slope of the demand curve, and μ_i is the elasticity of outsider firm *i*'s marginal cost with respect to output.

This index requires quite detailed knowledge about several specific structural features of the industry, both concerning cost and demand conditions. In some interesting special cases this index can be simplified. Let H_O be the sum of the outsiders' squared market shares (that is, the Herfindahl index of the outsiders) and $H_O{}^*$ be the sum of the outsiders' cubed market shares. The matrix in Figure 3.3 then provides measures of CI_O in terms of these indices and elasticities for four alternative cases, depending on whether the marginal cost function is constant or (linearly) upward sloping, and whether the demand curve is linear or of a constant elasticity form.

Consider first the left column, for linear demand. If marginal cost is constant, then the market share of the merging firms should be less than 50 per cent for the merger to create a positive externality. In this specific case, all that matters is the market share of the merging firms relative to the outsiders; the distribution of output across competitors is irrelevant. In contrast, if marginal cost is upward sloping, then the distribution of output

CI_O	Linear demand	Constant elasticity
Constant MC	$\frac{1}{2}$	$\frac{1}{2} - \left(1 + \frac{1}{\varepsilon}\right)\frac{H_O}{2}$
Upward sloping MC	$\frac{H_O}{\varepsilon}$	$\frac{H_O}{\varepsilon} - \left(1 + \frac{1}{\varepsilon}\right)\frac{H^*{}_O}{\varepsilon}$

Figure 3.3 Relationship between CI_o, cost and demand

across the outsiders does matter. The market share of the merging firms should not exceed the Herfindahl index of concentration among the outsider firms (normalized by the price elasticity of market demand). The more concentration there is across the outsiders, the more likely the merger will create a positive externality. The right column shows that the conditions are stricter in the case of a constant elasticity demand.

The strength of the approach proposed by Farrell and Shapiro is that it derives sufficient conditions for a positive externality that are expressed in relatively easy-to-observe variables, without requiring any knowledge of the actual cost efficiencies arising from the merger.

There are however also several disadvantages with their approach. First, the above examples showed that it is difficult to draw a general conclusion other than that the merging firms' market shares should be small relative to some concentration index CI_O. Nevertheless, this problem may be resolved by applying some robustness analysis using the above (or related) formulae. For example, it would be relatively safe to conclude that the merger creates a positive externality (assuming homogeneous goods and Cournot competition) if the joint market share of the merging firms does not exceed any of the four concentration indices in the above matrix.

A more important problem with the above externality analysis is that simple formulae are only available for a market with quantity competition and homogeneous goods. No simple rules exist under price competition and product differentiation. For these cases, one would need to resort to simulation analysis. Werden and Froeb (1994) consider simulation analysis to explore the effects of hypothetical mergers among US long distance carriers, and find examples of mergers that increase both price and welfare, without internal cost savings, similar to Farrell and Shapiro's result.

Another important problem with the approach of Farrell and Shapiro is that it looks at the total externality of a merger, assuming it leads to an increase in price. Since merger authorities seem to be primarily interested in consumer surplus, this is perhaps the main reason why their formulae have not been applied.

4.3 Evaluating Actual Efficiencies

The required efficiency standards computed using one of the methods proposed in the previous section ought to be confronted with the actual efficiencies realized by the merger. We discuss the evaluation of actual efficiencies in three sub-sections. First, we discuss what types of efficiencies are most likely to have beneficial effects. Second, we consider the question to what extent beneficial efficiencies are likely to be merger-specific. Third, we discuss the issue of verification of efficiencies. For obvious reasons, much of the discussion draws directly from the discussion in the 'checklist' in section 3.

4.3.1 What types of efficiencies are most likely to be beneficial?

4.3.1.1 Efficiencies and pass-on

In section 4.2 we discussed a methodology for calculating efficiency standards, that is, the minimum required efficiencies for mergers to decrease price. Broadly speaking, it was shown that the efficiencies should be sufficiently passed-on to consumers. Which types of efficiencies are more likely to result in pass-on?

First, it is necessary to distinguish between fixed and variable costs. Fixed cost savings, such as the avoidance of a duplication of administrative routines, do not affect the marginal costs of the firms. The possibility that these savings will be passed on to consumers is therefore limited. One possibility of pass-on of fixed costs may arise if there is market power also at the other side of the market. In this case bargaining between the firm and its customers may lead to lower prices. Nevertheless, such a consideration should be treated with care. Savings in variable costs directly affect the pricing decisions of the firm. For this reason, variable cost savings should be given priority in the assessment of efficiencies.

Second, it is important to know the magnitude of (variable) cost savings. Some examples illustrate what considerations may be taken into account. (1) If the merging firms argue that they will realize discounts from buying certain inputs, then one has to provide detailed documentation on the share of the cost of these inputs in overall costs. (2) If it concerns the realization of scale economies, then it is of course important to be convincing about the extent of scale economies. Also, since long-run economies of scale affect marginal costs only after some time, information on the expected timing of the cost savings must be given. (3) If the cost savings stem merely from rationalization of production, then it is known from theory that this will never be sufficient to generate price decreases, though it obviously may contribute to other factors.

Third, not only cost savings should be considered. Improvements in product quality constitute a synergy with similar economic effects. The relevant question in this case is whether the claimed efficiencies have the potential of lowering 'quality-adjusted prices'; see, for example, Rosen (1974).

4.3.1.2 Other considerations

Priority should be given to efficiencies that have real effects, rather than only redistributive (pecuniary) effects. For this reason, one should be careful in taking into account tax savings. Although these may be passed on to consumers, they of course also imply a transfer from the taxpayer to the firm.

Another issue concerns the distinction between efficiencies at the level of the merging firms and efficiencies at the level of the market. An example of the efficiencies at the level of the merging firms could be cost savings as a result of specialization between the plants that are owned by the merged entity. An example of efficiencies at the level of the industry is that the merger between two firms may affect the R&D incentives for the competitors. We discussed this in detail in sub-section 1.1.3.2. These types of efficiencies are potentially very important in some high-tech industries. To investigate the role of these efficiencies in practice is not an easy task. One way could be to adopt a simulation analysis, extending the typical oligopoly models used in simulations to a dynamic setting.

A possible reason why only firm-level efficiencies are considered by most jurisdictions is that they are easier to verify. Even if both types are considered, one may argue that market-level efficiencies should be treated separately, at least in assigning the burden of proof. The reason is that it is only on firm-level efficiencies that the firms are probably (much) better informed than the competition authorities.

Another subtle issue is cost savings (or other efficiencies) that are realized in other markets. On the one hand, one may argue that it does not matter where the saving of resources occurs. In a complete cost–benefit analysis, these savings should be included. However, there are at least two arguments against this view. First, if competition authorities need to study the effect of the merger on more markets (than the so-called relevant market), the analysis would be more complex and hence costly. Moreover, if cost savings in other markets are included one may argue that other issues also related to these other markets should be addressed by the competition authorities.[98] Second, including efficiencies in other markets makes it necessary to weigh the gains for consumers in those other markets against the losses for consumers in the market where competition is harmed.

Efficiencies arising from output reductions should not be given any weight if the focus is on price effects. If however producer surplus is also taken into account, then these savings do matter. Note, however, that they are never sufficient to outweigh the reduction in consumers' surplus.[99]

4.3.2 Can efficiencies be created through alternative means?

A question of central importance is whether efficiencies can be achieved through other means than the proposed merger. It is important not to put any *a priori* restrictions on the alternative possibilities and the practical feasibility. The following alternative possibilities may exist for realising the claimed efficiencies: (1) internal growth, (2) a joint venture, (3) a specialization agreement, (4) a licensing, leasing or other contractual agreement, (5) another merger.

Three elements need to be addressed when comparing the proposed merger with the alternative possibilities. First, it is necessary to determine which alternative arrangements would be chosen if the merger is blocked (for example, another merger). Some guidance about which alternatives are most practical may be gained by considering the regular practice of other firms in the industry. Unfortunately, however, economic theory cannot give much guidance on this issue.[100] Second, it is necessary to determine the relative costs (for example, restructuring costs) and expected efficiency benefits from setting up these alternative arrangements. Third, it is necessary to assess the possible anti-competitive effects of these alternative arrangements.

Whenever firms use efficiency arguments, they should be as explicit and as complete as possible regarding these alternative possibilities and their effects. For example, an alternative merger might be preferably with respect to anti-competitive effects when this would involve integration with a smaller firm or with a foreign firm (more distant competitor). In such a case it should be stated why this alternative merger does not create the potential for equal efficiencies at a similar restructuring cost and with less anti-competitive harm.

4.3.3 How can efficiencies be verified?

The most difficult issue regarding the analysis of efficiencies is their verification. Special care has to be taken so that the analysis of efficiencies can be undertaken with a reasonable degree of confidence and without relying on information collection activities that are too costly.

4.3.3.1 Burden of proof

It is acknowledged by most merger authorities that the merging firms have the burden of proof regarding the type, likelihood and magnitude of efficiencies, as well as the merger-specificity of the claimed efficiencies. The merging firms may be presumed to have more information about their businesses, especially about efficiencies if that was an important factor in deciding upon the merger.[101]

4.3.3.2 Standard of proof

Nevertheless, even if the merging firms have the burden of proof, informational problems remain a key issue, because of the asymmetry of information between the merging firms and the merger authorities. White (1987) and Fisher (1987) argue that efficiencies are typically easy to claim, but hard to prove. Fisher (1987) argues in favour of very high standards for proving actual efficiencies, based on several examples where efficiencies were claimed but presumably did not materialize or could have materialized in another way. [102] US policy has gradually shifted from a standard of 'clear and convincing' evidence, to a standard requiring that efficiencies are 'credible' or 'clearly demonstrated'.

Alternative standards are, of course, rather vague. In what follows below, we explain which elements may be taken into account so as to be able to assess efficiency claims in as reliable a way as possible.

4.3.3.3 The partial efficiency defence

Not all efficiencies are equally easy to verify. For this reason, it would be desirable to distinguish between alternative types of efficiencies not only based on their expected effects, but also based on their verifiability. For example, Areeda and Turner (1980) would especially favour efficiencies relating to economies of scale, at least if demand is not growing rapidly. Both the US and the Canadian merger guidelines[103] emphasize production efficiencies (economies of scale and rationalization) as sources of efficiency that may be more easy to verify, in contrast to dynamic efficiencies (research and development).

4.3.3.4 Verification and certification of information

To alleviate the asymmetric information problem between the merging firms and the merger authorities, it may be desirable to put different weight on the amount on efficiency claims, depending on the source that certifies the validity of the information. The Canadian merger guidelines[104] distinguish between the following sources of information: (1) plant- and firm-level accounting statements; (2) internal studies; (3) strategic plans; (4) capital appropriation requests; (5) management consulting studies (where available); or (6) other available data. There may be an important advantage of information that is certified by outsiders such as management consultants, since they need to protect a reputation of future reliability.

It may also be argued that less weight should be assigned to studies on efficiencies that have been prepared after the merger has been taken to a detailed investigation by the competition agency. This is because this would reveal that they were not the ostensible basis for the merger decision. Later documents should however not be discarded altogether, since they may, for example, be prepared to make efficiency claims more specific or in line with the formalities set out by merger guidelines or notices.

4.3.3.5 Post-merger review

Scherer (1991) has proposed to first approve mergers only on a temporary basis. Mergers for which persuasive preliminary evidence on expected efficiencies can be provided may be allowed for a temporary trial period of, for example, three years. At the end of this period, an evaluation can be conducted to find out whether the promised efficiencies have, in fact, been realized. If so, the merger could be definitely accepted. Otherwise, the company may be required to divest again into the two independent parties that existed before the merger.

A main advantage of such a system is that it forces the merging firms to think well ahead of potential future efficiencies, and to make only credible efficiency claims, since making empty promises may be punished later through a costly divestiture decision. At the same time, the competition policy authorities can economize significantly on information costs. There is no need to attempt to verify current claims on future efficiencies, since the final decision is made when the relevant information on realized efficiencies is available.

A disadvantage is that the merger process may be very costly.[105] These costs may well be sunk in the case where the *ex post* decision goes against the merger. Nevertheless, these costs may in fact serve to make the promised efficiencies credible, since the firms know the rules of the game, including the fact that they may need to divest if false promises are made. Furthermore, the costs of divestiture need not be exaggerated in modern times, as Scherer argues. Companies now have experience in applying a large variety of reorganizations, such as sell-offs, spin-offs or leveraged buy-outs, to make parts of their company independent organizations.

The system proposed by Scherer may fit better into the US antitrust system which already allows the possibility of breaking up existing firms to reduce market power. Nevertheless, we believe that it is worth thinking about the possibility of allowing mergers only conditionally for a trial period before definite approval.

4.3.3.6 Merger licence fees

Direct verification, certification or post-merger review all have in common that they require a direct evaluation (either *ex ante* or *ex post*) of the actual efficiencies that are (expected to be) realized through the merger. A drastically different approach to screening mergers would be to implement a revelation mechanism through the institution of merger licence fees to be paid to the government.

It is not clear how the licence fee for the merger to be accepted should be determined. This will for example depend on the objective the merger authority has in mind (maximization of consumer surplus and total welfare). To understand the determination of optimal merger licence fees, a more thorough theoretical analysis is required. One may expect that many of the insights from the asymmetric information (screening) literature would apply.

In practice, (small) fees for approving mergers (dependent on the merger size) have been used in the UK, though presumably not explicitly for screening purposes.

4.4 Should There be an Efficiency Defence?

4.4.1 Arguments for and against an efficiency defence

4.4.1.1 Informational aspects

The above analysis has shown the important potential role of efficiencies in the merger process. Even if there is no evidence that mergers create strong efficiencies on average, some particular mergers do just that. In practice, efficiency considerations are often implicit in merger evaluation. The relevant question is thus not whether, but rather how, potential efficiencies should be taken into account in merger control.

We have emphasized the central role of procedures which serve to economize on information costs. The general presumptions approach avoids potentially high information costs, but relies on possibly unreliable structural indicators for predicting the net benefits (including efficiencies). The case-by-case approach may imply significant information costs to measure efficiencies, but does not rely on structural indicators. The sequential approach aims to combine the advantages of both procedures by relying on general presumptions, with the exception of the borderline (or marginal) cases where a case-by-case analysis is taken regarding the anti-competitive and the efficiency effects. Which approach is actually taken, depends on the information costs and the reliability of the structural indicators. This may require some value judgements, but also common sense and experience with actual cases should help to determine which procedure is preferable.

If the intermediate solution of the sequential approach is found desirable, then a reconsideration of the threshold levels is required. As argued in more detail in sub-section 4.1.3, the introduction of an efficiency defence (if based on improved information collection methods) requires a revision of the current single threshold referring to 'dominance', which delineates those mergers to be accepted without efficiency analysis from those mergers to be rejected without efficiency analysis. Instead of this single threshold, two thresholds should now be used: a first threshold (L), below which mergers are automatically accepted, and a second threshold (H), above which mergers are automatically rejected. For the in-between cases an efficiency analysis would then be undertaken. We note that the lower threshold L will typically be below the 'dominance' threshold as currently adopted, whereas the upper threshold H (which one could possibly still label the dominance threshold) should exceed the dominance threshold as currently adopted. Note that the merger authorities could keep flexibility in determining the threshold levels L and H between which efficiency considerations are allowed. The more optimistic they are about information costs involved in analysing efficiencies, the further apart L and H could be. In an extreme case L could be very small and H very large so that effectively all proposed mergers are allowed efficiency considerations. There is then a full case-by-case approach as currently in the USA.

For those mergers that fall within the range in which an efficiency defence is allowed we propose an approach in which minimum required efficiencies (MREs) need to be compared with actual efficiencies in borderline cases. We propose a relatively simple approach to computing these MREs. This approach focuses on a worst-case scenario regarding anti-competitive effects, and would leave the burden of proof for demonstrating lower anti-competitive effects on the merging firms. The measurement and verification of actual efficiencies may follow rules that partly draw on experience in other countries.

4.4.1.2 Political considerations

The above discussion has compared the case-by-case, the general presumptions and the sequential approaches from an informational point of view. Each approach has its own strengths and weaknesses in treating the possible presence of efficiencies in a reliable, yet computationally tractable way. In this sub-section we point out that there are also political reasons why it may be advantageous (or not) to recognize the presence of efficiencies, at least in principle.

First, there has been the Kali + Salz decision, in which the Court for the first time accepted the concept of joint, or oligopolistic, dominance, rather than single firm dominance. This suggests that the merger control policy has become stricter. This development may make it more natural to consider efficiencies more explicitly today.

Second, many merging firms try to make use of efficiency arguments in convincing the merger authorities on the likely net benefits from the merger. At present, the Commission is simply not positioned to consider these efficiency claims in a formal way. It would potentially improve the transparency of merger review if efficiency considerations can be dealt with using a clear procedure. See, for example, Neven et al. (1993) or Camesasca (1999) on this.

Third, there is a political argument why it may not be desirable to allow efficiency considerations. One has to be careful that introducing efficiency considerations in a formal way does not open up the possibility of a more active industrial policy. Yet such a problem may be overcome as long as there is sufficient transparency in the procedures. According to Camesasca, the main problem with the current 'between-lines' approach is that the Commission has no fall-back line to defend itself against accusations of industrial policy considerations. Furthermore, the perception of political influence on the antitrust review of mergers and regulatory capture by a host of interest groups is aggravated by the limited judicial review of the Commission's decisions. Camesasca argues that it is necessary to clarify that 'efficiencies' are just that, and as such no open gateway for 'other competing values.'

4.4.2 Formalities

In this sub-section we discuss some possible actions that may be undertaken so as to take into account some of the findings of this chapter.

4.4.2.1 The merger regulation

According to Articles 2(2) and 2(3) of the merger regulation, a concentration which 'creates or strengthens a dominant position as a result of which effective competition would be significantly impeded' shall be prohibited. Otherwise it shall be allowed. According to Article 2(1)(b) of the merger regulation, the Commission shall, in making this appraisal, take into account:

(a) the development of technical and economic progress, provided that
(b) it is to consumers' advantage, and
(c) does not form an obstacle to competition.[106]

The question is if Article 2(1)(b) allows for efficiency considerations and, in particular, if it constitutes an efficiency defence. At first glance, the answer appears to be 'No'. In particular, if 'form an obstacle to competition' is synonymous with 'significantly impeding effective competition', the development of technical and economic progress can only be considered in those situations where the merger is to be allowed anyway. The main problem with this interpretation is that it makes Article 2(1)(b) meaningless.[107] Also according to the Commission (1996, p. 53):

> There is no real legal possibility of justifying an efficiency defence under the merger regulation. Efficiencies are assumed for all mergers up to the limit of dominance – the "concentration privilege". Any efficiency issues are considered in the overall assessment to determine whether dominance has been created or strengthened and not to justify or mitigate that dominance in order to clear a concentration which would otherwise be prohibited.

The Commission also points out that the dominance criterion is very strong. At that time (1996), the prohibition rate amongst cases considered under the merger regulation was only 1 per cent.[108]

However, in our view, the merger regulation may be re-interpreted to include an efficiency defence. Hence, in our view, the introduction of an efficiency defence may not require a change in the merger regulation. Remember that the term 'competition' takes on different meanings in the literature. In some literature the word 'competition' is synonymous with the absence of market power.[109] Market power may be measured by the price to cost mark-up that firms charge. With this definition, horizontal mergers most often reduce competition (that is increase mark-ups) at least slightly[110] and some of them significantly reduce competition (increase mark-ups). In other literature, however, the word 'competition' has been used in another sense, namely to mean the price level.[111] Using this definition, horizontal mergers can be either pro-competitive (those that reduce price) or anti-competitive (those that increase price). Now, if we assume that the merger regulation uses the word 'competition' in the first sense, this means that mergers that significantly increase mark-ups should be prohibited. Furthermore, Article 2(1)(b) cannot be used to save any horizontal mergers, since they do form an obstacle to competition, that is increase mark-ups. (This is just a restatement of the first interpretation above.)

In contrast, if we assume that the merger regulation uses the word 'competition' in the second sense, then Articles 2(2–3) state that a merger shall be prohibited if, and only if, the merger increases price. Article 2(1)(b) would amount to an efficiency defence. The Commission should consider efficiencies (the development of technical and economic progress), provided that these efficiencies do not lead to an increase in the price level.[112] The condition(s) for efficiencies to be considered guarantees that the potential negative side-effects of efficiencies do not dominate the beneficial effects of efficiencies.[113] Thus, with this interpretation the regulation allows an efficiency defence. However, a comparison with the efficiency defence under Article 81(3) of the EC Treaty suggests that the efficiency defence under the merger regulation (if any) is intended to be limited.

Two approaches can be taken to solving the problem of the ambiguity of Article 2(1)(b). The first approach is to reinterpret this provision to mean that efficiency considerations may be considered. We consider that such a reinterpretation is possible, that is, does not contradict the other articles of the legislation, as long as efficiencies are required to be sufficient to reduce price. If such a reinterpretation is made, it may be more convenient to talk about rebuttal than defence (see the checklist in section 3). Moreover, if such a reinterpretation is made it may be desirable to publish a notice commenting on the interpretation of Article 2(1)(b) as discussed below. A problem with this approach is that it could limit the treatment of efficiencies to dynamic efficiencies and not include static efficiencies as is done for agreements between firms in Article 81(3) of the Treaty. While Article 81(3) stipulates that an agreement must improve the production or distribution of goods (usually interpreted as static efficiencies) or promote technical or economic progress (usually interpreted as dynamic efficiencies) to be exempted, Article 2.1(b) of the merger regulation only requires the Commission to consider the development of technical and economic progress.

A second approach is to rewrite the merger regulation. The advantage of this approach is that the role of efficiencies can be considered in a more flexible way, for example without necessarily focusing exclusively on consumer interests.[114]

Whatever approach is taken, the merger regulation should limit attention to a recognition of the potential role of efficiencies in a flexible and unambiguous way. Details on how to incorporate efficiencies in the assessment of mergers do not belong in the merger regulation, since they should be subject to periodic evaluation.

4.4.2.2 Notice

To outline the specific procedure by which efficiencies are (or are not) taken into account, it would be desirable to publish a separate notice, comparable in goals to the relevant sections of the merger guidelines published in the USA or Canada.[115] Such a notice could be based on various findings discussed in the present section, outline the circumstances in which efficiencies are explicitly considered and how minimum required and actual efficiencies are compared.

The advantage of a separate notice is that it can be changed in a more flexible way, taking into account recent developments in the role of efficiencies and in our thinking about them.

The publication of a notice may be particularly important if the firms themselves have to carry out the burden of proving efficiencies. A notice which describes in detail how efficiencies are considered may also have a commitment value. The increased transparency would make it difficult to deviate from the described procedure and worries about industrial policy might be reduced.

4.4.2.3 Post-merger review

We have stressed that the procedure to be adopted for incorporating efficiencies depends on the role of information costs and the reliability of structural indicators as predictors of net effects. The actual mergers that have been proposed (and accepted) provide a unique database for the merger authorities to continuously evaluate their policy. For example, the merging firms may be asked to provide evidence on the realization (or lack thereof) of promised efficiencies. This would allow the merger authorities to obtain a more complete picture on the distribution of efficiency gains from mergers, in particular the average and the variance of efficiencies. Similarly, the merging firms may be asked to provide detailed historical data on competitive variables, in particular the evolution of prices and market shares. This would enable merger authorities to obtain a more precise idea of the degree of pass-on. A post-merger review could thus significantly contribute to experience and provide directions on how to update merger control and assess the role of efficiencies.

NOTES

1. All references to the merger regulation in this chapter are to the old regulation no. 4064/89.
2. But in some cases plant closure may also lead to new irreversible costs.
3. Such cost savings could also be classified as rationalisation. We choose to classify them as economies of scale since they reflect downward sloping marginal costs, which is in line with the ordinary use of the term 'economies of scale'. Moreover, the primary use of the term 'rationalisation' can be found in Farrell and Shapiro (1990). Their stability requirement in effect assumes away the cost savings that we discuss here, if they are sufficiently large.
4. An often cited example is the 'cube-square rule': a doubling in the surface area of a pipe will increase the volume by a factor of 4.
5. Tirole (1988, p. 389) uses the same definition for a process innovation. He defines a product innovation somewhat differently as the creation of an entirely new product. He then remarks that product innovation can be viewed as a special case of process innovation: the new product already existed prior to the innovation, and the process innovation reduces the cost of production such that it can be profitably supplied.
6. Another way to describe the same thing is to say that the inferior firm's production frontier has expanded.
7. We classify this as technological progress and not as rationalization. First, the cost savings correspond to an expansion of the firms' joint production possibility frontier. Second, the cost saving is achieved through reallocation of production of intermediary as opposed to final products.
8. The first effect has been called the 'efficiency effect' in the literature, referring to the fact that a monopoly enjoys higher profits than do two duopolists jointly (see for example, Gilbert and Newberry 1982, 1984b). The second effect has been called the 'replacement effect' (Arrow 1962). Reinganum (1983) and Tirole (1988) analyse the role of uncertainty in the R&D outcome to assess the relative importance of both effects.
9. For preliminary discussions of the role of countervailing power, see Galbraith (1952), von Ungern-Sternberg (1995), and Snyder (1996).
10. The term X-efficiency, introduced by Leibenstein (1966), was originally used in a broader sense than just to describe issues related to the separation of ownership and control.
11. For a discussion of relative performance evaluations, see Holmström (1982).
12. However, see Bagnoli and Lipman (1988) for a critique to the Grossman and Hart argument.
13. If competition is tough, firm revenues are low. Hence, if costs are high, firms are forced to pay low wages (including fringe benefits, courses that increase human capital, and so on). But then, to guarantee that employees receive their expected utility, the firms must pay high wages in cases where costs are low. Hence, in the presence of limited liability,

if competition is tough, the market forces firms to give their employees an incentive contract (wages contingent on cost realization).

14. In Hart (1983) and Scharfstein (1988a) the information is transmitted via the market price.
15. Brander and Spencer (1989) also establish the existence of a negative relation between competition and managerial incentives.
16. This relates to the failing firm defence, stating that a horizontal merger between two firms should not be considered anti-competitive, if the relevant alternative to the merger is that one of the firms is declared bankrupt and shut down. This defence has been used in several countries including the USA and in the European Union. In the EU the additional condition is added that the market share of the failing firm would inevitably accrue to the acquiring firm even without the merger. For discussions of the failing firm doctrine, see Kwoka and Warren-Boulton (1986), Shughart and Tollison (1985), Saloner (1987), and Persson (1997a, 1997b).
17. It is straightforward to verify that price will indeed increase under these circumstances in a Cournot model. In models with tacit collusion price will either increase, or remain constant if full collusion already existed. Under Bertrand competition with homogeneous goods, price will either remain constant or increase if it concerns a shift to monopoly. Finally, under Bertrand competition with differentiated products, the analysis by Davidson and Deneckere (1985a) shows that prices increase after a merger, at least in their linear demand model with symmetric competition. A similar observation is made for the logit demand model by Werden and Froeb (1994). See Reitzes and Levy (1992) for a model of localized competition to study the price effects of mergers.
18. Given that savings in fixed cost do not affect marginal cost, it is obvious that they cannot be claimed to reduce prices. The result that output rationalization cannot reduce prices is less obvious. A rationalization of output typically implies a reallocation from the high cost plant to the low cost plant, which (under rising marginal costs) reduces the marginal cost of the high cost plant, while increasing the marginal cost of the low-plant (except in extreme cases where rationalization involves the shutdown of one of the merging firms' plant). Apparently, the net effect of these changes according to Farrell and Shapiro's proposition is to always increase price under Cournot competition.
19. Brueckner and Spiller (1991) extend Farrell and Shapiro's model to analyse airline networks. They consider the role of higher prices under competition on other routes, and the role of scale economies. They show that consumers may benefit more easily in this setting.
20. If goods are homogeneous, the Bertrand model predicts a perfectly competitive price – equal to marginal cost – even if there are only two firms. The intuition for this is that for any price exceeding marginal cost, a firm would have an incentive to undercut the rival's price and conquer the whole market. Because of this result, the intensity of price competition is usually modelled by allowing the goods to be differentiated rather than homogeneous.
21. More specifically, they adopt a logit model of product differentiation, see for example Anderson et al. (1992).
22. Werden and Froeb demonstrate their result assuming constant (though possibly different) marginal costs. Note that the incentives for output rationalisation are reduced under product differentiation, since it implies a change in product diversity. Moreover, the welfare analysis is complicated by any change in product variety.
23. It is not clear exactly how one should interpret the term 'agreement'. Some people would argue that firms actually need to meet and discuss the arrangements in order for collusion to be effective. Others argue that it may suffice that firms are forward-looking and recognize their mutual long-term interdependence for them to start collusion.
24. A fully collusive regime is an output allocation on the firms' Pareto-frontier. Schmalensee considers this frontier by ignoring incentive constraints that ensure the agreement is sustainable (no cheating). Harrington does take into account the firms' incentives to cheat, but focuses on cases were the incentive constraints are not binding.
25. This assumes that side payments are not feasible.

26. Weiss (1992) provides some further results and computations on how to measure the efficiency/competition trade-off in a Williamsonian framework.
27. Verboven (1995) extends Farrell and Shapiro's Cournot model to allow for tacit collusive behavior. He finds reasonable conditions under which the externality effect of a merger is even more likely to be positive than in Farrell and Shapiro's Cournot model.
28. McAfee and Williams (1992) focus on some more specific aspects assuming increasing marginal cost. Barros and Cabral (1994) apply the framework of Farrell and Shapiro to investigate mergers in open economies.
29. One may argue that firms would not merge unless a merger is profitable. However, there are circumstances under which firms may merge, even if that lowers their profits relative to the pre-merger situation (Roll (1986), suggests a hubris hypothesis; Shleifer and Vishny (1988), suggest an empire-building hypothesis; Fridolfsson and Stennek (2000), suggest a pre-emption hypothesis).
30. Rau and Vermaelen interpret a low book-to-market value as an indication that the current management is efficient in managing the firm's assets.
31. Actually, Rau and Vermaelen argue that there is a growing body of evidence that short-term measurements of abnormal performance do not capture the full effects of the stock market reaction to an event.
32. This result may be upward biased due to the fact that anti-competitive price increases may come immediately after the merger while efficiency gains may only come in the long run.
33. Financially distressed airlines show a completely different pattern. They were initially setting prices well below the industry average. During the announcement period the merging firms cut their prices by an average of 19 per cent, further increasing the gap to the industry average. In failing firm mergers, prices were increased by 40 per cent during the completion phase.
34. For example, the Cournot model predicts that competitors would respond by increasing their output relatively more, whereas the Bertrand model predicts that competitors respond by increasing their prices relatively more.
35. This statement is at least true in simple models of oligopolistic competition.
36. Another reason why it is interesting to study market shares is that firm profitability is positively related to market share (Mueller 1983). Thus, a big reduction in market share may be taken to indicate a reduction of profitability.
37. One may question to what extent Singal succeeds to identify market power and cost reduction. First, if two airlines have a large number of common airports, they probably also have common routes. Hence, common airports should not only indicate scope for efficiencies, but also for anticompetitive effects. Second, the so-called free-rider problem should be smaller, not bigger if the change in concentration is large.
38. Barton and Sherman (1984), and Kim and Singal (1993) study product prices. Mueller (1985) studies market shares.
39. Eckbo (1983) finds little evidence of horizontal mergers being anti-competitive. This is surprising, since the sample only includes mergers that were challenged as anti-competitive. Based on this evidence, Eckbo and Wier (1985) draw strong policy implications: 'all but the "most overwhelmingly large" mergers should be allowed to go forward'.
40. See Caves (1989) and Scherer and Ross (1990) for useful overviews.
41. See also Akhavein et al. (1997) for a profit function approach.
42. See Caves and Barton (1990) and Lichtenberg (1992). Both studies are reviewed in Mueller (1997).
43. However, there is some evidence that expectations that successful R&D may increase a firm's market power may motivate R&D efforts.
44. That is if cost is reduced by 10 per cent, price is reduced by 3 to 7 per cent.
45. Remember, however, that there are relatively few direct studies of how mergers affect consumer prices (and the market shares of the insiders).
46. Remember, however, that the evidence only shows that mergers increase the aggregate stock value of the insiders relative to the pre-merger situation. This does not imply that the aggregate stock value after the merger is higher than it would have been in the case

of a strict merger control that would have prevented the merger. The reason is that the pre-merger stock value in the first case takes into account the probability that there will be a merger, while in the latter case the pre-merger value is formed under the knowledge that there will not be a merger (Fridolfsson and Stennek 2000).

47. In contrast, casual evidence suggests that many debaters are less favourable towards a merger in which a national firm is being bought. This may be due to a fear that the country will lose job opportunities, or to purely nationalistic reasons.
48. This discussion shows that efficiencies are likely to be important for how a merger affects employment in the merging firms. However, the effect of efficiencies (abstracting from the anti-competitive effect) is to increase employment in one case (complementary assets), and to reduce employment in the other case (elimination of duplicated functions).
49. Moreover, one may argue that hostile takeovers are likely to be triggered in those cases where the current management has negotiated wage contracts that are too generous. The takeover gain would then consist in renegotiations of these contracts. In that case, employees are hurt by the transaction. However, in order for that mechanism to work, it must be that the new management is more skilled in wage negotiations. Empirical studies find little evidence that takeovers are motivated by the expropriation of extra-marginal wages (Gokhale et al. 1995; Neumark and Sharpe 1996).
50. See our discussion in the Theory section 2.4.
51. In some jurisdictions the interests of other groups (apart from consumers and shareholders) are also taken into account. In some jurisdictions, it is explicitly stated that also the effects on workers is included (EU), while in other jurisdictions it is explicitly said that for example unemployment risks should not be considered (Sweden). In some jurisdictions (US) the effect of merger on small competitors is taken into account.
52. Editors' note: Since this study was carried out, the Canadian merger guidelines have been revised in light of the Propane judgment (see Chapter 2 section 2.4).
53. For terminological simplicity we let international competitiveness refer to both the international aspects mentioned.
54. Editors' note: Since the entry into force of the Enterprise Act 2002, international competitiveness no longer figures among the criteria applied in merger control in the UK.
55. In that case, competition authorities can simply wait to approve the merger until at least one of the firms is starting to lose money. On the other hand, if it is clear at an early stage that the firms are not viable as separate entities, then a quick merger might be preferred since that would reduce uncertainty for the firms' interest groups. This, however, seems to be an issue for the proper design of the failing firm defence.
56. Editors' note: Since the entry into force of the Enterprise Act 2002, the UK authorities can no longer prohibit a merger on the sole ground that it creates inefficiency.
57. See note 52.
58. If competition authorities use a consumer's surplus standard this issue is not entirely clear. Also reductions in the firms' costs that originate from redistribution (e.g. tax gains) do benefit consumers.
59. It appears that the first method is used in the USA. However, in the merger guidelines it is only stated that these cost savings are not included in the efficiency defence. It is not explicitly stated that they are considered in the first stage.
60. See note 52.
61. Today competition agencies focus attention on the effects of the merger on the so-called relevant markets (the market where competition is harmed). A reduction in competition is normally believed to produce dead-weight losses (allocative inefficiencies). However, from an economic perspective this is a very partial analysis. In particular, according to the theory of second-best, a reduction of competition in one market may actually be beneficial for allocative efficiency, if competition is already low in markets for close substitutes. If competition authorities were to include efficiencies in other markets, one may argue that they should also take into account second-best considerations.
62. The threshold criteria proposed by Farrell and Shapiro (1990) do take some external efficiencies (reallocation of production between merging and non-merging firms) into account.

63. See note 52.
64. See note 52.
65. See note 52.
66. This is important to assess the effect of merger on consumers. It is also important in a Williamsonian trade-off since the pass-on affects the size of the dead-weight loss.
67. This view is expressed in the US merger guidelines. It is said that marginal cost reductions may make co-ordination less likely or effective by enhancing the incentive of a maverick to lower prices or by creating a new maverick firm. These ideas are elaborated further in an FTC Staff Report (1997). It is said that lowered costs may disrupt market conditions so as to make collusion less likely or to disturb the terms by which firms previously were able to co-ordinate conduct. Likewise, if merger-related efficiencies eliminated a technology disadvantage, the merged firm might become a more significant constraint on market leaders.
68. See note 52.
69. There are a few 'theoretical' reasons why a horizontal merger would not reduce competition, such as if the merger triggers immediate entry, or if one of the firms is failing, or if the firms colluded perfectly before the merger.
70. Of course, the merger may not raise the mark-up *significantly*. In that case, a rebuttal is available. However, it is unlikely that the small increase in mark-ups is due to cost savings. It is more likely that a modest increase in mark-up is due to intense *ex post* competition.
71. However, the rebuttal frame is only convenient if the welfare standard is a price standard.
72. The rebuttal frame may imply that efficiencies are considered earlier in the process, and not as a second stage. However, as we see it, the issue of timing and the issue of frame may be decided separately.
73. For convenience, we have phrased our discussion in terms of an efficiency defence and not as a rebuttal.
74. Merger guidelines are also on their way in Sweden.
75. Unless we explicitly say so, we use the term 'efficiency defence' to also include 'rebuttal' (see point 18 of the checklist) in this chapter.
76. In practice, sequential decision making may occur in more than two steps, to consider various dimensions of the merger effects in detail. These steps may include a market share test, an entry barrier test, a failing firm test and an efficiency test. In our discussion here, we abstract from issues related to, for example, entry and failing firms.
77. An analysis on the usefulness of simple structural indicators along these lines has been done, among others, by Werden and Froeb (1996).
78. See, for example, Fisher (1987) for an outline of a detailed sequential procedure.
79. Note that it is also possible to consider three-step procedures. In a first step, general structural indicators are computed. A second step would consider the analysis of market power effects in more detail. A third step would consider the measurement of efficiencies and the balancing with market power effects. In France, such an approach is adopted. The second and third stage could also be reversed. We do not consider these possibilities here.
80. The calculation of the minimum required efficiencies may also be phrased as the question what should be the efficiency standard.
81. Assume that the merger tends to increase by dP/P per cent as a result of the first effect. Then, for the net effect to be non-positive, it is necessary that $(dc/c)(dP/dc)(c/p) \leq -dP/P$, where (dc/c) is the percentage cost reduction, and $\beta = (dP/dc)(c/p)$ is the pass-on elasticity. The pass-on elasticity indicates by how many per cent the price would be reduced if cost is reduced by one per cent.
82. Commission Notice on the definition of the relevant market for purposes of Community competition law, published in the *Official Journal*, 372 on 9 December 1997.
83. There has been a debate whether one should consider price increases above current or above competitive levels. See for example Hovenkamp (1994) and Sleuwaegen (1994), and the references therein, for a discussion. In practice, it has been usually chosen to take current levels as the point of reference.

84. The 5–10 per cent number thus corresponds to the threshold H in Figure 3.2c, above which mergers are certainly rejected.
85. If the dominance test entails a tolerance level for price increases of, say, 2 per cent, then the number 2 per cent corresponds to the threshold L in Figure 3.2 above.
86. Full pass-on means that the pass-on parameter $\beta = 1$. No pass-on means that $\beta = 0$. Partial pass-on means that β is some number between 0 and 1. More than full pass-on, which is possible at least in theory, means that $\beta > 1$. Negative pass-on is inconsistent with most models of firm behaviour.
87. To see this intuitively, suppose the firm were to fully pass on a cost decrease in a price decrease, hence keeping mark-ups constant. The result would be that the elasticity of demand is reduced at this lower price. But according to the inverse elasticity rule this would imply it is no longer optimal to charge the same mark-up, but rather to increase the mark-up. This implies that an optimizing firm will reduce its price by less than the cost decrease.
88. This can be illustrated in a simplified model of N price-setting firms without capacity constraints selling homogeneous goods. Including less than N firms in the market definition will not alter the firms' joint market power. When all N firms are included, they suddenly obtain market power, the degree of which depends on the elasticty of market demand; if market demand is very inelastic (little outside substitutes), the maximally profitable joint price increase may be significantly higher than 5 per cent.
89. In practice, the European Commission may not have enough information to distinguish between maximum profitable and optimal joint price increases.
90. See Section 1 for a more detailed discussion of both alternative assumptions.
91. Note that this formula is also consistent with frequently used structural indicators, that is, market shares and elasticities.
92. In a Cournot equilibrium, it is also the case that $s_A < \varepsilon$ and $s_B < \varepsilon$.
93. For a review, see for example also Sleuwaegen (1994).
94. This formula assumes firms compete in price, rather than in quantities. The derivation of the formula is tedious and is available on request. For some related work, see Fisher et al. (1989), Stockum (1993), Werden (1996) and Bian and McFetridge (1995, 1997).
95. Baker and Bresnahan (1985) originally proposed this procedure and applied it to the brewing industry. The methodology has been applied in several cases, see for example Hausman, Leonard and Zona (1994) for the brewing industry, or Hausman (1996) for the ready-to-eat cereal industry.
96. Froeb and Werden (1996) provide a detailed description on how to perform model simulations. They make use of the Mathematica software package.
97. Of particular interest are also the simulations done by Froeb and Werden (1996) to assess the validity of traditional structural criteria (as implemented in the first step of merger assessment). They find that the increase in the Herfindahl index is a far better predictor for beneficial mergers than either the combined market share of the merging firms or the post-merger Herfindahl index.
98. Today competition agencies focus attention on the effects of the merger on the so-called relevant markets (the market where competition is harmed). A reduction in competition is normally believed to produce dead-weight losses (allocative inefficiencies). However, from an economic perspective this is a very partial analysis. In particular, according to the theory of second-best, a reduction of competition in one market may actually be beneficial for allocative efficiency, if competition is already low in markets for close substitutes. If competition authorities were to include efficiencies in other markets, one may argue that they should also take into account second-best considerations.
99. The difference is the dead-weight loss.
100. The reason is that the theory of endogenous mergers is still very incomplete. That theory aims at explaining not only which mergers are likely to occur, but also, as an integral part of the analysis, what would happen without the merger. Early contributions include Stigler (1950), and Deneckere and Davidson (1985b). More recent contributions are Kamien and Zang (1990, 1991, 1993), Fridolffsson and Stennek (2000, 2005), Horn and Persson (1996, 1997), Gowrisankaran (1999).

101. A theoretical foundation for this principle is given by Song Shin (1998).
102. Scherer and Ross (1990) provide other cases. For example, the New York Central-Pennsylvania Railroad merger promised cost savings of about 4 per cent, but the actual results from the merger were much increased costs eventually leading to a quasi-nationalization.
103. See note 52.
104. See note 52.
105. For example, the merger between Pharmacia and Upjohn is estimated to have cost 1.6 billion dollars during the three years 1995–97 (Affärsvärlden 1998).
106. Moreover, according to preamble 13, the Commission must place its appraisal within the general framework of the achievement of the fundamental objectives referred to in Article 2 of the Treaty, including that of strengthening the Community's economic and social cohesion, referred to in Article 130a.
107. The same point was made by Neven et al. (1993, p. 62). They argue that the wording of the merger regulation is somewhat odd, since it suggests that the efficiency defence can be used only when there is no conflict between efficiency and competition; that is when an efficiency defence is unnecessary.
108. Additionally, in cases brought under Article 86, the Commission has a dominance test and efficiency gains will not justify the abuse of a dominant position. Under Article 85, by contrast, any agreement which restricts competition will have to demonstrate efficiency benefits in direct proportion to the degree of competition which is restricted.
109. Most economists would probably use this definition.
110. There are a few reasons why a horizontal merger would not reduce competition, such as if the merger triggers immediate entry, or if one of the firms is failing, or if the firms colluded perfectly before the merger.
111. This definition has at least implicitly been used in much antitrust literature.
112. Interpreting the Regulation this way, 'not form an obstacle to competition' and 'to consumers' advantage' are synonymous.
113. Cost savings are *per se* desirable. However, cost savings can have negative side-effects. In particular, if two firms merge and thereby lower their variable costs, they become a tougher competitor. Actually, if the cost reduction is big enough, the merger may imply that competitors are driven out of the market, or that new entry is blocked. In this sense, cost savings may be anti-competitive (price increasing). In this context, it is interesting to note that (for example) technical advantages are considered relevant in the assessment of dominance (see for example Hoffman La Roche vs. Commission).
114. Our review of the EU practice revealed that the efficiency defence under Article 81(3) of the Treaty of Rome may be more far-reaching than the efficiency defence that could be constructed under Article 2(1)(b) of the merger regulation.
115. See note 52.

REFERENCES

Adams, Walter and James W. Brock (1988), 'Reaganomics and the transmogrification of the merger policy', *Antitrust Bulletin*, **33**, 339–59.

Affärsvärlden (1998), Sjuka Pharmacia & Upjohn, 25 February, pp. 6–7.

Akhavein, Jalal D., Allen N. Berger and David B. Humphrey (1997), 'The effects of megamergers on efficiency and prices: evidence from a bank profit function', *Review of Industrial Organization*; **12**(1), pp. 95–139.

Anderson, Simon P., André de Palma and Jacques-Francois Thisse (1992), *Discrete Choice Theory of Product Differentiation*, Cambridge, MA: The MIT Press.

Areeda, P.A. and D.F. Turner (1980), *Antitrust Law: An Analysis of Antitrust Principles and Their Application*, Boston: Little Brown.

Arrow, Kenneth (1962), 'Economic welfare and the allocation of resources for inventions', in R. Nelson (ed.), *The Rate and Direction of Inventive Activity*, Princeton, NJ: Princeton University Press, pp. 609–25.

Asplund, Markus and Richard Sandin (1996a), 'Competition in interrelated markets: an empirical study', Stockholm School of Economics.

Asplund, Markus and Richard Sandin (1996b), 'Estimating the number of firms and capacity in small markets', Stockholm School of Economics.

d'Aspremont, Claude and Alexis Jacquemin (1989), 'Cooperative and Noncooperative R&D in Duopoly with Spillovers', *American Economic Review*, **78**(5), December, 1133–37.

Bagnoli, Mark and Barton L. Lipman (1988), 'Successful takeovers without exclusion', *Review of Financial Studies*, **1**(1) (Spring), 89–110.

Baker, J.B. and T.F. Bresnahan (1985), 'The gains from merger or collusion in product-differentiated industries', *Journal of Industrial Economics*, **23**(4), 427–43.

Baker, J. and T. Bresnahan (1988), 'Estimating the residual demand curve facing a single firm', *International Journal of Industrial Organization*, **6**(3), 283–300.

Baldwin, John and Paul Gorecki (1990), 'Mergers placed in the context of firm turnover', in Bureau of the Consensus, *1990 Annual Research Conference, Proceedings*, Washington DC: US Department of Commerce, pp. 53–73.

Banerjee, Ajeyo and Woodrow E. Eckard (1998), 'Are mega-mergers anticompetitive? evidence from the first great merger wave', *Rand Journal of Economics*, **29**(4) Winter, 803–27.

Barros, Pedro P. and Luis M.B. Cabral (1994), 'Merger policy in open economies', *European Economic Review*, **38**(5) (May), 1994, 1041–55.

Barton, David M. and Roger Sherman (1984), 'The price and profit effects of horizontal merger: a case study', *Journal of Industrial Economics*, **33**(2), 165–77.

Becker, Brian E. (1995), 'Union rents as a source of takeover gains among target shareholders', *Industrial and Labor Relations Review*, **49**(1) (October), 3–19.

Berger, Allen N. and David B. Humphrey (1992), 'Megamergers in banking and the use of cost efficiency as an antitrust defense', *Antitrust Bulletin*, **37**(3) (fall), 541–600.

Berger, Allen N. and David B. Humphrey (1997), 'The effects of megamergers on efficiency and prices: evidence from a bank profit function', *Review of Industrial Organization*, **12**, 95–139.

Berkovitch, Elazar and M.P. Narayanan (1993), 'Motives for takeovers: an empirical investigation', *Journal of Financial and Quantitative Analysis*, **28**(3) (September), 347–62.

Berry, Steven, James Levinsohn and Ariel Pakes (1995), 'Automobile prices in market equilibrium', *Econometrica*, **63**(4), 841–90.

Besanko, David and Daniel F. Spulber (1993), 'Contested mergers and equilibrium antitrust policy', *Journal of Law, Economics and Organization*, **9**(1) (April), 1–29.

Bettendorf, L. and F. Verboven (2000), 'Incomplete transmission of coffee bean prices: evidence from the Netherlands', *European Review of Agricultural Economics*, **27**, 1–16.

Bian, L. and D. McFetridge (1995), 'Implications of alternate efficiency standards in merger analysis', Department of Economics mimeo, Carleton University, Ottawa.

Bian, L. and D.G. McFetridge (1997), 'Efficiency standards for profitable mergers', Department of Economics mimeo, Carleton University, Ottawa.

Borenstein, Severin (1990), 'Airline mergers, airport dominance, and market power', *American Economic Review*, **80**(2) (May), 400–404.

Bradley, Michael, Anand Desai and E. Han Kim (1988), 'Synergistic gains from corporate acquisitions and their division between the stockholders of target and acquiring firms', *Journal of Financial Economics*, **21**(1) (May), 3–40.

Brander, James A. and Barbara J. Spencer (1989), 'Moral hazard and limited liability: implications for the theory of the firm', *International Economic Review*, **30**(4) (November), 833–49.

Bresnahan, T. (1981), 'Departures from marginal-cost pricing in the American automobile industry: estimates for 1977–1978', *Journal of Econometrics*, **17**, 201–27.

Bresnahan, Timothy F. (1989), 'Empirical studies of industries with market power', in: Richard Schmalensee and Robert D. Willig (eds), *Handbook of Industrial Organization*, vol 2, *Handbooks in Economics, no. 10*, Amsterdam, Oxford and Tokyo: North-Holland, pp. 1011–57.

Bresnahan, Timothy F. and Peter C. Reiss (1990), 'Entry in monopoly markets', *Review of Economic Studies*, **57**(4), 531–53.

Bresnahan, Timothy F. and Peter C. Reiss (1991), 'Entry and competition in concentrated markets', *Journal of Political Economy*, **99**(5) (October), 977–1009.

Bridgeman, John S. (1999), 'Merger efficiency – fact or fiction?', speech given at Keele University, 3 February, accessed at www.oft.gov.uk/html/rsearch/sp-arch/spe5–99.htm.

Brueckner, Jan K. and Pablo T. Spiller (1991), 'Competition and mergers in airline networks', *International Journal of Industrial Organization*, **9**(3), 323–42.

Cable, J.R., J.P.R. Palfrey and J.W. Runge (1980), 'Federal Republic of Germany, 1964–1974', in D.C. Mueller (ed.), *The Determinants and Effects of Mergers: an International Comparison*, Cambridge, MA: Oelgeschlager, Gunn & Hain, pp. 99–132.

Camesasca, Peter D. (1999), 'The explicit efficiency defence in merger control: does it make the difference?', *European Compeition Law Review*, **1**, 14–28.

Caves, Richard E. (1989), 'Mergers, takeovers, and economic efficiency: foresight vs. hindsight', *International Journal of Industrial Organization*, special issue, **7**(1) (March), 151–74.

Caves, Richard E. and David R. Barton (1990), *Efficiency in U.S. manufacturing industries*, Cambridge, MA and London: MIT Press.

Coate, Malcolm B. and Fred S. McChesney (1992), 'Enforcement of the US merger guidelines. Empirical evidence on FTC enforcement of the merger guidelines', *Economic Enquiry*, **30**, 277–93.

Cohen, Wesley M. and Richard C. Levin (1989), 'Empirical studies of innovation and market structure', in Richard Schmalensee and Robert D. Willig (eds), *Handbook of Industrial Organization*, vol 2, *Handbooks in Economics*, no 10, Amsterdam, Oxford and Tokyo: North-Holland, pages 1060–107.

Compte, Olivier, Frédéric Jenny and Patrick Rey (2002), 'Capacity constraints, mergers and collusion', *European Economic Review*, **46**(1), 433–72.

Cosh, Andrew, Alan Hughes and Ajit Sing (1980), 'The causes and effects of takeovers in the United Kingdom: an empirical investigation for the late 1960s at the microeconomic level', in D.C. Mueller (ed.), *The Determinants and Effects of Mergers: an International Comparison*, Cambridge, MA: Oelgeschlager, Gunn & Hain, 1980, pp. 227–270.

Cotterill, Ronald W. (1986), 'Market power in the retail food industry: evidence from Vermont', *Review of Economics and Statistics*; **68**(3) (August), 379–86.

Cotterill, Ronald W. (1990), 'Food mergers: implications for performance and policy', *Review of Industrial Organization*, **5**(2), 189–202.
Crampton, P. (1994), 'Alternative approaches to competition law: consumers' surplus, total surplus, total welfare and non-efficiency goals', *World Competition*, **17**, 55–86.
Davidson, Carl and Raymond Deneckere (1984), 'Horizontal Mergers and Collusive Behavior', *International Journal of Industrial Organization*, **2**(2) June 1984, pages 117–32.
Deneckere, Raymond and Carl Davidson (1985a), 'Incentives to form coalitions with Bertrand competition', *Rand Journal of Economics*, **16**(4) (Winter), 1985, pages 473–86.
Deneckere, Raymond and Carl Davidson (1985b), 'Coalition formation in noncooperative oligopoly models', *mimeo*.
DePrano, Michael E. and Jeffrey B. Nugent (1969), 'Economies as an antitrust defense: comment', *American Economic Review*, **59**, 947–53.
Eckbo, B. Espen (1983), 'Horizontal mergers, collusion, and stockholder wealth', *Journal of Financial Economics*, **11**(1–4), 241–73.
Eckbo, B. Espen and P. Wier (1985), 'Anti-merger policy under the Hart-Scott-Rodino Act: a reexamination of the market power hypothesis', *Journal of Law and Economics*, **28**, 119–49.
European Commission (1980), *Ninth Report on Competition Policy*, Brussels and Luxembourg: EC Commission.
European Commission (1988), 'The Economics of 1992', *European Economy*, 35.
European Commission (1996), contribution of the European Commission in 'Competition policy and efficiency claims in horizontal agreements', document OCDE/GD(96)65, prepared for the Organisation for Economic Co-operation and Development's Competition Policy Roundtables, Paris, pp. 53–7.
European Court of Justice (1998), judgement of the court of 31 March, joined cases C-68/94 and C-30/95, European Court Reports, page I – 01375.
Farrell, Joseph and Carl Shapiro (1990), 'Horizontal mergers: an equilibrium analysis', *American Economic Review*, **80**(1) (March), 107–26.
Federal Trade Commission (1996), 'Anticipating the 21st century: competition policy in the new high-tech, global market place', FTC staff report, Washington DC.
Feenstra, Robert C. (1989), 'Symmetric pass-through of tariffs and exchange rates under imperfect competition: an empirical test', *Journal of International Economics*, **27**(1–2) (August), 25–45.
Feenstra, Robert C., Joseph E. Gagnon and Michael M. Knetter (1996), 'Market share and exchange rate pass-through in world automobile trade', *Journal of International Economics*, **40**(1–2) (February), 187–207.
Fisher, Alan A. (1987), 'Horizontal mergers: triage and treatment', *Journal of Economic Perspectives*, **1**, 23–40.
Fisher, Alan A. and Robert H. Lande (1983), 'Efficiency Considerations in Merger Enforcement', *California Law Review*, **71**, (6) (December), 1580–1696.
Fisher, Alan A. Frederick I. Johnson and Robert H. Lande (1989), 'Price Effects of Horizontal Mergers', *California Law Review,* **77**, (July), 777–827.
Fridolfsson, Sven-Olof and Johan Stennek (2000), 'Why event studies do not detect anti-competitive mergers', Research Institute for Industrial Economics working paper no. 542, Stockholm.

Fridolfsson, Sven-Olof and Johan Stennek (2005). 'Why mergers reduce profits, and raise share prices – a theory of preemptive mergers', forthcoming in *Journal of the European Economic Association.*

Friedman, James (1971), 'A noncooperative equilibrium for supergames', *Review of Economic Studies*, **28**, 1–12.

Froeb, Luke M. and Gregory J. Werden (1996), 'Simulating the effects of mergers among noncooperative oligopolists', in Hal Varian (ed.), *Computational economics and Finance: Modeling and Analysis with Mathematica*, Santa Clara, CA: Springer-Verlag (Telos), chapter 8.

Galbraith, John Kenneth (1952), *American Capitalism: The Concept of Countervailing Power*, Boston: Houghton Mifflin.

Gal-Or, Esther (1988), 'The informational advantages or disadvantages of horizontal mergers', *International Economic Review*, **29**(4) (November), 639–61.

Geithman, Frederick E., Howard P. Marvel and Leonard W. Weiss (1981), 'Concentration, price and critical concentration ratios', *Review of Economics and Statistics*, **63**(3) (August), 346–53.

Gilbert, Richard J. and David M.G. Newberry (1982), 'Preemptive patenting and the persistence of monopoly', *American Economic Review*, **72**(3), 514–26.

Gilbert, Richard J. and David M.G. Newberry (1984a), 'Uncertain innovation and the persistence of monopoly: comment', *American Economic Review*, **74**(1), 238–42.

Gilbert, Richard J. and David M.G. Newberry (1984b), 'Preemptive patenting and the persistence of monopoly: reply', *American Economic Review*, **74**(1), 251–53.

Gokhale, Jagadeesh, Erica L. Groshen and David Neumark (1995), 'Do hostile takeovers reduce extramarginal wage payments?', *Review of Economics and Statistics*, **77**(3) (August), 470–85.

Goldberg, Lawrence (1973), 'The effect of conglomorate merges on competition', *Journal of Law and Economics*, **16**, 137–158.

Goldberg, Pinelopi Koujianou and Michael M. Knetter (1997), 'Goods prices and exchange rates: what have we learned?', *Journal of Economic Literature*, **35**(3) (September), 1243–72.

Goldberg, Pinelopi Koujianou and Frank Verboven (1998), 'The evolution of international price dispersion in the European car market', Centre for Economic Policy Research discussion paper 2029, London.

Gowrisankaran, Gautam (1999), 'A dynamic model of endogenous horizontal mergers', *Rand Journal of Economics*, **30**(1) (Spring), 56–83.

Grossman, S.J. and O.D. Hart (1980a), 'Disclosure laws and takeover bids', *Journal of Finance*, **35**(2) (May), 323–34.

Grossman, Sanford and Oliver Hart (1980b), 'Takeover bids, the free rider problem, and the theory of the corporation', *The Bell Journal of Economics*, **11**, 42–64.

Grossman, Sanford J. and Oliver D. Hart (1982), 'Corporate financial structure and managerial incentives', in J. McCall (ed.), *The Economics of Information and Uncertainty*, Chicago: The University of Chicago Press.

Harrington, Joseph E., Jr. (1991), 'The determination of price and output quotas in a heterogeneous cartel', *International Economic Review*, **32**(4) (November), 767–92.

Hart, Oliver D. (1983), 'The market mechanism as an incentive scheme', *Bell Journal of Economics*, **14**(2) (Autumn), 366–82.

Hausman, J. (1996), 'Valuation of new goods under perfect and imperfect competition', in T. Bresnahan and R. Gordon (eds), *The Economics of New Goods,*

Studies in Income and Wealth, vol 58, Chicago: National Bureau of Economic Research, pp. 209–37.

Hausman, Jerry, Gregory Leonard and J. Douglas Zona (1994), 'Competitive analysis with differentiated products', *Annales d'Economie et de Statistique*, **34**.

Hay, George A. and Gregory J. Werden (1993), 'Horizontal mergers: law, policy, and economics', *American Economic Review*, **83**(2) (May), 173–77.

Healy, Paul M., Krishna G. Palepu and Richard S. Ruback (1992), 'Does corporate performance improve after mergers?', *Journal of Financial Economics*, **31**(2) (April), 135–75.

Hekmat, Ali (1995), 'The effects of different types of mergers on union and non-union wages in the United States', *Journal of Economics* (Missouri Valley Economics Association); **21**(1) (Spring), 65–9.

Hermalin, Benjamin E. (1992), 'The effects of competition on executive behavior', *Rand Journal of Economics*, **23**(3) (Autumn), 350–65.

Holmstrom, Bengt (1982), 'Moral hazard in teams', *Bell Journal of Economics*, **13**(2) (Autumn), 324–40.

Holmstrom, Bengt R. and Jean Tirole (1989), 'The theory of the firm', in Richard Schmalensee and Robert D. Willig (eds), *Handbook of industrial organization*, vol 1, *Handbooks in Economics, no. 10*, Amsterdam, Oxford and Tokyo: North-Holland, 61–133.

Horn, Henrik, Harald Lang and Stefan Lundgren (1994), 'Competition, long run contracts and internal inefficiencies in firms', *European Economic Review*, **38**(2) (February), 213–33.

Horn, Henrik, Harald Lang and Stefan Lundgren (1995), 'Managerial effort incentives, X-inefficiency and international trade', *European Economic Review*, **39**(1) (January), 117–38.

Horn, Henrik and Lars Persson (1996), 'Endogenous mergers in an international oligopoly', mimeo, Institute for International Economic Study, Stockholm University, March.

Horn, Henrik and Lars Persson (1997), 'Endogenous mergers in concentrated markets', Centre for Economic Policy Reserch discussion paper no. 1544, London.

Hovenkamp, Herbert (1994), *Federal Antitrust Policy*, St. Paul, MI: West Publishing Company.

Houston, Joel F. and Michael D Ryngaert (1994), 'The overall gains from large bank mergers', *Journal of Banking and Finance*, **18**(6) (December), 1155–76.

Ikedi, Katsuhiko and Noriyuki Doi (1983), 'The performance of merging firms in Japanese manufacturing industry', *Journal of Industrial Economics*, **31**, 257–266.

Jacquemin, Alexis (1997), 'Theories of industrial organisation and competition policy: what are the links?', in *Economic Science, An Art or An Asset*?, Cheltenham, UK, and Lyme, USA: Edward Elgar.

Jarrell, Gregg A., James A.M. Brickley and Jeffry Netter (1988), 'The market for corporate control: the empirical evidence since 1980', *Journal of Economic Perspectives*, **2**(1) (Winter), 49–68.

Jenny, F. (1997), 'Antitrust in a global economy', in B. Hawk (ed.), *International Antitrust Law and Policy*, Fordham Corporate Law Institute.

Jenny, Frederic and André-Paul Weber (1980), 'France, 1962–1972', in D.C. Mueller (ed.), *The Determinants and Effects of Mergers: an International Comparison*, Cambridge: MA: Oelgeschlager, Gunn & Hain, pp. 133–62.

Jensen, Michael C. and Richard S. Ruback (1983), 'The market for corporate control: the scientific evidence', *Journal of Financial Economics*, **11**(1–4) (April), 5–50.

Kamien, Morton I. and Israel Zang (1990), 'The limits of monopolization through acquisition', *Quarterly Journal of Economics*, **105**(2) (May), 465–99.

Kamien, Morton I. and Israel Zang (1991), 'Competitively cost advantageous mergers and monopolization', *Game and Economic Behavior,* **3**(3) (August), 323–38.

Kamien, Morton I. and Israel Zang (1993), 'Monopolization by sequential acquisition', *Journal of Law, Economics and Organization*, **9**(2), (October), 205–29.

Kim, E. Han and Vijay Singal (1993), 'Mergers and market power: evidence from the airline industry', *American Economic Review*, **83**(3) (June), 549–69.

Kinne, Konstanze (1998), 'The "efficiency defence" in the U.S. American Merger Policy', Hamburg Institut für Wirtchaftsforschung (HWWA) Diskussionspapier 67.

Kitching, John (1967), 'Why do mergers miscarry?', *Harvard Business Review*, **45**, 87–90.

Kole, Stacy R. and Kenneth Lehn (1997), 'Workforce integration and the dissipation of value in mergers: the case of USAir's acquisition of Piedmont Aviation', University of Rochester financial research and policy working paper series FR97–07.

Kumps, Anne-Marie and Robert Wtterwulghe (1980), 'Belgium, 1962–1974', in D.C. Mueller (ed.), *The Determinants and Effects of Mergers: An International Comparison*, Cambridge, MA: Oelgeschlager, Gunn & Hain, pp. 67–98.

Kwoka, J. and F. Warren-Boulton (1986), 'Efficiencies, failing firms, and alternatives to merger: a policy synthesis', *Antitrust Bulletin*, **31**, 431–450.

Lamm, R. McFall (1981), 'Prices and concentration in the food retailing industry', *Journal of Industrial Economics*, **30**(1) (September), 67–78.

Leibenstein, Harvey (1966), 'Allocative efficiency vs. "X-efficiency"', *American Economic Review*, **56**, 392–415.

Lever, Jeremy (1999), 'The development of British competition law: a complete overhaul and harmonization', lecture given at Science Centre Berlin, 9 March.

Lichtenberg, Frank R. (1992), 'Industrial de-diversification and its consequences for productivity', *Journal of Economic Behavior and Organization*, **18**, 427–38.

Manne, Henry G. (1965), 'Mergers and the market for corporate control', *Journal of Political Economy*, **73**, 110–120.

Marris, R. (1964), *The Economic Theory of Managerial Capitalism*, New York: Free Press of Glencoe.

Martin, Stephen (1993), 'Endogenous firm efficiency in a Cournot principal-agent model', *Journal of Economic Theory*, **59**(2) (April), 445–50.

Marvel, Howard P. (1978), 'Competition and price levels in the retail gasoline market', *Review of Economics and Statistics*, **6**(2) (May), 252–58.

McAfee, R. Preston and Michael A. Williams (1988), 'Can event studies detect anticompetitive mergers?', *Economics Letters*, **28**(2), 199–203.

McAfee, R. Preston and Michael A. Williams (1992), 'Horizontal mergers and antitrust policy', *Journal of Industrial Economics*, **40**(2) (June), 181–87.

McCorriston, S., C.W. Morgan and A.J. Rayner (1998), 'Processing technology, market power, and price transmission', *Journal of Agricultural Economics*, **49**, 185–201.

McFetridge, Donald G. (1998), 'Merger enforcement under the Competition Act after 10 years', *Review of Industrial Organization*, **13**, 25–56.

Meeks, Geoffrey (1977), *Disappointing Marriage: A Study of the Gains from Merger*, Cambridge: Cambridge University Press.

Morgan, Eleanor J. (1996), 'The treatment of oligopoly under the European merger control regulation', *Antitrust Bulletin*, Spring, 203–46.
Mueller, Dennis C. (ed.) (1980a), *The Determinants and Effects of Mergers: An International Comparison*, Cambridge, MA: Oelgeschlager, Gunn & Hain.
Mueller, Dennis C. (1980b), 'The United States, 1962–1972', in D.C. Mueller, (ed.), *The Determinants and Effects of Mergers: an International Comparison*, Cambridge, MA: Oelgeschlager, Gunn & Hain, 299–314.
Mueller, Dennis C. (1983), 'The determinants of persistent profits', study for the Bureau of Economics, Federal Trade Commission, Washington D.C.
Mueller, Dennis C. (1985), 'Mergers and market share', *Review of Economics and Statistics*, **67**(2), 259–67.
Mueller, Dennis C. (1993), 'Merger policy and the 1992 merger guidelines', *Review of Industrial Organization*, **8**(2), 151–62.
Mueller, Dennis C. (1997), 'Merger policy in the United States', *Review of Industrial Organization*, **12**, 655–85.
Nalebuff, Barry J. and Joseph E. Stiglitz (1983), 'Information, competition, and markets', *American Economic Review*, **73**(2) (May), 278–83.
Neumark, David and Steven A. Sharpe (1996), 'Rents and quasi rents in the wage structure: evidence from hostile takeovers', *Industrial Relations*, **35**(2) (April), 145–79.
Neven, Damien, Robin Nuttall and Paul Seabright (1993), *Merger in Daylight, The Economics and Politics of European Merger Control*, London: Centre for Economic Policy Research.
Nevo, Aviv (1998), 'Measuring market power in the ready-to-eat cereal industry', National Bureau for Economic Research working paper no. 6387, Cambridge, MA.
Panzar, John C. (1989), 'Technological determinants of firm and industry structure', in Richard Schmalensee and Robert D. Willig (eds), *Handbook of Industrial Organization*, vol 1, *Handbooks in Economics, no. 10*, Amsterdam, Oxford and Tokyo: North-Holland, pp. 3–59.
Peer, Henk (1980), 'The Netherlands, 1962–1973', in D.C. Mueller (ed.), *The Determinants and Effects of Mergers: An International Comparison*, Cambridge, MA: Oelgeschlager, Gunn & Hain, pp. 163–92.
Peoples, James, Ali Hekmat and A.H. Moini (1993), 'Corporate mergers and union wage premiums', *Journal of Economics and Finance*, **17**(2), 65–75.
Perry, Martin K. (1989), 'Vertical integration: determinants and effects', in Richard Schmalensee and Robert D. Willig (eds), *Handbook of Industrial Organization*, vol 1, *Handbooks in Economics, no. 10*, Amsterdam, Oxford and Tokyo: North-Holland, pp. 185–255.
Persson, Lars (1997a), 'The auctioning of a failing firm', mimeo, Institute for International Economic Studies, Stockholm University.
Persson, Lars (1997b), 'Predation and mergers: is merger law counter productive?', mimeo, Institute for International Economic Studies, Stockholm University.
Pitovsky, Robert (1998), 'Efficiencies in defence of mergers: 18 months after', remarks given at *George Mason Law Review* antitrust symposium The Changing Face of Efficiency, 16 October, accessed at www.ftc.gov/speeches/pitovsky/pitofeff.htm.
Rau, P. Raghavendra and Theo Vermaelen (1998), 'Glamour, value and the post-acquisition performance of acquiring firms', *Journal of Financial Economics*, **49**, 223–53.

Ravenscraft, David J. and Frederic M. Scherer (1987), *Mergers, Sell-offs, and Economic Efficiency*, Washington, DC: Brookings Institution.

Reinganum, Jennifer F. (1983), 'Uncertain innovation and the persistence of monopoly', *American Economic Review*, **73**(4) (September), 741–48.

Reitzes, J.D. and D.T. Levy (1992), 'Anticompetitive effects of mergers with localized competition', *Journal of Law and Economics*, **8**, 427–40.

Reitzes, James D. and David T. Levy (1995), 'Price discrimination and mergers', *Canadian Journal of Economics*, **28**(2), 427–36.

Roll, Richard (1986), 'The Hubris hypothesis of corporate takeovers', *Journal of Business*, **59**(2Part 1) (April), 197–216.

Rosen, Sherwin (1974), 'Hedonic prices and implicit markets: product differentiation in pure competition', *Journal of Political Economy*, **82**, 34–55.

Rowley, J. William and Donald I. Baker (1996), *International Mergers – The Antitrust Process*, 2nd edn, London: Sweet & Maxwell.

Rydén, Bengt and Jan-Olof Edberg (1980), 'Large mergers in Sweden, 1962–1976', in D.C. Mueller (ed.), *The Determinants and Effects of Mergers: An International Comparison*, Cambridge, MA: Oelgeschlager, Gunn & Hain, pp. 193–226.

Salant, Stephen W., Sheldon Switzer and Robert J. Reynolds (1983), 'Losses from horizontal merger: the effects of an exogenous change in industry structure on Cournot-Nash equilibrium', *Quarterly Journal of Economics*, **98**(2) (May), 185–99.

Saloner, Garth (1987), 'Predation, mergers, and incomplete information', *Rand Journal of Economics*, **18**(2) (Summer), 165–86.

Salop, Steven C. (1987), 'Symposium on mergers and antitrust', *Journal of Economic Perspectives*, **1**(2) (Fall), 3–12.

Scharfstein, David (1988a), 'Product-market competition and managerial slack', *Rand Journal of Economics*, **19**(1) (Spring), 147–55.

Scharfstein, David (1988b), 'The disciplinary role of takeovers', *Review of Economic Studies*, **55**(2) (April), 185–99.

Scherer, Frederick M. (1980), *Industrial Market Structure and Economic Performance*, 2nd edn, Chicago: Rand McNally College Publishing Company.

Scherer F.M. (1991), 'Merger analysis, industrial organization theory, and merger guidelines: comment', *Brookings Papers on Economic Activity (Microeconomics 1991)*, 323–27.

Scherer, F.M., Alan Backstein, Erich Kaufer and R.D. Murphy (1975), *The Economics of Multi-Plant Operation: An International Comparison Study*, Cambridge, MA: Harvard University Press.

Scherer, F.M. and David Ross (1990), *Industrial Market Structure and Economic Performance*, 3rd edn, Boston: Houghton Mifflin Company.

Schmalensee, Richard (1987), 'Competitive advantage and collusive optima', *International Journal of Industrial Organization*; **5**(4) (December), 351–67.

Schmalensee, Richard (1989), 'Inter-industry studies of structure and performance', in Richard Schmalensee and Robert D. Willig (eds), *Handbook of Industrial Organization*, vol 2, *Handbooks in Economics, no. 10*, Amsterdam, Oxford and Tokyo: North-Holland, pp. 951–1009.

Schmidt, Klaus (1997), 'Managerial incentives and product market competition', *Review of Economic Studies*, **64**(2) (April), 191–213.

Schumann, Laurence (1993), 'Patterns of abnormal returns and the competitive effects of horizontal mergers', *Review of Industrial Organization*, **8**(6) (December), 1993, 679–96.

Schumpeter, Joseph A. (1942), *Capitalism, Socialism, and Democracy*, New York: Harper.

Schwert, G. William (1996), 'Markup pricing in mergers and acquisitions', *Journal of Financial Economics*, **41**(2) (June), 153–92.

Shleifer, Andrei and Robert W. Vishny (1986), 'Large shareholders and corporate control', *Journal of Political Economy*, **94**(3), 461–88.

Shleifer, Andrei and Robert W. Vishny (1988), 'Value maximization and the acquisition process', *Journal of Economic Perspectives*, **2**(1), 7–20.

Shughart II, W. and R. Tollison (1985), 'The welfare basis of the "failing company" doctrine', *Antitrust Bulletin*, **30**, 357–364.

Singal, Vijay (1996), 'Airline mergers and competition: an integration of stock and product price effects', *Journal of Business*, **69**(2) (April), 233–68.

Sleuwaegen, Leo (1994), 'The relevant antitrust market', in *Competition and Integration: Community Merger Control Policy, European Economy no. 57*, Brussels: European Commission.

Snyder, Christopher (1996), 'A dynamic theory of countervailing power', *Rand Journal of Economics*, **27**, 747–69.

Song Shin, Hyun (1998), 'Adversarial and inquisitorial procedures in arbitration', *Rand Journal of Economics*, **29**(2), 378–405.

Stennek, Johan (2000), 'Competition increases X-efficiency – a limited liability mechanism', *European Economic Review*, **44**(9), 1727–44.

Stennek, Johan (2001), 'Mergers without synergies may increase consumer welfare', Research Institute of Industrial Economics working paper no. 558, Stockholm University.

Stigler, George J. (1950), 'Monopoly and oligopoly by merger', *American Economic Review, Papers and Proceedings*, **40**, 23–34.

Stigler, George (1964), 'A theory of oligopoly', *Journal of Political Economy*, **72**, 44–61.

Stillman, Robert (1983), 'Examining Antitrust Policy toward Horizontal Mergers', *Journal of Financial Economics*, **11**(1–4) (April).

Stockum, Steve (1993), 'The efficiencies defense for horizontal mergers: what is the government's standard?', *Antitrust Law Journal*, **61**, 829–55.

Stulz, Rene M., Ralph A. Walkling and Moon H. Song (1990), 'The distribution of target ownership and the division of gains in successful takeovers', *Journal of Finance*, **45**(3) (July), 817–33.

Tirole, Jean (1988), *The Theory of Industrial Organisation*, Cambridge, MA: MIT Press.

US Department of Justice and Federal Trade Commission (1997), *Horizontal Merger Guidelines*, Washington, DC: US Department of Justice, April.

von Ungern-Sternberg, T. (1995), 'Countervailing power revisited', *International Journal of Industrial Organization*, **14**, 507–20.

Verboven, Frank (1995), 'Corporate restructuring in a collusive oligopoly', *International Journal of Industrial Organization*, **13**(3) (September), 335–54.

Verboven, Frank (1996), 'International price discrimination in the European car market', *Rand Journal of Economics*, **27**(2) (Summer), 240–68.

Verboven, Frank (1998), 'The markets for gasoline and diesel cars in Europe', CEPR discussion paper 2069, London.

Weiss, Avi (1992), 'Using the efficiencies defense in horizontal mergers', *The Antitrust Bulletin*, **37**(1), 123–132.

Werden, G. (1996), 'A robust test for consumer welfare enhancing mergers among sellers of differentiated products', *Journal of Industrial Economics*, **54**, 409–13.

Werden, Gregory J. and Luke M. Froeb (1994), 'The effects of mergers in differentiated products industries: logit demand and merger policy', *Journal of Law, Economics, and Organization*, **10**(2), 407–26.

Werden, Gregory J. and Luke M. Froeb (1996), 'Simulation as an alternative to structural merger policy in differentiated products industries', in Malcolm B. Coate and Andrew N. Kleit (eds), *The Economics of the Antitrust Process*, Topics in Regulatory Economics and Policy Series, Boston; Dordrecht and London: Kluwer Academic, pages 65–88.

Werden, Gregory J. and Luke M. Froeb (1998), 'The entry-inducing effects of horizontal mergers: an exploratory analysis', *Journal of Industrial Economics*, **46**(4), 525–43.

Werden, Gregory J., Andrew S. Joskow and Richard I. Johnson (1991), 'The effects of mergers on price and output: two case studies from the airline industry', *Managerial and Decision Economics*, **12**(5), 341–52.

Whish, Richard (1993), *Competition Law,* 3rd edn, London: Butterworths.

White, L.J. (1987), 'Antitrust and merger policy: a review and critique', *Journal of Economic Perspectives*, **1**, 13–22.

Williamson, Oliver E. (1968), 'Economies as an antitrust defence: the welfare tradeoffs', *American Economic Review*, **58**, 18–36.

Williamson, Oliver E. (1969), 'Economies as an antitrust defense: reply', *American Economic Review*, **59**, 954–59.

Willig, R. (1991), 'Merger analysis, industrial organization theory, and merger guidelines', in *Brookings Papers on Economic Activity – Microeconomics*, pp. 281–332.

4. Merger control and enterprise competitiveness: empirical analysis and policy recommendations

Johan Stennek and Frank Verboven

This chapter studies the importance of efficiency gains from horizontal mergers. A general theme throughout the chapter is that efficiency gains, and their pass-on to consumers, may vary substantially from merger to merger. For this reason it seems appropriate to reconsider current practice in European merger control, which does not allow the merging parties to appeal to an efficiency defence. We provide a detailed examination of two main parts of an efficiency analysis. The first part of the chapter considers the presence of efficiencies from mergers, with a focus on economies of scale. The second part considers the pass-on of efficiencies to consumers in the form of lower prices. In a final section, we develop an alternative approach based on the concept of the diversion ratio.

1. ECONOMIES OF SCALE

1.1 The Importance of Scale Economies

For a horizontal merger to benefit consumers and the economy as a whole it must reduce the firms' costs or generate some other form of efficiency gain. Cost savings are also one of many important determinants of enterprise competitiveness. One of the most important sources of cost savings is economies of scale.

The aim of this chapter is to investigate to what extent mergers are likely to generate cost savings through better exploitation of scale economies. This information is an important input to the discussion about the pros and cons of introducing an efficiency defence in the merger regulation. For this purpose we review the theoretical and empirical literature on scale economies. As will be demonstrated below, this literature contains information that is useful for the appropriate design of merger control. As always, however, there are more questions than answers. A second purpose of this review is therefore to carefully point out where the existing literature is still insufficient.

The first part is theoretical (section 1.2). We begin our analysis with an intuitive discussion of the sources of scale economies (section 1.2.1). Without constructing a full typology, we compile a 'checklist' of the most common sources of scale economies, such as mechanization and specialization achieved through division of labour. We also draw a sharp distinction between technologically determined economies of scale and overheads such as advertising and R&D. Next, we define the term scale economies more rigorously (section 1.2.2). This section is an important input for discussing the relationship between mergers and production costs, and also for presenting the empirical literature. The primary complication in defining scale economies arises when firms produce more than one product.

We then discuss the theoretical relation between mergers and scale economies (section 1.2.3). That is, if production is characterized by scale economies, under what conditions can they be exploited by means of merger? Drawing on the theory of sub-additivity, we analyse the effect of mergers on cost in the long run – when firms can adjust their capital stock freely. Our main conclusion is that theoretical analysis can establish the conditions under which mergers generate cost savings, related to scale economies, in the long run. Such conditions may also include a test for merger-specificity. To make these conditions operational for antitrust authorities, more research is needed, however.

In section 1.3, we review the empirical literature on economies of scale. We both provide a brief overview of empirical estimates of scale economies in several industries, and discuss the methodologies that are used. However, since many of these studies are rather old, and since scale economies in many industries are likely to change over time, as a result of technological development, we do not attempt to provide a detailed account of the measurement of scale economies for all industries. Rather, the main purpose is to extract the general conclusions from this literature that are relevant for the discussion of an efficiency defence in merger control. Our main finding is that the variability of scale economies across industries supports the idea that cost savings should be evaluated on a case-by-case basis. We also argue that the methods used in the economic literature should also be useful in antitrust cases.

The summary and conclusions from the theoretical part are found in section 1.2.4, and for the empirical part in section 1.3.5.

1.2 Theory of Scale Economies and Mergers

1.2.1 Sources of scale economies

A production process has scale economies if the unit cost of production is lower when more is produced. Scale economies may be product-specific, that is, associated with the volume of a single product produced and sold; plant-specific, that is, associated with the total output (of possibly many different products) of an entire plant; and firm-specific (or multiple-plant) economies, associated with a firm's operations of several plants.

Economies of scale may also be attributed to the different activities performed by the firm, such as production, purchasing, marketing and R&D. For reasons to be explained below, it is convenient to treat economies of scale arising from advertising and R&D as different from other 'production economies'. Therefore production economies are discussed in section 1.2.1.1 and advertising and R&D are discussed in section 1.2.1.2.

1.2.1.1 Production

Economies of scale

There are many different reasons why unit costs may decrease with volume. We list and explain some of the most commonly mentioned examples. The presentation is not intended to be complete, and the list should not be taken as a typology of scale economies.

1. *Indivisibilities* In some industries some factors of production are indivisible. The most well-known example is the critical mass in nuclear power generation. At the critical mass, some amount of electricity is generated. Producing less than this amount of electricity means that the cost of the indivisible input is spread over fewer units of output, implying a higher cost per unit of electricity. There are also many examples of indivisible tasks. Starting up a production run requires that machines are fine-tuned for the process. If this set-up cost is spread over many units, average cost is reduced. Some management and marketing tasks have to be done independent of the scale of operation. Again, the more units produced, the lower is the cost per unit.
2. *Specialization* Division of labour and specialization is an important source of scale economies. A production process may require 100 different tasks. If the firm has 5 employees each must perform 20 tasks on average. If the firm has 1000 employees, no individual will be required to perform more than one, and all may become more skilled at what they are doing – a specialist. Specialization may be both 'horizontal' into different production tasks and 'vertical' into production

and management tasks. Specialization may be an important part of multiple-plant economies. That is, if production of different products is allocated to different plants, specialization can be driven further than if all products are produced within one plant.

3. *Mechanization* Producing at a larger scale may make it meaningful to let a machine do some tasks. However, at a low volume the machine may perhaps only be used part of the time, and not pay its cost (indivisibility). The larger the volumes the more specialized the tools that can be used. Also parts can be transferred automatically between the different processing stages.
4. *Massed reserves* A manufacturer may need to keep one machine in reserve so that a breakdown does not interrupt production. Assume for example that a delivery failure of at most 1 per cent is acceptable. Assume also that a machine produces ten units if it works. Then, having just one machine does not enable the firm to write any contracts that satisfy the failure threshold. However, with two machines it can contract ten units (see Mulligan 1983).
5. *Increased dimensions* In many industries, the output of a processing unit tends to be roughly proportional to the volume of the unit, while the amount of materials and construction work is linked to the surface area of the unit's reaction chambers, storage tanks, connecting pipes, and so on. Since the area of a sphere varies as the two-thirds power of volume, there are considerable scale economies to be gained.
6. *Learning by doing* Economies of scale have an important dynamic dimension. There is considerable empirical support for the so-called learning curve, which shows that unit cost falls with cumulative output.

Economies of scope

Traditional economic analysis has concentrated on single-product firms. But, in reality, most businesses produce many products, and many antitrust issues involve only these enterprises. In recent years, economists and policymakers dealing with antitrust issues have increasingly recognized the need for a theory that can be used to evaluate the efficiency of market structures in industries dominated by a few firms operating in a diverse range of markets. For such firms, conventional concepts such as economies of scale do not adequately capture the complexity of the situation (Bailey and Friedlaender 1982). The new literature has introduced as a complement to the old concept of scale economies, the new concept of 'economies of scope', which measures the cost advantages to firms of providing a large number of diversified products as against specializing in the production of a single output.

1. *Joint production* Marshallian joint production exists if one or more factors of production are public input. That is, once acquired for use in producing one good, they are costlessly available for use in the production of others (up to some limit). For example, crude oil is a public input to producing petrol and asphalt. Similarly, certain tasks may be public tasks. For example, if the production of two outputs requires the same input, then the acquisition of these inputs may be cheaper if performed within the same firm. The reason for this may be both due to increased monopsony power but also real cost savings, for example, related to improved quality control.
2. *Indivisibilities* Indivisible input or tasks may not only result in economies of scale, but also in scope economies. Assembly line production with human labour is often economical for single-product runs of large scale. Combinations of robots and computer-controlled machine tools bring the benefits of large 'scale' to the production of small batches, even when demand for every particular product variety is small. Here it is the robot's ability to switch from one task to another that counts. The robot production line has the flexibility to handle a variety of separate products, and makes it possible to take advantage of the economies associated with automation.
3. *Networking* In the aviation industry, the cost of providing a seat is much lower on big planes than on small planes. This provides an incentive for airlines to organize the provision of services by offering a networking arrangement involving one-stop service. Individuals with a variety of destinations are boarded on a single larger plane. Planes from a variety of origins then stop at a central airport at approximately the same time. The passengers to each of the destinations are then combined, again making it possible to use larger planes. If one firm is more efficient in co-ordinating the scheduling of services to a variety of city-pair markets than several small firms, there are economies of scope (see Bailey and Friedlaender 1982).
4. *Knowledge-sharing* Multiple-product firms may be more cost efficient than combinations of single-product firms when several industries require similar know-how but there are transaction difficulties affecting the transfer of that know-how (how can one sell information without disclosing it?) (see Teece 1980).

Economies of vertical integration

There are many reasons why vertical integration or disintegration may affect the costs of production. For an overview of the economic literature on vertical integration, see Perry (1989). The aim of the present survey is to discuss efficiency gains associated with horizontal mergers. For such mergers, the degree of vertical integration remains constant. For this reason we will not discuss the economies and diseconomies associated with vertical integration. The reason for this limitation is that vertical mergers and horizontal mergers have very different effects on both competition and costs. This limitation obviously means that the conclusions drawn from this report are only valid for horizontal mergers.

Diseconomies of scale

While economies of scale may be common in many industries, especially at low levels of volume, there are also good reasons to believe that for large firms the opposite can be true: a reduction of the scale of a large firm may lower unit cost. In that case there exists diseconomies of scale. What are the sources of such diseconomies?

1. *Management is a fixed factor* Any firm must have some individual who assumes executive authority and responsibility. This individual has a limited time and cognitive capacity. At the same time, a large plant or firm is more difficult to manage than a small plant or firm. Thus, the larger the firm becomes, the more tasks must be delegated to lower level management, implying more loss of control.
2. *Transportation costs* If a firm produces more it must sell more implying that it may be necessary to reach out to more distant customers. Thus, including transportation costs, there may be diseconomies to plant size. The importance of transportation costs as a check to scale economies depends on the technological level in transportation. The more efficient transportation is, the more profitable it is to exploit economies of scale.
3. *Worker alienation* There exists psychological evidence that shows that workers become less satisfied with their jobs in larger plants (see Scherer and Ross 1990).

Since the sources of economies of scale become less important at a large scale, the sources of diseconomies of scale become especially relevant at large levels of production.[1]

Several of the above points reveal that a useful understanding of economies and diseconomies of scale and scope requires research going behind the neo-classical production function theory. Is knowledge sharing a valid argument for a conglomerate merger? To analyse that issue requires an analysis of the relative efficiency with which knowledge can be transferred between organizations and within organizations.

Unfortunately, there does not exist any research showing which effects are most important in different industries. The reason for this shortcoming is that most economic research, both theoretical and empirical, views the technology as given. There are few studies trying to go behind the production function and explain its properties. (An exception is provided by the theoretical studies deriving decreasing returns to scale as a result of loss of control.) Similarly, no research has been undertaken allowing us to identify which types of mergers generate the different types of scale economies.

1.2.1.2 Advertising and R&D

In recent times, the economic literature has started to draw a sharp distinction between technologically determined economies of scale and overheads such as advertising and R&D. The above discussion of scale economies concerns the first type: technologically determined economies of scale. The important point about these scale economies, for example economies due to mechanization, is that they are given by the firms' technological knowledge, and that they thus are fixed at any point in time. Merger policy may affect the extent to which such scale economies can be exploited by the firms. Merger policy does not, however, affect the existence of such scale economies.

There will also be economies of scale in advertising if some minimum amount of public exposure is needed before a sales campaign makes any impression at all on the public. The cost of this minimum amount of advertising is a fixed cost – the same, no matter how much the firm sells. Like any fixed cost, it will create a region of economies of scale in which the fixed advertising cost is spread over more and more units of output. Similarly, there may be a minimum amount of R&D that is needed before production can start. Again, spreading this fixed cost over a larger volume reduces unit cost.[2]

A merger may eliminate the duplication of certain R&D (and advertising) activities, and the production of the different products may benefit from knowledge sharing. The crucial question is: should such elimination of duplicated R&D activities be counted as cost saving, to be used as an efficiency defence?

The complicating factor is that advertising and R&D outlays are not fixed to the firms. Rather, they are choice variables to the firms. The firms actively use advertising and R&D outlays as competitive weapons. Their levels are determined in response to, for example, the size of the market and the intensity of price competition.[3] Thus, a merger will not only allow knowledge sharing. It will also affect the firms' incentives to undertake R&D activities and to produce new knowledge. Potentially, a merger may induce an anti-competitive reduction in the amount of R&D.

Unfortunately, however, the economic literature has only to a small degree studied the effect of mergers in industries where advertising and

R&D are important. As a result it is not clear how one should treat the endogenous scale economies that are an inalienable aspect of such industries. On the one hand, one may argue that an efficiency defence should take into account the fact that a merger may allow advertising and R&D outlays to be spread over larger volumes. The argument is clear: lower unit cost is good for welfare. On the other hand, by doing so, merger policy will affect the firms' incentives to undertake R&D and to advertise their products. On this point, the arguments are not clear. We do not know exactly how competition policy will affect the firms' incentives for advertising and R&D, and we do not understand the welfare consequences of changing the firms' incentives in these respects.[4]

However, this state of the art is very unfortunate since it is the industries that are characterized by high advertising or R&D intensities that are highly concentrated in the EU. Thus, it is in these industries that horizontal mergers are more likely to raise competitive concerns. Among the 20 most concentrated (3-digit level) industries in the EU (industries where the five largest firms' aggregate market share is over 33.3 per cent, for example, optical instruments, computers and tobacco) 16 are characterized by either high advertising or R&D intensity. Among the 25 least concentrated (3-digit level) industries in the EU (industries where the five largest firms' aggregate market share is lower than 10 per cent, for example, wooden furniture and clothing) none is characterized by high advertising or R&D intensity (see Davies and Lyons 1996, ch. 4).

Nevertheless, due to the lack of economic knowledge, the following discussion must be primarily confined to the case of exogenous scale economies (in the same way as any discussion of the anti-competitive effects of merger must be confined to price competition and leave out R&D competition).

1.2.2 Definition of scale economies[5]

A single-product technology is characterized by increasing returns to scale if unit cost is lower the larger is production. There are constant returns to scale if unit cost is unaffected by volume, and there are decreasing returns if unit cost is increased as production is increased.

This section presents the more rigorous definitions of the notion of economies of scale that are used in the economic literature. Rigour and formalism is necessary because the simple and intuitive idea of scale economies turns out to be rather complex in the context of multi-product firms. The more precise definition of returns to scale is also a necessary basis for discussing the relationship between returns to scale and mergers in section 1.2.3, and a necessary basis for the empirical studies reviewed in section 1.3.

To arrive at a useful definition of scale economies, that includes the various possible sources of scale economies discussed in section 1.2.1, it is convenient to start from the concept of the production technology, which is central to the economic theory of the firm. The production technology may be represented either by its production function or by its cost function (cf. duality theory). The production function describes which input–output combinations are technically feasible to the firm. The cost function describes the minimum cost for producing any possible output level (given the technology and factor prices).[6] There are several reasons for focusing on the cost function rather than the production function in defining economies of scale. The first reason is that it is the shape of the cost function that plays a key role in determining firm and industry structure. Second, in exploring the potential sources of increasing returns (section 1.2.1) it was recognized that the lower unit cost achieved at larger size is associated with organizing production in a way that is different from how production can be organized in small plants or firms. An inevitable aspect of scale economies is therefore that factor proportions in large plants must be different from factor proportions in small plants. For example, increased mechanization implies a higher capital/labour ratio. However, as will be discussed below, the definitions of scale economies based on the production function require factor proportions to be held constant. Such a restriction would eliminate much of the economies of large scale.[7] A third reason for focusing on the cost function is also motivated by empirical considerations.[8]

1.2.2.1 Single-product firms

The production function

In order to define scale economies precisely we need to introduce some formal notation. Consider a firm producing a single output. The quantity of this output is denoted q. The firm uses n different inputs, for example different types of labour and different types of machinery. The quantity used of input i is denoted x_i, and the complete consumption of resources is described by the vector of inputs $x=(x_1, \ldots, x_n)$. The technology is described by the so-called production function. We write

$$q=Q(x).$$

The production function should be interpreted as saying: if the firm uses input vector x, then it can produce at most $Q(x)$. Likewise, if the firm wants to produce q, then it needs to consume an input vector x such that $q=Q(x)$.

The cost function

If a firm wants to produce quantity q, there are two conditions that must be fulfilled in order for the firm to be cost-efficient. First, it should not use more inputs than is necessary to produce q. This amount of necessary inputs is given by the production function. Second, the firm should use different inputs in a proportion that balances their relative contribution to production to their relative prices. Let w_i denote the price of input x_i, and $w=(w_1, \ldots, w_n)$ the vector of all n input prices. The cost-efficient quantity of input i depends on how much the firm is producing (that is q) and on the prevailing factor prices (that is w). Normally, the higher q is, or the lower the price w_i is, the more the firm will use of the input x_i. We write $X_i(q,w)$ to indicate the cost-efficient quantity of input i and that it depends on quantity and factor prices. Similarly $X(q,w)$ denotes the whole vector of cost-efficient inputs. The total cost of a cost-efficient firm is given by the sum of expenditures for all efficiently chosen input, that is

$$c = C(q, w) = \sum_{i=1}^{n} w_i X_i(q, w)$$

where c is the production cost, and C is the cost function.

Economies of scale

In order to define scale economies, we first need to define two more basic notions, namely average cost and marginal cost. Average cost (or unit cost) is simply the cost per unit produced, that is

$$AC(q) = \frac{C(q)}{q}.$$

Marginal cost, which we denote by $MC(q)$, is the cost of the last unit. More formally, marginal cost is given by the derivative of the cost function. That is:

$$MC(q) = \frac{dC(q)}{dq}.$$

The definition of scale economies that we use in this chapter is based on the cost function. The intuitive idea that we want to capture is that there are increasing returns to scale if unit cost falls when output is increased. Similarly, there are decreasing returns to scale if unit cost is increasing when output is increased, and there are constant returns to scale if a change in output does not affect unit cost. Thus, economies of scale are determined by how unit cost is affected by a change in production. More formally, we say that there are increasing returns to scale if

$$\frac{dAC(q)}{dq} < 0,$$

and that there are decreasing returns to scale if the inequality is reversed. Note that this requirement is equivalent to marginal cost being lower than average cost, that is,

$$MC(q) < AC(q).$$

The reason is simple. If the cost of producing an additional unit is lower than the average cost of previous units, then producing the additional unit lowers average cost.[9] If the first unit produced costs €10 and the marginal cost of producing the second unit is €5, then average cost is reduced from €10 to €7.5 if production is increased from one to two units. Actually, the degree of scale economies is defined as the ratio between average and marginal costs, that is:

$$S(q, w) = \frac{AC(q, w)}{MC(q, w)}.$$

Returns to scale are said to be increasing, constant or decreasing as S is greater than, equal to or less than one. Note that S depends on quantity (and input prices). In particular, it is common that average cost is falling at low output levels, then constant, and finally increasing at high output levels. In that case, S would be larger than one at small output levels, and smaller than one at high output levels.

Economies of scale II

To complicate matters, there is a second definition of scale economies that is often used in the literature. This definition is based on the production function. Given a proportional increase in all input levels, does output increase more or less than proportionally? If output increases more (less), there are increasing (decreasing) returns to scale. For example, if output more than doubles when all inputs are doubled, there are scale economies. Formally, we define the elasticity of scale:

$$E(q, x) = \sum_{i=1}^{n} \frac{dQ}{Q} \Big/ \frac{dx_i}{x_i}.$$

If $E(q,x) > 1$ production increases more than input, and there are increasing returns to scale. To complicate matters even further, the production function-based measure $E(q,x)$ need not coincide with the cost function-based measure $S(q,w)$. The reason is that it may not be cost efficient to increase all inputs by the same proportion to achieve the increase in production. Thus, even if per unit cost does not fall when output is increased by expanding all inputs proportionally, it may decrease when inputs are chosen in a cost-minimizing manner. For example, it may be that doubling both capital and labour only leads to a doubling of output (that is, constant returns to scale, as defined from the production function). However, it may be that the larger output level can also be produced using a more capital intensive technique. If the more capital intensive technique is less costly, cost is not doubled as output is doubled (that is, increasing returns to scale, as defined from the cost function).[10]

Minimum efficient scale

We will sometimes assume that average cost is first decreasing and then increasing as the volume increases so that the average cost curve is 'U-shaped'. This corresponds to assuming that for low output levels there are increasing returns to scale and for large output levels there are decreasing returns to scale. Other times we will assume that the average cost curve is 'L-shaped', so that there are only increasing and then constant returns to scale. The lowest quantity where average cost is minimised is called the minimum efficient scale (MES). The MES is an important determinant for industry and firm structure.

A potentially complicating factor is that the measurement of scale economies depends on input prices. Hence, even if the technological knowledge is the same in two countries, returns to scale and the minimum efficient scale may well differ between the two countries, if input prices differ. As a consequence, one cannot take empirical estimates of MES from one country as a standard in another country without investigating the importance of factor price differentials.

1.2.2.2 Multiple-product firms

Most firms of reasonable size produce more than one product, and mergers normally create a firm that produces an even wider range of products. For this reason it is also essential to define what is meant by economies of scale for multiple-product firms. Unfortunately, however, the simplicity of the definition from the single firm case is lost. The reason is that in the multiple-product context, a firm's cost is not only determined by the scale of each single output, but also by the composition (or mix) of output. The concept of scale economies can be generalized to a multiple-product setting by considering two related measures, namely product-specific economies of scale and so-called ray economies of scale. Ray economies of scale refer to the behaviour of costs as the production levels of all the products in a given bundle are increased in the same proportion. However, to fully capture the effect of changes in the composition of output on cost, we also need to introduce the concepts of economies of scope and of so-called transray convexity.

To keep the formalism at a minimum we consider the case of a two-product technology. Let q_1 denote the quantity produced of the first good and q_2 the quantity produced of the second good. The cost of producing the two products is given by $C(q_1, q_2)$ for any output combination $q = (q_1, q_2)$. Naturally, the cost also depends on factor prices w, but for simplicity we do not indicate this dependence explicitly. The cost of producing an additional unit of output (that is, marginal cost) is denoted by $MC_1(q_1, q_2)$ and $MC_2(q_1, q_2)$ for products one and two respectively. It is customary to define the degree of scale economies as:

$$S(q_1, q_2) = \frac{C(q_1, q_2)}{q_1 MC_1(q_1, q_2) + q_2 MC_2(q_1, q_2)}.$$

This definition is a natural extension of the definition in the single-product case.[11] In the case of multi-product firms, however, the notion of scale economies is more complex than in the single-product case. In particular, overall scale economies $S(q, w)$ is constituted by three different parts, namely the product-specific economies of scale for products one and two respectively, and the economies of scope. We will discuss product-specific scale economies and economies of scope in turn.

Although the discussion in this chapter is confined to the case of two products, all definitions and results are valid also for the general case of m types of output. The discussion here is completely focused on the cost function. However, it is possible to define scale economies in the multiple-product case directly from the technology.

Product-specific economies of scale

The incremental cost of a single product, say q_1, is defined as the extra cost of producing q_1 given that q_2 is already produced, i.e. as $C_1(q_1, q_2) = C(q_1, q_2) - C(0, q_2)$. The average incremental cost of product one is defined as $AC_1(q_1, q_2) = C(q_1, q_2)/q_1$. The degree of scale economies specific to product one is defined as

$$S_1(q_1, q_2) = \frac{AC_1(q_1, q_2)}{MC_1(q_1, q_2)}.$$

Product-specific returns to scale are said to be increasing (decreasing) if S_1 is larger (smaller) than one.

There exists a relationship between the overall degree of scale economies S and the degree of product-specific scale economies S_i. This relation can be described by the following equation:

$$S(q_1, q_2) = \frac{[a_1 S_1(q_1, q_2) + a_2 S_2(q_1, q_2)]}{b} \tag{4.1}$$

where

$$a_1 = \frac{MC_1}{MC_1 + MC_2}, \quad a_2 = \frac{MC_2}{MC_1 + MC_2}$$

and

$$b = \frac{C_1(q_1, q_2) + C_2(q_1, q_2)}{C(q_1, q_2)}.$$

Hence, the numerator in equation (4.1) is the weighted average of the product specific returns to scale. Thus, the more product-specific economies of scope there are (large S_1 and S_2), the more overall scale economies there are (large S). The denominator is related to the so-called economies of scope.

Economies of scope

In addition to the more familiar cost savings deriving from the scale of operations, cost savings may also result from the production of several different outputs in one firm rather than each being produced in its own specialized firm. A striking example of scope economies is that it is cheaper to produce different forms of oil derivatives in one firm than in several specialized firms. We say that there exist economies of scope if the cost of producing q_1 and q_2 is smaller in the case where production of both goods is carried out in a single firm, rather than in two separate firms. Formally, there are economies of scope if

$$C(q_1, q_2) < C(q_1, 0) + C(0, q_2).$$

The degree of economies of scope measures the percentage increase in cost that would result from dividing the production of q_1 and q_2 into two separate firms, rather than producing both goods in a single firm. Thus, the degree of economies of scope is defined as

$$SC(q_1, q_2) = \frac{C(q_1, 0) + C(0, q_2) - C(q_1, q_2)}{C(q_1, q_2)}.$$

For example, if the cost of production is 50 per cent larger in a case the two products are produced separately, then SC = 0.5 (that is 50 per cent). If there are economies of scope, then $SC > 0$. If there are diseconomies of scope, then $SC < 0$. One can show that since all products have positive incremental cost, then $SC(q_1, q_2) < 1$.[12]

Using the definition of scope economies, overall scale economies (that is, equation (1)) can be written as

$$S(q_1, q_2) = \frac{a_1 S_1(q_1, q_2) + a_2 S_2(q_1, q_2)}{1 - SC(q_1, q_2)}. \tag{4.1'}$$

Equation (4.1′) shows that the overall scale economies are determined by three factors: the product-specific scale economies of products one and two, and the economies of scope. If the product-specific economies of scale are strong, overall scale economies also tend to, but need not, be strong. Actually, even if there are product-specific economies of scale, there may be overall diseconomies of scale. The reason is that there may be diseconomies of scope, and that the diseconomies of scope may dominate the product-specific economies of scale. For example, if $S_1\ (q_1,q_2)= S_2\ (q_1, q_2) = 2$, there are overall diseconomies of scale if $SC(q_1,q_2) < -1$.[13]

Another concept to describe how cost depends on the composition of output is transray convexity. Roughly speaking, the cost function is transray convex if, as a firm changes the composition of output while holding fixed the level of some aggregate measure of output, costs will be lower for diverse rather than specialized output mixes. For example, transray convexity would imply that

$$\frac{1}{2}C(q_1, 0) + \frac{1}{2}C(0, q_2) > C\left(\frac{q_1}{2}, \frac{q_2}{2}\right).$$

Minimum efficient scale

In the multi-product case, the idea of minimum efficient scale (MES) also becomes more complex. To discuss MES, one defines the so-called ray-average cost, by

$$RAC(q_1, q_2) = \frac{C(q_1, q_2)}{b_1 q_1 + b_2 q_2}.$$

The weights b_1 and b_2 are two completely arbitrary numbers. Their only role is to combine the two quantities into a single measure of size.

Although this construct is artificial, it surprisingly makes it possible to formally relate the slope of the *RAC* curve to the degree of scale economies. In particular, one may consider how *RAC* is affected by increased production, assuming that the production of the two products is increased by the same proportion (for example 10 per cent). One may show that, if ray-average cost is reduced (increased) as production is increased in a proportional way, there are increasing (decreasing) returns to scale.

Using the notion of ray-average cost, one may talk about 'U-shaped' average cost also in the case of multiple products. The ray-average cost is U-shaped if ray-average cost is first decreasing, then constant, and eventually increasing. The only complication in the multiple-product case is that the size of the output bundle at which scale economies are exhausted will tend to vary with the composition of the bundle. For example, it may be that the MES is small if the firm is producing a relatively large amount of product one in comparison to product two, while MES is large if the firm is producing relatively more of product two. Thus, instead of a single point of minimum efficient scale, there will be a 'locus' of such points.

1.2.2.3 Multiple-plant firms

In the discussion above we did not distinguish between the production technology of a firm and the production technology of a single plant. However, since firms can and often do run more than one plant, the distinction is important.

Some scale economies can already be achieved in a single plant. Examples may be some economies related to specialization and mechanization. When the scale economies at the plant level are exhausted, for example due to worker alienation, it is better to divide production between two plants than to produce all output in a single plant. Another reason for dividing production between two plants is that having two plants located in different geographical markets can lower transportation costs. The fact that plant economies are exhausted does not imply, however, that firm size is optimal. The reason is that there may exist economies of scale associated with running more than one plant in each firm. For example purchasing of inputs may be better organized by one centralized department than to have one small department in each plant. However, multi-plant economies are also often exhausted above some level. The cost per unit will rise when the firm operates so many plants that corporate management starts to lose track of local operations.

The relation between the plant-level cost function and the firm-level cost function can be described in the following way. Assume that a firm has only one plant, and denote the cost function for this firm by $C(q, 1)$ where 1 indicates that the firm has only one plant. This cost function (which may also be called plant-level cost function) indicates the lowest cost of producing q units of output in a single plant. Similarly $C(q, 2)$ indicates the lowest cost of producing q units in a two-plant firm. This cost function presupposes that the production is allocated in a cost-minimizing way between the two plants. It also presumes that the firm has chosen to organize the purchasing function (joint or separate) in the most cost-efficient way. The cost function at the firm level is given by

$$C^{\mathrm{Firm}}(q) = \min_n\{C(q,1), C(q,2), \ldots, C(q,n), \ldots\}$$

Thus, the firm-level cost function is built on the assumption that the firm, for any output level q, will choose the number of plants that produces q at the lowest possible cost.

The discussion in the previous sections defines what we mean by economies of scale for a given cost function. Actually, that discussion is general enough to be interpreted both in terms of the technology of a single plant and in terms of the technology of a firm. In the first case the cost function $C(q)$ in the above section should be understood as $C(q,1)$ and in the second case it should be understood as $C^{\mathrm{Firm}}(q)$. Thus, there is no reason to have a separate discussion of measures of scale economies at the firm level.

In some empirical studies of economies of scale associated with $C^{\mathrm{Firm}}(q)$ it is found that there is one region of low output in which unit cost is falling, and that there is one region of high output where unit cost is increasing. There is also a substantial range of intermediary output levels where unit cost is at the minimum. The reason for this shape may be multi-plant operations. The scale economies at low output levels may have to do with scale economies at the plant level. Then there is the intermediate region where the firm operates a number of plants at minimum cost. Finally there is a region where multi-plant diseconomies are important.

In the context of mergers one should distinguish between plant-level scale economies and firm-level economies. Most economies of scale at the plant level can only be exploited in the long run, when the use of capital can be adjusted. In contrast, important multi-plant economies of scale may be exploited even in the short run. First, the elimination of administrative duplication may not require long lags. Second, there are also often product-specific economies of multi-plant operation. If a firm produces different products in a single plant, production time will inevitably be lost as assembly lines are switched from one product to another. By operating more than one plant, a firm can specialize the production of high-volume products in single plants. This will reduce downtime due to shifting production, resulting in run-length economies. Run-length economies are important in many industries, including fabric weaving and finishing, shoe making, bottle blowing and bearing manufacturing (Scherer et al. 1975, p. 51). However, it is also important to point out that such short-run gains related to economies of multi-plant operation can be expected to be insufficient for a merger to reduce price. The elimination of duplicated administrative functions affects fixed rather than variable costs. The specialization of production in different plants is an instance of so-called rationalization, which is insufficient to reduce price (Farrell and Shapiro 1990).

1.2.3 Scale economies and mergers

In this section we discuss the relationship between, on the one hand scale economies, and on the other hand the effect of merger on cost. If production is characterized by scale economies, under what conditions can they be exploited by means of merger? In part, this question was analysed by Farrell and Shapiro (1990).[14] However, a limitation in their analysis is that they focus on the case when the capital stock in each plant is fixed – the short run. Drawing on the theory of sub-additivity, we analyse the effect of mergers on cost in the long run – when firms can adjust their capital stock freely.

The short-run analysis of Farrell and Shapiro and the long-run analysis undertaken in this chapter are complements. The first analysis considers the extreme case when the capital stock in every plant is fixed. The second analysis considers the other extreme case when firms freely can adjust their capital. In the long run, cost savings are larger than in the short run. Hence, the latter form of analysis is more likely to produce a positive picture of the effects of the merger. As a consequence, antitrust authorities may reach different decisions regarding a merger, depending on whether they consider the long-run or the short-run effects. To complicate the picture further, it is likely that capital adjustments require different amounts of time in different industries. If the antitrust authority must evaluate the effects of the merger within the first two-year period, long-run analysis may be relevant for some industries and short-run analysis may be relevant for other industries.

A strength with the analysis is that we are able to analyse not only the effect of merger on cost. Using the concept of sub-additivity, we are also able to say if a full merger is the best way to restructure production in order to produce the given output as cheaply as possible (section 1.2.3.3). This is important since there are often several alternatives, short of a full merger, that may reduce cost without imposing all the anti-competitive effects of a horizontal merger. Antitrust authorities are often required to make such a broad evaluation of mergers. The reason is the requirement that cost savings should be merger-specific.

We should also mention that all cost comparisons are made at a given quantity of output. In reality, a merger will affect output for several reasons. The reduction of competition will tend to reduce output. The reduction of cost, on the other hand, will tend to increase production. The net effect may be negative or positive depending on the circumstances. It is customary, however, to decompose the change in cost into two parts. The first part is the change in cost due to increased efficiency. This effect must be measured at some given level production. Following Williamson (1968) the normal procedure is to measure this effect at the level of production chosen by the merged entity. The second part is the change in cost due to the change in quantity. (The second part is normally subtracted from the change in consumers' surplus to generate a measure of the change in deadweight loss resulting from the merger.) However, there are also some limitations in this analysis. Any adjustment costs associated with merger are not included in the analysis.

1.2.3.1 Single-product firms

In the single-product case, economies of scale (in the relevant range) implies that a merger reduces cost. To see this, consider an industry where there are economies of scale up to production of at least q units. In other words:

$$\frac{C(q)}{q} < \frac{C(tq)}{tq} \quad \text{for all } t < 1.$$

That is, the unit cost of producing q is lower than the unit cost of producing only $tq < q$. Consider a merger between two firms, one producing tq and the other producing $(1-t)q$. Thus, they together produce q units. Before the merger the total cost of production is $C(tq) + C((1-t)q)$ and after the merger the total cost of production is $C(q)$. In this case, a merger reduces cost, that is[15]

$$C(q) < C(tq) + C((1-t)q).$$

The reason is simple. Since the unit cost of production is lower at q than at any level below q, it must be less costly to produce $tq + (1-t)q = q$ units in one firm than in two separate firms. Thus, in the single-product case there exists a simple and important relation between scale economies and merger:

Observation 1.1 Economies of scale (in the relevant range) are sufficient for a merger to reduce cost in the long run, in the single-product case.

However, we should emphasize that this analysis suffers from several limitations. First, the analysis does not have anything to say about what happens to cost in the short run, before the input of capital can be changed. Second, the analysis abstracts from any adjustment costs.

The qualifier 'in the relevant range' is important. In many industries the technology is characterized by increasing returns to scale at low production levels, then a segment of approximately constant returns to scale, and eventually, there are diseconomies of scale. In short, the unit cost function is U-shaped. In order for a merger to reduce cost, it is only important that there are scale economies up to the level of production that firms will carry out. Above that level, possible diseconomies of scale will not affect the merger.

Although scale economies are sufficient for a merger to lower cost, it is important to note that scale economies are not necessary for a merger to reduce cost. Here, we will consider two reasons for this to be so. If the two firms have access to different technologies (that is, different knowledge) a merger may also reduce cost in the absence of economies of scale. It may be that both firms have constant returns to scale but that one firm has a superior technology with a lower marginal cost. Then, transferring knowledge to the other plant, or transferring production to the superior plant, lowers cost. It may also be that the two firms have different, but complementary, patents so that a merger expands the production technology to both plants.

A more surprising result is that even if the two firms have access to the same technology, a merger may reduce cost in the presence of diseconomies of scale. Assume that the firms have the cost function $C(q)=a+cq$ for $0<q<y$ and $C(q)=a+b+cq$ for $y<q$, where $a>b>0$. That is, there is a fixed cost (a) associated with production up to y, and then there is an additional fixed cost ($b<a$) associated with production beyond that level. For example, consider a shipping market. In order to ship the quantity $0<q<y$ it is necessary to build a firm including various administrative functions and to invest in one shipment (that is, the fixed cost a is equal to the cost of administration plus the cost of one shipment). In order to ship the quantity $0<q<2y$ it is necessary to invest in a second shipment (that is, the fixed cost b is equal to the cost of one shipment). However, the administration may not need to be duplicated. Then, average cost is increasing as production is expanded from a level slightly lower than y to a level slightly higher than y (a second ship must be bought). Nevertheless, it is cheaper to produce in one firm, than to keep two independent firms since $b<a$ (running only one firm avoids the duplication of administrative costs). Thus:

Observation 1.2 Economies of scale are not necessary for a merger to reduce cost, even if the firms have access to the same technology.

To sum up the case of single output technologies: economies of scale are sufficient, but not necessary, for a horizontal merger to reduce cost in the long run.

1.2.3.2 Multi-product firms

In the multi-product case, economies of scale are not sufficient for a merger to reduce cost. One reason for this is that there may be overall scale economies at the same time as there are diseconomies of scope. In that case, a merger between two formerly separate product lines may increase costs. This fact is demonstrated in a theoretical example (Example 1 in Appendix

1.2.3.4). Thus, despite possible econometric evidence showing the existence of scale economies, a merger would nevertheless increase cost.

More surprising is that economies of scale and economies of scope together do not suffice to guarantee that a merger will reduce cost. This fact is demonstrated in a theoretical example (Example 2 in Appendix 1.2.3.4). The gist of the example is the following. Consider a farmer producing proteins and textile fibres. The farmer can use three processes. The farmer can raise sheep, producing both proteins and fibres (Marshallian joint production). Alternatively, the farmer can grow beans to produce proteins or flax to produce textile fibres. However, since the sheep will destroy the crop, the farmer must fence in the smaller of these operations, which is costly. The presence of a (small) fixed cost entails economies of scale. The economies of scope come from the Marshallian joint production in raising sheep. It is more expensive to produce one unit of fibre and one unit of protein by growing flax and beans. At the same time there is an element of diseconomies of scope due to the negative externality between raising sheep and growing a crop. However, in the example the first effect dominates the latter. To minimize production cost in this case there should be one firm raising sheep to produce proteins and fibres. Then there should be one firm growing either beans or flax depending on whether there is need to produce additional protein or additional fibres. In this way Marshallian joint production is exploited and fencing is avoided. Thus:

Observation 1.3 Economies of scale and economies of scope (in the relevant range), together, do not suffice to guarantee that a merger will reduce cost.

Thus, in the multi-product case, there is no logical connection between economies of scale and cost savings from mergers:

Observation 1.4 Economies of scale are neither necessary nor sufficient for a merger to reduce cost, in the case of multi-product firms.

In view of this result, it is clear that a stronger set of sufficient conditions is required to guarantee that mergers reduce costs. Actually, when pushing this analysis further, it is reasonable to generalize the discussion, and to replace the concept of scale economies with the concept of sub-additivity. This discussion is found in the next section 1.2.3.3.

1.2.3.3 Merger specificity

The above discussion was exclusively focusing on the question of whether a merger reduces cost. From a policy point of view, however, that is not the relevant question. The reason is that in most countries with an efficiency defence, there is a so-called merger specificity clause. According to this requirement, cost reductions cannot save a horizontal merger unless the merger is the least anti-competitive means of achieving the cost savings. Thus, if there exists some alternative restructuring of production, short of a full merger, that achieves the same cost cuts (or more), the merger should not be allowed. In Example 3 in Appendix 1.2.3.4 we show that it may well be that a merger reduces cost as compared to the initial production structure, but that there may exist another restructuring that lowers cost even more. In the example there are two product varieties and two firms that both produce both varieties. A merger would reduce cost due to product-specific economies of scale. However, due to diseconomies of scope, cost would be reduced even further if the two firms specialize in one of the varieties each. This alternative restructuring may also be preferred from a competition point of view, if consumers consider the two varieties as substitutable.

In order to accommodate this complication, the rest of the discussion is not focusing on the question of whether a merger reduces cost. Rather, we ask the question if a merger minimizes the cost of producing a given output (equal to the aggregate output of the two firms before the merger). The central concept in this discussion is so-called strict sub-additivity. To define this concept, consider the case of two products. Assume that we want to produce the quantity q_1 of product one and q_2 of product two. We may divide production in any way we want into k separate firms. Let q_1^2 denote the quantity of product one produced by firm two, and so on. Then,

$$q_1^1 + q_1^2 + \ldots + q_1^k = q_1,$$
$$q_2^1 + q_2^2 + \ldots + q_2^k = q_2.$$

A cost function $C(q_1, q_2)$ is said to be strictly sub-additive in the production of (q_1, q_2) if

$$C(q_1^1, q_2^1) + C(q_1^2, q_2^2) + \ldots + C(q_1^k, q_2^k) > C(q_1, q_2),$$

independent of how production is divided between the k firms, and independent of how many separate firms (that is, k) there are.

Observation 1.5 If the cost function is sub-additive (in the relevant range), a merger reduces cost. Moreover, there does not exist any less concentrated alternative to the merger that reduces cost even more.

Hence, if the merging firms can show that their cost function is sub-additive, they have established that, from the point of view of productive efficiency, a full merger is the best way of organizing the production of (q_1, q_2). Expressed in a different way, sub-additivity but not scale economies is the relevant concept to use in judging if a full merger is the best way of achieving cost efficiency. Naturally, productive efficiency must still be traded off against possible anti-competitive effects.

Still, however, sub-additivity and scale economies are related, and the economic literature contains several sets of sufficient conditions (for example in terms of scale economies) for the cost function to be sub-additive. These conditions may be of practical use to merger control, even though the sufficient conditions are more restrictive than sub-additivity itself. The reason is that it may often be easier to find econometric evidence on for example scale economies than econometric evidence on sub-additivity. The first condition is also intuitively appealing.

Observation 1.6 If (i) there are product-specific economies of scale for all products, and (ii) there are (weak) economies of scope, then the cost function is sub-additive.[16]

Actually one can show that if there are product-specific economies of scale for a particular product, then industry cost minimization requires that production of this good is consolidated in a single firm. Economies of scope implies that all production lines should be allocated within a single firm.

Additional sets of sufficient conditions for sub-additivity, for example in terms of transray convexity, can be found in the literature (see Baumol et al. 1982, ch. 7; Sharkey 1982, ch. 4).

1.2.3.4 Appendix: theoretical examples

The following examples are chosen because of their simplicity. They are not intended to portray real-world merger decisions.

Example 1

This is the simplest possible example to illustrate that economies of scale are not sufficient for a merger to reduce cost. Assume that firms' costs are given by

$$C(q_1, q_2) = \begin{cases} 0 & q_1 = q_2 = 0 \\ f + cq_1 & q_1 > 0, q_2 = 0 \\ f + cq_2 & q_1 = 0, q_2 > 0 \\ f + g + c(q_1 + q_2) & q_1, q_2 > 0 \end{cases}$$

In this case, there are overall economies of scale since $S(q_1,q_2) = 1 + (f + g)/c(q_1 + q_2)$ is larger than one. There are also product-specific economies of scale since $S_1(q_1,q_2) = 1 + g/cq_1$ is larger than one (and similarly for product two). However, there are diseconomies of scope if $g > f$ since then $SC(q_1, q_2) = (f - g)/[f + g + c(q_1 + q_2)] < 0$. In this case, a merger increases cost if the two firms before the merger produced one of the two products each. In particular,

$$C(q_1,q_2) - C(q_1,0) - C(0,q_2) = [f + g + c(q_1,q_2)] - [f + cq_1] - [f + cq_2]$$
$$= g - f > 0$$

Thus, despite possible econometric evidence showing the existence of scale economies, a merger would nevertheless increase cost.

Example 2

To demonstrate the second point (that economies of scale and economies of scope together do not suffice to guarantee that a merger will reduce cost) consider the following example. Raising sheep costs € 10 per animal and yields one unit of protein and one unit of fibre. Growing beans or flax costs €6 per unit of protein or fibre obtained. Fencing costs €1 per unit of the smallest activity. The set-up cost, e, is small. To minimize the cost of producing proteins, p, and fibres, f, the farmer should raise sheep, s. In particular he should raise $s = \min\{p, f\}$ sheep. The farmer must also grow crops, either flax or beans. In particular he must grow the quantity $c = \max\{p, f\} - \min\{p, f\}$. Thus, the cost function is:

$$C(p, f) = 10s + 6c + \min\{s, c\} + e,$$

where the third term is the fencing cost. Due to the fixed cost, e, the cost function exhibits increasing returns to scale everywhere. If the same amount of fibres and proteins are produced in separate firms, the cost is:

$$C(p, 0) + C(0, f) = 6(p + f) + 2e = 6(\max\{p, f\} + \min\{p, f\}) + 2e.$$

The cost function exhibits economies of scope everywhere since:

$$C(p, 0) + C(0, f) - C(p, f) = 2\min\{p, f\} - \min\{\min\{p, f\}, \max\{p, f\}$$
$$- \min\{p, f\}\} + e \geq \min\{p, f\} + e \geq 0$$

Assume now that the market demands more protein than fibres, so that $p > f$. Consider dividing production of (p, f) between two firms with output levels (f, f) and $(p - f, 0)$. This division results in total costs of:

$$C(f, f) + C(p - f, 0) = [10f + e] + [6(p - f) + e].$$

This division of production into two firms lowers cost since:

$$C(f, f) + C(p - f, 0) - C(p, f) = [4f + 6p + 2e] - [10f + 6(p - f) + \min\{f, p - f\} + e] < 0,$$

when e is small. (Remember that the fixed cost is small.) A merger between the two firms would increase cost due to the need for fencing.

Example 3
Consider again the cost function in Example 1 in Section 1.2.3.2. Assume that at the outset, both firms produce both products. Let q_1^2 denote firm two's production of good one, and so on. The firms propose a merger. Such a merger will reduce cost:

$$\begin{aligned} C(q_1^1 + q_1^2, q_2^1 + q_2^2) - C(q_1^1, q_2^1) - C(q_1^2, q_2^2) = \\ &[f + g + c(q_1^1 + q_1^2 + q_2^1 + q_2^2)] - [f + g + c(q_1^1 + q_2^1)] - \\ &[f + g + c(q_1^2 + q_2^2)] \\ &= -(f + g) < 0. \end{aligned}$$

However, if the two firms instead of a merger, agree to specialize in one of the products each, then the costs of production would be reduced even further (this follows immediately from Example 1).

1.2.4 Summary and conclusions

We begin our analysis with an intuitive discussion of the sources of scale economies. A production process is said to have scale economies if the unit cost of production is lower when more is produced. There are several sources of scale economies, such as mechanization and specialization achieved through division of labour. Without constructing a full typology, we compile a 'checklist' of the most common sources of scale economies.

We also draw a sharp distinction between technologically determined economies of scale and overheads such as advertising and R&D. Due to the state of economic knowledge, we are forced to focus this overview primarily on the first type of scale economies. However, we also argue that this state of knowledge is very unsatisfactory. Advertising and R&D are important features of most concentrated European industries.

Next, we define the term 'scale economies' more rigorously. This section is an important input for discussing the relationship between mergers and production costs, and also for presenting the empirical literature. In the economic literature there exist two different definitions of scale economies, one based on the so-called production function, the other based on the so-called cost function. We argue that for the purpose of analysing efficiency gains from mergers, it is vital to use the concept based on the cost function. The reason is that the exploitation of some scale economies (for example, mechanization) requires changing the factor proportions. Such gains are only captured by the concept based on the cost function. The primary complication in defining scale economies arises when firms produce more than one product. In this case, there may exist overall diseconomies of scale even if there are (product-specific) economies of scale for all individual products. The reason is that there may exist so-called diseconomies of scope. Another complication is that the minimum efficient scale of a firm depends on the mix in which the firm produces the different products.

We then discuss the theoretical relation between mergers and scale economies. That is, if production is characterized by scale economies, under what conditions can they be exploited by means of a merger? In part, this question was analysed by Farrell and Shapiro (1990).[17] However, a limitation in their analysis is that they focus on the case when the capital stock in each plant is fixed – the short run. Drawing on the theory of sub-additivity, we analyse the effect of mergers on cost in the long run – when firms can adjust their capital stock freely.

In the single-product case, the relation is rather straightforward. Economies of scale (in the relevant range) are sufficient, but not necessary, for a merger to reduce cost.[18] In the multiple-product case, the primary finding is that the relation between scale economies and mergers is rather complex. Even if there are unexploited scale economies, mergers may well raise rather than reduce cost. A positive finding is that one can establish different sets of sufficient conditions for mergers to reduce cost. These conditions are based on the notion of sub-additivity of the cost function. For example, if there are product-specific economies of scale for all products, and there are economies of scope, then a merger reduces cost. In effect, these theoretical results show that in evaluating the effect of a merger on cost, competition authorities need to take into account both product-specific economies of scale and potential economies of scope. However, in order to make these conditions more precise, additional analysis, similar to that undertaken by Farrell and Shapiro for the short-run case, is needed.

A strength with the analysis is that we are able to analyse more than just the effect of merger on cost. Using the concept of sub-additivity, we are also able to say if a full merger is the best way to restructure production in order to produce the given output as cheaply as possible. This is important since there are often several alternatives, short of a full merger, that may reduce cost without imposing all the anti-competitive effects of a horizontal merger. Antitrust authorities are often required to make such a broad evaluation of mergers. The reason is the requirement that cost savings should be merger-specific.

The short-run analysis of Farrell and Shapiro and the long-run analysis undertaken in this report are complements. The first analysis considers the extreme case when the capital stock in every plant is fixed. The second analysis considers the other extreme case when firms can freely adjust their capital. In the long run, cost savings are larger than in the short run. Hence, the latter form of analysis is more likely to produce a positive picture of the effects of the merger. As a consequence, antitrust authorities may reach different decisions regarding a merger, depending on whether they consider the long-run or the short-run effects. To complicate the picture further, it is likely that capital adjustments require different amounts of time in different industries. Therefore, if the antitrust authority evaluates the effects of the merger within the first two-year period, long-run analysis may be relevant for some industries and short-run analysis may be relevant for other industries.[19]

In sum:

Conclusion Theoretical analysis can establish the conditions under which mergers generate cost savings, related to scale economies, in the long run. Such conditions may also include a test for merger-specificity. To make these conditions fully operational for antitrust authorities, more research is needed.

1.3 Empirical Estimates of Scale Economies

The question that we are interested in answering is to what extent production costs can be reduced as a result of horizontal mergers. Unfortunately, however, there is very little direct empirical evidence on the effect of mergers on cost. The purpose of this section is to review the empirical studies of scale economies in various industries, and to investigate if such evidence can be used to shed indirect light on the likely efficiency gains from mergers.

There are several approaches to measuring cost-scale relationships. One approach has been to analyse profitability as a function of firm size. The attractiveness of this approach is that data on profits at the firm level are relatively easy to collect. However, we will not focus on this approach since profits are affected by so many other circumstances than just scale economies. In particular, since profits are sensitive to market power, and since firm size may well be related to market power, this approach does not seem well suited in the present context of an efficiency defence in merger control, which is all about the relative strength of market power and cost efficiency. A second approach is the so-called survivor test (see Stigler 1958). Firm or plant sizes that survive and gain larger market shares over time are assumed to be efficient, and those that lose market shares over time are considered to be too large or too small. Again, one may suspect that selection operates on profitability (or possibly relative profitability) and hence that it is difficult to separate scale economies from market power using this approach.

In this review we focus on direct estimates of the cost-scale relationship. There are three approaches within this class, namely econometric cost function (or production function) analysis, the mathematical programming approach (DEA), and the engineering approach.

- *Engineering approach* Bain (1956) who covered 20 different industries, undertook the pioneering study. This approach is built on interviews (or questionnaires) with engineers whose profession it is to plan and design new production units and plants.
- *Econometric approach* Economists have used econometric techniques to estimate cost or production functions. The investigation of estimated functions may concern their scale economy properties. In this category we include traditional least-squares econometric production models and stochastic frontiers methods.
- *Mathematical programming approach* This approach is similar to the econometric approach in that the aim is to estimate a frontier cost or production function, using input and output data collected from different firms. However, the so-called data envelopment analysis (DEA) builds on mathematical programming rather than standard statistical techniques.

For a much more detailed (technical) discussion and comparison of the econometric and mathematical programming approaches, see Coelli et al. (1998). A methodological discussion and an extensive survey of the engineering approach can be found in Pratten (1988).

1.3.1 Econometric approach: methodology

This section will review the empirical results from cost-function-based estimates of scale economies. The discussion of the empirical results is sorted by industry. We start with some methodological issues.[20]

Cost vs. production function

One issue is whether to undertake direct estimate of production function, or to estimate a cost function. As we have already argued in section 1.2.2, in the present context the cost-function approach is preferred. It is the cost function that determines industry structure. From an econometric perspective, estimation of a cost function may be preferable since it accounts for the endogeneity of inputs. Another reason is that cost functions are more easily generalized to multiple output situations.[21]

Varying vintage

To estimate a cost function one has to gather data on the cost of production from existing plants operating at varying scales of output. Such data usually relate to plants built at different points in time. The plant and equipment is of varying vintages and the latest plant and equipment may incorporate knowledge which was not available when the earlier units were built. As a result the estimates will usually not reflect the technology of a particular point in time. Expressed in other words, cost differences between different firms may not only reflect varying scale but also differences in vintages.

Aggregation: the homogeneity problem

The early empirical literature on scale economies has been severely criticized on several accounts. According to Gold (1981), the single most important reason for the inadequacies of the early research was the tendency to carry out the analysis at too-high levels of aggregation. Often analysis was carried out at four, three or event two-digit levels of industrial classification. At this level of aggregation firms do not produce homogeneous goods, and comparisons of costs at different 'scales' may reflect differences in products rather than economies of scale. This aggregation prevents conformance with the requirements not only of theory, but of practical evaluations by both industrial executives and government officials.

Sources of scale economies

Researchers have lacked an interest in identifying the sources of scale economies (Gold 1981). The dominant concern has been to mechanically describe the relation between firm or plant size and unit cost. This is unfortunate in the present context. Scale economies may often be achieved in different ways, some of which may be less damaging to competition than mergers. In some cases a joint venture may achieve the gains. Thus, for antitrust authorities to evaluate different alternatives, it should be valuable to have an understanding of the sources of scale economies.

Aggregation: the multiple-product problem

Since most large firms produce a large variety of products, estimation of their cost functions involves a large number of parameters. Due to data limitations, researchers must aggregate the output data in some way. There are two methods that have been used to do so. The typical method in the early literature was to construct a single scalar measure of output by only considering firm revenues. Unfortunately, this approach implicitly imposes the restriction that the so-called transformation rate between different products is constant. In other words, it is assumed that the cost function can be written as $C(q_1, q_2) = \tilde{C}(a_1 q_1 + a_2 q_2)$ where a_1 and a_2 are two constants. As a result, it is impossible to distinguish between different products' product-specific economies of scale. It is also impossible to distinguish between economies of scale and economies of scope.

There is one case in which it is possible to infer properties of C from estimates of $\tilde{C}$. If all firms at all times (included in the sample) produce the same output mix, the economies of scale calculated from $\tilde{C}$ will coincide with the degree of multiple-product economies of scale at the observed product mix. However, it is in general not valid to extrapolate this measure to other product mixes.

The more modern method is the so-called 'hedonic cost function' approach.[22] Assume that we want to estimate the cost function for airlines. Every destination-origin pair is a separate market. Thus, in an economy with 100 cities, there are 9900 different types of output. Thus the cost function $C(q_1, \ldots, q_{9900})$ is likely to contain a very large number of parameters. However, it is likely that passenger miles and the number of cities served by the firm determine the cost for airlines. One may then estimate a hedonic cost function $\tilde{C}(m, c)$ where m is passenger miles and c is the number of cities served. In this case 9900 variables have been turned into only two. After $\tilde{C}$ has been estimated one may indirectly compute measures of scale economies for C. However, this final step is not trivial, and the reasoning behind it is an important contribution in itself (see Caves et al. 1984).

Long- vs. short-run functions

Another empirical problem is that the available data often allow a short-run but not long-run cost function to be estimated. For example, if a cost function is to be estimated using monthly data from a single firm, it would be unrealistic to assume that the firm's capital inputs were adjusted to the cost-minimizing level associated with each month's output level. Unfortunately, the short-run cost function does in general not carry the information needed to analyse economies of scale (see Braeutigam and Daughety 1983).

1.3.2 Econometric approach: empirical estimates

Regulated or formerly regulated industries have been studied much more than many other industries. The primary reason for this is that much more data are available on these industries because of regulatory requirements. In a sense this is fortunate since antitrust issues are especially important in these industries after deregulation. Here we review the development in the trucking and electric power industries that have generated much of the methodological development. However, there have also been econometric studies of the economies of scale of several other industries, including railroads (see Jara-Diaz and Whinston 1981; Jara-Diaz and Cortes 1996), automobiles (see Friedlaender et al. 1983), telecommunications,[23] and others.

Trucking

In empirically analysing the costs of a multiple-product firm, the basic problem is one of aggregation. Since most firms typically produce a wide range of diverse products, it is generally impossible to incorporate all outputs in the analysis, because of the limited number of observations relative to the potential number of parameters that would have to be estimated. For example, trucking output is very heterogeneous. Not only do trucks haul different commodities with different handling requirements, but they also haul them in different shipment sizes, in different loads, and for different lengths of haul. Drawing on theoretical work on production theory, Spady and Friedlaender (1978) attempted to take the composition of output into account by introducing the operating characteristics of the firm explicitly into the cost function. They introduced a so-called hedonic output function that attempted to measure effective output as a function of physical output (q) and the characteristics of that output ($x_1, \ldots, x_m$) where q was measured in ton-miles and the xs represented variables such as shipment size, average load, average length of haul, and so on. Thus, instead of estimating a traditional cost function as $c = C(q, w)$ they estimated a cost function as $c = \tilde{C}(H(q, x), w)$ where $H(q, x)$ represents hedonically adjusted output and w represents a vector of factor prices.

They found that the inclusion of operating characteristics made a significant difference. When costs are estimated using physical output (q) alone, marked economies of scale where found. However, when operating characteristics (the xs) were included, the measured scale economies disappeared. Since larger firms tend to utilize longer hauls and larger shipment sizes, they tend to have lower costs. However, if smaller firms could have the same operating characteristics as large firms, they could presumably achieve comparable advantages. (The small firms in the sample were kept from achieving the operating characteristics of the large firms because of limited regulatory operating rights.)

The study by Spady and Friedlaender (1978) has two important limitations. Due to the specification of the hedonic cost function the operating characteristics (or output composition) are not allowed to affect the substitutability between different factors of production. However, Friedlaender and Spady (1981) solved this problem by specifying the cost function as $c = \tilde{C}(q, x, w)$.

The second limitation is that the aggregate measures of output not only vary with the scale of output but also with its composition. Thus, measures of scale economies based on their approach are necessarily ambiguous since they may reflect the effects of both scale and scope upon costs. Later contributions have resolved this problem. Thus the hedonic cost function approach can be adapted to distinguish between different types of economies of largeness (see the study by Caves et al., 1984).

There is also a study of the trucking industry attempting to distinguish between economies of scale and scope. This study incorporates disaggregated output, but also variables that reflect the configuration and utilization of the network over which the firm operates. Wang Chiang (1981)[24] shows that firms enjoy marked economies of networking. Networks having many connected links and networks permitting direct routing lead to significant saving in costs. These network effects explain much of the economies of scale and scope that Wang Chiang observed.

Electric power

Nerlove (1963) studied economies of scale in electricity generation, using data from 1955.[25] The study is based on modern duality theory. The estimated cost function includes factor prices as arguments. The basic estimation equation was a Cobb–Douglas log-linear specification of the cost function:

$$\ln C = \kappa + (1/\sigma) \ln q + (1/\sigma) \Sigma\, \alpha_i\, [\ln p_i].$$

Here σ is the (single product) degree of scale economies. The p_is refer to the prices of labour, fuel and capital. The sum $\Sigma\alpha_i$ is constrained to equal unity. The main finding is that there exist important economies of scale in electricity generation. In particular the model yielded an estimate of $\sigma \approx 1.4$. That would mean that the firm's cost would exceed its revenues by 40 per cent if its output were priced at marginal cost.

The functional form used restricts the degree of economies of scale to be the same for all output levels. To check the importance of this restriction, Nerlove divided the sample into five output categories. Doing so revealed that the economies of scale are exhausted at large plant sizes. In the largest group there were diseconomies of scale.

Nerlove's study has had a methodological influence in two ways. First, it established the cost function, with its factor price arguments, as the proper framework in which to study economies of scale. Second, it showed that the degree of scale economies declines with output, thereby demonstrating the need for more flexible functional forms than the one used by Nerlove himself.

Christensen and Greene (1976) employ more flexible functional forms, allowing the degree of scale economies to vary with the level of output. In particular, they employed the translog cost function:

$$\ln c = \kappa + \alpha \ln q + \beta [\ln q]^2 + \Sigma\, a_i \ln p_i + \Sigma\Sigma\, b_{ij} \ln p_i \ln p_j + \Sigma\, \gamma_i \ln q \ln p_i.$$

In order for this function to represent a proper cost structure some restrictions on the parameters of the model must be imposed. Using data from 1970, they found that the cost function is U-shaped, with a large segment that is approximately flat. Approximately 45 per cent of the output was produced in the minimum-cost segment.

A problem with the above studies is that they do not take the multiproduct nature of the studied industry into account. Many electric utilities sell natural gas as well. Another complication is that firms producing electricity at peak times incur much higher costs than firms generating electricity off peak. If the peak/off peak mix varies across firms, estimates of the single-output cost function may be biased. Empirical work on multiproduct issues did not begin until the developments reported in the section above had taken place.

Mayo (1984) extends the analysis to incorporate the multiproduct nature of operations. In particular, he allows for two types of output, namely electricity and gas. Using data from 1979, he found that diseconomies of scope set in at small output levels. Chappell and Wilder (1986) used 1981 data for the same sample but left out utilities that generate more than 10 per cent of their electricity using nuclear power plants. In contrast to the earlier results, their estimates indicate product-specific economies of scale and economies of scope that are not exhausted even at very large levels of production. This has triggered a debate whether or not one should include very different techniques (nuclear vs. other) in the same study (see Mayo 1986; Gold 1981; Panzar 1989).

1.3.3 Mathematical programming approach

In the previous sections we have implicitly presumed that all firms are fully efficient. In this section we relax this assumption and describe methods that may be used to estimate so-called production frontier functions and measure the efficiencies of firms relative to these estimated frontiers. The two principal methods that have been used are data envelopment analysis (DEA) and stochastic frontiers. We focus here on the first type. Since the methodology is based on mathematical programming rather than standard econometric analysis it is very different from the methods discussed above.

For simplicity, consider an industry that produces one output q using one input x. Assume that we have data on the inputs used and outputs produced for n firms. The data points are: $(q_1, x_1), \ldots, (q_n, x_n)$.

The essential assumption behind DEA analysis is that the production possibility set is convex. That is, if two input–output combinations (q_1, x_1) and (q_2, x_2) are technically feasible, then also any input–output combination (q, x), where $q = \lambda q_1 + (1-\lambda)q_2$ and $x = \lambda x_1 + (1-\lambda)x_2$ with $0 \leq \lambda \leq 1$, is technically feasible. Due to the convexity assumption, the production frontier can be approximated as the piece-wise linear function that connects the most efficient firms. Next, we can measure the firms' (technical) efficiency and their scale efficiency. The degree of technical efficiency is defined in the following way. Firm one consumed x_1 to produce q_1. If it would have been possible to produce the same quantity q_1 using only $x_1^t < x_1$, then the technical efficiency of the firm is equal to x_1^t/x_1. Note that only if $x_1^t = x_1$ is the technical efficiency 100 per cent. Otherwise it is lower. Note also that the cost of production could have been lowered by $(x_1 - x_1^t)/x_1$ per cent. Thus the degree of technical efficiency directly corresponds to the cost-savings potential. If the efficiency is 90 per cent, cost could be lowered by 10 per cent. The degree of scale inefficiency is defined in a similar way. If it would have been possible to produce the same quantity q_1 using only $x_1^s < x_1^t$ at the most efficient scale, then the firm's scale efficiency is equal to x_1^s/x_1^t. This measure of scale inefficiency is very convenient since it is expressed in terms of how much cost can be reduced if production is carried out at the most efficient scale. One may also note that total efficiency is the product of the technical efficiency and scale efficiency, that is $x_1^s/x_1 = (x_1^s/x_1^t)(x_1^t/x_1)$.

We can illustrate the application of DEA analysis with a study of Australian universities (Coelli 1996).[26] In 1996 the University of New England (UNE) formed a committee to look at the performance of UNE relative to 36 other universities in Australia. Of particular concern was some evidence that suggested that the UNE's administration appeared to be larger than some comparable universities. The study concerned the calendar year 1994. The specification of the outputs of a university administration was a challenging task. But it was decided that the output would be proxied by two measures: the number of students and the number of staff. Some of the results on scale efficiency are reported in Table 4.1.

In total the study found that 14 of 36 universities were operating on a too-low scale with increasing returns to scale, and that 13 of the universities were operating on a too-large scale with decreasing returns to scale. The mean scale efficiency was 0.94 indicating that if universities had been operated at optimal scale they would have been able to save on average 6 per cent (not weighted) of their cost.

Table 4.1 DEA results for the Australian universities study

	Scale efficiency	Type
Australian Catholic University	0.94	Increasing returns
Australian National University	1.00	–
University of New England	0.99	Increasing returns
University of Western Sydney	0.99	Decreasing returns
Mean	0.94	–

Source: Coelli et al. (1998)

1.3.4 Engineering approach

The pioneering study was Bain (1956) who covered 20 different industries. This approach is built on interviews (or questionnaires) with engineers whose profession it is to plan and design new production units and plants. The engineering approach has also been followed by Pratten (1971), Scherer et al. (1975), Weiss (1975) and more recently, by Gasmi et al. (1999). Most of the engineering studies are relatively old, and there are reasons to believe that the estimates for many industries may have changed since the times of the studies. Thus, in our view, there is not much point in presenting a detailed account of the studies at the level of particular industries. Moreover, an extensive survey of the results can be found in Pratten (1988, section 5). Instead we point at the more general implications of these studies for merger control. However, to give some feeling for these studies, we do provide some results from one of them below.

The central concept in the studies based on the engineering approach is the minimum efficient scale (MES). In theory, the MES is the level of output at which unit cost is at its minimum. In practice, the MES is measured as the minimum level of output (or other measure of size) that must be reached in order to have only a 'slight' cost disadvantage compared to the minimum unit cost. The definition of the minimum efficient scale differs between different studies (Pratten 1988). Another source of variation between studies is that some include all types of costs, while others only focus on production costs and exclude selling and distribution costs (for example, Scherer et al. 1975). Still others go even further and exclude development costs.

The engineering studies produce two important measures. First, in order to estimate how much is gained by exploiting scale economies, the studies measure the increase in cost of operating below the minimum efficient scale. For example, the cost may be 10 per cent higher if a plant is operated at half or one third of the MES. Second, in order to measure the implications of scale economies for (the cost efficient) industry structure, the studies measure the size of the minimum efficient scale plant or firm relative to the size of the market. For example, if the minimum efficient scale of a firm is 5 per cent, then the market can support 20 independent firms and still allow production at minimum cost.

The main result of the engineering studies is that the extent of economies of scale varies across industries. The increase in cost of operating below the minimum efficient scale varies, and the size of the minimum efficient scale plant or firm relative to the size of the market varies. These results have two important implications for merger policy.

First, the differences between industries support the idea that cost savings related to scale economies should be evaluated on a case-by-case or at least industry-by-industry basis. A general presumptions approach, with thresholds common for all industries, is likely to produce important decision-making errors. At the same time the engineering studies show that it should be possible for antitrust authorities to collect information that describes the extent of scale economies in a particular industry.

Second, the engineering studies show that concentration in many markets is often higher than the concentration necessary for exploiting scale economies. It is therefore important that only scale economies in the relevant range are used as an argument to support horizontal mergers.

1.3.4.1 Cost savings due to plant size

Scherer et al. (1975) cover 12 major industries in seven industrialized nations. The results on the minimum efficient plant scales in the USA are summarized in Table 4.2. Two measures are given. The second column reports the size of a minimum efficient scale plant, assuming mid-1960s best-practice technology. Scale is measured by capacity, output or employment. The third column reports the percentage elevation of long-run unit cost as a consequence of building and operating plants at one-third the MES rather than the full MES.

It is not obvious how one should summarize these results. It would have been instructive to relate the cost differentials connected to size to, for example, the actual total cost differentials between different plants in these industries. However, even without such a benchmark, it seems reasonable to say that in most of the industries concerned, during the mid-1960s, the long-run cost disadvantage of operating at sub-optimal scale is not huge. In half of the industries, the elevation is 5 per cent or less. But there are exceptions. The cost disadvantage of operating at one-third MES in the cement industry is 26 per cent.

These results indicate that in some industries, but not in most of them, cost savings related to plant economies of scale can be an important effect

Table 4.2 Minimum efficient plant scales, and the cost disadvantage of suboptimal scale plants

	Minimum efficient scale	Percentage by which unit cost rises at 1/3 MES
Beer brewing	4.5 million barrels per year capacity	5.0
Cigarettes	36 billion cigarettes per year	2.2
Cotton and synthetic broadwoven fabrics	37.5 million square yards per year	7.6
Paints	10 million US gallons per year	4.4
Petroleum refining	200 000 barrels per day crude oil capacity	4.8
Leather shoes	1 million pairs per year	1.5
Glass bottles	133 000 tons per year	11.0
Portland cement	7 million 376-pound barrels per year capacity	26.0
Integrated steel	4 million tons per year capacity	11.0
Anti-friction bearings	800 employees	8.0
Refrigerators	800 000 units per year	6.5
Automobile storage batteries	1 million units per year	4.6

Source: Scherer et al. (1975)

of horizontal mergers. In other words, there exists a gain from evaluating such cost savings on a case-by-case basis.

Observation 1.7 Engineering-approach studies indicate that cost savings related to plant economies of scale differ substantially between different industries. These differences indicate that such cost savings should be evaluated on a case-by-case or at least industry-by-industry basis.

However, the picture provided by Table 4.2 is very incomplete. The analysis must also take into account economies of multiple-plant operation. And, perhaps more important, in order to understand the implications for merger policy, the MES must be related to the size of the market.

1.3.4.2 Scale economies in relation to the size of the market

It is crucial to point out that the cost minimizing industry structure, and thus the rationale for mergers, depends on the interplay between scale economies and the size of the market. Consider a single product industry with increasing returns to scale up to the production of q^{MES} and thereafter decreasing returns to scale. Thus, q^{MES} is the minimum efficient scale (MES). If consumers demand exactly q^{MES} units of the good, or less, then the cost minimizing organization of the industry requires that all production is carried out in a single firm. Thus, mergers up to this level reduce cost. On the other hand, if consumers demand $2q^{\mathrm{MES}}$ units of the good, cost minimization requires that production is divided between two separate firms. In this case, a merger between two duopoly firms will increase the cost of production. Thus, in order to support a merger with efficiency claims, it is not sufficient to show that the technology exhibits scale economies in some range. It must be demonstrated that there are scale economies in the relevant range. In many industries, it is likely that this qualification is crucial.

Economists have estimated minimum efficient scale and compared the estimates with observed levels of market concentration. Typical results from one study, using the engineering approach, are reported in Table 4.3, showing how important multiplant economies of scale were in the late 1960s for 12 US industries. Column (1) shows estimates of how many MES plants a firm needs to operate in order to have not more than a slight overall handicap vis-à-vis companies securing all multiplant economies. Column

Table 4.3 Firm size required to experience not more than slight cost handicap in relation to the size of the US market

	Number of MES plants needed to have not more than 'slight' overall handicap (1)	Share of US market required in 1967 (%) (2)	Average market share per US Big Three member, 1970 (%) (3)
Beer brewing	3–4	10–14	13
Cigarettes	1–2	6–12	23
Fabric weaving	3–6	1	10
Paints	1	1.4	9
Petrolium refining	2–3	4–6	8
Shoes	3–6	1	6
Glass bottles	3–4	4–6	22
Cement	1	2	7
Ordinary Steel	1	3	14
Bearings	3–5	4–7	14
Refrigerators	4–8	14–20	21
Storage batteries	1	2	18

Source: Scherer et al. (1975, pp. 334–6)

(2) translates the column (1) judgements into an estimate of how large a share of the US market an enterprise needs to realize these economies. In effect it summarizes the imperatives for high concentration at the nation-wide level. In only three of the 12 industries (refrigerators, brewing and perhaps cigarettes) were oligopolistic national industry structures (defined as four-firm concentration ratio above 40) a natural result of high MES. However, in several other industries, transportation costs were sufficiently high to confine the sales of any single plant to a regional market. As a result, exploiting scale economies also required oligopolistic industry structures in many glass bottle, petroleum, steel and cement markets. Column (3) indicates the average market share held by individual firms among the industries' three leading producers in 1970. By comparing column (3) with column (2) it appears that in the United States, concentration was much larger than the operation of efficient firms would dictate. In weaving and batteries, the Big Three firms were ten times as large as they needed to be to enjoy all economies of scale.

The important conclusion from this table is the following:

Observation 1.8 Comparing minimum efficient scale with the size of the market shows that real world concentration may be considerably higher than the imperatives of scale economies require.

Table 4.3 does not reveal the reason for the excessive concentration. However, at least one potential explanation is the firms' strategies to build market power. Another potential reason may be that economies of scale in marketing have not been properly accounted for in the studies. Be that as it may, these empirical results show that it is important that only scale economies in the relevant range should be used as a defence for a horizontal merger.

1.3.5 Summary and conclusions

In this section, we review the empirical literature on economies of scale. We both provide a brief overview of empirical estimates of scale economies in several industries, and discuss the methodologies that are used. However, since many of these studies are rather old, and since scale economies in many industries are likely to change over time, as a result of technological development, we do not attempt to provide a detailed account of the measurement of scale economies for all industries. Rather, the main purpose is to extract the general conclusions from this literature that are relevant for the discussion of an efficiency defence in merger control.

The primary finding is that the exploitation of scale economies is a source of substantial cost savings in some, but not all, industries. Economies of scale are often present at low volumes of output, and exhausted at larger volumes. In our view, the empirical results have an important implication for merger policy. The variability of scale economies across industries and different output volumes support the idea that cost savings should be evaluated on a case-by-case basis, that is, an efficiency defence. Moreover, the empirical literature shows that concentration in many industries has gone further than motivated by scale economies alone. Thus, in evaluating mergers it is important that only scale economies in the relevant range should be used as a defence for a horizontal merger. In sum:

Conclusion The variability of scale economies across industries supports the idea that cost savings should be evaluated on a case-by-case basis. Only scale economies in the relevant range should be used as an efficiency defence.

In order for antitrust authorities to take cost savings related to scale economies into account, they need some methodology to assess the importance of these economies. Therefore, we also provide a short introduction to the empirical methodologies that have been used to estimate economies of scale. Essentially, three different methods have been used to study the relationship between size and unit cost. The econometric approach uses statistical techniques to analyse cost–output data from some collection of firms. The mathematical programming approach is similar in that it also analyses cost–output data, but using linear programming. The engineering approach relies on interviews with engineers who design new production units.

In our view, all of these methodologies are useful for antitrust authorities, albeit in different ways. The already existing studies based on the econometric and mathematical programming approaches have produced useful 'background knowledge'. Whenever a case has to be decided concerning some industry, these studies can give a first hint to whether scale economies are important in that particular industry. What is the order of magnitude of potential cost savings? Is it reasonable to carry out a more detailed study?

However, for several reasons the econometric approach is probably not a suitable one for the antitrust authorities to carry out being a such detailed investigation. The main reason is data limitation. In order to estimate scale economies, cost and output data is also necessary from firms not participating in the merger. Another reason is that the econometric approach does not identify the sources of scale economies, which is important in order for assessing merger specificity. Estimates of scale economies do not indicate the time it takes for a merger to achieve cost savings related to scale economies. In contrast, the engineering approach should lend itself for such more detailed studies in particular cases. In particular, the engineering approach may supply an 'incremental analysis', that is, focus on the factors that will be affected by the merger. In sum:

Conclusion Antitrust authorities can use existing econometric evidence on scale economies to indicate if the order of magnitude of potential cost savings warrant a more detailed study, in particular merger cases. If detailed investigation is warranted, studies based on the engineering approach can be commissioned.

2. PASS-ON OF COST SAVINGS INTO CONSUMER PRICES

2.1 The Importance of Pass-on of Cost Savings

The relevant question for competition policy is to what extent the total cost savings, as discussed in Section 1, affect the policy objectives. For this reason, it is necessary to be more explicit about policy goals of merger regulation. As discussed in Chapter 3 of this volume, several objectives are frequently mentioned in the competition policy debate.

- *Consumer surplus* A first objective upon which merger analysis may be based is the protection of consumer interests. If this is the case, the central focus of merger analysis is on the competitive, or price effects, of mergers.
- *Total surplus* Another objective may be to further both consumer and producer interests. Total surplus may operationally be defined as the sum of consumer and producer surplus. More generally, one may give different weights to consumer and producer surplus.
- *Other objectives* These include the promotion of European integration, employment, regional balance, viability of small firms, and competitiveness of national firms on international markets. The concern with the preservation of employment has often been a political concern in proposed mergers. In principle, employment considerations should be taken into account in a full cost–benefit analysis of mergers. In practice, a merger policy designed to preserve old production structures is presumably not the best way to deal with the employment objective in the long run. See for example Crampton (1994) for more on the employment objective.

Depending on which policy objective one has in mind, the total cost savings should be evaluated differently. In our analysis below we focus exclusively on the first policy goal, the protection of consumer surplus, since this goal is typically the main objective in merger control.

Our focus on consumer surplus implies that we are mainly interested in the price effects of mergers. There are, however, also reasons to be interested in the price effects if one adopts the producers' own point of view. Indeed, understanding the price effects is essential to evaluate changes in the merging firms' competitive position. If a merger leads to a reduction in price, the merging firms typically increase their market share. In contrast, if a merger leads to a price increase, the merging firms are likely to experience a shrinking market share. While the merging firms' profits may still increase in this case, this would be caused by increased market power and not by increased competitiveness.

The price effects of a merger can be decomposed into two components:

- The price increase from an increase in market power, holding the merging firms' costs constant;
- The price reduction from an improvement in the firms' competitive position.

The price reduction from the improvement in the firms' competitive position will be strong to the extent that (1) the realized cost savings are marginal cost savings; and (2) the cost savings are passed on to at least some extent to consumers.

The total price effect from the merger is therefore negative if pass-on of marginal cost savings is sufficiently high to outweigh the market power effects.[27] This shows the importance of assessing pass-on of cost savings into consumer prices in merger analysis. Generally speaking, the greater the pass-on, the more likely it is that a merger will reduce price in the presence of cost savings. For example, if 50 per cent of the cost savings are passed on to consumers, then a merger reduces price if the cost savings are at least twice the percentage amount of the price effects from increased market power. If cost savings are fully passed on to consumers, then a merger decreases price if the cost savings are at least the same percentage amount as the price effects from increased market power.

These examples illustrate the importance of understanding the degree of pass-on to evaluate the full price effects from mergers. What are the relevant determinants of pass-on? Do technological conditions affect the degree of pass-on? What is the role played by competition? How important is the distinction between pass-on of firm-specific and industry-wide cost savings? What is the empirical evidence regarding pass-on? We take up these questions in this section with the purpose of obtaining a better understanding into the role of efficiencies in mergers.

2.2 Theoretical Analysis of Pass-on

2.2.1 Two measures of pass-on

As an introductory remark, it is instructive to note that pass-on of marginal cost savings can be measured in various ways. The choice of measure depends on what one wants to emphasize.

One approach is to compute how the absolute price level would change when the marginal cost is changed by, say, one unit. We refer to this measure as 'absolute pass-on'. A second approach is to compute how the price would change in percentage terms, when the marginal cost is changed by, say, 1 per cent. This gives a measure of 'relative pass-on', or, in other words, the 'pass-on elasticity'. Both measures will be used throughout the text.

In fact, it can be shown that the absolute pass-on is simply equal to the pass-on elasticity, multiplied by the ratio of price to marginal cost. Since this ratio is typically greater than one (when firms have positive mark-ups), the absolute pass-on is typically greater than the pass-on elasticity. Only under perfect competition (when mark-ups are zero) are both measures the same.

2.2.2 Pass-on of industry-wide cost savings

We begin with a discussion of pass-on of cost savings that are realized by all firms in the industry. While cost savings from mergers are typically achieved only at the level of the merging firms, understanding pass-on of industry-wide cost savings is a useful starting point. We can draw from a well-established theoretical literature on competition and monopoly and add generalizations for the oligopoly case. Furthermore, we will show how industry-level and firm-level pass-on are related to each other. This is useful, since the largest part of the empirical literature, which we review in section 2.3, has been concerned with industry-level pass-on.

Sections 2.2.2.1 to 2.2.2.3 consider pass-on of industry-wide cost savings under alternative forms of competition, assuming products are homogeneous. Section 2.2.2.4 investigates how the results generalize to differentiated products.

2.2.2.1 A competitive industry

Consider first pass-on of industry-wide cost savings in a competitive industry. This case is treated in the context of taxation by Bishop (1968), and is well explained and illustrated in several economics textbooks, see, for example, Pindyck and Rubinfeld (1992). It is useful to review this case, before considering more complicated market structures with market power.

In a competitive industry firms choose production levels to maximize profits, taking the market price as given. An individual firm's supply is then given by the production level at which the marginal cost of production

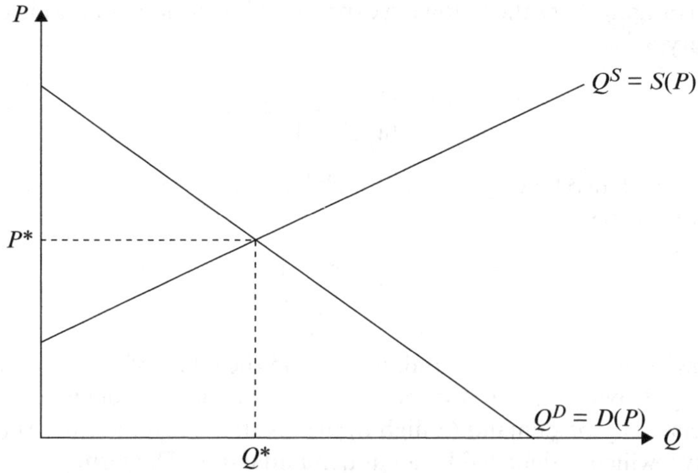

Figure 4.1 Market equilibrium

equals the market price. The aggregate supply curve is simply the sum of the individual firms' supplies, as depicted by the curve $Q^S = S(P)$ in Figure 4.1. Aggregate demand is the sum of the individual consumers' demand, shown by the curve $Q^D = D(P)$ in Figure 4.1. The equilibrium market price is the price at which supply is equal to demand, $Q^S = Q^D = Q^*$. It is given by the solution to $S(P) = D(P)$, as shown by the intersection of the two curves in Figure 4.1.

We are interested in assessing pass-on of an industry-wide cost saving, that is, the effect of a decrease in the marginal costs on the price level. More precisely, we want to compute the industry-wide pass-on elasticity, defined as the percentage increase in the market price caused by a percentage increase in marginal costs. To address this question, it will be convenient to use the inverse of the aggregate supply curve $S(P)$, which is the aggregate marginal cost curve, denoted by $P = wMC(Q^S)$. The parameter w is used to analyse the effects of percentage changes in marginal costs. Using this curve, the equilibrium market price is given by the condition:

$$P = wMC(D(P)).$$

Industry-wide pass-on can be computed by totally differentiating this condition:

$$\left(1 - \mathrm{w}\frac{\mathrm{d}MC}{\mathrm{d}Q}\frac{\mathrm{d}D}{\mathrm{d}P}\right)\mathrm{d}P - MC\mathrm{d}w$$

Rearranging gives the following expression for the industry-wide pass-on elasticity:

$$\tau^R = \frac{dP}{dw}\frac{w}{P} = \frac{1}{1+\varepsilon\omega},$$

which would also be the measure for absolute pass-on.

In this expression

$$\varepsilon = -\frac{dD}{dP}\frac{P}{Q}$$

is the price elasticity of demand, measuring the effect of an increase in the price by 1 per cent on the percentage reduction in demand. A high price elasticity of demand (a high ε) means that consumers are very price sensitive, which is depicted by a flat demand curve. The term

$$\omega = \frac{dMC}{dQ}\frac{Q}{MC}$$

measures the effect of an increase in the quantity produced by 1 per cent on the percentage change in marginal cost. It is, in fact, the inverse of the elasticity of supply, and it may be positive or negative. If ω is negative, then marginal costs decline as output increases, which can be depicted by a downward sloping supply curve. In contrast, if ω is positive, then marginal costs increase with output, depicted by an upward sloping supply curve. This indicates the presence of capacity constraints. If ω is close to zero, firms face few capacity constraints, which can be depicted by a flat marginal cost curve.

The formula for the industry-wide pass-on elasticity under perfect competition thus stresses the importance of the slope of the demand and supply curves. To illustrate, we begin our discussion by assuming that ω is positive or zero. Figure 4.2a assumes that demand is somewhat elastic while supply is upward sloping, meaning that firms face increasing marginal costs as they increase their production. Consider a reduction in marginal cost by 20 per cent. Holding production levels constant, perfect competition would induce firms to lower their prices by 20 per cent. However, such a price reduction would induce consumers to buy more. To bring the market back in equilibrium, firms need to produce more. Yet since they face increasing marginal costs (capacity constraints), they are only willing to do this if the price can increase. As a result, price will not decrease by 20 per cent but by a lower amount.

Pass-on can only be complete if either one of two conditions is met: (1) demand is perfectly inelastic, consumers are very price sensitive ($\varepsilon = 0$

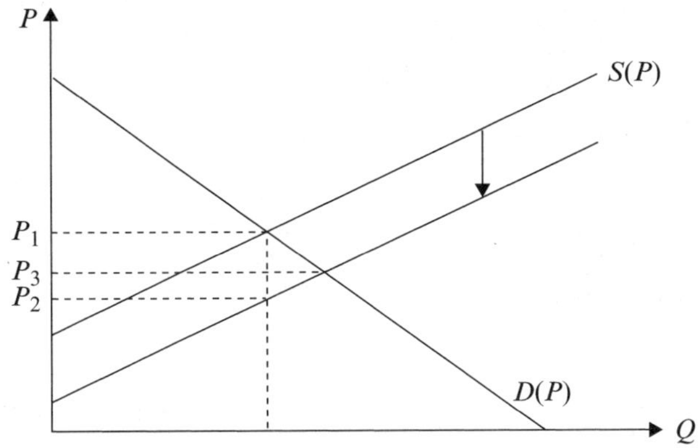

Figure 4.2a *Pass-on with elastic demand*

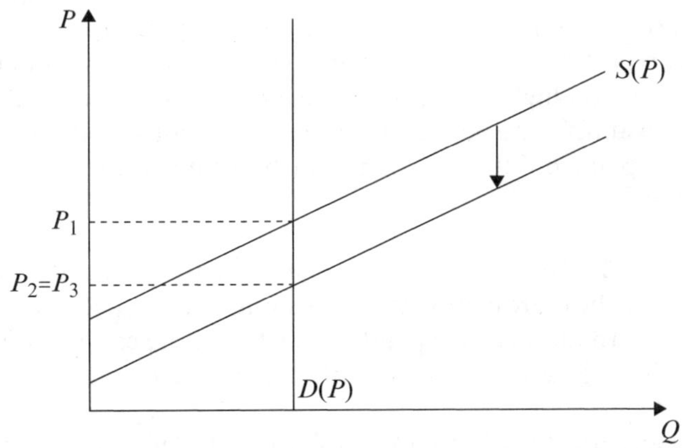

Figure 4.2b *Pass-on with perfectly inelastic demand*

as in Figure 4.2b); (2) supply is perfectly elastic, capacity is available in unlimited amounts so that marginal costs are constant ($\omega = 0$ as in Figure 4.2c). For example, if marginal costs are constant, then a cost reduction by 20 per cent corresponds to a price reduction by 20 per cent, since new demand at the lower price can be easily produced without affecting marginal costs. But more generally, pass-on is less complete the more consumers respond to price changes (high elasticity of demand) and the more producers are capacity constrained (low elasticity of supply). For a perfectly elastic (flat) demand curve and increasing marginal costs (ε = infinity and $\omega > 0$), a marginal cost reduction is not passed on at all to consumers.

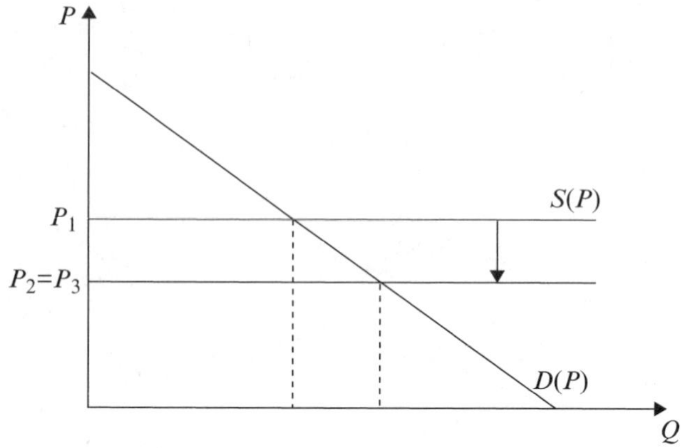

Figure 4.2c Pass-on with perfectly elastic supply

Similarly, there is no pass-on if there are very severe capacity constraints, that is, for a perfectly inelastic (vertical) supply curve (ω = infinity).

This discussion highlights that the degree of pass-on crucially depends on the consumers' responses to price reductions and on the firms' ability to expand production. This can be summarized in the following observation.

Observation 2.1 In a competitive industry, pass-on of a reduction in marginal costs will be more complete, as consumers respond less to price reductions and as producers can expand production more easily without raising their marginal costs by too much (little capacity constraints).

Several empirical studies have emphasized the importance of capacity constraints in explaining incomplete pass-on. For example, in international trade, a study by Knetter (1995) has investigated whether incomplete pass-through of exchange rates is caused by the presence of quantitative import quota restraints. Import quota constraints may be viewed as an example of severe capacity constraints in the country of import.

This discussion is based on the assumption that the supply curve is upward sloping, that is, the firms' marginal costs increase as production increases. In practice, when the industry is subject to increasing returns to scale, it is possible that the firms' marginal costs are decreasing as production increases, that is, $\omega < 0$.[28] In this case, there will be overshifting: a reduction in marginal cost by, say, 20 per cent would lead to a reduction in price by more than 20 per cent (unless demand is perfectly inelastic). The intuition for this is clear. At a constant production level, competitive firms would lower their price by 20 per cent. This induces consumers to buy more. The required additional output can be produced at a lower marginal cost since marginal cost is decreasing in production. This induces competitive firms to reduce the price further until a market equilibrium is reached.

Observation 2.2 In a competitive industry, there will be overshooting if the supply curve is downward sloping, that is, marginal costs decrease as producers expand production.

The extent of pass-on in a competitive industry is thus a largely empirical question: there may be incomplete pass-on, complete pass-on, or even overshooting. Nevertheless, there seems to be a common acceptance that pass-on is complete (pass-on elasticity of one) in a competitive industry. This can be rationalized if one is willing to make some additional assumptions: (1) the competitive industry is characterized by free entry and (2) all firms have access to the same technology and production factors. Under these assumptions the marginal cost curve is flat and supply is perfectly elastic (ω = infinity), so that pass-on is complete.

Observation 2.3 In a competitive industry, pass-on of a reduction in marginal cost savings is complete if the marginal cost curve is flat. For some industries, this may occur in the long run, when entry is free and firms have access to the same technologies and production factors.

While these assumptions may be more or less justified in the long run, they are not likely to hold in the short run, since entry and exit take time, imitation of competitors' technologies may be difficult, and production factors are not perfectly mobile. For these reasons, even in competitive industries the assessment of the pass-on rate is an empirical question.

2.2.2.2 Monopoly

We now take another extreme and assume that there is only one single firm in the industry. We ask the question whether and by how much a monopolist will pass on cost reductions to consumers. In contrast to a competitive firm, which takes the market price as given, a monopolist takes into account that it can influence the market price. Its profits are PQ minus total costs $C(Q)$. Assuming as before that demand is equal to supply so that demand is given by $Q = D(P)$, the monopolist's profits are given by total revenues minus total costs:

$$PD(P) - wTC(D(P))$$

The profit-maximizing price is given by the following condition:

$$D(P) + \frac{\mathrm{d}D}{\mathrm{d}P}(P - wMC(D(P))), \tag{4.2}$$

where $wMC(Q)$ is as before the marginal cost curve.

The first term measures the gain from a price increase by one unit: it is proportional to the total sales at the current price level. The second term measures the loss from a price increase: this is proportional to the mark-up multiplied by the reduction in sales caused by the price increase. We can rewrite (4.2) in elasticity form as:

$$\frac{P - wMC(D(P))}{P} = \frac{1}{\varepsilon}. \tag{4.2$'$}$$

In other words, the percentage mark-up is inversely related to the price elasticity of demand. Only if the price elasticity of demand is infinite, is the mark-up zero, so that price is equal to marginal cost. We note from (4.2′) that a monopolist always operates at the elastic portion of the demand curve: since marginal costs are positive, it must be that $\varepsilon > 1$. Intuitively, at the inelastic portion of the demand curve ($\varepsilon < 1$), it always pays for a monopoly to raise its price.

We can follow a similar approach as under perfect competition and totally differentiate the monopoly condition.[29] This gives the following formula for relative pass-on, or the pass-on elasticity:

$$\tau^R = \frac{\mathrm{d}P}{\mathrm{d}w}\frac{w}{P} = \frac{1}{1 + \varepsilon\omega + \frac{1}{\varepsilon - 1}\eta}, \tag{4.3}$$

which measures the effect of a percentage marginal cost change in the percentage price change. To measure absolute pass-on, one simply has to multiply the pass-on elasticity by the price to marginal cost ratio, as discussed in section 2.1.

The first two terms in the numerator of expression (4.3) are exactly the same as in the case of perfect competition. Consequently, it is again true that pass-on is more complete as consumers respond less to price reductions and as producers can expand production without raising their marginal costs by too much (see Observation 2.1). To abstract from these effects, assume the marginal cost curve is flat ($\omega = 0$), so that pass-on would be complete under perfect competition (see Observation 2.3).

We can then focus on the third part in the numerator of expression (4.3). This contains the term η, which measures the elasticity of the price elasticity of demand, that is,

$$\eta = \frac{d\varepsilon}{dP}\frac{P}{\varepsilon}.$$

It may be positive or negative. If $\eta > 0$, then a price increase leads to a higher price elasticity of demand, that is, consumers become more price sensitive. This is the most intuitive scenario. If $\eta < 0$, then a price increase leads to a decrease in the price elasticity of demand; if $\eta = 0$, then the price elasticity of demand is independent of price changes.

To interpret the role of the parameter η in assessing pass-on, suppose that the monopolist experiences a reduction in marginal cost of 20 per cent and initially completely passes this on to consumers by lowering its price. This will cause an increase in demand, which the monopolist can easily accommodate since we assume a flat marginal cost curve ($\omega = 0$). However, the lower price may cause the monopolist to reconsider its mark-up strategy. There are three possibilities, as can be seen from the mark-up formula (4.2′). First, if the elasticity of demand is unaffected by price changes ($\eta = 0$), then the optimal monopoly mark-up is a fixed percentage of cost. The monopolist never adjusts its percentage margins, so that (relative) pass-on is complete. Second, if the elasticity of demand is increasing in price ($\eta > 0$), then a price reduction would reduce the elasticity of demand. A lower price elasticity calls for an upward adjustment of the optimal monopoly mark-up. The monopolist thus prefers to raise its percentage mark-up and pass on only part of the cost reduction. Third, if the elasticity of demand is decreasing ($\eta < 0$), lowering the price increases the elasticity of demand, so that the optimal monopoly mark-up decreases. In this case, the monopolist prefers to pass on more than the cost reduction by lowering its mark-up, so that there will be overshooting.

We can summarize this discussion as follows.

Observation 2.4 Suppose the marginal cost curve is flat ($\omega = 0$). If consumers become more price sensitive when price increases ($\eta > 0$), a monopolist raises its percentage mark-up after a marginal cost reduction so that relative pass-on is incomplete. If consumers become less price sensitive when price increases ($\eta < 0$), a monopolist reduces its percentage mark-up after a marginal cost reduction so that there is overshooting.

This discussion shows the important role of market power in assessing pass-on. A monopolist may respond to cost reductions by lowering or raising its mark-up, depending on the curvature of the price elasticity of demand. The central question for assessing pass-on when monopoly market power is present is thus whether the price elasticity of demand increases or decreases as the price rises. To gain some further intuition, it is useful to compute the elasticity of the price elasticity of demand η as:

$$\eta = 1 + \varepsilon + \frac{dD/dP}{d^2D/dP^2}P. \tag{4.4}$$

This expression shows that the sign of η depends on the curvature of the demand curve, as measured by d^2D/dP^2. If the demand curve is concave or linear all terms are positive, so that $\eta > 0$, that is, the price elasticity of demand increases in price. Hence for concave or linear demand curves ($d^2D/dP^2 \leq 0$), firms increase mark-ups after a marginal cost reduction so that pass-on is incomplete (assuming flat marginal costs). Only if the demand curve is sufficiently convex (d^2D/dP^2 sufficiently high) is it possible that firms reduce their mark-ups after a marginal cost reduction so that there is overshooting.

In practice, while one cannot rule out the case of overshooting, it is more reasonable to expect that pass-on of cost reductions will be incomplete. To see this, consider now the value of the price elasticity of demand for two extreme values of marginal cost. First, if marginal cost equals zero, then by the inverse elasticity rule, the price elasticity of demand is equal to one. Second, if marginal cost is so high that only the smallest possible amount is consumed, then the price elasticity of demand must be very large. Hence, the price elasticity of demand drops considerably as one moves from the highest to the lowest possible cost level. Only for a range of prices may the price elasticity of demand increase as price falls. Assuming that marginal costs are flat, we conclude that overshooting, that is, lowering the mark-up in response to a marginal cost reduction, is a rather unusual scenario.

Even if one rules out the possibility of overshooting as implausible, the degree of pass-on cannot easily be pinned down to a small range. To illustrate, consider the commonly used specification of linear demand ($d^2D/dP^2 = 0$) while still assuming flat marginal costs (ω). Substituting (4.4) into (4.3) one can compute that the pass-on elasticity of a monopolist is then equal to $(\varepsilon - 1)/2\varepsilon$. This implies that the pass-on elasticity is always less than 0.5. In contrast, the commonly used specification of a constant elasticity demand ($\eta = 0$) implies that pass-on is complete. This illustrates that one can obtain drastically different conclusions regarding pass-on, by simply changing the demand specification. Assessing the pass-on of cost savings by a firm with monopoly market power is thus, more than under competition, an empirical question.

2.2.2.3 Oligopoly models

To explain the role of competition for assessing pass-on, we consider an oligopolistic industry where firms can influence the market price. One may distinguish between two types of oligopoly models: the Cournot and the

Bertrand model. In the Cournot model, each firm chooses a quantity to maximize profits, taking as given the quantity set by the other firms. In the Bertrand model, each firm chooses a price to maximize profits, taking as given the price set by the other firms.

Consider first a Cournot model with N firms, where each firm i operates at a constant, but not necessarily identical marginal cost c_i. Market demand $P = P(Q)$ is now represented as the inverse of the demand function $Q = D(P)$; it is downward sloping. The constant marginal cost assumptions allow us to abstract from the possibility of incomplete pass-on or overshooting stemming from, respectively, upward or downward sloping marginal cost functions. Except for this assumption, this is a fairly general set-up, as described in more detail by, for example, Levin (1990).[30] We are interested in finding the industry-wide pass-on elasticity, which we define as the percentage reduction in price when all firms reduce their marginal cost by 1 per cent.

A firm i producing a quantity q_i obtains a profit equal to:

$$(P(Q) - c_i)q_i.$$

Each firm i chooses a quantity q_i to maximize profit given the quantity chosen by the other firms. The profit maximising quantity for each firm i must satisfy the condition that the firm's marginal revenue equal its marginal cost, or:

$$\frac{\mathrm{d}P}{\mathrm{d}Q}q_i + P - c_i = 0.$$

This condition must hold for every firm to have a Cournot equilibrium. As under monopoly, we can write this in elasticity form:

$$\frac{P - c_i}{P} = \frac{s_i}{\varepsilon}$$

where $s_i = q_i/Q$ is the market share of firm i. Intuitively, a firm obtains a high mark-up if the price elasticity of demand ε is low (as in the monopoly case) and if its market share is high. In the special case in which $s_i = 1$, a single firm has 100 per cent of the market and the monopoly condition holds.

We can add up these conditions for all firms to obtain the following equation from which the Cournot market quantity can be solved:

$$\frac{\mathrm{d}P}{\mathrm{d}Q}Q + NP - \Sigma c_i = 0.$$

The market price can then be computed by substituting the Cournot market quantity in the inverse demand function $P = P(Q)$. We can compute the pass-on elasticity by totally differentiating this condition. Some calculations show that the industry-wide pass-on elasticity is equal to:

$$\tau^R = \frac{dP}{d\Sigma c_i/N}\left(\frac{\Sigma c_i/N}{P}\right) = \frac{1}{1 + \frac{1}{N\varepsilon - 1}\eta}, \tag{4.5}$$

where η is the elasticity of the price elasticity of demand as defined previously for the monopoly case. To obtain a measure of absolute pass-on, one would need to multiply the pass-on elasticity by the ratio of price to the average of the firms' marginal cost.

One can see that the industry-wide pass-on elasticity depends on the number of competing firms N, but is independent of the distribution of market shares in the industry. It thus does not matter whether the industry consists of, say, four equally sized firms, or whether instead there is one dominant firm and three small ones.

The pass-on elasticity (4.5) covers monopoly and perfect competition as special cases (for the case of constant marginal costs). More specifically, if $N = 1$ the monopoly formula holds. As the number of firms N increases (and assuming $\eta > 0$), the pass-on elasticity increases, until it becomes unity as the number of firms N approaches infinity. As in the monopoly case, when the price elasticity of demand increases with price ($\eta > 0$), firms find it optimal to increase their mark-up after a reduction in marginal cost. We can summarize this as follows.

Observation 2.5 Suppose that the marginal cost curve is flat and the price elasticity of demand increases with price. Cournot firms raise their mark-ups after an industry-wide marginal cost reduction so that relative pass-on is incomplete. As the number of firms in the industry increases, pass-on becomes more complete.

McCorriston et al. (1998) consider an oligopoly with identical firms and constant marginal costs. Conduct is modelled through a conjectural variation parameter θ. This parameter is often used in empirical work (see Bresnahan 1989) to cover a broad range of oligopoly models as special cases, including perfect competition, Cournot, Bertrand and cartel. In the symmetric Cournot model the conjectural variation would be equal to $1/N$. McCorriston et al. consider the case in which the cost of only one production factor decreases; the share of this production factor is called α.

Assuming the production factors are used in a fixed proportion their formula reduces to:

$$\tau^R = \frac{dP}{d\Sigma c_i/N}\left(\frac{\Sigma c_i/N}{P}\right) = \frac{\alpha}{1 + \dfrac{1}{\varepsilon/\theta - 1}\eta}.$$

This is very similar to what we found before. The formula first shows the role of conduct through the conjectural variation parameter: pass-on increases as the market becomes more competitive (lower θ). The formula also shows that it is important to know whether or not the cost reduction applies to all production factors. If the cost reduction only applies to a fraction α of the marginal costs, then the pass-on elasticity has to be adjusted correspondingly.

Observation 2.6 The pass-on elasticity increases as conduct becomes more competitive. Furthermore, the pass-on elasticity is proportional to the share of the production factors for which the cost reduction applies.

It is important to bear in mind this observation when interpreting the results obtained in the empirical literature. In particular, if a low pass-on elasticity is found, this may simply be because the empirical study only considered one component of costs.

Next consider the Bertrand model of oligopoly, where firms compete by choosing prices taking as given the prices of their competitors. Assume again that firms have constant but not necessarily identical marginal cost. If products are homogeneous, then the price will equal the marginal cost of the firm with the second lowest marginal cost and the market share of the lowest cost firm will be 100 per cent. This is true no matter how many firms are in the industry. In this case, one can easily see that pass-on of an industry-wide marginal cost change will be complete, no matter how many firms are in the industry. The Bertrand model with homogeneous goods thus has the rather unappealing property that the number of firms has no influence on the degree of pass-on. In the next section, it will become clear that this is no longer the case if one assumes that products are differentiated.

2.2.2.4 Industries with product differentiation

Up to now we have assumed that consumers view the products offered by different firms as perfect substitutes. As a result, there is only one price in the industry; if there were two prices, than the products at the highest price would obtain zero market share. With homogeneous products, pass-on of marginal cost savings is therefore defined straightforwardly in terms of the single prevailing price, independent of the firms' market shares. If products are differentiated, things are more complicated. Different products are typically sold at different prices and have different sales. A natural way to define pass-on would be to construct a price index for the industry, where the products are weighted according to sales. Pass-on could then be defined as the effect of a reduction in marginal cost on this price index (holding the weights fixed). A justification for this approach is that the change in this price index when all prices change by one unit is exactly the opposite of the change in consumer surplus, if we ignore income effects. To see this, let consumer surplus be equal to:

$$CS = V(p_1, p_2, \ldots, p_N, y)$$

where $V(p_1, p_2, \ldots, p_N)$ is the indirect utility function of a representative consumer in the industry. Applying Roy's identity, it can be checked that the change in consumer surplus is given by:

$$\mathrm{d}CS = q_1\mathrm{d}p_1 + q_2\mathrm{d}p_2 + \ldots + q_N\mathrm{d}p_N,$$

where q_i are the sales of product i. When we assess pass-on of cost reductions on the sales-based price index, we are thus looking at pass-on to consumers.

The pattern of product differentiation in a market may take many forms and can differ from market to market. Generally speaking, one may view competition in industries with product differentiation to be either localized or global. If competition is localized, then products are direct substitutes of only a few other products in the market. Many products then only compete indirectly with each other through a chain of price responses by competitors. In contrast, if competition is global, then all products are direct substitutes for all other products in the market.[31] A simple form of global competition occurs when all products are symmetric substitutes for each other. An example of this is the popular logit model, which we will use to illustrate how to measure pass-on. It will be convenient to focus on absolute pass-on (rather than relative pass-on).

Suppose there are N differentiated products, $i = 1 \ldots N$; consumers either choose one unit of their most preferred product, or they decide not to buy anything, in which case they choose the outside good 0. According to the logit model, the market share s_i for product i (in the total sales including the outside good) is given by the following formula:

$$s_i = \frac{\exp((v_i - p_i)/\mu)}{\sum \exp((v_k - p_k)/\mu)}$$

where v_i measures the intrinsic utility for the product, and μ is a parameter measuring the degree of substitution. The total sales q_i for product i are equal to the market share s_i times the total number of potential consumers, L. Assuming a flat marginal cost curve c_i for each product i, the profits from product i are given by $(p_i - c_i)s_iL$.

We consider pass-on of an industry-wide marginal cost reduction in two kinds of market structure: a monopoly and a Bertrand oligopoly. A monopolist takes into account that a price increase does not only reduce the sales of the product itself, but also increase the sales of the other products it sells. The monopolist thus sets prices to maximize its total profits, taking into account the profit effects for all products it sells. The result is that the monopolist charges a mark-up that is inversely proportional to the price elasticity of demand for all products. This generalizes the monopoly mark-up rule for homogeneous products given by (4.2′). Specifically for the logit model, this rule translates into the following condition:

$$p_i - c_i = \frac{\mu}{s_0}.$$

Intuitively, the monopolist charges equal mark-ups for all its products, and these mark-ups are higher the less attractive is the outside good (low elasticity of market demand). One can totally differentiate this condition to obtain the following expression for the absolute pass-on, that is, the effect of a unit marginal cost change on the industry price index:

$$\tau^A = \sum \frac{\mathrm{d}CS}{\mathrm{d}c_k} = (1 - s_0)s_0. \tag{4.6}$$

This simple condition implies that pass-on of a unit cost reduction for all products will not be passed completely into the consumer price index. In particular, a monopolist selling differentiated products of the logit form never passes on more than one quarter of a cost reduction (which occurs when the outside good has a market share of one half).

This can be contrasted with pass-on in an oligopoly. Suppose that there are N firms each selling one of the differentiated products. Each firm takes into account that a price increase reduces the sales of its own product, but does not consider the effect on the sales of the other products. The resulting mark-up is inversely related to the price elasticity at the level of the individual product, which is greater than the price elasticity of demand for all products together. The closer the products are substitutes, the higher the product-level price elasticities of demand, and the lower the mark-ups. More specifically, the price rule for firm i must satisfy the following condition:

$$p_i - c_i = \frac{p_i}{\varepsilon_i}$$

which for the logit model translates into:

$$p_i - c_i = \frac{\mu}{1 - s_i}.$$

From this condition one can derive the following expression for pass-on of an industry-wide unit marginal cost change on the price index:

$$\tau = \sum \frac{\mathrm{d}CS}{\mathrm{d}c_k} = \sum \frac{s_k(1 - s_k)^2}{(1 - s_k)^2 + s_k} \Big/ \sum \frac{s_k(1 - s_k)}{(1 - s_k)^2 + s_k}.$$

This is a rather complicated formula, yet it has several interesting properties. First, it can be shown that the pass-on expression is greater than the expression in (4.6). The logit example thus illustrates that also for differentiated products there is more pass-on under oligopoly competition than under monopoly. Second, it can easily be seen that pass-on is always less than one. For symmetric products, it can also be verified that pass-on becomes more complete as the number of firms increases; pass-on becomes complete as the number of products becomes very large.

Observation 2.7 Suppose that the marginal cost curve is flat and products are differentiated according to the logit model. Absolute pass-on is incomplete, yet greater under competition than under monopoly. As the number of competing products becomes very large, absolute pass-on becomes complete.

Note that Observation 2.7 is only true for the logit model. It is well-known, see for example Werden and Froeb (1994), that the logit model generates price elasticities of demand that increase as the price rises. For this reason, it implies that firms absorb cost changes partially by adjusting their mark-ups. In other models of product differentiation, such as the linear demand model or the CES model, mark-up adjustment may be lower, so that it is possible that absolute pass-on would be more than complete.

2.2.3 Pass-on of firm-specific cost savings

We now go to the question that is most relevant for merger analysis: how are firm-specific cost savings passed on to consumer prices? In answering this question we are also concerned with the relationship between pass-on of industry-wide cost savings. Understanding this relationship will prove to be very important since our empirical review will make it clear that previous research efforts have traditionally been most concerned with pass-on of industry-wide cost savings.

2.2.3.1 A competitive industry

In a perfectly competitive industry, each firm's demand curve becomes horizontal. In other words, the elasticity of each firm's perceived demand becomes infinitely large (consumers become very price sensitive). Under such conditions, a firm has no incentive to pass-on any cost changes. It acts simply as a price taker, and would only adjust its produced quantity in response to a marginal cost change. See Yde and Vita (1996) for a graphical illustration.

2.2.3.2 Oligopoly with homogeneous products

First, we consider firm-level pass on in a Cournot oligopoly as introduced in section 2.2.2.3. Each firm chooses an output level to maximize its profits. The condition for profit-maximization can be totally differentiated as before, but now varying only the marginal cost of a specific firm i, holding the marginal costs of the other firms constant. This yields the following formula for the pass-on elasticity of firm i:

$$\tau_i^R = \frac{dP}{dc_i}\frac{c_i}{P} = \frac{(\varepsilon - s_i)/(N\varepsilon - 1)}{1 + \frac{1}{N\varepsilon - 1}\eta} \tag{4.7}$$

where the notation is the same as before. To measure the absolute pass-on, one would have to multiply the pass-on elasticity by firm i's price to marginal cost ratio.

The formula (4.7) looks quite close to the industry-wide pass-on elasticity given by (4.5). The denominator is in fact the same, showing that the price elasticity of demand ε, the elasticity of the elasticity η and the number of firms has a similar influence on the firm-specific pass-on elasticity as on the industry-wide pass-on elasticity. The numerator is different from (4.5). It contains the market share of firm i, which experiences the cost reduction. It shows that the pass-on elasticity is larger for firms with a smaller market share. Intuitively, this is because small firms are firms with high marginal costs and little market power.

The relationship between the firm-specific pass-on elasticity τ_i and the industry-wide elasticity τ can be discussed by computing the ratio between the two:

$$\tau_i^R/\tau^R = (\varepsilon - s_i)/(N\varepsilon - 1).$$

Note that this ratio is independent of the elasticity of the elasticity. In fact, the denominator of this ratio is simply the sum of the numerator over all firms. Since ε must be greater than s_i, this implies that this ratio is always less than one, that is, the firm-specific pass-on is necessarily less than industry-wide pass-on in the Cournot model.

It is possible to say a bit more about the relationship between firm-specific and industry-wide pass-on. The ratio τ_i/τ implies that a firm with a market share equal to the average market share in the industry (that is, $1/N$) has a pass-on elasticity that is exactly equal to a fraction $1/N$ of the industry-wide pass-on elasticity. For example, if there were four firms in the industry, then a firm with a market share of 25 per cent would have a pass-on elasticity of exactly 25 per cent of the industry-wide pass-on elasticity. A firm with a higher market share than the average market share in the industry will necessarily pass-on less than the fraction $1/N$, so that pass-on of a cost reduction by such firms is likely to be small. In contrast, a firm with a lower market share than the average in the industry will pass-on more than the fraction $1/N$. If all firms are identical (with market shares of $1/N$), then the firm-specific pass-on elasticity is exactly $1/N$ of the industry-wide pass-on elasticity.

Observation 2.8 Suppose that the marginal cost curve is flat. In a Cournot industry a firm-specific cost reduction is passed on less than an industry-wide cost reduction. The higher a firm's market share is, the lower is the firm-specific pass on.

One can also easily compute the pass-on elasticity for multiple firms, that is, the N^F merging firms. One simply has to reinterpret the market share in (4.7) as the joint (post-merger) market share of the N^F firms. This shows that pass-on from cost savings is lower the greater is the merging firms' joint market share. The special case of the analysis by Dornbusch (1987) obtains if one considers pass-on of cost savings by N^F symmetric firms and a constant price elasticity of demand ($\eta = 0$).[32] In this case, the pass-on elasticity is equal to the firms' joint market share N^F/N: the greater the firms' joint market share, the closer pass-on is to unity.

Now consider firm-level pass-on in a Bertrand oligopoly where firms choose prices rather than quantities. As explained in section 2.2.2.3, in such an industry firms set a price equal to the marginal cost of the second lowest cost firm, and the market share of the lowest-cost firm is 100 per cent. In such an industry a cost saving by the dominant, low-cost firm is not passed on at all to consumers, whereas a cost saving by the second-lowest-cost firm is passed on completely. This is in line with the results of the Cournot model: larger firms pass-on less than smaller firms and firm-specific pass-on is less than industry-wide pass-on. Pass-on of cost savings by multiple firms will be complete if and only if the second-lowest-cost firm is involved. Since the Bertrand model with homogeneous products yields a quite unrealistic situation in which one firm obtains the whole market, we now turn to the case where products are differentiated.

2.2.3.3 Oligopoly with differentiated products

To illustrate pass-on of firm-specific cost savings we again use the logit model of product differentiation, which has the property that products compete symmetrically with each other. We will again focus on absolute rather than relative pass-on in the logit model because this is more convenient.

As before, the condition for profit maximization can be totally differentiated, now varying only the marginal cost of a single firm and holding the cost of the other firms constant. First consider the product-specific pass-on rate under the hypothesis that prices are set by a monopolist:

$$\tau_i^A = \frac{dCS}{dc_i} = s_i s_0.$$

Product-specific pass-on is simply a fraction of industry-wide pass-on, where this fraction is proportional to the product's market share, that is, $\tau_i^A/\tau^A = s_i/(1-s_0)$. Consistent with the findings for the Cournot model, a cost reduction for a single product is thus passed on by less, into the price index, than an industry-wide cost reduction. However, the product-specific pass-on rate is now *greater* as the product's market share increases.

Now consider the product-specific pass-on rate under the hypothesis that prices are set oligopolistically:

$$\tau_i = \frac{dCS}{dc_i} = \frac{s_i(1-s_i)^2}{(1-s_i)^2+s_i} \Big/ \sum \frac{s_k(1-s_k)}{(1-s_k)^2+s_k}.$$

This rather complicated formula has again the property that product-specific pass-on is only a fraction of industry-wide pass-on. A cost reduction for a single product is thus passed on by less than an industry-wide cost reduction. However, in contrast to the monopoly case, there is now no longer a simple relationship between the product's market share and the degree of pass-on. To gain some further insights we computed firm-specific pass-on for alternative values of the firm's market share and alternative numbers of competing firms. We assume the competing firms are all identical (so that they have an equal market share). The results of the computations are given in Table 4.4.

Reading Table 4.4 row by row, one can see that a firm with a given market share passes on less as the number of competing firms increases. Intuitively, when there are a large number of firms, competition between these firms is strong and market power is weak, so that they do not respond to price changes initiated by one firm. Reading the table column by column, one can

Table 4.4 Firm-specific absolute pass-on with symmetric competitors

Market share	Number of competing firms					
	1	2	3	4	5	1000
0.001	0.000	0.000	0.000	0.000	0.000	0.000
0.100	0.197	0.138	0.120	0.111	0.107	0.090
0.200	0.287	0.222	0.200	0.189	0.183	0.160
0.300	0.327	0.271	0.250	0.240	0.234	0.210
0.400	**0.337**	**0.293**	**0.276**	0.267	0.262	0.240
0.500	0.325	0.292	0.279	**0.272**	**0.268**	**0.250**
0.600	0.293	0.271	0.262	0.257	0.254	0.240
0.700	0.243	0.230	0.224	0.221	0.219	0.210
0.800	0.176	0.170	0.167	0.166	0.165	0.160
0.900	0.095	0.093	0.092	0.092	0.091	0.090
0.999	0.000	0.000	0.000	0.000	0.000	0.000

Note: Bold indicates maximum pass-on with a given number of competitors

see the role of the market share of the firm experiencing the cost reduction. Pass-on is very limited when the market share of the firm is either very small or very large. The case of no pass-on under a very small market share corresponds to the case of a price-taking firm as under perfect competition (section 2.2.3.1). Intermediate market shares lead to the greatest pass-on.

Observation 2.9 In a product-differentiated industry, product-specific pass-on is less than industry-wide pass-on, both under monopoly as under oligopoly.

Market share matters in assessing the magnitude of firm-specific pass-on under product differentiation. The logit model indicates that intermediate levels of market shares yield the greatest product-specific pass-on.

We note that the specific results depend on the assumption of the logit model, which implies that firms have a tendency to adjust their mark-ups when cost changes. In other models, such as the linear demand model or the CES model, it may be expected that higher levels of firm-specific pass-on would obtain. A robust finding would nevertheless be that firm-specific pass-on would be less than industry-wide pass-on. Also, it should be clear that the market share of the firm experiencing a cost reduction is a key determinant of firm-specific pass-on; the logit example suggests that pass-on is largest when the firm has an intermediate market share.

It is useful to compare this preliminary analysis on differentiated goods industries with the theoretical results obtained by Feenstra et al. (1996).

They studied exchange rate pass-through, which is equivalent to pass-on of cost changes. In particular, they investigated the role of the market share of the exporting firms who experience the exchange rate shock (the cost change). We stress that their results are not directly comparable to ours: they treat each individual exporting firm as small and look at the role of the total market share of all exporting firms. They find that under some modest assumptions, pass-through is equal to one half if the exporting firm has a very small market share. As the market share of the exporting firm increases, pass-through may initially decrease or increase; yet as the market share becomes very large, pass-through starts to increase and ultimately becomes complete. These results on the role of market share are not necessarily inconsistent with ours. Indeed, as the market share of the exporting firms increases in Feenstra et al.'s model, the exchange rate (or cost) change becomes more like an industry-wide cost change. Their conclusion that pass-on is complete as the market share of the exporting firms becomes very large is then similar to our Observation 2.7 regarding complete pass-on of an industry-wide cost shock.

2.2.4 Summary

This section has reviewed the theoretical determinants of pass-on of cost savings. It is important to bear in mind that one may measure either absolute pass-on or relative pass-on (the pass-on elasticity). We begin by looking at pass-on of industry-wide cost savings, that is, cost savings realized by all firms in the industry. Under perfect competition, the price elasticity of demand and the shape of the marginal cost curve are the main determinants. As consumers become more price inelastic, and as the supply curve becomes more elastic (little capacity constraints), pass-on of industry-wide cost savings will be more complete. If supply is perfectly elastic (no capacity constraints), pass-on of industry-wide cost savings is complete under perfect competition. The picture is different under monopoly or oligopoly with market power. In this case, pass-on of industry-wide cost savings may be incomplete even if supply is perfectly elastic. The reason is that firms charge mark-ups, which depend on the price elasticity of consumer demand. In the 'typical' case, consumers become more price sensitive as the price increases. If this is the case, then firms will absorb cost changes by adjusting their mark-ups and pass-on will be incomplete. This is especially true in the monopoly case. Nevertheless, it is worth stressing that even in the monopoly case (or the dominant-firm case) firms pass on at least part of the cost savings onto consumers. As the number of firms increases, pass-on of industry-wide cost savings generally becomes more complete.

This section finally emphasized the importance of distinguishing between industry-wide and firm-specific pass-on. An understanding of firm-specific pass-on is especially relevant in the context of mergers, since it is typically only the merging firms who benefit from any cost reduction. Our analysis shows that firm-specific pass-on is generally less than industry-wide pass-on. For example, when firms are identical, firm-specific pass-on is equal to industry-wide pass-on divided by the number of firms in the industry. Hence the more firms there are, the lower is the degree of firm-specific pass-on. When firms are not identical, no general results on firm-specific pass-on are available. Nevertheless, it is clear that the market share of the firm realizing the cost reduction matters. On the one hand, a high market share of the cost-reducing firm makes the cost saving close to an industry-wide cost saving and thus makes pass-on more complete. On the other hand, a high market share also means a lot of market power, which may provide an incentive to pass on cost changes incompletely. The results of these forces is that pass-on in an industry is typically the largest for firms with intermediate market share, that is, not the very small firms but also not the dominant firms.

2.3 Empirical Evidence

We do not aim at this point to provide a complete review of the empirical results on pass-on. Instead, we consider some of the most important recent contributions in more detail. This will give the opportunity to explain strengths and weaknesses of alterative approaches in measuring pass-on. Nevertheless, we will also discuss the specific empirical results obtained in various papers. This should be useful to put further results in perspective.

The empirical literature on pass-on of cost savings from mergers is, to our knowledge, virtually non-existent. It is thus necessary to draw lessons from empirical work on pass-on of cost changes that are triggered by other events than mergers. Various fields in economics have, in fact, been concerned with quantifying pass-on. First, there is a large literature in international economics on exchange-rate pass-through. This deals with the question whether and to what extent exporting firms pass-through exchange rate fluctuations in consumer prices. Related to the exchange rate pass-through literature is the pricing to market literature (Krugman 1987). The focus is different in that the implications of incomplete exchange rate pass-through on local prices are investigated when exporting firms sell to different markets. Also in international economics, there has been research on the impact of tariffs on consumer prices. Second, in public economics, there has been a great amount of research on tax incidence. A central question here is which agents are most affected by a tax policy, taking into account behavioural responses. The literature relevant for our purposes deals with the incidence of excise taxes. It asks how consumer prices respond to changes in excise taxes. Third, in various specialized applied areas in economics, there has been considerable interest in the transmission of intermediate goods prices into the prices for final goods. For example, in agricultural economics, empirical research has looked at the price transmission of intermediate food products, such as cacao, coffee beans, sugar, and so on; in energy economics empirical research considers the transmission of price fluctuations for crude oil, and so on.

Exchange rates, tariffs, excise taxes and intermediate goods prices have in common the important properties that they affect the marginal costs of firms, often fluctuate considerably and can be well observed.[33] They thus have the potential to provide useful information on the pass-on of cost changes onto consumer prices. Nevertheless, special care has been taken when drawing inferences. First, it is essential to know whether the measured cost changes are specific to some firms only, or whether they apply to all firms in an industry. In the previous section we emphasized that firm-specific pass-on may differ significantly from industry-wide pass-on. Changes in excise taxes or intermediate goods prices typically affect the costs of all firms in the industry. Exchange rate changes, in contrast, only affect the costs of the foreign firms, leaving the costs of the domestic firms constant.[34] Second, one has to know whether the measured cost change applies to the whole product, or only to part of it. Excise taxes apply to the full product. An exchange rate fluctuation affects the full marginal cost incurred in the exporter's country, yet has no impact on local distribution or other costs of services. Intermediate goods typically constitute only a fraction of the marginal costs. Third, one should be sure whether one is measuring short-run or long-run effects of cost changes on consumer prices. If short-run effects are considerably lower than long-term effects, and if adjustment goes quickly, then results on short-run effects may be highly misleading.

2.3.1 Evidence on industry-wide pass-on

2.3.1.1 Excise taxes and pass-on

Several papers have looked at the pass-on of industry-wide cost changes by looking at the relationship between excise taxes and consumer prices. A first study in this spirit is by Sumner (1981). He regresses the price for cigarettes in 47 states of the USA during 1954–78 on the per-unit excise tax and some control variables. The regression thus takes the following form:

$$P_t = \alpha + \beta T_t + \gamma W_t + u_t \qquad (4.8)$$

where P_t is the consumer price for observation t, T_t is the per-unit excise tax, and W_t are control variables. Of our immediate interest is the coefficient β.

Sumner interpreted this coefficient also as a measure of the price to marginal cost mark-up. This interpretation was criticized by Bulow and Pfleiderer (1983) and Sullivan (1985) since it relies on strong functional form assumptions. We instead interpret the parameter simply as a reduced form parameter measuring the extent to which excise taxes are passed on into the consumer price. More precisely, since the variables are expressed in levels, the parameter β measures the pass-on of a unit cost (tax) change on the unit price change. This differs from the pass-on elasticity, which measures pass-on in percentage terms rather than in absolute levels.

Sumner finds a precise estimate of β of 1.074 (with a standard error of 0.013). This means that an increase in the excise tax by, say, 10 cents per unit leads to an increase in the price for cigarettes of 10.74 cents. (Or, since the analysis uses a panel, the price in a state with a 10 cents higher excise tax will be 10.74 cents higher.) Pass-on in absolute terms is thus greater than one. This implies that one can reject the hypothesis of perfect competition under constant marginal cost. To compute the pass-on elasticity, referring to pass-on in percentage terms, one would need to divide the number 1.074 by the price/marginal cost ratio. This number is not known, but it is generally greater than one. It is thus possible that the pass-on in percentage terms is incomplete.

Sullivan (1985) also estimates a reduced form version of (4.8). He allows for a more flexible specification, since he adds a quadratic term for the excise tax:[35]

$$P_t = \alpha + \beta_1 T_t + \beta_2 (T_t - \overline{T})^2 + \gamma W_t + u_t$$

where $\overline{T}$ is the average tax rate. The effect of an increase in the excise tax by one unit on the consumer price is thus $\beta_1 + 2\beta_2(T_t - \overline{T})$. Sullivan obtains a parameter estimate of β_1 equal to 1.089 (standard error of 0.26) and an estimate of β_2 equal to 0.0090 (standard error of 0.0035). For example, if the tax in one state is 10 cents higher than the average, the price in that state will be higher by the amount of 10 cents times 1.089 + 2*0.009 = 1.107, so it will be 11.07 cents higher. In contrast, if the tax rate is 10 cents lower than the average, then the price will be 10.71 cents lower. Pass-on is thus found to be asymmetric, yet of the same order of magnitude as in Sumner (1981).[36]

Barnett et al. (1995) estimate a structural model of oligopoly to assess the pass-on ('incidence') of excise taxes. This approach allows them to estimate the cost parameters and demand parameters that potentially explain pass-on. The advantage of this approach is thus that is can unravel the determinants of pass-on. A main disadvantage is that the results are more dependent on the functional form assumptions. Their estimates show that the price elasticity of demand is equal to 0.71, implying that a price increase by 1 per cent leads to a demand reduction of 0.71 per cent. They also find that manufacturers are subject to increasing returns to scale, and that conduct is consistent with Cournot oligopoly behaviour, indicating a moderate degree of market power. They use their elasticity parameter estimates to simulate the effects of a 1 cent increase in the excise tax, holding all other variables constant. They find that such an increase leads to an increase in the consumer price in the range of 0.9–1.0 depending on whether it concerns a federal or a state tax increase. This result is due to a combination of two factors. First, marginal costs are declining which induces overshifting of the taxes into consumer prices. Second, firms have market power and adjust their mark-ups downward when taxes increase (and upward when they decrease).

In a structural model of the automobile industry, Verboven (1998) considers the effects of the differential taxation on petrol and diesel cars on the manufacturers' pricing decisions. Verboven shows that the premium charged for diesel cars can be largely explained by higher mark-ups and less so by higher marginal costs for producing diesel cars. Firms thus exercise significant market power on their premium models (though not necessarily on their base models). Simulations on the effects of increasing the tax differential between petrol and diesel cars show that firms adjust their mark-ups significantly. In other words, although marginal costs are assumed constant, pass-on is small because of mark-up adjustment.

In sum, the studies on cigarette excise taxes show that pass-on of industry-wide cost changes (excise taxes) in the cigarette industry is more than complete in absolute terms. It is asymmetric in that an increase in costs is passed on more than a decrease. It is not possible to draw strong conclusions on pass-on in percentage terms, that is, the pass-on elasticity. All we can say is that the pass-on elasticity has to be adjusted by the price/marginal cost ratio; it will thus be smaller than the reported range of 1.07–1.09. Nevertheless, it seems that pass-on is rather large in the cigarette industry, which is confirmed by the structural analysis by Barnett et al. The results follow the moderate amount of market power and the possible presence of increasing returns to scale (declining marginal costs). In contrast, in the automobile market, the study by Verboven indicates that pass-on of cost changes is rather limited, at least regarding differential costs between petrol and diesel cars. This follows from the significant market power firms have regarding the pricing of their premium models.

2.3.1.2 Intermediate goods prices and pass-on

Several papers have looked at how the price for a final consumer good responds to the movements in the price of a single intermediate good, for example crude oil in energy economics, or unrefined sugar in agricultural economics. For simplicity, we assume in the following discussion that the intermediate good is used in a fixed proportion to the other inputs. This means that producing one unit of the final consumption good always requires the use of x units of the intermediate good, where x is called the transformation rate. In contrast to an excise tax, a movement in the price of an intermediate good only affects a fraction of the marginal cost. As explained in section 2.2.2.3, to know the full pass-on elasticity, one needs to adjust the pass-on elasticity by the cost share of the intermediate good. Without such an adjustment, one could falsely conclude that pass-on is low, whereas in fact only the cost share of the intermediate good is low. To illustrate, in unpublished results we estimated the following pass-on regression relating the price of roasted coffee to the price of its main intermediate input, coffee beans:

$$p_t = \alpha + \beta m_t + \gamma w_t + u_t$$

where p_t, m_t and w_t refer to the consumer price of roasted coffee, the price of the intermediate good, coffee beans, and control variables (for example, time and country dummies). All variables are now in lower-case letters, to denote that they are expressed in logarithms. The coefficient β can then be interpreted as a pass-on elasticity, rather than measuring pass-on in absolute levels. Regression results based on either quarterly or annual data for a set of 15 OECD countries since 1970 show that the pass-on elasticity varies between 0.5 and 0.7, depending on the country. This should not, however, be seen as evidence that pass-on of marginal cost savings is incomplete. One rather has to ask what is the share of coffee beans in the full marginal cost. Taking into account that labour and packaging costs also affect the marginal costs, most industry experts agree that coffee beans constitute slightly more than 60 per cent of the marginal costs. If this is true, then one could conclude from the estimates that the pass-on elasticity for industry-wide cost savings is close to one in the coffee markets of OECD countries.

Several studies have looked at pass-on of intermediate goods price fluctuations in levels, rather than in percentage terms.

$$P_t = \alpha + \beta M_t + \gamma W_t + u_t \tag{4.9}$$

This is similar to the experiments of Sumner (1981) and Sullivan (1985) on the pass-on of excise taxes in levels. There is, however, one important difference. An excise tax directly translates into a marginal cost. An intermediate goods price needs to be multiplied by its transformation rate to measure the impact on marginal cost. For example, for the production of 1 kg roasted coffee, 1.2 kg of coffee beans are required, so the transformation rate is 1.2.[37] To correctly assess whether pass-on in levels is complete one thus has to compare the estimate of β to the transformation rate (if this is known).

Borenstein et al. (1997) consider a version of regression (4.9) to assess the effect of fluctuations in crude oil prices on gasoline prices. They propose a lag adjustment specification, which distinguishes between short-run and long-run responses to fluctuations in crude oil prices. Our interest is mainly in the long-run response. They find that that an increase in the crude oil price by 1 cent leads to an increase in consumer prices by 0.55 cent in the first two weeks, and a further increase of 0.12 cent in the next two weeks; after six weeks pass-on is about 0.71 cents without any further effects at later points in time. Pass-on is asymmetric: decreases in the crude oil prices are passed on to consumers more slowly, but eventually at the same rate. A decrease in the crude oil price by 1 cent has no immediate effect; it leads to a 0.29 cent price reduction after four weeks, a 0.43 cent price reduction after six weeks and a 0.70 cent price reduction only after eight weeks. Overall, in the long run (after ten weeks) pass-on is less than one, about 0.81 cent. This is despite the fact that they are looking at pass-on in levels and not in percentage terms, so that one cannot use the fact that crude oil is only one component of the marginal cost of producing gasoline. Furthermore, the transformation rate of crude oil into gasoline is presumably greater than one. One explanation for the incomplete pass-on is that the marginal cost curve is upward-sloping (capacity constraints). As explained in the theoretical section, a reduction in price following a crude oil price decrease would lead to greater demand. To accommodate this demand, a larger production is needed. This could lead to a partially offsetting increase in cost, explaining incomplete pass-on. An alternative explanation would be that consumers become more price sensitive as prices increase (increasing price elasticity of demand). If this is so, then it is optimal to pass-on cost changes incompletely by adjusting markups.

In a related model, von Cramon-Taubadel (1997) considers the transmission of producer prices for pork into the wholesale prices in Northern Germany. He also distinguishes between short-term and long-term adjustments. Pass-on turns out to be complete in the long run: over a period of about ten weeks. The absolute margin between the producer and the wholesale price remains constant at DM1.30/kg. In the short run, however, pass-on is found to be incomplete: a unit increase in the producers' price leads to an increase in 0.58 units during the first week. Furthermore, it turns out that the adjustment process is asymmetric. The response to an increase in the producer price for pork is significantly faster than the response to a decrease. The most relevant message for our purposes is that pass-on of producer price into whole prices is complete in the long-run, that is, when considering a period of at least ten weeks. This result is confirmed in various other studies relating producer to wholesale prices in agricultural economics, see for example, Kinnucan and Forker (1987) for dairy product price transmission or Pick et al. (1990) for the citrus market.

Bettendorf and Verboven (2000) consider the price transmission for coffee beans into consumer prices for roasted coffee. In contrast to the other studies on price transmission in agricultural products, they consider a structural model to explain the causes underlying price transmission. They find that the rather weak relationship between bean and consumer prices follows largely from the fact that coffee beans are only a fraction of marginal costs. Nevertheless, they also show that mark-up adjustment is present, although it has only a modest importance since market power is limited. Genesove and Mullin (1998) consider a structural model of price setting for refined sugar. Although they do not explicitly consider the pass-on question, their estimation results imply similar results on pass-on as those obtained by Bettendorf and Verboven.

From the analysis of price transmission of intermediate goods prices common to all firms in the industry, we conclude that pass-on in the long run is relatively large, and in many cases complete. In the short run pass-on may be less complete, yet adjustment takes place relatively quickly, within a period of ten weeks for the studies we reviewed. Structural studies suggest that the large degree of pass-on follows from the relatively low degree of market power in the industries considered.

2.3.2 Evidence on pass-on by a fraction of the firms

2.3.2.1 Exchange rate pass-through in general

The large empirical literature on exchange rate pass-through also provides interesting evidence on pass-on of cost savings. This literature aims to measure by how much foreign firms pass on exchange rate fluctuations into the import price charged to local consumers. Understanding exchange rate pass-through is very relevant for our purposes, since a fluctuation in the exchange rate may be viewed as a change in the marginal costs of the foreign firm. Note that an exchange rate fluctuation only affects the cost position of the foreign firms. An exchange rate fluctuation should thus no longer be viewed as an industry-wide cost shock in contrast to the above discussed studies considering the effects of taxes and fluctuations in intermediate goods prices.

To analyse exchange rate pass-through, a common approach has been to regress the local consumer price to the exchange rate of the foreign firm, after controlling for other variables:

$$p_t = \alpha + \beta e_t + \gamma w_t + u_t. \tag{4.10}$$

In this specification, p_t is the logarithm of the consumer price at time t, expressed in the local currency of the importing country. The variable e_t is the logarithm of the exchange rate, measured in units of the local currency per unit of the foreign firm's currency. An increase (decrease) in e_t thus means an appreciation (depreciation) of the foreign firm's currency relative to the currency of the importing country. It may equivalently be viewed as an increase (decrease) in the marginal cost of the foreign firm. The vector w_t is a control vector of cost or demand shifters and u_t is a disturbance term.

In its simplest form the parameters α, β and γ can be estimated through ordinary least squares (OLS). Our main interest is the parameter β, which measures the extent of exchange rate pass-through, or the pass-on elasticity as discussed before in the theoretical analysis. For example, if $\beta = 0$, then a foreign firm does not pass on any of the exchange fluctuations in the local consumer prices. In this case, we have local currency price stability or zero pass-on of cost changes. In contrast, if $\beta = 1$, then a foreign firm would increase its price by 10 per cent whenever its currency appreciates by 10 per cent; and vice versa for a currency depreciation. In this case, we have complete exchange rate pass-through or full pass-on of changes in marginal costs.

The empirical literature has considered various alternative forms for regression (4.10). One alternative is to estimate the regression in first differences of the included variables:

$$\Delta p_t = \alpha + \beta \Delta e_t + \gamma \Delta w_t + u_t.$$

This regresses the change in local consumer prices on the change in the value of the foreign firm's currency and a change in the control variables.

More recently, authors have estimated 'error correction' versions of the model. Such regressions take into account that responses to exchange rate fluctuations may not necessarily be instantaneous. One can then distinguish between exchange rate pass-through in the short term and in the long term. Because of adjustment costs, one may expect exchange rate pass-through to be larger in the long term. One simple version of an error correction model is:

$$\Delta p_t = \beta^S \Delta e_t + \gamma^S \Delta w_t + \varphi(p_t - \alpha - \beta e_t - \gamma w_t) + u_t.$$

The parameters β^S and γ^S measure short-term responses of prices, whereas β and γ measure the long-term responses.[38]

Among the most interesting studies in the spirit of the above regressions are the contributions by Kreinin (1977), Woo (1984), Hooper and Mann

(1989), Feenstra (1989) and Athukorala and Menon (1994). All studies estimate some form of the above regressions, to find out the degree of exchange rate pass-through, after controlling for other factors.

Kreinin (1977) considers exchange rate pass-through to eight countries, using detailed commodity data. He estimates that exchange rate pass-through by foreign firms to US import prices is 50 per cent. In comparison, pass-through by foreign firms to import prices is 60 per cent in Germany, 70 per cent in Japan, 90 per cent in Canada and Belgium, and 100 per cent in Italy. One interpretation of the differences across the importing countries (which is also advanced by Kreinin) relates to differences in the size of the countries. For a large country like the USA, the market share of the foreign firms is likely to be small. An exchange rate shock thus only affects the marginal costs of a relatively small fraction of the firms. In contrast, foreign firms are likely to have a significant market share in smaller countries like Canada, Belgium or Italy. An exchange rate shock then affects the marginal costs of a larger fraction of firms. In an extreme case, when there are only foreign firms, an exchange rate fluctuation would affect the marginal cost of all the firms in the market, so that one may speak of an 'industry-wide cost change'. The fact that pass-on is smaller into the USA than into Belgium, Canada or Italy, is thus consistent with the hypothesis that firm-specific pass-on is smaller than industry-wide pass-on.

In our theoretical analysis we discussed whether incomplete pass-on of cost changes can be explained by mark-up adjustment, or by adjustments in marginal costs if these are not constant. Since Kreinin does not include direct controls for marginal cost changes, one cannot determine whether the observed incomplete pass-through can be explained by mark-up or marginal cost adjustment. Woo (1984) studies exchange rate pass-through by foreign firms exporting to the USA. He estimates pass-on to be between 40 and 75 per cent, in line with the results by Kreinin. He attributes the incomplete pass-through fully to mark-up adjustments, since he controls for changes in the marginal costs.

Hooper and Mann (1989) control for cost changes more completely, by accounting for foreign labour and materials costs, foreign capacity and US domestic costs. They also try to distinguish between long-run and short-run effects using an error correction approach. They find that the long-run exchange rate pass-through elasticity by foreign firms in the USA is 60 per cent. Because they control for costs, they interpret this incomplete exchange rate pass-through as mark-up adjustment. Interestingly, they also impose the symmetry restriction. The symmetry restriction says that a change in all factor prices (labour, materials) by, say, 10 per cent, should have the same effect on local consumer prices as a change in the exchange rate of the foreign firm by 10 per cent. Intuitively, this is because a change in all factor prices has the same effect on marginal costs as a change in the exchange rate, and should therefore also lead to the same degree of pass-on. They find that imposing the symmetry restriction does not affect the estimated pass-on elasticity of 60 per cent.

Feenstra (1989) investigates the symmetry restriction further. He tests whether a change in all factor prices has the same effect on local consumer prices as a change in the exchange rate and as an import tariff. Intuitively, an import tariff also has the same effect on marginal costs, and should therefore have a symmetric effect on local consumer prices. In contrast to the previous studies, Feenstra considers disaggregated data on individual industries. The symmetry hypothesis is tested for Japanese firms selling into three US markets: trucks, cars and heavy motorcycles. With respect to exchange rate changes, he finds a pass-on elasticity between 0.52 and 0.63 for trucks, between 0.7 and 0.8 for cars and between 0.7 and 1.1 for heavy motorcycles. With respect to tariffs, the pass-on elasticity is 0.57 for trucks, and between 0.95 and 1.39 for heavy motorcycles (no tariffs on cars). Feenstra finds statistical support for the symmetry hypothesis. Imposing the symmetry hypothesis,[39] he obtains estimates of the pass-on elasticities of 0.58 for trucks, 0.73 for cars and between 0.97 and 1.27 for heavy motorcycles. It is instructive to consider the interpretation provided by Feenstra for his differential findings regarding the pass-on elasticity with respect to tariffs. For trucks, the tariffs only applied to Japanese models produced in Japan, with a relatively small market share. In contrast, for heavy motorcycles, the tariff also applied to US based production by the Japanese companies. Furthermore, the Japanese firms have a modest market share in the US truck market, and a strong market share in heavy motorcycles, the only US competitor being Harley-Davidson. Once again, this indicates that it is important to distinguish between firm-level and industry-wide pass-on.

Another study that looks at more disaggregated data is by Athukorala and Menon (1994). They consider exchange rate pass-through in various sectors, in particular textiles, chemicals, metal products, general machinery, electrical machinery and transport equipment. They also take into account that an exchange rate fluctuation affects the marginal costs because inputs need to be imported at a different cost to the exchange rate change. Table 4.5 shows the pass-on coefficients for the various sectors, after controlling for changes in factor prices for imported inputs.[40]

First, Athukorala and Menon note that the aggregate pass-on elasticity of 0.788 is larger than the average pass-on elasticity across the industries, which is 0.47. From this they suggest that there is an upward bias in the pass-on elasticity due to aggregation. Second, going to individual sectors, they argue that the low pass-on elasticity for textiles, compared to the other

Table 4.5 Pass-on elasticities for Japanese firms in various industries, 1980–92

Industry	Export share in 1985	Pass-on elasticity
Textiles	3.37	0.140
Chemicals	5.47	0.483
Metal products	10.82	0.678
General machinery	21.13	0.461
Electrical machinery	15.95	0.549
Transport equipment	34.23	0.605
Miscellaneous products	9.03	0.566
Total manufacturers	100.00	0.788

Source: From Table 2 of Athukorala and Menon (1994)

sectors, is due to the limited market power of the Japanese firms in the textile industry.

2.3.2.2 Exchange rate pass-through due to mark-up adjustment

A new approach to estimating incomplete exchange rate pass-through was proposed by Knetter (1989). He criticizes the previous approaches because they only partially control for cost changes that coincide with the exchange rate fluctuation. According to Knetter, the previous approaches cannot identify very well whether pass-on is incomplete because of mark-up adjustment, or because of cost changes that coincide with the exchange rate change. Consider for example an exchange rate appreciation of a foreign firm's currency by 10 per cent. This has the direct effect of making the firm less competitive, similar to an increase in its marginal cost by 10 per cent. However, two additional cost effects may occur. First, an appreciation makes the imported inputs cheaper, so that marginal cost decreases. Failure to account for this would lead to an estimate for the pass-on elasticity that is biased downward. This was in fact shown to be the case by Athukorala and Menon (1994). Second, if an appreciation is at least partly passed on to consumers by raising import prices, then demand decreases. This has no further implications for costs only if marginal costs are flat. If, however, marginal costs are upward sloping, then the demand reduction also means a reduction in marginal costs, which partly compensates for the initial cost reduction.

To measure costs accurately, Knetter proposes considering exchange rate pass-through behaviour by an exporting firm selling into multiple local markets, as in the following regression:

$$p_{it} = \alpha_i + c_t + \beta_i e_{it} + \gamma w_{it} + u_{it}.$$

This regression model differs from the regression (4.10) in that now data are used for multiple local markets, as indicated by the additional subscript i. One thus uses a panel data set of countries and years. The term α_i is a fixed market effect to control for the fact that prices in one country may be persistently higher. The marginal cost c_t is unobserved, but it is assumed that it is common across all local destination markets to which the firm exports. Marston considered a two-country version of this model, and used the price in the country of production as a measure for the marginal costs in the local destination market. Knetter proposes estimating the model for multiple local markets, and estimates the common cost effects c_t as a fixed effect using time dummies. The regression model then is:

$$p_{it} = \alpha_i + \alpha_t + \beta_i e_{it} + \gamma w_{it} + u_{it}$$

or in first differences:

$$\Delta p_{it} = \alpha_t + \beta_i \Delta e_{it} + \gamma \Delta w_{it} + u_{it}.$$

The time effects thus aim to control for annual changes in marginal cost common for all countries. If one uses these fixed effects, then the coefficient β_m may be interpreted as a pass-through coefficient, after holding marginal costs constant; it thus purely aims to capture mark-up adjustment following exchange rate fluctuations. A coefficient for β_m equal to 1 does thus not mean that exchange rate pass-through is complete; it only means that mark-ups are not adjusted after exchange rate movements. In contrast, a coefficient for β_m equal to 0 means that mark-ups are fully adjusted after an exchange rate movement.

The advantage of the panel data approach proposed by Knetter is thus that it is possible to identify one key component of pass-on: the possibility that firms adjust their mark-ups.[41] Without such an identification, it is not clear whether one should explain incomplete pass-on by mark-up adjustment or by the presence of an upward sloping marginal cost curve.

Knetter (1993) applies his approach to study a rather large set of import markets and various industries. Knetter thus also aims to bring a synthesis of the existing empirical evidence using his methodology. One may summarize his findings as follows. First, there is a tendency by firms to pass-on incompletely by adjusting mark-ups in response to exchange rate fluctuations. This tendency is stronger for Japanese, German and UK firms than for US firms, with pass-on elasticities of respectively 0.52, 0.64, 0.64 and 1. Second, incomplete pass-through stemming from mark-up adjustment depends on the specific industry. For example, consider industries that have a common classification across all countries. Pass-on is complete for whisky, 84 per cent for titanium dioxide, 40 per cent for synthetic dyes and film, 25 per cent for paper, and absent for aluminium foil. One can conclude from this work that an important source of incomplete pass-on of cost savings is in fact mark-up adjustment. Thus even in an industry with constant marginal costs, it is possible that firms will pass on cost changes incompletely into consumer prices. The exact magnitude will, however, depend on the specific industry. In a subsequent paper, using data on the same industries, Knetter (1994) tests whether pass-on is asymmetric, that is, different for exchange rate appreciation from depreciation. He does not find evidence on this possibility.

In subsequent work, Gagnon and Knetter (1995) aim to distinguish between short-term and long-term adjustments of markups in response to exchange rate changes, following an error correction approach.[42] In a simple form, one may write the error correction model as:

$$\Delta p_{it} = \beta_i^S \Delta e_{it} + \gamma^S \Delta w_{it} + \varphi(p_{it} - \alpha_i - \alpha_t - \beta_i e_{it} - \gamma w_{it}) + u_t.$$

They apply their analysis using data on Japanese, German and US automobile exporters, in three engine size categories (less than 1 litre, 1–2 litre, and greater than 2 litres). They find that pass-on due to mark-up adjustment is especially low in the short run due to adjustment costs (price rigidities). In the long run, pass-on tends to be more complete, especially by US firms. Japanese firms have pass-on elasticities in the range of 0.09–0.12, meaning that they tend to pass-on only about 9 to 12 per cent of an exchange rate fluctuation into final consumer prices. This is true for all three engine size categories, and most local import markets. German firms tend to pass on more. In the low and medium-size engine categories, pass-on is usually 50 per cent or more. In the large size engine category, pass-on is close to being complete, with even overshooting to the import markets of France and Sweden. US firms show an even larger tendency to pass-on exchange rate movements, with elasticities ranging between 0.80 and 1.2. Gagnon and Knetter interpret the different results regarding the firms from the three sources, based on the type of demand they face. Japanese exporters attract only a few consumers with high reservation prices (high willingness to pay). This implies that an increase in the local price to compensate for a yen appreciation makes most consumers more price sensitive (higher price elasticity). This forces Japanese firms to adjust their mark-up. German and US exporters are more active in niche markets with few substitutes and many consumers with high reservation prices. They can more easily raise prices after an appreciation without making consumers more price sensitive.

Ghosh and Wolf (1994) also emphasize the importance of distinguishing between the short and the long run. They look at weekly prices set for the magazine *The Economist*. If one does not make a distinction between the short and the long run, then one may obtain the 'spurious' result that pass-on is close to zero, since adjusting to new conditions takes time.

Feenstra et al. (1996) bridge the gap between empirical studies that consider industry-wide pass-on (section 2.3.1) and studies that consider only a fraction of (exporting) firms. In particular, they consider the role of the market share of the foreign firms in determining pass-on in the long run, using data on the automobile industry. They find that exporting firms with a very small market share pass on about 70 per cent of an exchange rate fluctuation by adjusting mark-ups. As market share of the exporting firms increases, the pass-on elasticity decreases, to reach a minimum of about 0.30 when the market share is about 40 per cent. When the market share increases beyond 40 per cent the pass-on elasticity increases and becomes roughly complete when the exporting firms have 100 per cent of the market. These findings are very intuitive and consistent with the theory on pass-on of cost changes. If the market share of the exporting firms is 100 per cent, then the exchange rate fluctuation is essentially an industry-wide cost shock. One may then expect complete pass-on if the marginal cost curve is flat, and if firms act rather competitively. In contrast, if the market share of the exporting firms is small, then an exchange rate fluctuation corresponds more to a firm-specific cost shock.[43] In this case, pass-on is expected to be smaller.

Schembri (1989) analyses pass-on of exchange rate fluctuations for a Canadian export industry (using confidential data) selling an intermediate good to the USA and Canada. In contrast to the previous studies on exchange rate pass-through, Schembri explicitly estimates the cost and demand parameters of the export industry, from which the pass-on elasticity can then be computed using formulae similar to the ones we provided in section 2.2. This approach is feasible because there are more data than simply prices and exchange rates. Good cost data (factor prices and factor demands) and demand data (sales) are also available. Schembri reports that the pass-on elasticity by the Canadian export industry to the USA is approximately 0.85. This incomplete pass-on is partly due to the fact that marginal costs are not flat but increasing, and partly because of mark-up adjustment. Unfortunately, we do not know what the market share of the Canadian export industry is in the US market.

In a study of the US automobile market, Goldberg (1995) estimates a model with product differentiation, the nested logit model, which classifies the market in various segments, according to class and country of origin. Using the estimated demand and cost parameters, Goldberg simulates the pass-on of exchange rate fluctuations into consumer prices for various exporting firms selling into the USA. She computes exchange rate pass-through for Japanese and German firms, following both appreciations and depreciations. She distinguishes between the time when the Japanese firms

Table 4.6 Pass-on by Japanese and German firms, with and without quota constraints

	Without Japanese quota		With Japanese quota	
	($ appr.)	($ depr.)	($ appr.)	($ depr.)
Jap. subcompact	0.155	0.250	0.015	0.01
Jap. compact	0.18	0.30	0.010	0.02
Jap. trucks	0.195	0.245	0.235	0.255
Ger. intermediate	0.700	1.21	0.600	1.20
Ger. luxury	0.755	1.01	0.551	1.11
Ger. sports	0.65	0.805	0.60	1.06

Source: Goldberg (1995).

were capacity constrained due to import quotas and the time when they were unconstrained. Table 4.6 summarizes the results.

The first finding from this table is that Japanese firms typically pass-on a small amount, and considerably less than German firms. This is consistent with, for example, Knetter's study which uses a different methodology. Japanese firms cannot raise (lower) the prices in the USA in response to a cost increase (decrease) induced by the exchange rate, and need to adjust mark-ups. German firms have a higher ability to adjust their prices, since they are able to adjust their mark-ups by less. The second finding is that pass-through is asymmetric: a cost decrease induced by an appreciation of the dollar is passed on less than a cost increase induced by a depreciation of the dollar. The third finding is that pass-on by the Japanese firms was much smaller when they were subject to import quota constraints. This is very intuitive: an import quota constraint means that Japanese firms are capacity constrained, that is, they face a steeply increasing marginal cost curve. Under these conditions, any pass-on of cost changes has to be small since supply cannot be adjusted to demand responses.

Goldberg and Verboven (1998) consider the role of exchange rates in the European automobile market. They find evidence of incomplete pass-on, with pass-on elasticities of about 0.5. They show that one-third of the incomplete pass-on can be explained by mark-up adjustment. About two-thirds of the incomplete pass-on follows from the fact that exporting firms also have important local costs (transportation, distribution, marketing) which do not depend on the exchange rate fluctuations of the exporting firms. Abstracting from the presence of local costs, one can thus say that pass-on is relatively large, that is, mark-ups are only adjusted moderately. This is intuitive, since an exchange rate fluctuation of, say, the pound, affects the competitive position of all exporting firms selling into the UK.

2.3.3 Firm-specific pass-on

Studies that have looked at firm-specific pass-on of cost savings are scarce, especially when compared to the relatively large literature on pass-on of industry-wide cost changes (taxes, intermediate goods prices) and on pass-on of cost changes for a fraction of firms (exchange rates). In the following, we discuss two articles, one reduced-form approach to assessing firm-specific pass-on and one structural approach.[44]

Ashenfelter et al. (1998) propose a methodology to estimate firm-specific pass-on as opposed to the pass-on of an industry-wide cost change. They apply their approach to the Staples/Office Depot merger, a prominent US case in applying quantitative analysis.[45] Their analysis was a response to the merging firms' expert who had asserted, without providing empirical evidence, that Staples reduced price by two-thirds of any cost reduction (see Baker 1998). In essence their approach amounts to regressing the price an individual firm charges on both its own costs and the costs of other firms in the industry. Consider the following simplified regression, using the notation we introduced in section 2.3.1:

$$p_t = \alpha + \beta_1 m_t^F + \beta_2 m_t + \gamma w_t + u_t$$

where m_t^F measures the cost of the individual firm, that is, Staples; m_t measures industry-wide costs; and w_t captures control variables. Industry-wide cost m_t is approximated by the cost of Staples' competitor Office Depot. All variables are in logarithms, so the parameters may be interpreted as elasticities. The coefficient β_1 measures the pass-on of a cost change specific to the firm, controlling for industry-wide cost changes, which are measured by the coefficient β_2. Ashenfelter et al. also consider a restricted specification in which β_2 is set equal to zero, to see what bias would result if one does not control for industry-wide cost savings.

The data are provided by Staples and Office Depot. They are average monthly prices and variables costs for 30 identical products sold during the years 1995 and 1996 in various stores. The products were 17 pens, 7 paper items, 5 toner cartridges and 1 computer diskette. Store, product and time dummies are included to control for price variation due to differences across stores, products and months.

In the regression where β_2 is excluded, they find a pass-on elasticity of 0.571 (*t*-value of 194). This relatively high number does not distinguish between firm-specific and industry-wide cost changes. In the regression where β_2 is included they find a much lower elasticity of 0.149 (*t*-value of 38). It implies that when Staples' costs fall by 10 per cent, without a change in the rival's costs, then Staples would lower price by roughly only 1.5 per cent. The difference between the two regression models demonstrates that the bias from estimating firm-specific pass-on without controlling for industry-wide cost changes can be quite large. Ashenfelter et al. also consider whether there was any asymmetric pass-on of cost changes (that is, increases versus decreases), although they did not find evidence on this.

Kadiyali (1997) studies strategic pricing and exchange rate pass-through in the US photographic film industry. There are two main competitors: Kodak and Fuji. A structural econometric model is constructed, in which the demand and cost are directly estimated. Kadiyali then simulates the effects of changes in the yen/$ exchange rate on the prices set by Fuji. Since there are only two firms, one can view his simulation exercise as an analysis of firm-specific pass-on, in contrast to all the other articles on pass-on reviewed above. Kadiyali finds that the firms-specific pass-through elasticity for Fuji is relatively low. During the period 1980–84, when it had an average market share of 7.17 per cent, the pass-on elasticity was 0.076. During the period 1985–90, when its average market share increased to 15.59 per cent, the pass-on elasticity was 0.178.

2.3.4 Summary

In this section we started by reviewing the rich empirical literature on tax incidence, intermediate goods price transmission and exchange rate pass-through. The empirical results vary sometimes substantially from sector to sector. Yet it is still possible to make some empirical generalizations. It seems fair to say that the literature on the effects of excise taxes and intermediate goods prices finds that pass-on is close to 100 per cent, at least when one considers a sufficiently large time horizon (ten weeks or more). The literature on exchange rate pass-through tends to find incomplete pass-on, of an order of magnitude of 60–70 per cent. Part of this literature also relates the extent of exchange rate pass-though to the market share of the exporting sector. Finally, the scarce literature on firm-specific pass-on finds a relatively low degree of pass-on, especially when the market share of the firms is small. The estimates are in the range of 10–20 per cent.

This evidence makes clear the empirical importance of considering firm-specific rather than industry-wide pass-on. While industry-wide pass-on is more or less complete, firm-specific pass-on may be substantially smaller. At the same time, however, it is not sensible to draw strong general conclusions about the extent of firm-specific pass-on. The extent of firm-specific pass-on is likely to vary substantially from merger to merger, and it seems unreasonable to aim for a general presumption on the extent of firm-specific pass-on. In particular, there is a central role for market share in explaining firm-specific pass-on. Low firm-specific pass-on may be due to low market shares; yet in those cases the market power effects from mergers may also be low.

Our empirical review does not only stress the importance of assessing pass-on on a case-by-case basis; it has also introduced several possible methodologies for assessing pass-on of cost savings. We hope our analysis makes it clear that the methodology lends itself quite well for a fast implementation, as is required in merger cases. This is especially true for the reduced-form analysis, although structural approaches could also be feasible in some cases. The major potential constraint to assess pass-on in merger cases is thus not necessarily in the application of sophisticated technical analysis. Rather, it is important to make sure that the data required for the analysis are collected from the parties in an efficient way.

3. AN APPLICATION OF PASS-ON

In the previous section we have shown that the degree of pass-on depends on a variety of factors. For example, one cannot make general claims that pass-on of cost savings will be complete, unless one can be sure about certain market conditions (such as the absence of capacity constraints). Similarly, one cannot make a general claim that a monopolist (or a dominant firm) would not pass on any cost savings; to the contrary, it is likely that even a monopolist will pass on at least part of its cost saving to consumers. The extent of pass-on thus ultimately becomes an empirical matter. The previous section showed that there are several general tendencies, confirming the theory. An example is that that firm-specific pass-on is typically less than industry-wide pass-on. Nevertheless, it is also clear that one cannot hope to have completely general empirical conclusions on the extent of pass-on, applicable to any firm in any industry. One is thus left with the task of empirically measuring the extent of pass-on.

One approach would be to try to quantify all the relevant structural market conditions, for example the price elasticity of demand, the extent of capacity constraints, and so on. While such an approach may be feasible in certain applications, it is often impractical, especially in light of the time frame that competition agencies have to respect. The goal of this section is to illustrate that there is a practical empirical alternative to measure pass-on of cost savings in competition cases. The approach can be based on data that are often readily available to the firms, and can be carried out within a reasonable time using econometric techniques.

Using data for refrigerated juices, we will illustrate how a practical estimate can be made of the extent of pass-on using standard econometric techniques. The econometric framework further elaborates on the framework of Ashenfelter et al. (1998). They have used it to assess firm-specific pass-on in the Staples/Office Depot merger, as discussed above. We show

how the framework can be extended to also consider the multiproduct nature of firms. Yet to estimate firm-specific pass-on, we would also need data on competing firms.

We begin by outlining the required data and the actual data in section 3.1. We next discuss the econometric framework in section 3.2. Finally, we present and interpret the empirical results in section 3.3.

3.1 The Data

3.1.1 Data requirements

Price and cost data
Whether one measures absolute pass-on or relative pass-on (that is, the pass-on elasticity), two key types of data are required: price data and cost data. The price data refer to the price for the products sold by the merging firms. The cost data in principle refer to marginal cost, though in practice variable costs may be a reasonable proxy.

In merger analysis, it is important to focus on firm-specific pass-on, rather than industry-wide pass-on, since cost efficiencies are typically only realized by the merging firms. In the previous section it was shown that firm-specific pass-on is typically lower than industry-wide pass-on. We also discussed there the framework of Ashenfelter et al. (1998) to measure firm-specific pass-on. The required data for their approach are price and cost data for several firms in the industry, for example the two merging firms. We do not have this information. Instead, we show how one can easily extend the Ashenfelter et al. framework to account for the multiproduct nature of firms. We also show that it is important to focus on the price level in the whole industry, rather than on the prices of the individual products.

Sales data
In addition, as will be shown in section 3.2, it will be useful to have sales data. With sales data, it is possible to summarize the firm-level price data to an industry price index. This may be more relevant from a competition policy point of view, especially if the price index is closely related to measures of consumer surplus. Note that the pass-on measures in the previous chapter were often closely related to consumer surplus or the industry price index.

The size of the data set
Given price and cost data (and possibly sales data), the remaining question is how many of these price and cost observations are required. In principle, one could follow the prices and costs over an extended period in time. For example, one could collect annual price and cost data over a period of

30 years. Yet in practice, it is probably asking too much to obtain the price and cost information dating back 30 years. When information is available over a more limited historical period, the number of observations to identify pass-on can be increased by increasing the frequency of the observations. For example, one could collect quarterly data on prices and cost over the last ten years, to have 40 observations to identify pass-on. Similarly, one could gather monthly data over three years and have 36 observations on prices and costs. One could increase the number of observations even further by having a higher frequency, say weekly, but in practice, the informational value of this would depend on the actual variation of price and cost data in short intervals. For example, costs and prices for gasoline show a high variation, even within a month, so that a high frequency of data may provide useful additional information. In contrast, the prices for cars are typically adjusted by the manufacturers only a few times a year, so that there is probably little to be gained from increasing the frequency beyond the quarterly level.[46] Note also that when one increases the frequency of the data, it may become useful to specify a dynamic model, which distinguishes between short-run and long-run pass-on.

In addition to following the price and cost observations over a certain time period, there is the possibility of pooling the data. To see how this works, note that data are often available at a finer level of detail than at the level of the firm. A firm may sell different products, in different stores. Suppose that each firm operates in three different product categories and sells in ten different stores. One could then collect historical price and cost data to estimate pass-on for each product in each store. This would amount to 30 (3×10) separate pass-on studies. But alternatively, one could pool the information on products and stores and construct a large panel data set in three dimensions: time, stores and product categories. If one is willing to make certain assumptions, for example that the degree of pass-on is the same across stores and/or product categories, then one can conduct a single large study of pass-on instead of 30 small ones. By pooling the data, one can thus also try to identify pass-on by comparing price and cost observations across stores and products, in addition to following the evolution of price and cost over time. This can greatly increase the amount of information, so that one does not necessarily have to go back very far in time. In our example of three product categories and ten stores, the number of observations can be multiplied by a factor of 30 when one pools the data. For pooling to be effective it is necessary that prices and costs show enough variation across stores and product categories, in addition to the previous requirement of sufficient variation over time.

To summarize, a suitable data set to estimate the extent of pass-on would contain the following variables for several firms in the industry:

prices (marginal or variable), costs and (possibly) sales. The information can be collected as a panel data set with the following dimensions: time, stores and product categories. This information should be available for many cases.

3.1.2 Actual data

The panel data set collected by Ashenfelter et al. (1998) consisted of the following.

- There was information on two firms: Staples and Office Depot. Since there was no information on the other firms, the information on Office Depot was treated as a good proxy for all other firms.
- There was information on prices and variable cost.
- The following dimensions of the panel were included:
  - Time: 24 months during 1995–96.
  - Stores: 500 stores.
  - Product categories, here called 'stock keeping units' (SKU): 30 SKUs, including 17 pens, 7 paper items, 5 toner cartridges and 1 diskette.

The total number of observations in the panel on the prices and costs for both firms can thus be up to 360 000 ($24 \times 500 \times 30$).

The analysis in this section has made use of an alternative data set on the market for refrigerated juice. In contrast to Ashenfelter et al. we have only information available on one supermarket: Dominick's Finer Foods, one of the two largest retail chains in the Chicago metropolitan area.[47] There are three main brands sold by the retail chain: Tropicana, Minute Maid and the private label. There are 146 different stores and the brands are sold in many different varieties (called UPCs).

Our panel data set on the refrigerated juice market thus consists of the following:

- There is information on three brands: Tropicana, Minute Maid and the private label. The other brands have a negligible share of the market and are ignored (only 11 per cent of the market for the remaining brands).
- There is information on prices, variable cost (measured by the manufacturer's price) and sales.
- The following dimensions of the panel are included:
  - Time: 218 weeks between 1989–93.
  - Stores: 146 stores.
  - Product categories, here called UPCs: about 200.

The total number of observations in the panel is thus also very large. To keep the data manageable, we followed Kadiyali et al. (2000) and averaged the data across stores and across varieties. This reduces the number of observations to only 218 (the number of weeks). It thus appears that we no longer make use of panel data information, and that all identification of pass-on would become the result of variation in prices and cost over time. Yet this is not the case. Because our price and cost data are now averages (across store and UPC), the variation across stores and UPC also plays a role in identifying pass-on.[48] We emphasize that in principle we could also have followed the same approach as in Ashenfelter et al. (1998) yet in practice it turned out to be more convenient to follow the 'averaging approach'.[49] This may also be the case in competition policy cases.

The main difference between the application of Ashenfelter et al. and our current application lies in the ownership structure of the firms. In Ashenfelter et al., two independent firms are chosen that are competing with each other. In our application, three brands are considered. At the retail level, the prices of these brands are set jointly by the retailer, rather than competitively (see Kadiyali et al. 2000). One could thus view our analysis as complementary to Ashenfelter et al.: we do not focus on the extent of pass-on of cost changes by competing firms, but rather on the extent of pass-on of cost savings by brands whose prices are set cooperatively (by the retailer). For both applications, the same econometric framework can be used.

3.2 The Empirical Framework

Suppose there are three products, products 1, 2 and 3, and we are interested in studying pass-on of cost changes into consumer prices. A 'traditional' approach would be to estimate the following basic regression equation for firm 1:

$$p_{ijt}^{1} = \alpha_i + \alpha_j + \beta^1 m_{ijt}^{1} + \gamma w_{ijt} + u_{ijt}.$$

In this specification, p_{ijt}^{1} is the price charged by product 1 for a product sold in store i, belonging to product category j at time t. Similarly, m_{ijt}^{1} is the marginal (or variable) cost incurred by product 1 in store i in product category j at time t. The variable w_{ijt} measures other factors that may affect the price. The terms α_i, α_j, β^1 and γ are parameters that are to be estimated using common econometric regression techniques. For example, the ordinary least squares method (OLS) may be used under certain assumptions.

The parameters α_i and α_j are called fixed effects for, respectively, the store i, the product category j. Ashenfelter et al. (1998) also include a time effect, α_t. It is important to include them as parameters to be estimated, since they measure the systematic effect that a store, product category or time period could have on the price. (For example, one product category can be systematically more expensive than the other product category.)

The main parameter of interest is β^1, which measures pass-on. It may either reflect absolute or relative pass-on, depending on how the variables are measured. If the price p^1_{ijt} and the cost m^1_{ijt} are measured in monetary units, for example in euros, then β^1 measures absolute pass-on: the effect of an increase in the variable cost by one euro on the price in euros. In contrast, if the price and cost are measured in logarithms, then β^1 measures the relative pass-on, or the pass-on elasticity.

Ashenfelter et al. showed that the above specification fails to distinguish between firm-specific pass-on and industry-wide pass-on. The reason is that the specification looks at the effects of cost increases by firm 1 on the price charged by firm 1, without controlling for any possible accompanying cost changes by the other firms. In practice, this will lead to biased estimates for firm-specific pass-on.

A more general approach is therefore to modify the regression equation and also include the costs of the other products in the regression, that is, the variables m^2_{ijt} and m^3_{ijt}. In Ashenfelter et al. these other products were from the merging partner. Here we include other products of the same firm.

Pass-on equation for firm 1's price p^1_{ijt}

$$p^1_{ijt} = \alpha_i + \alpha_j + \beta^1 m^1_{ijt} + \beta^2 m^2_{ijt} + \beta^3 m^3_{ijt} + \gamma w_{ijt} + u_{ijt} \tag{4.11}$$

More specifically, one can interpret the parameters as follows:

β^1: This reflects product-specific pass-on: the pass-on of a cost increase by product 1 on the price of product 1's product.

$\beta^1 + \beta^2 + \beta^3$: This measures product 1, 2 and 3's overall pass-on: the pass-on of a cost increase by product 1, product 2 and product 3 together on the price of product 1's product (if the costs are highly correlated).

As before, the pass-on may be either in absolute terms, or in elasticity form (in relative terms), depending on whether one measures the prices and costs in monetary values (euros) or in logarithms.[50]

One may easily extend the analysis beyond pass-on by product 1. One can thus also ask how a cost change will be passed on to the price of product 2 and product 3. It is straightforward to formulate similar regression equations for product 2 and 3. To avoid too much notation, these equations are not shown here.

We now discuss how one can extend beyond the Ashenfelter et al. framework. Instead of asking what will happen to the individual price of product 1, or product 2 or product 3, one may wonder what would happen to a composite price index when the cost of one product (or several products) changes. This may indeed be the more natural question to ask if one is interested in consumer welfare questions relating to the industry as a whole. In fact, consumer theory has discussed extensively the choice of an appropriate price index to measure changes in consumer surplus. A detailed discussion on the choice of an appropriate price index is beyond the scope of this study. Yet it is fair to say that there is a consensus that one should include a representative basket of related products in the price index, using sales as weights. In the theoretical discussion on pass-on in the previous section the emphasis was also on what happens to the price level for the industry as a whole.

Suppose the price index for store i of product category j at time t is measured by the variable p^{I}_{ijt}. Such a price index is typically some weighted average of the prices of product 1, product 2 and product 3 (p^1_{ijt}, p^2_{ijt} and p^3_{ijt}), where the weights may be the sales at a certain base period. Using the price index as the relevant focus it is possible to formulate the following variation of the above regression equation.

Pass-on equation for a composite price index p^{I}_{ijt}

$$p^{\mathrm{I}}_{ijt} = \alpha_i + \alpha_j + \beta^1 m^1_{ijt} + \beta^2 m^2_{ijt} + \beta^3 m^3_{ijt} + \gamma w_{ijt} + u_{ijt} \tag{4.12}$$

The only difference with the previous regression equation is that one now looks at the effects of cost changes on the whole price index, rather than on the price of a single product. We now have the following interpretation of the included parameters:

β^1:	Product 1's specific pass-on into the price index.
β^2:	Product 2's specific pass-on into the price index.
β^3:	Product 3's specific pass-on into the price index.
$\beta^1 + \beta^2 + \beta^3$:	Product 1, 2 and 3's overall pass-on.

The above equations (4.11) and (4.12) can be estimated directly using the large panel data set. Alternatively, the data can be averaged across the store and/or the product category. As discussed in section 3.1.2, in our application we average the observations across both dimensions of the panel.[51] The equations (4.11) and (4.12) then become:

Pass-on equation for product 1's averaged price $\overline{p}_t^1$

$$\overline{p}_t^1 = \overline{\alpha} + \beta^1 \overline{m}_t^1 + \beta^2 \overline{m}_t^2 + \beta^3 \overline{m}_t^3 + \gamma \overline{w}_t + u_t \qquad (4.11')$$

Pass-on equation for an averaged composite price index $\overline{p}_t^I$:

$$\overline{p}_t^I = \overline{\alpha} + \beta^1 \overline{m}_t^1 + \beta^2 \overline{m}_t^2 + \beta^3 \overline{m}_t^3 + \gamma \overline{w}_t + u_t \qquad (4.12')$$

One may of course also estimate the pass-on equations for product 2 and 3's price. These equations will be the regression equations to which the data set is applied in the next section.

3.3 The Results

3.3.1 Base results

We have estimated the pass-on regressions with the variables expressed either in monetary values or in logarithms. The main results are displayed in Table 4.7.

Table 4.7 shows the estimates of pass-on when cost increases and cost decreases have symmetric effects on the price (as was implicitly assumed in the empirical framework of section 3.2). The first twelve rows show the effects of product-specific cost changes on the price of the private label, Minute Maid, and Tropicana, respectively. They are based on the specifications (4.11′). The final four rows show the effect of cost changes on the general market price index, based on the specification (4.12′). The first two columns show the estimates (and standard errors) when all variables are expressed in monetary values; the final two columns show the estimates when the variables are expressed in logarithms.

Most relevant for our purposes are the numbers printed in bold. They measure the product-specific pass-on rate. The other numbers refer to the parameters estimates for the control variables, namely the competitors' costs. They are not of immediate interest, but as was discussed in the previous section, it is necessary to include them as control variables, since otherwise the parameters of our main interest will be biased.

We begin by discussing the pass-on regressions for the private label, Minute Maid and Tropicana, as shown in the first twelve rows. These specifications are most comparable to the one considered by Ashenfelter

Table 4.7 Pass-on of cost changes – effect on price of the private label, Minute Maid, Tropicana and on the market price index

	variable	Level specification		Logarithmic specification	
		Estimate	Standard error	Estimate	Standard error
Private label	constant	−0.113	(0.144)	0.279	(0.042)
	cost PL	**1.493**	(0.056)	**1.120**	(0.043)
	cost MM	−0.003	(0.041)	−0.014	(0.030)
	cost TR	−0.044	(0.050)	−0.038	(0.050)
Minute Maid	constant	0.649	(0.168)	0.523	(0.048)
	cost PL	−0.135	(0.065)	−0.121	(0.049)
	cost MM	**1.297**	(0.048)	**0.945**	(0.035)
	cost TR	−0.097	(0.059)	−0.108	(0.058)
Tropicana	constant	−0.354	(0.142)	0.139	(0.035)
	cost PL	−0.038	(0.055)	−0.017	(0.035)
	cost MM	−0.087	(0.041)	−0.055	(0.025)
	cost TR	**1.631**	(0.050)	**1.275**	(0.041)
Market price index	constant	−0.369	(0.157)	0.177	(0.041)
	cost PL	**0.505**	(0.061)	**0.359**	(0.042)
	cost MM	**0.488**	(0.045)	**0.332**	(0.030)
	cost TR	**0.549**	(0.055)	**0.493**	(0.049)

Source: Author's calculations on basis of University of Chicago data.

Note: Figures in bold are product-specific pass-on rates.

et al. (1998) especially the logarithmic specification. Consider first the regression for the private label (first four rows), with the variables in monetary values (levels). It can be seen that a cost increase for the private label by one unit would lead to a price increase by 1.493 units.[52] This is thus the absolute pass-on, which is estimated with a high precision as can be seen from the low standard error. The effect of the rival firms costs' is negligible (insignificantly negative). The logarithmic specification gives an estimate of the relative pass-on, or elasticity, namely 1.120. It says that a cost increase for the private label by 1 per cent would lead to a price increase of 1.12 per cent, after controlling for cost changes for the competing firms.

The pass-on estimates for Minute Maid and Tropicana are shown by the bold numbers in the next eight rows. The absolute pass-on numbers for Minute Maid and Tropicana are estimated to be 1.297 and 1.631, respectively. The relative pass-on numbers, or the pass-on elasticities, are estimated to be 0.945 and 1.275, respectively.

One can conclude from these numbers that product-specific pass-on of cost changes is considerably larger in this market than in the market considered by Ashenfelter et al. (1998). For example, the product-specific pass-on elasticities are around one, so that pass-on is roughly complete. This compares to the product-specific pass-on elasticity of around 0.15, as had been obtained by Ashenfelter et al. One interpretation for this finding is the different focus of our analysis. Ashenfelter et al. also took into account cost changes by competing retail chains. In contrast, the analysis here only focuses on competing brands within the same retail stores. If the prices are set more or less cooperatively within a retail store (as in Kadiyali et al. 2000), then a higher degree of pass-through would be reasonable, and also consistent with the theoretical results derived in the previous chapter. Nevertheless, it is possible that the estimates would go down if the analysis could also control for the cost increases by a competing retail chain (which was not feasible in our application because of limited data).

How can one interpret the results in light of the theoretical discussion of section 2.2? To address this question, it is necessary to consider product-specific pass-on with respect to the market price index, rather than with respect to the individual prices. In our opinion, this approach is also more appealing from a competition policy point of view, at least if the market price index is a reasonably good approximation for consumer surplus. The estimates are shown in the last four rows of Table 4.7.

Looking at the extent of absolute product-specific pass-on, one can see that a cost increase for the private label by one unit would lead to a rise in the market price index by 0.505 units. A cost increase by one unit for Minute Maid would lead to a slightly lower rise in the market price index (0.488 units), whereas a cost increase by one unit for Tropicana would have a larger effect (0.549 units). The product-specific pass-on estimates expressed in relative terms, or the elasticities, are lower. A 1 per cent cost increase for the private label would lead to a general price increase by 0.359 per cent, whereas a 1 per cent cost increase for Minute Maid would lead to a general price increase by only 0.332 per cent, and a 1 per cent cost increase for Tropicana would lead to a general price increase by 0.493 per cent.

If cost shocks are highly correlated, the sum of these pass-on rates is a rough measure of the industry-wide pass-on. In absolute terms this amounts to a number of 1.542, whereas in relative terms it amounts to 1.184. This says that a joint cost change by 1 unit or by 1 per cent would lead to a change in the market price index by respectively 1.542 units and 1.18 per cent. This indicates some tendency of overshifting, at least in absolute terms.

To what extent are these results consistent with the theoretical analysis in the previous section? First, note that it is confirmed that product-specific pass-on is smaller than the overall pass-on of all products' costs.[53] This underscores the importance of formulating a pass-on regression after controlling for the cost changes by all firms, if one is interested in an unbiased estimate for product-specific pass-on.

Second, note that product-specific pass-on is the smallest for the products with the smallest market shares in this example. The average market shares of the private label, Minute Maid and Tropicana during the sample period were respectively 28.0, 24.8 and 47.2 per cent (ignoring the market shares of other brands, which constitute about 11 per cent of the sales; see Kadiyali et al. 2000). Tropicana is the firm with the highest market share and the highest pass-on, especially when expressed in elasticity terms. The theoretical analysis in section 2.2.3.3 was ambiguous about the role of market shares, with a tendency of the highest degree of pass-on for intermediate market shares (see Observation 2.9). The empirical analysis correspondingly provides important information that theoretical considerations cannot bring.

Third, the overall pass-on estimates in absolute terms indicate a tendency of overshifting. This appears to be in contradiction with the theory, in particular the predictions on pass-on with differentiated products, unless one assumes strong increasing returns to scale (declining marginal cost curve). For example, Observation 2.7 established that industry-wide pass-on is incomplete in a logit model of product differentiation. Yet it was also noted that this was dependent on the functional form assumptions of the logit model, which generate price elasticities that are increasing in price, or equivalently, mark-ups that are declining in price; under the logit assumptions firms thus absorb cost changes by adjusting their mark-ups. Under other models of product differentiation, such as the CES model, mark-up absorption may be lower (or absent) so that industry-wide pass-on in absolute terms can be greater than 1. This application thus shows that since we do not know in general how the elasticity or mark-up varies with price, it is better to take an empirical approach and measure the extent of pass-on.

3.3.2 Extensions

The above analysis of pass-on takes the most stylized form. In merger investigation, it is desirable to do various extensions so as to confirm the robustness of the results. We have already pointed out that it would be useful to have information on another retail chain, in particular if the proposed merger was between two retail chains (in which case it should not be too difficult to collect the data, as demonstrated by Ashenfelter et al. (1998)). Nevertheless, our analysis may be a reasonable approximation if competition between retail chains is relatively weak, for example due to consumer search costs. Our application may also be a reasonable point of departure if one is analysing a merger between two manufacturers (say Minute Maid and Tropicana) rather than between two retail chains.[54]

Regarding the econometric specification, several possible extensions may be undertaken. First, it is possible to estimate the model on the full data set, rather than averaged across stores and product categories. Furthermore, it is possible to consider other control variables for the reduced form pass-on equation, for example a measure for the macro-economic state of the economy (GDP, interest rate, and so on). It could also be possible to introduce dynamics in the analysis, for example by adding lagged price and cost variables, or by specifying a complete error correction model, which can distinguish between short-run and long-run effects of cost changes.

Finally, one may consider the role of alternative functional forms. We have already considered two possible functional form specifications: the linear and the logarithmic specifications. Note that both functional forms generated comparable measures for goodness of fit. An R^2 in the range of 0.6–0.75 was obtained for the pass-on regressions on the individual prices; an R^2 of around 0.5 was obtained for the pass-on regressions on the market price index, whether one considers the linear or the logarithmic functional form. A further extension is to consider the role of asymmetries in pass-on regarding cost increases and cost decreases. We have considered this possibility in Table 4.8, for the linear case. (The results for the logarithmic case are analogous.)

The interpretation of Table 4.8 is similar to that of Table 4.7. The new parameters are the parameters related to the cost 'up' variables. These parameters indicate whether there is a different effect on prices (in absolute terms) when costs go up, than when costs go down. In merger analysis, the relevant estimates refer to what would happen to prices when costs go down (since the claims by the parties concern efficiencies rather than inefficiencies). We limit our discussion here to the last eight rows; the discussion for the other results straightforwardly generalizes the previous table. One can see that a one-unit cost decrease by the private label would decrease the price by 0.518. In contrast, a one-unit cost increase has a smaller effect: it would increase the price by only $0.518-0.014=0.504$ units. Note, however, that the difference is not significant. Similarly, for Minute Maid and Tropicana the effects of cost increases are somewhat less pronounced than for decreases, though the effects are not significant. In sum, this extension would indicate that the pass-on estimates remain more or less robust whether or not one allows pass-on to differ when the effect of cost increases is allowed to differ from the effect of cost decreases.

3.4 Concluding Remarks

The above empirical analysis illustrates how an analysis of pass-on can be implemented in practice. The analysis complements the original work of

Table 4.8 Pass-on regressions with possible asymmetries

		Level specification	
		Estimate	Standard error
Private label	constant	−0.091	0.144
	cost PL	**1.442**	0.062
	cost PL up	**0.026**	0.015
	cost MM	0.006	0.042
	cost MM up		
	cost TR	−0.031	0.051
	cost TR up		
Minute Maid	constant	0.675	0.167
	cost PL	−0.143	0.066
	cost PL up		
	cost MM	**1.253**	0.058
	cost MM up	**0.026**	0.020
	cost TR	−0.082	0.059
	cost TR up		
Tropicana	constant	−0.196	0.153
	cost PL	−0.050	0.055
	cost PL up		
	cost MM	−0.089	0.040
	cost MM up		
	cost TR	**1.545**	0.061
	cost TR up	**0.032**	0.013
Whole market	constant	−0.475	0.170
	cost PL	**0.518**	0.069
	cost PL up	**−0.014**	0.016
	cost MM	**0.505**	0.055
	cost MM up	**−0.015**	0.019
	cost TR	**0.606**	0.068
	cost TR up	**−0.026**	0.015

Source: Author's calculations on basis of University of Chicago data.

Note: Figures in bold are product-specific pass-on rates.

Ashenfelter et al. (1998). They demonstrate that relatively simple regressions can be estimated, to measure firm-specific pass-on using data on price and variable firm-specific costs to be provided by the two merging firms. We extended the analysis to include other products sold by the same firm to account for the multiproduct nature of the firm.[55]

Our analysis was done in the context of retailing. Note that this also has implications for analysing mergers by (upstream) firms in manufacturing. If two upstream firms merge, one should not simply ask to what extent these firms will pass-on cost savings into the wholesale prices charged to the downstream retailers. One should also ask whether these downstream retailers will pass-on the changed wholesale prices onto the final consumer prices.

NOTES

1. See Teece (1980) for a discussion of less easily quantifiable sources of economies of scope, for example managerial expertise, a good financial rating and a sales staff.
2. Another issue is that there may exist scale economies internally in these activities. There is some evidence that the average cost of advertising falls as its volume increases (Martin 1993).
3. See Sutton (1991, 1998). To illustrate the crucial difference between endogenous and exogenous (sunk) costs, consider the different effects that these costs have on industry structure. The equilibrium level of concentration declines with the ratio of market size to technologically determined set-up costs and rises with the toughness of price competition. Intuitively, the larger the market is, the more firms can cover the (exogenously given) set-up costs, and thus the more firms are induced to enter. This relationship breaks down for endogenous set-up costs. By incurring greater advertising or R&D costs a firm can raise the perceived quality of its products, thereby enhancing the demand for them. Competition between the firms involves an escalation of outlays by firms and so leads to higher sunk costs being incurred. Moreover, the larger the market, and thus the larger the potential profits are, the greater the incentive the firms have to channel demand towards their products. Thus, the larger the market, the higher are sunk costs. As a result, it is not possible to support more firms, the larger the market is.
4. In the case of some forms of advertising there are additional problems. In particular, it is not clear how one should evaluate the effects of non-informative image building advertising on consumer welfare.
5. This section is based on Panzar (1989).
6. In the theoretical literature it is often emphasized that the production and cost functions represent a given state of technological knowledge. However, at least the first firm to organize production at some scale will necessarily have to adapt the technology to that scale. It may be difficult both theoretically and empirically to discriminate between innovations that lower the cost function from the adaptations necessary to achieve the lower unit cost at a higher scale. For a more detailed discussion of these problems, see Gold (1981).
7. For a more detailed discussion of this point, see Gold (1981).
8. Estimating a production function ignores the endogeneity of the input factors. A cost function gives a theory on how these input factors are determined, with the resulting 'elegant instruments', being the input prices (being exogenously determined on a perfectly competitive input market).
9. Formally this can be shown by taking the derivative of the average cost function, that is

$$\frac{\mathrm{d}\left[\frac{C(q,w)}{q}\right]}{\mathrm{d}q} = \frac{MC}{q} - \frac{C}{q^2} = \frac{MC - AC}{q}.$$

10. If one assumes that all inputs are chosen in a cost-minimizing manner, that is according to $x = X(q, w)$ then the two measures coincide, that is

$$E(q, X(q, w)) = S(q, w).$$

11. In the single-product case, the degree of scale economies can be expressed as:

$$S(q, w) = \frac{AC(q, w)}{MC(q, w)} = \frac{C(q, w)}{qMC(q, w)}.$$

12. To see this, first note that:

$$SC(q_1, q_2) = [C(q_1, q_2) - C_1(q_1, q_2) - C_2(q_1, q_2)]/C(q_1, q_2).$$

Using the definition of incremental cost, the degree of scale economics can be written

$$SC(q_1, q_2) = 1 - \frac{C_1(q_1, q_2) + C_2(q_1, q_2)}{C(q_1, q_2)}.$$

Since the last term is positive when incremental costs are positive, it follows that $SC(q1, q2) < 1$.

13. One may derive conditions (weak cost complementarities) in terms of the properties of the multi-product cost function that can be used for empirically inferring the presence of economies of scope.
14. Their analysis is discussed in Chapter 3 of this volume.
15. To see this, rewrite the inequality as

$$\frac{C(q)}{q}[tq + (1-t)q] < \frac{C(tq)}{tq}tq + \frac{C((1-t)q)}{(1-t)q}(1-t)q.$$

Hence:

$$0 < \left[\frac{C(tq)}{tq} - \frac{C(q)}{q}\right]tq + \left[\frac{C((1-t)q]}{(1-t)q} - \frac{C(q)}{q}\right](1-t)q.$$

It is easy to see that economies of scale implies that this inequality is fulfilled, since both []-parentheses are positive.

16. This condition was established by Baumol et al. (1982).
17. Their analysis is discussed in Chapter 3 of this volume.
18. If the two firms have access to different technologies (i.e. different knowledge) a merger may also reduce cost in the absence of economies of scale. It may be that both firms have constant returns to scale but that one firm has a superior technology with a lower marginal cost. Then, transferring knowledge to the other plant, or transferring production to the superior plant, lowers cost. It may also be that the two firms have different, but complementary, patents so that a merger expands the production technology to both plants.
19. Unfortunately, the empirical literature does not report anything on the length of time that is required in order to achieve scale economies in different industries. Another important issue unexplored in the literature is the possible difference in time required for achieving scale economies by means of a merger and by means of internal growth.
20. A discussion of the econometric issues involved in empirical analysis of production can be found in Coelli et al. (1998).
21. For more on these issue see Coelli et al. (1998). They also discuss the choice of functional forms. The first study to use the cost function, with factor prices as arguments, in the study of scale economies appears to be Nerlove (1963).
22. This approach was pioneered by Spady and Friedlaender (1978).
23. See Fuss and Waverman (1981), and Fuss (1983) for a survey. See also Foreman and Beauvais (1999).
24. This study is usefully summarized in Bailey and Friedlaender (1982).
25. This study is usefully summarized in Panzar (1989).
26. This study is usefully summarized in Coelli et al. (1998).
27. Assume that the merger tends to increase price by dP/P per cent as a result of the first effect. Then, for the net effect to be non-positive, it is necessary that $(dc/c)(dP/dc)$

$(c/p) \leq -\mathrm{d}P/P$, where $(\mathrm{d}c/c)$ is the percentage cost reduction, and $\beta = (\mathrm{d}P/\mathrm{d}c)(c/p)$ is the pass-on elasticity. The pass-on elasticity indicates the percentage by which the price would be reduced if cost is reduced by 1 per cent.

28. We make the standard stability assumption that marginal cost is not decreasing too much, that is, $-\omega < \varepsilon$ at the equilibrium, so that the supply curve intersects the demand curve from below.
29. See, for example, Feenstra (1989), Marston (1990) or Knetter (1993).
30. For example, some weak stability assumptions for guaranteeing existence and uniqueness of equilibrium are required.
31. See Anderson et al. (1992) for a detailed analysis of models of product differentiation. Models of localized competition are sometimes referred to as the Kaldorian approach, whereas models of global competition are referred to as the Chamberlinian approach.
32. Dornbusch (1987) did a Cournot analysis with symmetric firms in the context of analysing exchange rate pass-through.
33. Feenstra (1989) goes into a detailed theoretical and empirical investigation of the 'symmetry' hypothesis, which states that exchange rate fluctuations, tariff and factor prices should have the same impact on consumer prices.
34. This would at least be the case in the short run. The long-run exchange rates may also affect the costs of the domestic firms, because exchange rate changes affect the prices of inputs used by the domestic firms.
35. He also considers a reduced form demand equation to draw inferences on market power.
36. See also the preceding studies by Barzel (1976), Johnson (1978), Harris (1987), Sumner and Wohlgenant (1985), and Sumner and Ward (1981).
37. The transformation rate is 1.2 because water is evaporated during the production process, typically an amount of 20 per cent.
38. We note that to estimate an error correction model, one has to check whether there is a co-integrating relationship between the (non-stationary) variables.
39. Feenstra also imposes a homogeneity restriction.
40. Athukorala and Menon prefer to call these coefficients pricing to market coefficients, since they take out exchange rate effects stemming from changed factor prices for imported inputs. For our purposes, the exchange rate pass-through coefficient that includes factor price effects is not relevant. The differences between both measures are generally small.
41. Marston provides an early approach in the spirit of Knetter. He controls for cost changes by looking at the ratio of the local import price to the foreign export price.
42. If the variables are non-stationary, then significant parameter estimates may be a consequence of spurious correlation. One then has to test whether there is a co-integrating relationship between the variables. If so, one can sensibly apply an error correction model to distinguish between a short-run and long-run relationship.
43. Note however that even when the exporting firms have a small market share, the exchange rate fluctuation cannot be viewed as a firm-specific cost shock, since there may still be several competing exporting firms.
44. The residual demand literature, in particular, Baker and Bresnahan (1985); Scheffman and Spiller (1987), has also offered results that are of related interest. A detailed discussion would however lead us too far.
45. The case is not only known for its careful analysis of assessing pass-on. A detailed analysis on market power effects was also conducted. This was done by showing that Staples prices were significantly lower in cities where Staples competed with Office Depot, than in non-competitive zones, where there were no other superstore chains. This market power analysis indicated that prices could increase by 9 per cent in markets where there had been competition.
46. Note that, as the frequency of the data is increased, dynamic models that distinguish short-term from long-term effects may be necessary.
47. The data set is maintained by the marketing group at the University of Chicago.
48. In the panel data terminology, we have something resembling a 'between-groups' estimator.

49. Otherwise, it would have been necessary to precisely match the product varieties (UPCs) of the various brands.
50. Note that this set-up differs slightly from Ashenfelter et al. They assumed that only the cost changes of the other firms should be interpreted to capture firm-specific pass-on, whereas the current framework also includes the cost change of firm 1 itself.
51. This can be referred to as a between-groups estimator, as discussed before.
52. Note that the effect of other product cost changes is negative, though it is insignificant.
53. Note however that this only holds in this application for considering pass-on with respect to the market price index. As can be confirmed from the first nine rows of Table 4.7, it does not hold for pass-on with respect to the individual firms' prices, in contrast to Ashenfelter et al.'s (1998) result. This is because Ashenfelter et al. consider competing products, whereas we consider products that are priced by the same firm.
54. Yet for this case, a complete analysis would also require data on the manufacturers' cost.
55. Yet unlike Ashenfelter et al. (1998) we could not account for competing products due to data limitations. These problems are not likely to be present with an actual merger investigation, since then one can request data from the competing merging firms.

REFERENCES

Anderson, Simon P., André de Palma and Jacques-Francois Thisse (1992), *Discrete Choice Theory of Product Differentiation*, Cambridge, MA: MIT Press.

Ashenfelter, O., D. Ashmore, J.B. Baker and S.-M. McKernan (1998), 'Identifying the firm-specific pass-through rate', Federal Trade Commission discussion paper.

Athukorala, P. and J. Menon (1994), 'Pricing to market behaviour and exchange rate pass-through in Japanese exports', *Economic Journal*, **104**, 171–81.

Bailey, E.E. and A.F. Friedlaender, (1982), 'Market structure and multiproduct industries', *Journal of Economic Literature*, **20**, 1024–48.

Bain, J.S. (1956), *Barriers to New Competition*, Cambridge, MA: Harvard University Press, especially pages 71–83 and 227–49.

Baker, J.B. (1998), 'Econometric analysis in FTC versus staples', prepared remarks before American Bar Association's Antitrust Section, 18 July 1997, accessed at www.ftc.gov/speeches/other/stspch.htm

Baker, J.B. (1999), 'Policy watch: developments in antitrust economics', *Journal of Economic Perspectives*; **13**(1) (Winter), 181–94.

Baker, J.B. and T.F. Bresnahan (1985), 'The gains from mergers or collusion in product differentiated industries', *Journal of Industrial Economics*, **35**, 427–44.

Baker, J. and T. Bresnahan (1988), 'Estimating the residual demand curve facing a single firm', *International Journal of Industrial Organization*, **6**(3), 283–300.

Barnett, P.G., T.E. Keeler and T.-W. Hu (1995), 'Oligopoly structure and the incidence of cigarette excise taxes', *Journal of Public Economics*, **57**(3), 457–70.

Barzel, Y. (1976), 'An alternative approach to the analysis of taxation', *Journal of Political Economy*, **84**, 1177–97.

Baumol, W.J., J.C. Panzar and R.D. Willig (1982), *Contestable Markets and the Theory of Industry Structure*, New York: Harcourt Brace Jovanovich.

Bettendorf, L. and F. Verboven (2000), 'Incomplete transmission of coffee bean prices: evidence from the Netherlands', *European Review of Agricultural Economics*, **27**, 1–16.

Bishop, R.L. (1968), 'The effects of specific and ad valorem taxes', *Quarterly Journal of Economics*, **82**, 198–218.

Borenstein, S.A., C. Cameron and R. Gilbert (1997), 'Do Gasoline Prices Respond Asymmetrically to Crude Oil Price Changes?' *Quarterly Journal of Economics*, **112**(1), 305–9.

Braeutigam, R. and A.F. Daughety (1983), 'On the estimation of returns to scale using variable cost functions', *Economic Letters*, **11**, 25–31.

Bresnahan, T.F. (1989), 'Empirical studies of industries with market power', in R. Schmalensee and R.D. Willig (eds), *Handbook of Industrial Organization*, vol 2, *Handbooks in Economics*, no. 10, North-Holland, pp. 1011–57.

Bulow, J. and P. Pfleiderer (1983), 'A note on the effect of cost changes on prices', *Journal of Political Economy*, **91**, 182–5.

Caves, D., L.R. Christensen and M.W. Tretheway (1984), 'Economies of density versus economies of scale: why trunk and local service airline costs differ', *Rand Journal of Economics*, **15** (4), 471–89.

Chappell, H.W. Jr. and R.P. Wilder (1986), 'Multiproduct monopoly, regulation, and firm costs: comment', *Southern Economic Journal*, **52**(4), 1168–74.

Christensen, L. and W. Greene (1976), 'Economies of scale in U.S. electric power generation', *Journal of Political Economy*, **4**, 655–76.

Coelli, T. (1996), 'Assessing the performance of Australian universities using data envelopment analysis', mimeo, Centre for Efficiency and Productivity Analysis, University of New England.

Coelli, T., D.S.P. Rao and G.E. Battese (1998), *An Introduction to Efficiency and Productivity Analysis*, Dordrecht: Kluwer Academic Publishers.

Crampton, P. (1994), 'Alternative approaches to competition law: consumers' surplus, total surplus, total welfare and non-efficiency goals', *World Competition*, **17**, 55–86.

Davies, S. and B. Lyons (eds) (1996), *Industrial Organization in the European Union: Structure, Strategy and the Competition Mechanism*, Oxford University Press.

Dixit, A.K. (1986), 'Comparative statics for oligopoly', *International Economic Review*; **27**(1) (February), 107–22.

Dornbusch, Rudiger (1987), 'Exchange rates and prices', *American Economic Review*, **77**(1), 93–106.

Farrell, J. and C. Shapiro (1990), 'Horizontal mergers: an equilibrium analysis', *American Economic Review*, **80**(1) (March), 107–26.

Feenstra, R. (1989), 'Symmetric pass-through of tariffs and exchange rates under imperfect competition: an empirical test', *Journal of International Economics*, **27**, 25–45.

Feenstra, Robert C., Joseph E. Gagnon and Michael M. Knetter (1996), 'Market share and exchange rate pass-through in world automobile trade', *Journal of International Economics*; **40**(1–2), 187–207.

Foreman, R.D. and E. Beauvais (1999), 'Scale economies in cellular telephony: size matters', *Journal of Regulatory Economics*, **16** (3) (November), 297–306.

Friedlaender, A.F. and R.H. Spady (1981), *Freight Transport Regulation: Equity, Efficiency, and Competition in the Rail and Trucking Industries*, Cambridge, MA: MIT Press, 1981.

Friedlaender, A.F., C. Whinston and D.K. Wang (1983), 'Cost, technology and productivity in the U.S. automobile industry', *Bell Journal of Economics*, **14**(1) (Spring), 1–20.

Fuss, M.A. (1983), 'A survey of recent results in the analysis of production conditions in telecommunications', in L. Courville, A. de Fontenay and R. Dobell (eds), *Economic Analysis of Telecommunications: Theory and Applications*, Amsterdam: North-Holland.

Fuss, M. and L. Waverman (1981), 'Regulation and the multiproduct firm: the case of telecommunications in Canada', in G. Fromm (ed.), *Studies in Public Regulation*, Cambridge, MA: MIT Press, pp. 277–313.

Gagnon, Joseph E. and Michael M. Knetter (1995), 'Markup adjustment and exchange rate fluctuations: evidence from panel data on automobile exports', *Journal of International Money and Finance*, **14**(2), 289–310.

Gasmi, F., J.-J. Laffont and W.W. Sharkey (1999), 'The natural monopoly test reconsidered: an engineering process-based approach to empirical analysis in telecommunications', industrielle Institut d'economie working paper 91, Toulouse.

Genesove, D. and W. Mullin (1998), 'Testing static oligopoly models: conduct and cost in the sugar industry, 1890–1914', *Rand Journal of Economics*, **29**, 355–77.

Ghosh, Atish R. and Holger C. Wolf (1994), 'Pricing in international markets: lessons from *The Economist*', National Bureau of Economic Research working paper no 4806.

Gold, B. (1981), 'Changing perspectives on size, scale and returns: an interpretive survey', *Journal of Economic Literature*, **19**(March), 5–33.

Goldberg, Pinelopi K. (1995), 'Product differentiation and oligopoly in international markets: the case of the U.S. automobile industry', *Econometrica*, **63**(4), 891–951.

Goldberg, Pinelopi K. and Frank Verboven (1998), 'The evolution of international price dispersion in the European car market', Centre for Economic Policy Research discussion paper 2029, London.

Harris, J.E. (1987), 'The 1983 increase in the federal cigarette excise tax', in L.H. Summers, (ed.), *Tax Policy and the Economy*, vol 1, Cambridge, MA: MIT Press, pp. 87–111.

Hausman, J.A. and K.L. Gregory (1999), 'Efficiencies from the consumer viewpoint', *George Mason Law Review*, **7**, 707–27.

Hooper, Peter and Catherine L. Mann (1989), 'Exchange rate pass-through in the 1980s: the case of U.S. imports of manufactures', *Brookings Papers on Economic Activity*, **1**, 297–337.

Jara-Diaz, S. and C. Whinston (1981), 'Multiproduct transportation cost functions: scale and scope in railway operations', in N. Blattner et al. (eds), *Eighth European Association of Research in Industrial Economics*, vol 1, University of Basle, Basle, Switzerland.

Jara-Diaz, S. and C.E. Cortes (1996), 'On the calculation of scale economies from transport cost functions', *Journal of Transport Economics and Policy*, **30**(2), (May), 157–70.

Jenny, F. (1997), 'Antitrust in a global economy', in B. Hawk (ed.), *International Antitrust Law and Policy*, Fordham Corporate Law Institute.

Johnson, T.R. (1978), 'Additional evidence on the effect of alternative taxes on cigarette prices', *Journal of Political Economy*, **86**, 325–8.

Kadiyali, V. (1997), 'Exchange rate pass-through for strategic pricing and advertising: an empirical analysis of the U.S. photographic film industry', *Journal of International Economics*, **43**, 437–61.

Kadiyali, V., P. Chintagunta, and N. Vilcassim (2000), 'Manufacturer-retailer channel interactions and implications for channel power: an empirical investigation of pricing in a local market', *Marketing Science*, **19**(2), 127–48.

Kinnucan, H.W. and O.D. Forker (1987), 'Asymmetry in farm-retail price transmission for major dairy products', *American Journal of Agricultural Economics*, **69**, 285–92.

Knetter, M. (1989), 'Price discrimination by U.S. and German exporters', *American Economic Review*, **79**, 198–210.

Knetter, M. (1993), 'International comparisons of pricing to market behavior', *American Economic Review*, **83**(3), 473–86.

Knetter, M. (1994), 'Is export price adjustment asymmetric? Evaluating the market share and marketing bottlenecks hypotheses', *Journal of International Money and Finance*, **13**, 55–70.

Knetter, M. (1995), 'Pricing to market in response to unobservable and observable shocks', *International Economic Journal*, **9**(2), 1–25.

Kreinin, M.E. (1977), 'The effect of exchange rate changes on the prices and volume of foreign trade', *International Monetary Fund Staff Papers*, **24**(2), 297–329.

Krugman, P. (1987), 'Pricing to market when exchange rate changes', in S.W. Arndt and J.D. Richardson (eds), *Real Financial Linkages Among Open Economies*, Cambridge, MA: MIT Press, pp. 49–70.

Levin, D. (1990), 'Horizontal mergers: the 50% benchmark', *American Economic Review*, **80**(5), 1238–45.

Marston, R. (1990), 'Pricing to market in Japanese manufacturing', *Journal of International Economics*, **29**, 217–36.

Martin, S. (1993), *Advanced Industrial Economics*, Oxford: Blackwell.

Mayo, J.W. (1984), 'Multiproduct monopoly, regulation, and firm costs', *Southern Economic Journal*, **51**(1), 208–18.

Mayo, J.W. (1986), 'The technological determinants of the U.S. energy industry structure', *Review of Economics and Statistics*, **66**, 51–8.

McCorriston, S., C.W. Morgan, and A.J. Rayner (1998), 'Processing technology, market power and price transmission', *Journal of Agricultural Economics*, **49**, 185–201.

Mulligan, J.G. (1983), 'The economies of massed reserves', *American Economic Review*, **73** (September), 725–34.

Narnett, P.G., T.E. Keeler and The-wei Hu (1995), 'Oligopoly structure and the incidence of cigarette excise taxes', *Journal of Public Economics*, **57**, 457–70.

Nerlove, M. (1963), 'Returns to scale in electricity supply', in C. Christ (ed.), *Measurement in Economics: Studies in Mathematical Economics and Econometrics in Memory of Yehuda Grunfeld*, Stanford, CA: Stanford University Press.

Panzar, J.C. (1989), 'Determinants of firm and industry structure', in R. Schmalensee and R.D. Willig (eds), *Handbook of Industrial Organization*, vol 2, *Handbooks in Economics*, no. 10, North-Holland, 3–59.

Panzar, J.C. and R.D. Willig (1981), 'Economies of scope', *American Economic Review*, **71**(2), 268–72.

Perry, M.K. (1989), 'Vertical integration: determinants and effects', in R. Schmalensee, and R.D. Willig (eds), *Handbook of Industrial Organization*, vol 1, North-Holland.

Pick, D.H., J. Karrenbrock, and H.F. Carman (1990), 'Price asymmetry and marketing margin behavior: an example for California-Arizona citrus', *Agrobusiness*, **6**, 75–84.

Pindyck, Robert S. and Daniel L. Rubinfeld (1992), *Microeconomics*, New York: Macmillan Publishing Company.

Pratten, C.F. (1971), *Economies of Scale in Manufacturing Industry*, Cambridge: Cambridge University Press.

Pratten, C. (1988), 'A survey of the economies of scale', in *Research on the 'Cost of Non-Europe', Basic Findings, Volume 2, Studies on the Economics of Integration*, Luxembourg: Office for Official Publications of the European Communities.
Scheffman, D.T. and P.T. Spiller (1987), 'Geographic market definition under the US Department of Justice merger guidelines', *Journal of Law and Economics*, **30**(1), 123–47.
Schembri, Lawrence (1989), 'Export prices and exchange rates: an industry approach', in Robert C. Feenstra (ed.) *Trade Policies for International Competitiveness*, Chicago: University of Chicago Press, pp. 185–206.
Scherer, F.M., A. Beckenstein, E. Kaufer and R.D. Murphy (1975), *The Economics of Multi-Plant Operation: An International Comparison Study*, Cambridge, MA: Harvard University Press.
Scherer, F.M. and D. Ross (1990), *Industrial Market Structure and Economic Performance*, 3rd edn, Boston: Houghton Mifflin Company.
Shapiro, C. (1995), 'Mergers with differentiated products', address before the American Bar Association, 9 November.
Sharkey, W.W. (1982), *The Theory of Natural Monopoly*, Cambridge, MA: Cambridge University Press.
Spady, R.H. and A.F. Friedlaender (1978), 'Hedonic cost functions for the regulated trucking industry', *Bell Journal of Economics*, **9**(1) (Spring), 159–79.
Stigler, G.J. (1958), 'The economies of scale', *Journal of Law & Economics*, **1**, (October), 54–71.
Sullivan, D. (1985), 'Testing hypotheses about firm behavior in the cigarette industry', *Journal of Political Economy*, **93**, 586–98.
Sumner, D. (1981), 'Measurement of monopoly behavior: an application to the cigarette industry', *Journal of Political Economy*, **89**, 1010–19.
Sumner, D. and R. Ward (1981), 'Tax changes and cigarette prices', *Journal of Political Economy*, 89, 1261–5.
Sumner, D.A. and M.K. Wohlgenant (1985), 'Effects of an increase in the federal excise tax on cigarettes', *American Journal of Agricultural Economics*, **67**(2), 235–42.
Sutton, J. (1991), *Sunk Costs and Market Structure: Price Competition, Advertising and the Evolution of Concentration*, Cambridge, MA: MIT Press.
Sutton, J. (1996), *Sunk Costs and Market Structure*, Cambridge, MA: MIT Press.
Sutton, J. (1998), *Technology and Market Structure*, Cambridge, MA: MIT Press.
Teece, D.J. (1980), 'Economies of scope and the scope of the enterprise', *Journal of Economic Behavior and Organization*, **1**, 223–47.
Verboven, Frank (1998), 'The markets for gasoline and diesel cars in Europe', Centre for Economic Policy Research discussion paper 2069, London.
Von Cramon-Taubadel, S. (1997), 'Estimating asymmetric price transmission with the error correction representation: an application to the German pork market', *European Review of Agricultural Economics*, **25**, 1–18.
Wang Chiang, J. Shaw-er (1981), 'Economies of scale and scope in multiproduct industries: a case study of the regulated U.S trucking industry', PhD dissertation, Massachusetts Institute of Technology, Cambridge, MA.
Weiss, L.W. (1975), 'Optimal plant size and the extent of suboptimal capacity', in R.T. Masson and P.D. Qualls (eds), *Essays on Industrial Organization in Honor of Joe S. Bain*, Cambridge, MA: Ballinger, pp. 128–31.
Werden, G.J. and L.M. Froeb (1994), 'The effects of mergers in differentiated

products industries: logit demand and merger policy', *Journal of Law, Economics, and Organization*, **10**(2), 407–26.
Williamson, Oliver E. (1968), 'Economies as an antitrust defense: the welfare trade-offs', *American Economic Review*, **58**, 18–36.
Willig, R.D. (1991), 'Merger analysis, industrial organization theory, and merger guidelines', *Brookings Papers in Microeconomics*, pp. 281–332.
Woo, Wing T. (1984), 'Exchange rates and the prices of nonfood nonfuel products', *Brookings Papers on Economic Activity*, **2**, 511–30.
Yde, P. and M.G. Vita (1996), 'Merger efficiencies: reconsidering the passing-on requirement', *Antitrust Law Journal*, **64**, 735–47.

5. Efficiencies in merger control

Jrissy Motis, Damien Neven and Paul Seabright

In a lecture in the Beesley series, Paul Seabright observed, on the occasion of the tenth anniversary of EU merger control, that little was known about the source of efficiencies in mergers (Seabright 2002). In that lecture, he also put forward a simple framework for consideration on the motivation behind mergers, as a particular form of corporate restructuring, and the source of synergies between merging partners. In this chapter, we report on some of the work that we have undertaken on synergies and the source of efficiencies in mergers. We outline the framework that we have developed for thinking about mergers, summarize some of the empirical evidence that we have gathered and discuss the insights that the framework yields into the role of competition authorities. This work provides some confirmation that the reallocation of intangible assets is a significant motivation for mergers and a source of merger-specific efficiencies. With respect to the role of competition authorities, we will suggest that they should systematically ask about the activities that can only be undertaken through the proposed merger and seek evidence from the merging parties about the plans that they have developed to integrate their activities. We will also suggest that synergies are of particular importance compared to technical efficiencies because the latter are, in principle, achievable by means other than a merger and, if in practice they are not likely to be achieved otherwise, this will tend to signal that rivalry is weak in the market where the merging firms are active.

Developing a better understanding of efficiencies seems to be essential for improving the precision of EU merger control; indeed, when the current treatment of efficiencies in the EU is considered in the light of empirical regularities with respect to the importance and distribution of efficiencies across mergers, it would appear that the EU approach is likely to generate significant Type II errors (circumstances where anti-competitive mergers are allowed) as well as Type I errors (circumstances where pro-competitive or neutral mergers are prohibited or remedies are imposed).

Let us first consider some empirical regularities (see Pautler 2003 for an excellent survey). Three methodologies are typically used in order to assess whether mergers lead to efficiencies; these methods consider profits, or the share of the profits that accrue to shareholders, and hence do not directly capture efficiencies. Changes in returns can be estimated *ex ante*, from the change in stock market value of the merging partners when the merger is announced. They can also be estimated *ex post*, when returns accruing to the shareholders of the merging entity are compared with those obtained from companies that are similar but did not merge. Finally, the comparison between the merging partners and other similar companies can be undertaken in terms of accounting profits – rather than returns to shareholders.

These methods have some shortcomings; in particular, they focus on profits rather than efficiency, and profits can be obtained, for instance, through the exercise of market power, without efficiencies. In contrast, enhanced profits arising from the exploitation of efficiencies can sometimes be competed away within a short period of time (for instance, when efficiencies diffuse among competitors). In addition, the choice of an appropriate comparator group to assess performance is often difficult, because the performance of firms that are comparable to the merging partners is often directly affected by that of the merging entity. Keeping these shortcomings in mind, the following hard facts emerge; first, mergers generate small returns on average and often these returns are not statistically different from zero. Second, the targets obtain on average a very large share of the gains that can accrue. However, these averages conceal a substantial amount of variance across deals. With regard to returns, one observes that many mergers simply fail and generate important negative returns. According to some estimates, as many as 60 per cent of mergers fail. As many as 30 per cent of mergers lead to subsequent divestitures that are acknowledged by firms as resulting from a failure of the merging plans. However, some mergers lead to substantial gains. A similar variance is observed with respect to the distribution of gains and some bidders obtain a significant share of the gains.

Consider now the essential features of the EU procedure. The substantive criterion under which EU merger control operates is that '[a] concentration which would significantly impede effective competition, in the common market or in a substantial part of it, in particular as a result of the creation or strengthening of a dominant position, shall be declared incompatible with the common market' (Article 2.3 of the EC merger regulation – ECMR). This criterion is further informed by Article 2.1(b) which stipulates that in evaluating mergers, the Commission should take into account the 'development of technical and economic progress provided that it is to consumers' advantage and does not form an obstacle to competition'.

The insistence on positive consumers' advantage suggests that the EU operates with a consumer surplus standard and that efficiencies can be used in order to claim that consumers are likely to benefit. At the same time, in the vast majority of cases, the EU does not consider efficiencies and waives mergers through after it has convinced itself that anti-competitive effects are unimportant (in the absence of efficiencies). The EU has only considered efficiencies where, under the assumption that there were none, significant anti-competitive effects were observed.

Consider first the cases where efficiencies are not considered. Given that in the absence of some efficiencies (broadly speaking), mergers cannot be to consumers' advantage, the EU procedure must rely on a presumption that efficiencies are sufficiently significant and widespread to compensate for the (relatively minor) anti-competitive effects that it has identified in those cases. Yet, as mentioned above, there is ample empirical evidence that efficiencies may not be large on average and also that many mergers fail to generate efficiencies. In those circumstances, one can expect the EU to make many type II errors, namely to allow mergers on the presumption that they would generate efficiencies which never materialize. And indeed, there is evidence that the EU has very different expectations from stock market analysts regarding the anti-competitive effects of mergers that it waives through; for instance, Duso et al. (2003) find that a significant proportion of mergers that were cleared by the EU (without remedies) generated a positive reaction in the stock market price of competitors, which suggests at least a reasonable probability that they were expected to lead to higher prices in the industry.[1]

Consider next those cases where efficiencies have been considered because without them the merger would be expected to lead to important anti-competitive effects. There are few cases where, according to the published decisions, efficiencies were explicitly considered and, to the best of our knowledge, none where efficiencies have been considered to be sufficient to change the Commission's mind. There may also be a number of cases in which efficiencies were discussed during the proceedings and many cases where the parties did not put forward any claim regarding efficiencies because they were unclear about the Commission's policy in this area. However, these observations certainly suggest that the Commission will have made some Type I errors; it is highly unlikely that since the merger regulation came into force, the Commission would not have encountered a merger where efficiencies did indeed make a difference. This presumption is supported by the existing empirical evidence on merger efficiencies, discussed above, which reveals a very high dispersion across mergers. There are some very efficient mergers and with a sample of more than 1500 units, the Commission should have encountered a few in which there were also anti-competitive problems.

Overall, it appears that developing a better understanding of efficiencies and reliable procedure to evaluate them would significantly contribute to a more effective screening of mergers.

At the outset, it also seems important to distinguish between efficiencies that could be achieved by other means than a merger and those that can only be achieved through this particular form of corporate reorganization. We will suggest that antitrust authorities should focus on the latter.

There is no well-accepted terminology with respect to efficiencies and in this study we adopt the terminology used by Farrell and Shapiro (2001), who refer to 'technical efficiencies' to describe those gains that could be obtained otherwise and 'synergies' to describe efficiencies that can only be achieved by merging. Technical efficiencies correspond to changes within the joint production possibilities of the merging parties. In the short term, they can be achieved by a reallocation of output across different units or the achievement of scale economies if capital is mobile. In the longer run, they can be achieved by undertaking investment on a larger scale. By contrast, synergies are associated with a shift in the production possibilities of the merging parties.

Technical efficiencies could thus in principle be achieved by other means than a merger. In the long term, the production possibilities of the merging parties are the same as the production possibilities of an individual firm and efficient production plans can be achieved, for instance, by internal growth. That is not to say however that technical efficiencies would have been achieved without the merger and what the antitrust authorities should consider is not whether efficiencies could be achieved otherwise but whether they would.

Still, as emphasized by Farrell and Shapiro (2001), there are good reasons to believe that if technical efficiencies would not be achieved without the merger, it is likely that the merger will have significant anti-competitive consequences. The reason is simply that the incentive to achieve efficiencies for individual firms and their incentive to grow and achieve scale economies is partly determined by their competitive environment. With a competitive structure inducing limited rivalry, firms will have little incentive to achieve these efficiencies. But these are also the circumstances where a merger is likely to have serious anti-competitive consequences.[2]

This does not mean that technical efficiencies should be given less weight than synergies in evaluating the benefits of the transaction in question. Rather it implies that the very circumstances which justify regarding the technical efficiencies as merger-specific will increase the probability that the threats to competition are sufficient to outweigh the benefits from efficiencies whatever their source. This increases the importance of improving our understanding of synergies and their role in the merger process. However, despite their practical importance, the discussion of synergies has been relatively neglected in the economic literature. There is a general recognition that synergies involve either a process of learning across merging parties or the close integration of specific, 'hard to trade' assets owned by the merging parties. But the consequences of this approach for the analysis of mergers and merger control have not been investigated systematically (at least in the industrial organization/antitrust literature), and the importance of synergies in mergers has not yet been properly investigated empirically. Our work attempts to contribute to these research questions.

In order to understand where synergies in mergers come from, we ask why firms have chosen that form of corporate reorganization. An answer to that question will identify the private gains that firms could only achieve by merging and help identify synergies, that is, the enlargement in firms' production possibilities that mergers allow for. But the answer will also provide an important key to understanding the role of the competition authorities in evaluating efficiencies. For it will never be reasonable to suppose that the authorities are simply better at evaluating efficiencies than the firms themselves. The view of regulatory authorities as simply wiser than private firms has long been discredited. What the authorities can do instead is to evaluate the procedures that the firms have used in their own evaluation – in order to determine, for example, whether firms have genuinely identified merger-specific efficiencies rather than using the merger as a lazy way to gain market share.

Section 2 develops a simple analytical framework in order to investigate the source of merger-specific gains and synergies. Section 3 discusses the evidence that we have gathered to validate this framework. Section 4 discusses whether competition authorities should take efficiencies into account, and if so, how this should be done. Section 5 discusses the consequences of this approach for merger control procedures.

1. CORPORATE RESTRUCTURING, INTANGIBLE ASSETS AND SYNERGIES

A firm may have decided to acquire or merge with another because the underlying assets of its partners could not be acquired. Reputation, knowledge, organizational assets are typically difficult to trade in part because contracts regarding the transfer of these assets are highly incomplete. In addition, the interaction between assets, in particular when it involves reputation, knowledge and organizational assets, is typically poorly understood and difficult to codify, so that the ability to make these assets interact efficiently with one another and with physical and human assets is typically not contractually enforceable. Because of the difficulty of describing and codifying their operation, these assets can be described as 'intangibles'.

For instance, the productivity of a research team can be contingent on dimensions that are poorly understood and controlled. It may be associated with a mode of communication among researchers which is highly informal and made possible by particular circumstances (the age distribution, the location of the researchers, or the culture of the organization). The interaction between physical assets and the knowledge associated with a patent may also be dependent on parameters that are poorly understood. A good example of this is provided by the production of carton packages in aseptic conditions. Aseptic packaging machines have been sold for more than two decades by Tetra Laval but competitors have been unable to reproduce machines with the same level of reliability, despite the fact that all the necessary technology is in the public domain or licensed. It is widely believed in the industry that the process by which aseptic carton packages are effectively produced is not fully understood even by Tetra Laval itself.

When intangible assets are involved, the bundle of assets operated by the firm will enable it to undertake a range of activities, offer a set of products or services and achieve a level of productivity in producing them that are not easy for others to replicate. The corporation itself only owns the assets that can be traded and enters into formal contracts with others, but its production possibilities are associated with a particular combination of intangible assets that work together in a certain way.

In this framework, when one corporation chooses to buy another it is because it could not replicate what this other corporation does (if it could, it would simply buy its component tradable assets independently – or would accumulate the assets through internal growth). It must be that it is really trying to buy tradable assets in the hope that it will benefit from the combination of tangible and intangible assets operated by that corporation as well. So, paradoxically, the key to understanding this kind of trade is to see it as a contractual exchange of assets, in which the assets enumerated are not the primary motive for the transaction.

In this perspective, firms will thus engage in mergers and acquisitions because they anticipate that additional value will be generated by recombining assets and the source of these gains must be found in the operation of intangible assets. That is, firms must anticipate that the particular bundle of assets operated by each firm can be combined in new ways which generate additional value; firms are trying to generate a specific combination of the assets which will generate value in excess of the value that they generate in their current use. One extreme example of such a situation would be one in which a target firm is a bundle of tradable but intangible assets, which generate low returns. Think, for instance, of a portfolio of IP rights and a manufacturing facility. If IP rights were not to some extent intangible, their interactions with the manufacturing facility could be easily predicted and the inadequate performance could be immediately corrected by management. But the interaction of IP rights with the manufacturing facility is difficult to predict; an improvement in performance may require, for instance, a different combination of IP rights in the portfolio from that used by the target. The identification and implementation of this remedy may itself require another intangible asset, for instance an organizational asset. An acquirer who has access to this asset will then be in a position to apply his own organizational skills to the target and improve its performance. This would be a situation where the interaction between the intangible assets of acquirers and targets is limited. More generally, however, one would expect that the intangible assets of both firms will be re-organized in complex ways in order to expand the production possibilities of both.

Before turning to the empirical validation of our framework, a number of comments may be in order. First, although the recombination of intangible assets provides a motivation behind mergers, it is by no means the only one. For instance, mergers can be motivated by market power, concerns about investment in specific capital or the pursuit of objectives by managers that may have little to do with profits. These alternative motives should be kept in mind while undertaking an empirical analysis of mergers.

Second, even if in general, the merger-specific gains that firms anticipate from recombining their assets will be associated with some synergies (an expansion of their production possibilities), they may come at the expense of consumers and competitors. As in the case of technical efficiencies, it will be necessary from a public policy perspective to disentangle the effects that corporate restructuring will have on the merging entity, competitors and consumers. This will be further discussed in the concluding section.

2. EMPIRICAL EVIDENCE

Three distinct hypotheses can be derived from the theoretical framework discussed above.

First, mergers that achieve significant positive returns should be associated with the presence of intangible assets in the merging parties. Hence, we will test whether returns are correlated with the intensity of intangibles.

Second, given the central role that intangible assets play in mergers and acquisitions, the returns that they generate should be highly variable. Since the operations of intangible assets are hard to predict, the recombination of assets which is taking place in mergers and acquisitions is to some extent a gamble; some recombination may be uncharted territory but attempted on the basis of the firms' limited understanding of how the intangible assets operate. The recombination of assets may have been experienced in other circumstances but the very nature of intangibles is such that the parameters which determine their operation are not all fully understood and controlled. Hence, past experience will offer a poor guide to future performance. Overall, mergers and acquisitions involving intangibles will involve high risks; it should not come as a surprise that many of them fail to generate the returns that were contemplated when they were undertaken. In addition, the returns to deployment of intangible assets may take relatively extreme values (see Lev 2001), with success generating substantial returns but failure generating massive losses.[3] Accordingly, we will test whether mergers involving large intangible assets also display a higher variance of returns.

Third, the allocation of the potential gains from mergers between acquirer and target, or between merging partners, may be affected by the importance of intangible assets; the insight comes from auction theory which suggests that the winner of an auction is the bidder who has the highest willingness to pay among all bidders for the object being sold and that the winner will pay a price equal to the second highest willingness to pay realized among the bidders.[4] Hence, when there is only a single bidder that can manage to generate value from a merger, he should pay a price equal to zero, or in other words, he should not pay a premium in excess of the market value of the target. He will appropriate the value that he can generate and in those circumstances most of the gains from the merger should thus accrue to the bidder. More generally, if both the assets of the bidder and those of the target are necessary in order to generate value, one would expect that targets and bidders (having equal bargaining power) will share the gains equally. By contrast, when a number of alternative bidders can generate value, the price paid by the winner may be close to the value that he expects to generate from the merger (because the second highest bidder will have a willingness to pay which is close to his own). In those circumstances, the target will appropriate most of the expected gain from the merger.

As discussed above, when the merger is associated with the deployment of intangible assets, it is unlikely that many acquirers, or many merging partners, will anticipate the same gains from recombining their assets. This will arise because different potential acquirers or different potential merging partners will operate different bundles of assets. Even if assets are similar, the uncertainty involved in operating intangible assets will make it very unlikely that different partners have the same understanding of how the assets are operated and end up with a similar assessment of the potential gains. Hence, one would expect that none of the merging partners will face an alternative candidate (bidder) who would anticipate similar gains. In such an environment, it is likely that the gains will be split evenly between merging partners or between the acquirer and the target. By contrast, when no intangible assets are involved, we expect that several merging partners will be able to replicate the gains from the merger. The competition between these alternative partners will then exhaust the rent that they will obtain. In this case, one of the merging firms, typically the target, will obtain most of the gains.

We investigated these hypotheses in a sample of mergers (Neven and Seabright 2003). The empirical investigation uses two sources of information with respect to the value of intangible assets. We use accounting data on intangible assets in firms' balance sheets, and a market-based measure of intangibles, which also considers the difference between the firm's market value prior to the merger and its book value. With respect to the evaluation of gains from mergers, we rely on stock market data. That is, we assume that the gain in the value of the firms concerned from some suitable date prior to the announcement of the transaction to a suitable date afterwards provides an unbiased estimate of the gain yielded by the transaction to the firm's shareholders, controlling for other factors that may influence that value of the shares of the firms concerned. We control for these other factors by calculating the gain in firm value compared to what would have occurred if the firms' shares had simply mirrored the evolution of the market index for the relevant sector between the two dates (we call such measures 'index-adjusted'). Our data are drawn from the SDC Thomson and Datastream databases. Our sample includes about 330 firms for which we have data on gains and intangibles.[5] Our sample of transactions with index-adjusted gains is about one-third smaller than that with unadjusted gains (that is, about 250 deals).

We do not find a strong support for our first hypothesis; there is no clear pattern suggesting that deals undertaken by firms for whom intangible assets are relatively important generate significantly higher returns than deals involving firms for whom such assets are relatively unimportant.

Our second hypothesis is supported by the data. In particular, we find that the variance of returns conditional on the share of intangibles is strongly increasing in the share of intangibles.

Our third hypothesis is also supported by the data; we observe that when intangibles are relatively unimportant in the acquirer's assets the bulk of the gains from the transaction accrues to the target firm, while acquirers for whom intangibles are important are able to capture a significant proportion of the gains for themselves. The distribution of gains between partners that we uncover, as a function of intangibles, also matches the theoretical predictions; in particular we find, for some specifications of the model, that an acquirer in the upper quartile of the intangible distribution would get 48 per cent of the gains accruing from the transaction – while theory would suggest that gains should be evenly split. At the opposite end of the spectrum, we observed that an acquirer in the lower quartile of the intangible distribution would get 15 per cent of the absolute gains – while theory would suggest that they should not obtain any. This evidence certainly confirms that the importance of intangibles plays a significant role in accounting for variance in the share of gains accruing to the acquirer (across deals).

We conclude, therefore, that our data do not provide clear support for the hypothesis that intangible assets are likely to be associated with higher gains to merger transactions. However, they do support the hypothesis that these gains are likely to be more variable. And we have found support for the view that acquiring firms perform better, relative to targets, when they have more intangible assets, a view that makes sense in the light of the reduced competition from other bidders when the acquirer has significant intangibles. The question arises as to why we do not find clear support for the first hypothesis. One possibility is that the market may actually already discount the fact that firms with high intangibles are likely to be involved in profitable reorganizations: as a result, when a merger is actually announced, the price of firms with high intangibles may not react more than the price of others.[6]

3. THE ROLE OF COMPETITION AUTHORITIES

One response to the complex character of synergies and the considerable uncertainty surrounding their nature and magnitude might be to conclude that competition authorities should not even begin to consider them as factors influencing their attitude towards merger cases, but should rather confine their attention to technical efficiencies. In fact, as we argued above, technical efficiencies are ones about which the authorities would do well to be sceptical (though this does not imply that good defences involving technical efficiencies can never be made). However, synergies are ones that, if achieved at all, are necessarily specific to the merger. Refusing to take them into account would consequently rule out any mergers whose likely synergies would be large enough to outweigh the likely adverse effects of increased market power. Given the uncertainties surrounding predictions about synergies one can reasonably doubt whether such effects could ever be large enough and probable enough to outweigh large risks to competition. However, many cases are not of this kind. There is a wide zone of uncertainty about risks to market power as well (as recent adverse court judgments on EU merger decisions have underlined). Even where the uncertainty is not great, there are many cases where the risk to competition, though not trivial, is not very large, and where the authorities are quite reasonably under some hesitation as to whether the transaction should be blocked. These cases are marginal in terms of the appropriate decision but far from marginal in terms of their importance and their claims on the authorities' time – should evidence about likely synergies not be given some weight in these cases? The evidence may not be 100 per cent compelling but it might still be compelling enough to tip a marginal case in one direction or the other. If so, what kind of evidence might this be?

It is impractical to suppose that competition authorities might ever realistically have access to information better than that which the merging parties could have collected themselves. The two questions it seems reasonable to ask are therefore: first, how can the authorities induce the merging parties to give them, accurately, the relevant information, and second, how should the authorities evaluate this information?

The key to the answer lies in the fact that efficiency gains from merging intangible assets will never be realized entirely through their passive combination under common ownership. This is because such intangible assets always represent ways of working and managing the other assets of the firm; consequently, bringing the intangibles of one firm together with those of another requires a change in behaviour (other than just pricing behaviour) of some of the parties involved, and this will require a change in incentives. This is not always true when intangibles are used to create or consolidate market power. For instance, if two pharmaceutical firms bring together a portfolio of products with no other intention than to raise their prices, they have no need to do anything to change the behaviour of the parts of the firm that research, develop, produce or manage the products themselves – only the sales teams need to be implicated. If there is an intention to bring about real change in the productive parts of the firm's activities, an integration of the intangible assets – the research teams, the production processes or the management methods – has to be put into action, and this will require changing the incentives for some of the individuals who will take part in these activities.

To put the point another way, if the intangible assets of the merging parties are substitutes for each other and have no capacity for being used together in genuinely complementary ways, the attraction of the merger to the parties will consist purely in being able to increase the return to these assets' activities by raising the prices of the goods they are used to produce.[7] If, on the other hand, they are indeed complements, the merging parties cannot know this unless they have some idea how to alter incentives within the merged firm so as to realize their complementarities. Furthermore, for these complementarities to be genuinely merger-specific, the parties need to have identified ways of altering incentives within the merged firm that would not be possible between two independent firms ('improving contacts between research teams', for instance, would hardly count as a merger-specific source of efficiency gains). We can conclude from this that for the firm to have identified merger-specific means of implementing the integration of the parties' intangible assets is a necessary condition of their having identified even the existence of any merger-specific efficiencies at all.

We can now turn to the first of the two questions above: how can the authorities induce the merging parties to give them, accurately, the relevant information? If the parties have indeed identified merger-specific means of implementing the integration of their intangible assets, they will have information about this (in the form of board-level memoranda, for example), and it is straightforward to require such evidence to be produced. Ensuring that such evidence is not falsified or manipulated is, of course, an important concern. However, note that what is being asked of firms is to present evidence of definite intentions to undertake actions which, once they have been identified, the firm would have an interest in undertaking anyway even in the absence of intervention by the authorities. Firms that have no synergies to claim will not, in the great majority of cases, be firms that promise to implement actions that in fact they will not undertake. Rather they will be firms that can find no relevant, value-creating actions to implement in the first place. This makes the requirement to provide evidence of synergies more naturally incentive-compatible than it would be if such evidence consisted, say, in judgements about the characteristics of the merging parties.

It will remain possible, of course, for merging parties to assert falsely that their intangible assets have certain characteristics which make synergies possible, and then to invent implementing actions that would allow these synergies to be realized if indeed they were possible. However, this will be a costly subterfuge for the merging parties to undertake: falsely asserting characteristics of the merging parties is something that could be undertaken by a report of external consultants without significantly impinging on management time, but asserting plausible implementing actions to realize these will involve a significant commitment of management time (the degree of commitment will of course depend on how rigorously the management expect their assertions to be scrutinized by the authorities). Such an investment of management time would have been undertaken in any event by firms that had genuinely identified synergies, and would not represent an additional cost for them. But for firms falsely asserting the existence of such synergies it would represent a significant additional cost (at a time when the management would in any event be preoccupied with planning the forthcoming merger). So it seems reasonable to suggest that, while fabrication or manipulation of intentions is certainly not impossible, it may be costly enough to make it difficult and infrequent.

It is quite likely, of course, that some firms will reply that, until the merger is actually consummated, it will be difficult or impossible to know what actions need to be taken to implement the relevant synergies. This is indeed a reasonable response in some cases, but it also represents the assertion of a hope that synergies can be realized rather than a well-grounded belief that they can. There may be nothing reprehensible about such a situation, but it does not provide sufficient grounds for asserting efficiencies as a counterweight to risks of market power.

Overall, therefore, our arguments suggest that in considering efficiencies the authorities may adopt the following procedure.

1. Firms notifying mergers should be asked to state on their notification form, reasonably briefly, what is the business rationale for the merger and what are the main types of efficiency gain they expect the merger to make possible. They should be warned that they may be asked about this in any notification discussions. Firms should not be required (though they may be permitted) to submit supporting documentation at the notification stage.
2. The extent of any supporting documentation will obviously depend on the stage of the investigation (notably in that Phase II investigations will typically scrutinize claims about efficiencies much more thoroughly than those in Phase I). Nevertheless we can say something about the kind of documentation that is appropriate. This should consist of documents dated prior to the notification of the merger, and identifying two types of information: first, evidence about the existence of potential complementarities between the various assets and capacities of the merging parties; such evidence may consist of external consultants' reports. Second, evidence about the plans of the merging parties for implementing the integration of their assets and capacities. This evidence must consist in documents signed by executive members of the board and proposing actions, with a reasonable indication of likely timing, which would enable the realisation of efficiencies in a way that would not be possible without the merger. Naturally any such documents could be commented on, or supplemented, by other documents submitted by the parties in support of their case (for instance, documents explaining why certain proposed actions were in fact merger-specific).
3. In evaluating the evidence submitted, the authorities should note that:
   (a) If the complementarities identified appear to be principally in the nature of what we have called 'technical efficiencies', it is likely that these will be merger-specific only if there are significant elements of imperfect competition. The claimed merger-specific character of such efficiencies should therefore be used as a guide

to identify where precisely the most significant obstacles to competition are to be found.

(b) If the complementarities appear to be principally synergies, the depth and plausibility of the proposed implementing actions will themselves be evidence as to the degree of conviction of the parties about the existence of such synergies. Firms will only devote significant management time to planning the implementation of synergies they genuinely believe to exist.

(c) If the parties provide particularly weak or unconvincing evidence of synergies, this fact of itself may be used as grounds, albeit slight, for concluding that their motive for undertaking the merger is likely to have been the strengthening of their market power. Such grounds may be used to support the case for prohibition or modification of a merger provided the case would already have been reasonably strong on conventional criteria alone. The knowledge that this inference may be made can act as a disincentive for firms to have frivolous recourse to the efficiency defence.

(d) If the evidence for the existence of synergies appears reasonably strong, it should be used in support of approval of a merger provided the risks to market power are not very great, bearing particularly in mind that the evidence provided by the parties is evidence of their belief in the existence of synergies rather than of their existence *per se*.

(e) Such evidence should also be used when conditional approval is granted, in order to ensure that, where possible, conditions attached to a merger should not be ones that undermine the business rationale for the deal.

4. CONCLUSION

This chapter has argued that developing a better understanding of synergies and a method to evaluate them should be an essential component of merger reform in the EU. We suggest that synergies can be grasped by asking why firms undertake mergers rather than alternative forms of corporate reorganization. In this perspective, we have gathered some evidence suggesting that the reallocation of intangible assets could be an important source of synergies and we have argued that synergies can be assessed by asking the firms about precise plans for the integration of their assets.

However, the merit of the procedure that we outline for competition authorities does not rest on the importance of intangibles as source of synergies. Its central feature, namely that authorities should enquire why the merger is taking place and evaluate the evidence provided by the firms, is independent of the source of gains. It suggests another approach that authorities may systematically wish to pursue, possibly in parallel with the usual approach (such that an analysis of dominance is possibly followed by an analysis of efficiencies); it is for the authorities to enquire directly into the sources of gains to shareholders as identified by the management, and to form a judgement as to what proportion of these gains are of the kind that can be achieved without significant costs to consumers – the magnitude of the remainder being an indicator of the likely dangers to competition. This approach, which focuses on the core of the motivation behind corporate reorganization, is more likely to identify synergies that benefit consumers and hence to reduce Type I errors. The ability of the authorities to ask firms explicitly about the business rationale for the deal would make it easier to identify merging parties that did not seem to have thought about the deal other than as a means of buying market power and hence would reduce Type II errors. And it is at least possible that some firms might give more careful thought to the rationale for such deals in the first place if they believed they might subsequently have to defend it in front of the authorities.

NOTES

1. The market evaluation of the effect on competitors may in some cases have been based on the belief that the merger would cause efficiencies that would diffuse throughout the industry, but it seems unlikely that this is true for all or even most transactions.
2. A particular sharp illustration of this argument is found in Farrell and Shapiro (1990), who show that in the context of the Cournot model, mergers which do not exhibit synergies will always raise price. Hence, in this context, synergies are necessary to generate pro-competitive mergers.
3. Jovanovic (2001) notes that such discrete distribution of returns will generate very high market-to-book ratios. If an investment involving intangibles generates a normal return *ex ante* but has a probability of success of some 10 per cent, a successful project will have a market-to-book ratio equal to 100.
4. The process of acquisition is best seen as an affiliated private value auction (in which the value of the target has a common element for all bidders). The result that the acquirer will get a higher share of surplus if few other bidders have a high private value also holds in this environment.
5. Note that the samples using accounting intangibles can be smaller than those using market intangibles despite the fact that market intangibles include accounting intangibles. This arises because accounting intangibles are scaled by total assets – whereas market intangibles are scaled by market value.
6. Note that the interpretation of the results that we report for the third hypothesis would be unaffected if we assume that the market discounts the benefit that might accrue to firms with high intangibles.
7. Other anti-competitive actions might fall under this heading, such as when a firm suppresses some product varieties altogether in order to be able to raise the prices of others more effectively.

REFERENCES

Duso, T., D. Neven and L.-H. Röller (2003), 'The political economy of European merger control: evidence using stock market data', discussion paper FS IV 02–34, Wissenschaftszentrum, Berlin.

Farrell, J. and C. Shapiro (1990), 'Horizontal mergers: an equilibrium analysis', *American Economic Review*, **80**, 107–26.

Farrell J. and C. Shapiro (2001), 'Scale economies and synergies in horizontal merger analysis', *Antitrust Law Journal*, **68**, 685–710.

Jovanovic, B. (2001), 'Comments', in B. Lev, *Intangibles. Management, Measurement and Reporting*, Washington DC: Brookings Institution Press.

Lev, B. (2001), *Intangibles. Management, Measurement and Reporting*, Washington DC: Brookings Institution Press.

Neven, D. and P. Seabright (2003), 'Synergies and dynamic efficiencies in merger analysis', final report of a study carried out for the European Commission, Directorate-General for Economic and Financial Affairs, Brussels.

Pautler, P. (2003), 'Evidence on mergers and acquisitions', *The Antitrust Bulletin*, (Spring), 119–221.

Seabright, P. (2002), 'Ten years of European merger control', in C. Robinson (ed.), *Utility Regulation and Competition Policy,* Institute of Economic Affairs, London, Chapter 9.

Index